GERMAN RAIDERS OF WORLD WAR II

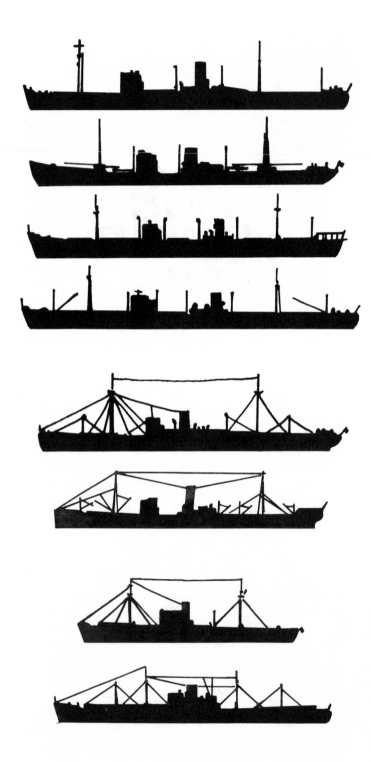

GERMAN RAIDERS OF WORLD WAR II

August Karl Muggenthaler

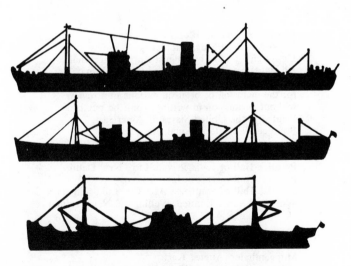

PRENTICE-HALL INC., Englewood Cliffs, N.J.

For Elizabeth

German Raiders of World War II
by August Karl Muggenthaler
Copyright © 1977 by August Karl Muggenthaler
All rights reserved. No part of this book may be
reproduced in any form or by any means, except
for the inclusion of brief quotations in a review
without permission in writing from the publisher.
Printed in the United States of America
Prentice-Hall International, Inc., London
Prentice-Hall of Australia, Pty. Ltd., Sydney
Prentice-Hall of Canada, Ltd., Toronto
Prentice-Hall of India Private Ltd., New Delhi
Prentice-Hall of Japan, Inc., Tokyo
Prentice-Hall of Southeast Asia Pte. Ltd., Singapore
Whitehall Books Limited, Wellington, New Zealand
10 9 8 7 6 5 4 3 2 1

Library of Congress Cataloging in Publication Data

Muggenthaler, August Karl.
  German raiders of World War II.

  Bibliography: p.
  Includes index.
  1. World War, 1939–1945—Naval operations,
German. 2. Armed merchant ships. I. Title.
  D771.M83   940.54′59′43   76–30612
  ISBN 0-13-354027-8

Du Br.
7-27-79.
orig.

ACKNOWLEDGMENTS

A few years ago, when the present writer first approached Captain J. Armstrong White, O.B.E. (whose ship, the *City of Bagdad,* was sunk by the raider *Atlantis* in the Indian Ocean), to ask him about his post-captive experiences, he replied immediately and generously, and added that he had sent copies of our correspondence to his former captor, Vizeadmiral Bernhard Rogge, of the reborn German Navy. White made it clear that he was "very British and not pro-German," but added that it was only fair to let Rogge, "a nice fellow with good human qualities of decency and honor," in on our communications. Delighted with what his former enemy had had to say, Admiral Rogge soon wrote to me to offer assistance with this history, and later sat patiently for an interview.

Since then, hundreds of persons from both sides of the conflict have assisted through interviews, with magnificent private photographs, or in extensive correspondence, to make this book possible. Some are mentioned in the text; some are quoted; others, for lack of space, have had to be omitted. The author is both thankful for the aid and sorry for the omissions. Special thanks, too, should go to those who may not have been directly involved in the events depicted here—the staffs of the Personnel and Historical divisions of the Australian, British, German, Japanese, Netherlands, New Zealand, Norwegian, and United States navies, the national archivists, and the corporate heads and managers who gave their time patiently and magnanimously. Though a compilation of names is an inadequate means of showing appreciation, I cannot but list them in the Bibliography, and offer my thanks to one and all.

And, finally, I would like to add my appreciation for the patient help of Prentice-Hall editors John G. Kirk and Roy H. Winnick, production editor Shirley D. Stein, and the never-mentioned alert proofreaders, observant copy-editors, the art department and all the publisher's production people.

I would like to extend special thanks, too, to James Bresnan, formerly with *Newsweek* magazine's art department, for his fine work on the line drawings and track charts.

FOREWORD

There is a unique nostalgia that surrounds the final exercise of a traditional type of naval warfare. This has never been more true than in the case of the disguised commerce raider. The raider survived the transition from oar to sail, sail to steam, coal to oil fuel, and entered World War II with a background of glamour developed over centuries. The growing capabilities of ocean surveillance in the second World War spelled the demise of the raider by the fourth year of the war as radar, wide-ranging aircraft, and rapidly improved communications and communications intelligence snipped away at the cloak that had hidden these lone venturers.

The German Raiders is a chronicle of this final bit of history. It is an account of the men and ships that played a little-publicized but telling role in the war at sea. A natural preoccupation with the German U-boat and the pocket battleship on the part of most of us who exercised command at sea in the battle against the Germany Navy, and of the historians who then and since have traced that battle, overshadowed the role of the raider.

Only nine of these converted merchantmen successfully put to sea, yet the damage they accounted for was 7 percent of the impressive U-boat total. They sank a cruiser, an armed merchant cruiser, so gallantly fought two more armed merchant cruisers that the latter were forced to break off the engagement, and captured or destroyed 890,000 tons of Allied shipping. They created a nuisance, diversion, and destruction out of all proportion to their capabilities and numbers.

Their story is one of ingenuity, courage, and persistence against formidable odds. Disguise, secret rendezvous, hardship, boredom, and terror mixed to constitute their life. But the principal appeal of their history is the empathy one has for the warrior behind enemy lines, engaged in a form of combat that was anachronistic in the chivalry by which the captains, with rare exception, abided. They plied their war with a high regard for international law and remarkable concern for the safety of the enemy during capture and his well-being in captivity.

The most effective part of the raider campaign was conducted before the United States declared war on Germany. But five U.S. Merchant ships fell victim, and one, the S.S. *Stephen Hopkins,* sank the raider! The last of the raiders, *Michel,* was sunk by the United States submarine *Tarpon.*

The author is to be complimented for the thorough research conducted. His was a unique opportunity with lineal ties to both Germany and the Allies, to conduct personal interviews and correspondence with Axis and Allied participants as well as shipping companies, navies, and other government agencies that are the repository of the pertinent documents. The product is a history of the raider in World War II that utilizes many personal accounts and eyewitness details as well as historical materials, that not only makes enjoyable and informative reading, but will be of lasting benefit to naval and maritime history.

Sheldon H. Kinney
Rear Admiral, U.S.N. (Ret.)
President, SUNY Maritime College

PREFACE

Almost everyone interested in the history of naval warfare has read of the exploits of Sir Francis Drake, of the Confederate ship *Alabama,* of the Q-boats and Count Felix von Luckner in World War I, and of Germany's U-boats, pocket battleships, and other terror-inspiring surface units in World War II. Yet few of us, naval men included, know more than a little about the German Hilfskreuzer—auxiliary cruisers—of the 1939–45 period, which ranged from the Arctic to the Antarctic and around the world from the Galápagos to the Caribbean in search of their unsuspecting prey.

These well-disguised and well-armed raiders, which masqueraded as harmless and friendly commercial vessels, are part of a particularly interesting chapter in the history of warfare at sea. The operations of these singular ships in the last great conflict brought to a final climax the long and romantic era of ocean raiding.

Fewer than a dozen of these deadly vessels, which looked like the harmless, often plodding and slab-sided freighters they had once been, were at sea during the years from 1940 to 1943, yet they managed to extract the awesome toll of nearly a million tons of Allied shipping. They destroyed or captured 138 ships, including a British AMC (armed merchant cruiser), sent thirty prizes on their way to German bases, and sank an Australian cruiser as well. Their activities on the oceans of the world spread confusion and terror, caused the severe disruption of Allied commerce, and tied up a veritable fleet of warships assigned to their pursuit. Though they could not by themselves have been decisive to the outcome of war, the raiders constituted a serious threat and thus served their limited purpose extraordinarily well.

A more risky enterprise than the operation of one of these raiders is hard to imagine. Day by day—one crew managed to survive 622 days of action—hovering at sea, "stealing geese like a fox," as one raider skipper, Hellmuth von Ruckteschell, put it, surrounded by a relentless foe whose signals could be heard but usually not decoded, the raiders were alone—desperately alone. Eternal, wearisome vigilance and painstaking attention to the most apparently minor detail were their only means of staying afloat and alive. Their chances always poor, they could never guard against a coincidence that might spell their destruction. As raider captain Otto Kähler noted after his third successful encounter with British AMCs, a raider was, after all, "always behind enemy lines."

The anxieties suffered by the raider's victims, the merchant seamen, are equally difficult to conceive. Alone, too, with their vital cargoes, in raider-infested waters usually far from the lurking hell of the U-boat zones, they were almost safe, but only almost. Practically any vessel they might sight by day or night, no matter what its appearance, might prove to be a raider. Any wisp of smoke or light winking in the dark could mean the end of a voyage. After a sudden bloody engagement, any survivors of a raider attack were packed into the victor's hold to share its fate. Some hoped that their captors, no matter how decent as men, would be brought to book. But then a man still likes to live, and anyone in one of the thin-hulled raiders, ex-merchantmen that they were, stood little chance in an engagement. And the Germans would fight, too, if intercepted; they had been trained to and they had the guts for it. To Captain P. Beeham, then Second Officer of the S.S. *Port Wellington,* which was captured in 1941 by the raider *Pinguin,* it was simply a fair and square matter of "both sides carrying out their jobs on behalf of their countries in any way that seemed best. They were all cogs in a vast machine, hoping that their various activities could be conducted without disastrous results to themselves. The Germans ran a good deal of risk in what they were up to and, for them, it was not a question of avoiding detection and capture, but avoiding destruction." To Fregattenkapitän Theodor Detmers, of the raider *Kormoran,* every undertaking meant "staking everything on victory or total defeat; there was little comfort in running, and none in surrender. If discovered, it would be a fight to the finish."

Germany's raiding campaign was a war within a war, tough, tedious, and nerve-racking. It was carefully planned to spread fear and confusion, a deadly weapon skillfully employed by a numerically inferior navy as a supplement to more conventional naval operations. Executed with pluck and dash, it provided rare moments of gallant chivalry in a war too often marked by meanness and atrocity.

It is unlikely in this present age of the jet, the spy satellite, and the atomic-warhead missile that any navy will ever again deploy raiders-in-disguise to win a battle for command of the high seas. The raider, no doubt, has gone the way of the ram, the sailing man-of-war, and the large-scale naval engagement.

CONTENTS

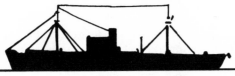

CHAPTER 1

Buildup

TIMED BY HITLER   When Britain and France declared war on September 3, 1939, to put an end to Adolf Hitler's rapacious assaults in Europe, the German surface fleet was so weak, according to its commander in chief, Grand Admiral Erich Raeder, that it "would be able to do little more than show that it could die courageously." The Treaty of Versailles had limited the German Navy to a strength of fifteen thousand men and a handful of old destroyers, cruisers, and battleships that had been considered obsolete as early as 1914. Various attempts were made to circumvent the restrictions during the Weimar Republic, but no major building program was undertaken until Hitler came into power and signed the London Naval Agreement of 1935, a treaty that abrogated the Versailles settlement and gave Germany the right to construct up to 45 percent of the Royal Navy's surface tonnage and up to parity in submarines.

A fast modern fleet of that size, though by no means large, would have been adequate to meet the operational needs then envisioned for a war with France, Poland, or Russia. It would by no stretch of the imagination have been strong enough for a contest with Great Britain, but no one in the German Navy had seriously considered such an eventuality.

The idea of challenging the island empire for a second time had seemed inconceivable for nearly two decades and for a number of obvious reasons involving money, manpower, and common sense. Furthermore, Hitler himself had always maintained that he could not foresee any trouble with His Majesty's Government. He usually explained that he could not really see any need for the navy until the mid- or late forties, and to those most immediately involved, it seemed that he was probably right. The crafty ex-corporal, it was reasoned, was a dexterous politician who had managed to avoid any serious confrontations with the major powers despite several outrageous provocations. It

1

was a persistent and strange delusion that lasted for years. Nevertheless, on May 23, 1938, Hitler called Raeder to the Reichschancellory to advise him that the British might someday in the far future be foolish enough to stand up and fight, regardless of his own conviction that he could maintain peace with the decadent West. He did not say that he would force them into war, much less when. But to be properly prepared, that was precisely what the navy had to know.

Raeder was well aware that Britain's greatest weakness was her dependence on imports—some 68 million tons annually. The food, oils, metals, wood, and fertilizers so vital to the country's existence were carried in some 21 million tons of shipping, and the number of British-registered vessels at sea on any given day totaled 2,500. If enough of those deeply laden ships could be destroyed or prevented from reaching their home ports, the United Kingdom's ability to wage war would falter and eventually collapse as it nearly had under the onslaught of the U-boats in 1917. To achieve that end and to be at least partially ready to meet any contingency, the admiral worked out two plans which he presented to Hitler in the winter of 1938–39. The first would have created a stop-gap fleet, generally within the limits of the 1935 agreement, that would be ready for limited action sometime in 1940. The second option was far more ambitious. In its various versions, "Plan Z" would have resulted in a navy that could interdict Britain's overseas communications and become a menace in traditional battle as well. Predictably awed by the statistics of big ships, and confident in his own political prowess, Hitler opted for the heavy, long-term buildup. But because the Führer lost whatever control he thought he had over world events and Europe tumbled inexorably into the abyss of war, Raeder never got that fleet.

On the last day of March 1939, Britain and France announced their guarantees of Poland's integrity. Disregarding that pointed warning, Hitler ordered his armed forces to prepare for "Case White" (war with Poland), and another top secret directive dated May 10 advised the Kriegsmarine (navy) to be ready for "a war against British and French shipping." While the Nazis shrieked invectives and chanted demands, and diplomats passed the bad time in fashionable hotels, Admiral Raeder worried over secret orders issued August 4 warning the captains of the pocket battleships *Deutschland* and *Graf Spee* of the likelihood that Poland's guarantors would intervene if that country were invaded.

On August 21 Germany's Chancellor announced his greatest diplomatic coup: a nonaggression pact with Russia. Secure now in the East, he could afford to risk trouble with the West, and just ten days before sending his field-gray troops and armor crunching into Poland, he called his senior commanders to his retreat on the Obersalzberg to outline his intentions. All agreed that the view of the Bavarian Alps was magnificent, but the assembled officers could not agree later as to what they had heard. Some said Hitler had claimed that he saw no reason why the British should go to war over a bunch of Poles; others remember him insisting they certainly would not. In any case, fearing the worst, Raeder was not about to let his tiny fleet remain at its moorings. By the end of the month he had eighteen U-boats at sea and *Graf Spee* and *Deutschland* near their respective waiting stations in the South Atlantic and off Greenland. All were fully prepared for "the disruption and destruction of enemy merchant ships by all possible means."

Across the North Sea, in London, the British Admiralty was fully alert, its fleet mobilized. While Hitler fretted lest something interfere with his plans for Poland, Whitehall issued "Navigation Order No. 1, 1939," thereby taking over control of all merchant ships. On August 24 the Royal Navy went to its war stations, submarines departed from their bases to begin the blockade off Norway, and all the ships of the huge reserve fleet were ordered fully manned. Two days later, four cruisers steamed off, on patrol to seal off the exits between the Faroe Islands, Iceland, and Scapa Flow in search of any German ships they might find. Britain was not about to forget the lessons of the Great War or the droll dictum penned by Rudyard Kipling in the "Big Steamers" nearly half a century before:

> *Send out your big warships to watch your big waters,*
> *That no one may stop us from bringing you food.*
> *For the bread that you eat and the bisquits you nibble,*
> *The sweets that you suck and the joints that you carve,*
> *They are all brought to you daily by all of us Big Steamers*
> *And if anyone hinders our coming you'll starve.*

At 1100 hours on September 3, a lovely sunny Sunday, the sad but electrifying signal flashed out from London to hundreds of His Majesty's ships: "Commence hostilities with Germany forthwith." Almost simultaneously, radio officers in the blue coats, shiny buttons, and neatly stitched golden eagles of the Kriegsmarine adjusted their earphones to jot down the laconic message conveyed by *dit-daahs* beaming in from Berlin. The message: "Begin hostilities with England immediately." It was the beginning of the end of "Plan Z," of Raeder's minuscule fleet (two battle cruisers, three pocket battleships, seven cruisers, twenty-one destroyers, and fifty-seven U-boats had so far been completed), and of the Third Reich as well. Hitler's new socialistic dictatorship, boisterously billed as a thousand-year Reich, had only sixty-nine months to go.

As the navigation lights flickered out at sea and the sirens wailed in darkened cities on shore, Whitehall implemented orders that had long since been cut to provide for the immediate arming of more than fifty luxury liners as armed merchant cruisers, just as soon as passengers could be disembarked and cargos unloaded. On the German side, however, few preparations had been made. The brassbound men in the offices of Berlin's Tirpitzufer had gone over the 1914–18 records and found that some of the Imperial Navy's cruiser warfare tactics had paid off handsomely by creating panic and confusion in sharp forays against the enemy's shipping. But because certain staffs underestimated the potential of this type of operation, just as had their predecessors twenty-five years earlier, only a few studies were made during hectic 1939 before it was decided that two small and three large freighters should be requisitioned initially and armed as raiders. Prospective commanding officers and some of the enlisted personnel were sifted out of the rapidly growing naval establishment for future assignment to these Hilfskreūzer, but, for political reasons and to avoid arousing suspicion abroad, nothing further was immediately done to carry out the long-range plans for twenty-six such raider vessels.

⎯ Caught unprepared by the early outbreak of war, the Seekriegsleitung (SKL)—the Naval Operations Staff initially headed by Admiral Otto Schniewind—nevertheless moved swiftly and with the precision that was characteristic of the German General Staff. Their first typically concise orders rattled out over teletype machines to the shipbuilders on September 5. Hamburg's Blohm & Voss yard was instructed to take over Hamburg Amerika Line's S.S. *Neumark* and *Kurmark;* Hansa Line's *Goldenfels* was ordered into the Deschimag Werke, Bremen, and work was begun on two uncompleted 3,000-tonners (but soon abandoned when it was discovered that the ships would be too small for their assignment and their armament necessarily too weak to intimidate Allied vessels being equipped with 4-, 5-, and 6-inch mounts of their own). The architects, foremen, and shipwrights were given some sixty days in which to perform the countless jobs of cutting, riveting, welding, and hammering required to transform money-making merchant vessels into effective fighting ships that still looked like freighters. The only precedent they had for their unusual contracts was the five disguised raiders that had captured the public and the enemy's imagination a quarter of a century earlier, when the Kaiser's magnificent fleet lay at anchor in the Schillig Roads and the Western armies bled inconclusively in Belgium and France.

"THE GREAT WAR"

At the beginning of that earlier conflict, the Kaiserliche Marine had had six light cruisers already at sea or on foreign stations available as commerce raiders. The most famous and effective was S.M.S. *Emden,* which fought a dashing campaign that terrorized the Indian Ocean and earned her almost legendary commander, Karl von Müller, the ungrudging respect of friend and foe alike. Before she was forced onto a reef at North Keeling Island by the larger and more heavily armed H.M.A.S. *Sydney* on November 9, 1914, she had sent down a Russian cruiser, a French torpedo boat (not to be confused with the small, speedy, often wooden motor torpedo boats henceforth called MTBs.), and twenty-three Allied ships totaling 101,182 tons. Second in order of tonnage destroyed was *Karlsruhe,* which sank seventeen vessels in the Atlantic before an unexplained explosion in her torpedo room tore her and 146 of her men apart. The four other light gray cruisers, *Dresden, Leipzig, Königsberg,* and *Nürnberg,* though not as successful (they took fewer than a dozen ships between them), logged some adventurous careers, but all of them were brought to book early in the war.

Several liners, fast but very lightly armed, were also set to work preying on Allied shipping. The Kaiser's Admiralty hoped that their speed would assure their success. Though it was a reasonable assumption, it proved wrong. The ships were capable of outrunning most warships and all of their prospective victims, but their engines burned up vast quantities of coal and their huge complements spent much of their time (more than two of the eight months *Kronprinz Wilhelm* was at sea) attempting to take on enough coal just to keep going. Besides, the liners were too distinctive and could be instantly recognized. The fight of those handsomely appointed oceangoing spas was romantic, but they were only moderately successful and the early termination of their campaign was a foregone conclusion.

By the fall of 1915, it had become obvious that something had to be done to show the flag in foreign waters with something other than U-boats. But Berlin was still thinking in terms of cruisers or liners. The former, however, needed the bases and colliers by then either in enemy hands or driven from the seas, and the latter had proven ill-suited to the demands of war. While the Kaiser's officials deliberated, the very junior, thirty-year-old reserve Lieutenant Theodor Wolff, then serving in torpedo boat V-162, thought he could help the fatherland. He penned a well-considered memorandum that was to presage the most successful aspects of commerce raiding in both world wars. An ordinary freighter would be slow, he reasoned, but it would use up comparatively little coal and its vast holds could carry a lot of it to extend its range. Such a ship would be inconspicuous, too. Wolff's note went through channels to Adm. Hugo von Pohl, commander in chief of the fleet, whose endorsement, "I think . . . that such steamers can create great damage," accompanied it to the Admiralty. There it was promptly shelved.

In the meantime, the fleet's staff decided that it was time for a repeat of some earlier mining missions that had been carried out by a disguised steamer, and on September 21, 1915, they summoned Commander Graf zu Dohna-Schlodien to undertake the chancy venture. Seven days later, the fleet requested the return of Wolff's paper for further study and they kept it for six days. Simultaneously, and entirely on his own, Dohna had raiding as well as mining on his mind as he searched for and outfitted his ship. He set out from Kiel on December 15 with 235 men and instructions making it clear that mining was to be his principle job. If he succeeded in that, then, and only then, could he go about raiding at his own discretion.* Dohna's command was the 4,778-ton *Pungo* of the Laeisz Line that was so famous for its huge immaculate square-riggers. Renamed *Möwe,* she was armed with four 5.9-inch and one 4.1-inch gun and five hundred mines, and she was to use her weapons well. When she returned to Germany on March 4, 1916, Dohna could report one battleship and a total of fifteen merchant ships scratched from his enemies' registers. Starting out again November 22, Dohna got another shot at the Allies and managed to better his score in just four months of raiding by sinking twenty-seven vessels totaling 121,707 tons.

Just eight days after *Möwe* sailed on her second voyage, Germany tried again and came up with another winner. That ship was S.M.S. *Wolf,* commanded by Karl August Nerger. The first raider so named had run aground in the Elbe. Though the accident had not been her captain's fault, the man was sent to the Russian front with a mining detachment because, as his seniors put it, "it is absolutely necessary that the leader of an undertaking [such as *Wolf*'s] be not only competent but lucky as well." Nerger was. He drove his ship and men so hard that he was able to remain at sea for a record fifteen months, a remarkable feat for any vessel and especially so for a coal burner entirely dependent on supplies that could be gotten only from captured ships. *Wolf*'s mines sank thirteen ships and damaged five more. Another fourteen merchantmen, ranging from small liners to old wind bags, were sent down by the raider's guns before Nerger churned back home on February 24, 1918,

---

* That sort of an operation had not been attempted since the American Confederate Navy had nearly driven the Union's merchant fleet from the high seas with such steam-and-sail driven ships as *Alabama, Florida,* and *Shenandoah.*

just seven days after the Admiralty sent out notices advising the families of his 374-man complement that their relatives and ship were presumed lost at sea.

Only three more raiders worthy of note were employed in World War I. Trapped in the North Sea by a cruiser, two destroyers, and two AMCs that had been expecting her, *Greif* gamely signaled that she was indeed the German the Royal Navy had been waiting for. Down with the former freighter and 180 of her crew on February 29, 1916, went AMC *Alcantara* and sixty-nine tars. The next commerce destroyer to sail literally did so as her men manned the yards of the full rigger *Seeadler,* a product again of the imagination of a junior officer, Alfred Kling, and not, as is commonly supposed, of her publicity minded skipper, Count Felix von Luckner. *Seeadler* duped fifteen vessels into surrendering before being wrecked on Mopelia Island (in the Societies) through negligence. *Leopard,* a 4,652-ton ex-prize of *Möwe,* steamed out on March 10, 1917. She was cornered by armored cruiser H.M.S. *Achilles* and auxiliary *Dundee.* All that remained of the Kaiser's ship was a bottled message signed by some of her men: "On March 16, 2 o'clock in the afternoon we are between Iceland and Norway. Battle 64°50′ North; 1° West. Battle with English cruiser. Fighting for the glory and honor of Germany. A last greeting to our next-of-kin."

WORLD WAR II

For both sides in World War II, the order to create a new wave of AMCs or raiders was easier to issue than to carry out, but to the Kriegsmarine it seemed nearly impossible. Not being the senior service and under the command of a continent-minded dictator, the German Navy's priorities for war matériel were often downgraded in favor of the pampered Luftwaffe, the proconsular SS, and the powerful army. Besides, in order to fight at all, Raeder needed U-boats—lots of them —more than raiders. Allocations of steel, motors, weapons, and skilled workers were hard to win from an economy still too disorganized to cope with the severe dislocations brought about by war. Shortages of everything from aluminum to yard space forced an approach to Japan and Russia. Would those countries, friendly in purpose if not in philosophy, be willing to help, for a start by outfitting and supplying raiders? No, the Imperial Government said, and Russia's acceptance of the proposal had to be declined because Stalin's security was deemed inadequate and his labor force unskilled. But SKL did not let such setbacks interfere with their planning. By November 27, 1939, there were twelve large raiders on order, and the contracts made it clear that the first wave of those ships was to be in action that winter. The second group—all motor ships capable of sustained operations and with a range of 40,000 miles or more at twelve knots—would follow within half a year.

But the projections proved chimerical. Production squeezes immediately dampened optimistic intentions, and bad weather—it was one of the worst winters on record and several raiders were ice-bound for weeks—did the rest to delay initial operations by more than three months. In fact, the entire program was continually bedeviled by similar reversals, and the more serious interruptions caused by such operations as "Weserübung" (attack on Norway and Denmark) and "Sea Lion" (proposed invasion of Britain) created even greater delays and cancellations until the ever-growing Allied aerial and naval supremacy finally crushed the effort.

But actually, the campaign was a startling success. In their heyday the "mystery ships" struck and struck hard at the very heart of Britain's ability to survive—her maritime transport which, to Winston Churchill, was the "crunch of the whole war." And they did so at relatively little cost to Germany. Tactically, the few ships did very well by destroying nearly 900,000 tons of shipping and cargoes worth anywhere from 5 billion on up and causing the Allies the loss of thousands of trained seamen at a time they needed them most. The men and ships were important, but the cost, no matter what it was—it cannot be measured by peacetime standards—was not. What mattered most was whether the foodstuffs, raw materials, and arms got to their destinations, and got there on time. And that is where the raiders played their role. Strategically, the lonely captains carried out their threefold mission—disruption of enemy shipping movements, wide dispersal of Allied forces, and the destruction of merchant tonnage—far more effectively than even their most sanguine proponents at SKL would have dared hope. When the Royal Navy, facing unprecedented crises, was already stretched and worn thin by fighting in the Mediterranean, by escort duties around the world, and by an apparently futile attempt to keep the U-boats at bay, Hilfskreuzer were drawing His Majesty's ships from theaters where they were badly needed to prevent the whole structure of British maritime control from crumbling.

Since the Kriegsmarine, as will be seen, was so successful with its raiders, it may be surprising to note that no other nation was able to achieve any noteworthy results with similar vessels. One reason was that the Allies, as superior naval powers, had little need for them and hardly a single German against whom to employ them. The wife of one German officer asked this writer during the course of an interview "whether the United States had had any raiders." "My dear child," her husband chuckled, *"der Ami hat über hundert Träger gehabt."* ("The Americans had over one hundred aircraft carriers.") Decoy, or "Q," ships, which had received so much publicity for a few spectacular battles with U-boats in World War I, were again put to use in the 1939–45 conflict by both Britain and the United States, but their accomplishments were so indifferent that naval historian Samuel Eliot Morison felt obliged to write off the American effort as "the least useful of all methods adopted to fight submarines. It had cost the lives of 148 officers and men, about one in four of the total personnel involved."*

The Royal Navy's decoy ships did not perform at all. Not one, according to Britain's official historian S. W. Roskill, "ever sighted a U-boat or accomplished any useful purpose at all."† Two were sunk, and one achieved the dubious distinction of being intercepted by light cruiser H.M.S. *Neptune,* which carelessly remained in her vicinity at close range and far too long. Had that lesson been widely disseminated, it is possible that many lives would have been saved later in the war when H.M.A.S. *Sydney* stopped the "Dutch" *Straat Malakka.*

Germany's Axis partners, both of which boasted far larger fleets, lacked either the opportunity or the imagination to employ raiders effectively. When they did try, the outcome of their attempts was so feeble that only two incidents are worth mentioning. The first involved an Italian, *Rambi,* who was more bent on escaping than raiding and was sunk less than a week after sortieing from Massawa, and in the second case, two Japanese raiders, *Hokoku* and *Aikoku Maru* (eight six-inch, two 3-inch, four 25mm and two twin 21-inch torpedo tubes) were fought so irresolutely in the Indian Ocean on November 11, 1942, by their commander, Captain Hiroshi Imasoto, that both their virtually helpless victims, the Dutch tanker *Ondina* (one 4-inch) and the Royal Indian Navy's fleet minesweeper *Bengal* (one 3-inch, two Oerlikons) escaped after sinking the 10,439-ton *Hokoku* with 76 of her 354-man crew including Imasoto.‡

* Samuel Eliot Morison, *History of United States Naval Operations in World War II;* (Boston: Little, Brown & Co., 1950), Vol. I.

† Capt. S. W. Roskill, *The War at Sea* (London: Her Majesty's Stationery Office, 1954), Vol. I.

‡ *Bengal,* Lt. Commander W. J. Wilson commanding, and *Ondina* (Captain William Horsman) fought splendidly but there is still a smoldering dispute over who sank the raider. The 650-ton minesweeper's first dispatches indicated that it had been she. Both the Dutch and the Japanese National Defense Agency credit *Ondina* with the shot that resulted in the sinking. Horsman and four *Ondina* men were killed and the burning tanker was abandoned. Her First Officer, M. J. Rehwinkel and Second Officer, B. B. Bakker, however, reboarded and extinguished the fire while *Aikoku Maru* unaccountably quit the fight to steam off and pick up her luckless consort's survivors. She was sunk in February 1944 at Truk by U.S. carrier planes.

FITTING OUT IN GERMANY

No one could have accused the Kriegsmarine of such bungling with their raiders, but the Germans naturally were not perfect, either. There were errors in judgment, a lack of modern equipment, and interference from desk-and-book-bound bureaucrats (*Silberlinge* for their silver-braided uniform stripes), who just as often as not thought of the raiders as "never-come-back liners." Some of the ships, their machinery old or untried, proved inadequate for their missions, and drafts of men were often poorly chosen. "Why not get rid of the troublemakers?" the Personnel Bureau reasoned. "Why kill off twenty good officers?"

Some of those officers had trouble convincing the authorities of their need for even the simplest items like Very pistols; others could not get enough compass slaves to hook up with a master gyro. But even without such difficulties the problems of outfitting a raider were enormous. In an ordinary freighter of, say, eight thousand gross tons, approximately 40 percent of the total space is taken up by engines, bridge, crews' quarters, boatswains' stores, and food, fuel, and water to last at the most only a couple of months. The rest, or net tonnage, may for all practical purposes be regarded as a big, empty, self-propelled box to be filled with cargo. That freighter's crew, if European or American, would normally consist of about forty men living in rather cramped quarters amidships or on the poop. The raiders, on the other hand, were warships with complements of up to four hundred crewmen, and all their requirements had to be packed into the holds that once held bales of cotton, sewing machines, or sacks of cocoa beans.

Guns, torpedo tubes, range finders, and all the accouterments of war were naturally given the first consideration. Each raider carried a main battery of six 5.9-inch guns distributed fore and aft. They mounted anywhere from two to six 21-inch torpedo tubes and an assortment of up to fourteen 40-, 37-, and 20-mm automatic weapons. One or two seaplanes were provided each vessel, and mines were stowed in five of them. In addition, *Schiff* (ship) *41* and *Schiff 45* carried mine-laying motorboats, and *Michel* was provided with a motor torpedo boat (MTB). All such gear had to be invisible, even at close inspection by air, and it all had to be accessible and capable of being put into service within seconds. There was no one in the yards, in the navy's construction service, or in the ships' complements who had any experience in organizing or designing anything of the sort. A few plans were available from World War I, and the venerable corsair Nerger did his best to aid the new generation with advice. But as each problem arose, the supervisors, inspectors, and officers of 1939 had to sit down to draw up workable solutions for new engineering, communications, and gunnery systems. Automatic cannon, 3-meter range finders, and 60-cm searchlights were relatively simple to hide, and collapsible ventilators, removable king posts, telescoping funnels, and masts did not confound the designers overly long.

The heavy weapons were another matter. First of all, the decks had to be stiffened to carry the five-ton weights and absorb the shock of the guns' discharge, no matter where they were mounted. And their location itself was a major difficulty which had to be solved in a different manner in each ship. The 5.9s had to be free to traverse a maximum number of degrees, and their elevation could not be encumbered. Ideally, they should all have been set on the center line to permit training to both starboard and port, but that was impossible on a merchantman cluttered with deckhouses and cargo-handling gear. Never more than 30 percent of the guns could be placed in hatches with specially raised coamings. Of the rest, a few were hidden inside folding deckhouses or behind false bulwarks, but many had to be installed below the weather decks or in newly drawn decks where their positioning depended as much on the contours of the ship as it did on naval requirements. Below-deck mounts affected the arrangements of ammunition rooms and hoists, limited living and storage space, and necessitated the cutting of large apertures into the slab-sided hulls where they did not belong. A lot of ingenuity and calculations was needed before a practical system of securing the openings was devised. The flaps and hinges had to be exceptionally strong to withstand the pounding of seas that have battered oceangoing vessels to scrap, tight enough to keep out water, and indiscernible to an outsider. After many knee-to-knee, shirt-sleeve sessions and attempts with scale models, the exhausted engineers and seamen were able to draw up some promising blueprints for a contraption that resembled an old-fashioned bread-box door. At the touch of a lever to expose the guns, the heavy steel flaps, precisely balanced, slid upward and in effortlessly. That problem solved, the men turned to tackle some of the thousands of other questions that were more prosaic but of very nearly as much importance to the success of those unusual ships.

Just finding space for storage, boatswains' stores, sick bays, carpenter, shoe-repair, and machine shops, laundries, livestock pens (pigs and chickens thrived well, rabbits did not), auxiliary radio stations, and the hundreds of charts necessary for navigating in unfamiliar waters from Bear Island to the Weddell Sea was like trying to fit the furnishings of a sixty-room Schloss into the cozy Stube of a Garmisch ski hut. Tons of paint and bulky structural materials to facilitate frequent changes of disguise had to be stowed, and a large number of rubber boats had to be hidden away because a sufficient number of regulation lifeboats to carry the large crews would have looked suspicious on a ship purporting to be a harmless, possibly short-handed, and plodding cargo carrier. But no matter how much forethought went into the construction and supplies, there were bound to be some problems that could not be overcome due to the vast difficulties the raiders would face in their unusual taxing undertakings. *Widder*'s machinery failed completely; *Orion*'s was marginal, at best. Radio technicians rightly complained that many of their sets were not even as powerful as those installed in many merchant ships. Pilots objected to the inherent weakness of the Heinkel and Arado planes, and *Stier*'s experimental AR-231s, miniatures designed for U-boats, managed only a few feeble flutters. Cramped, stuffy, and damp quarters were to make the older ships hellish for the men, and the lack of adequate reefer space was to have the officers and ratings and the prisoners who shared their menus grumbling about the monotonous diets while more reserved captains argued as bitterly over a few fresh potatoes, heads of cabbages, and bottles of beer brought out by supply ships as they did over tons of oil. But despite such vexations and some complaints of shoddy workmanship, the combined efforts of sailors, bureaus, and engineers achieved good results often enough to make the exceptions prove the rule. The design, conversion, and supplying the Hilfskreuzer was an accomplishment, though by no means one comparable to the dash and determination displayed by the commanders in overcoming seemingly insurmountable difficulties at sea.

BERLIN PULLS THE STRINGS

The operations of the raiders and their train were directed by the Operations Division, 1/SKL, which in its lofty position in Berlin was in the best spot to oversee the successful employment of all ships serving overseas. Its chief not only had access to all intelligence available but was responsible for every strategic plan. He knew, for example, how far south the Arctic ice barrier extended at any given moment, that His Majesty's carrier *Eagle* had left its base at Capetown, or that Japan would be willing to trade the fuel oil so badly needed by *Orion* for gasoline carried by a Norwegian prize called *Ole Jacob*.

SKL naturally took all such factors into account when it drew up its orders and when it guided the ships with new instructions based on the latest information. The skippers on the spot were given as much freedom of action as possible—they had to have such freedom—but they often complained bitterly that far-off, land-locked Berlin simply could not understand the local tactical situation and that its signals interfered with shipboard decision-making. Some of the misunderstandings could easily have been cleared up instantly over any normal channels of communication, but the raiders were understandably hesitant to tap out messages that would give their positions away to the alert, worldwide network of British radio direction finders. When they did report, it was always with a *Kurzsignal* (short signal), which was a special code designed to pass information along with a minimum number of letters or digits and in the shortest possible time to avoid detection. A five-letter message could, for example, tell the people at home that a raider was just south of the equator on May 1, that it had sunk a certain number of ships grossing x-thousands of tons, and that she had enough oil for another fifty-seven days of steaming. "WIH" meant "I am moving my operations to the Indian Ocean, large chart square XY." Since this system could not allow for every contingency, and since the raiders were reluctant to open up with their transmitters, SKL was often left groping in the dark for an indication as to where their charges were and what they had been up to. As a matter of fact, the staff was, at times, dependent on intercepts of British messages to determine the probable location of a Hilfskreuzer.

And there were many times when the demands of global strategy forced SKL to change their orders for the prima donnas at sea. The first such situation occurred during "Operation Weserübung" to which Germany had committed virtually its entire fleet. To relieve the pressure in Norwegian waters, SKL sent signal "1814/16/57" to the only ships available in overseas waters, raiders *Atlantis* and *Orion*, whose written orders had not anticipated their going into action for many weeks to come. So the raiders' war was on. Capt. Bernhard Rogge and Lt. Commander Kurt Weyher would be in action and fully engaged sooner than they had expected, and they knew that they would be in for a rough time. That much had been foreseen years before in the official German history of World War I, which concluded its study of raider operations with the warning that the relatively favorable circumstances then prevailing would not occur again, and that scientific advances would most likely make it far harder for raiders to operate in any future conflict. By April 16, 1940, Rogge and Weyher had already managed narrowly to effect a passage through the British blockade and they had, of course, read that history. They had been briefed by SKL to expect the worst, and they were well aware that henceforth they would be entirely on their own.

CHAPTER 2

Atlantis, 1940

BEATING PLOWSHARES INTO SWORDS   On April 16, 1940, a Tuesday, the war was 229 days old. To the commander of *Atlantis* (*Schiff 16*), Captain Bernhard Rogge, it seemed as if the struggle had gone on for that many years. Only seventeen days had passed since he had broken his anchor out of the ooze of Schleswig-Holstein's Süderpiep bay to try his luck at running the British blockade. He had been successful in that. Full-out at seventeen and a half knots, his ship's diesels throbbing, he had pounded into gigantic seas in the Shetlands-Bergen narrows, up the Norwegian Sea, and then west-south-west down the ice-choked Denmark Strait. Those days had been horribly cold, wet, and tense. But by the sixteenth, *Atlantis* was free, pitching slowly in the gentle swells of the trade-wind zones, and the many hours of wretched uneasiness that had clutched at the men as the ice had at their ship were nearly forgotten. Deck work had become pleasant for the first time, and the off-duty watch had taken to snoozing in the sun. Preparations for getting a pool together in time for the traditional equator crossing ceremonies were being made, and many of the raider's 347 officers and men were beginning to feel that they were being paid for a cruise that only the rich could afford. A few officers had taken a fling at pistol practice; others had marveled at the gorgeous sunsets, deep blue seas, and bright white clouds few Germans ever got to see. Those on the bridge, where the first white uniforms had already appeared, were beginning to wonder whether they would ever be able to shed their jackets and black bow ties.

Captain Rogge, similarly garbed, was both a military perfectionist and a pleasant, genial man. Born in Schleswig, the son of a government official, he had joined the Imperial Navy as a cadet in 1915 and served on several cruisers until his discharge as an ensign in 1919. Reenlisting less than a year later, he then spent his time with the navy's educational and training establishments, later as the service's representa-

14

tive during the construction of the sail training ship *Gorch Fock*. An educator, conscientious disciplinarian, and yachtsman—he had sailed in numerous international competitions—he had enjoyed his long tours as master of the barques *Gorch Fock* and *Albert Leo Schlageter,* the latter a sister of the United States Coast Guard's gleaming white *Eagle*. During the Czech crisis, Commander Rogge inquired what his duties were to be in case of mobilization. Skipper of auxiliary cruiser No. II, he was told. Rogge was glad that he had asked. The forewarning gave him time to consider the future while he sailed the Baltic during the summer of 1939 in his spotless square-rigger. On August 25 he was recalled as a result of submarine warnings, and that was the end of the life he loved and lived so well. A week later, the war broke out, and within a few days his wife, Anneliese, died.

Rogge, as ordered, took himself to Bremen, registered in the Hotel Columbus across the square from the main station, and then set off in mufti to find his ship. It was a mess. Built in 1937 for the Hansa Line, *Goldenfels* had hardly finished unloading her last cargo before the shipwrights started tearing her innards apart to convert her into a raider. It was dirty and noisy work, and no one really knew how to go about it. Fuel capacity had to be increased from 1,368 tons to 3,000, water tanks to 1,200, and coal bunkers (to fire the condensors) to 1,000. The tween decks had to be rebuilt to hold mines, prisoners, sand ballast, live chickens, reefers, and crew's quarters with bunks for as many men as possible. Hold No. 2 was redesigned to house a seaplane, and its spare parts and artificial ventilation had to be trunked in to all the spaces below the weather decks where all the men, stores, and paraphernalia of war and the comforts for making it possible had to be squeezed in.

Rogge was lucky that he had been able to make connections with the right people and that he knew how to use them to get what he needed. And he was fortunate in having obtained a former boatswain and shipmate, Erich Kühn, who was now Lieutenant (s.g.) Kühn and a legendary figure in the German Navy. He was priceless. He knew how to manage a ship, and in his thirty years of service he had learned where the Kriegsmarine had squirreled away all its stores and the equipment no one would willingly part with; and he knew how to get it, too—trainloads of it, by moonlight requisitioning if necessary.

Rogge's promotion to captain in November helped speed the supplies and equipment, but the hubbub and the irritations of rebuilding, Rogge felt, were almost unbearable. There were his guns, for example —World War I models. Installed in the wrong place and intended to be disguised as deck cargo, the forward 5.9-inch mounts had to be cut out and moved inboard when tests with models proved a new deck with

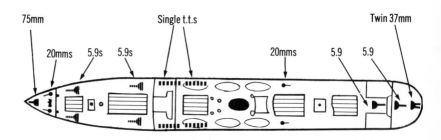

ATLANTIS, SHIP 16, ex-GOLDENFELS

Built:	1937, Bremer Vulkan, Bremen-Vegesack
Tonnage:	7,862
Length:	488.1 feet, Lloyds Register
Beam:	61.3
Draft:	31.1
Speed:	17
Armament:	Six 5.9-inch; one 75mm; one twin 37mm; four 20mm; four single 21-inch torpedo tubes; 92 mines*
Planes:	2 Heinkel 114; later Arado 196
Complement:	347 (varied due to prize crews and new drafts)
	*Shaded guns and tubes indicate a mounting below deck
Ships sunk or taken:	22 (including three prizes) = 145,697 tons
	SCIENTIST, TIRRANNA, CITY OF BAGDAD, KEMMENDINE, TALLEYRAND, KING CITY, ATHELKING, BENARTY, COMMISSAIRE RAMEL, DURMITOR, TEDDY, OLE JACOB, AUTOMEDOM, MANDASOR, SPEYBANK, KETTY BRÖVIG, ZAM ZAM, RABAUL, TRAFALGAR, TOTTENHAM, BALZAC, SILVAPLANA
Length of cruise:	622 days, 3.11.40-11.22.41 (including time spent in getting crew home after sinking)
Fate:	Sunk by H.M.S. DEVONSHIRE

ports that could be lifted most advisable. Everyone knew that the Heinkel 114B seaplanes assigned to the ship were unsuitable for the shocks of takeoffs or landings at sea, but when flying officer Richard Bulla requested the slightly stauncher Arado 196s, he was told the only available craft were being held in reserve for the pocket battleship *Graf Spee*, which, everyone was embarrassed to admit, had already been scuttled in the La Plata River off Montevideo.

At breakfast and in the evenings at the hotel where he gathered all his officers, Rogge discussed each man's assignments. Some of the junior grades did not appreciate the evening sessions, he knew, but it gave them all a chance to get acquainted, to understand what he wanted done and how he intended to run the show at sea, and it gave him the opportunity of taking their measure.

An old hand, well versed in the workings of the navy's training establishment, Rogge quickly realized that the personnel bureaus had fobbed off many of their most undesirable elements on *Atlantis*. He could not use those men, and he sent roughly 50 percent of them packing. To add some backbone to the lot, he demanded and got, after a protracted struggle, a dozen senior ratings from the sail training ships. In his final selection, he ended up with a goodly number of reservists from the merchant marine, 32 men under twenty years old, 160 between twenty and twenty-five, 95 between twenty-six and thirty, and 38 over thirty-one. It was an excellent mix, but experience later showed that older reservists and married men with families failed to stand up to the strain of an extended tour as well as those unburdened by personal worries.

The problems faced by the various department heads were endless: which charts and sailing instructions to take; how many sextants, how much line—manila or hemp—chain and cable, ammunition and binoculars. The tons of supplies were a headache and presented an unprecedented challenge. *Goldenfels,* as originally built for peacetime service, could hold enough provisions to sustain a crew of forty-five and twelve passengers for three months in her reefer compartments and storerooms, and usually her trading voyages took her to a port where fresh water, fruit, and vegetables could be replenished every fortnight or so. When she set out as *Schiff 16,* she carried a complement of 347, subsequently took over three times that number in prisoners, and actually did not meet up with a supply ship for more than a year. Everything from armatures, blankets, cameras, summer and winter clothing—pith helmets and fur-lined watch coats—combs, erasers, jacks, light bulbs, nails, paper and pencils, pigs, quartz, razors, soap, steel plate, toothbrushes, tools, and zinc oxide that the ship would need for a year at sea had to be found, ordered, and acquired.

SOME OF THE DISGUISES EMPLOYED BY THE RAIDERS

The officers in ATLANTIS found only 26 ships which bore a striking resemblance to
the raider and might also have been found in the latter's area of operation. Minor alterations to stacks, ventilators, derrick posts, masts and superstructure were usually made
to complete the disguise. Here are some of the vessels ATLANTIS pretended to be:

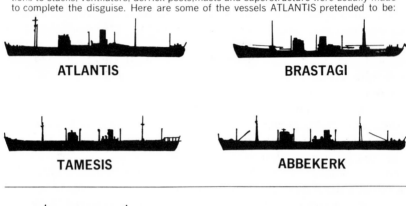

ATLANTIS	BRASTAGI

TAMESIS	ABBEKERK

ORION	BEEMSTERDIJK

Similarly, other raiders like ORION, successfully passed inspection as BEEMSTERDIJK....

KOMET	TOKYO MARU

while KOMET played at being TOKYO MARU, and................

PINGUIN	TAMERLANE

PINGUIN, sistership to ATLANTIS, tried to get by as TAMERLANE.......... By comparison
it would have been very difficult for any of these ships to disguise themselves as vessels
such as GETUYO MARU or CORNWALL

GETUYO MARU	CORNWALL

When *Atlantis* was all decorated, bolted, welded, screwed, and hammered together again, the worst was over. But it was still to be over three months before she was ready to sail.

Finally, on March 11, 1940, the raider, following in the wake of the old battleship *Hessen,* then being used as an icebreaker, and followed in turn by raiders *Orion* (36) and *Widder* (21), sailed through the Kiel Canal to try out her flack and main armament in the North Sea.* Ten days later, she was in the Süderpiep being redisguised as the Russian *Kim,* a good trick because no one in those days, and especially not the Allies, would want to meddle with any of Stalin's property. And there behind the sand banks she stayed for ten tedious days until the weather worsened enough to allow her escape.

On March 31 they sailed and headed north past drifting mines, fishing boats and other vessels, escorted by a submarine whose skipper would much have preferred to be sinking ships. It was so cold that *Atlantis'* adjutant, Ensign Dr. Ulrich Mohr, an educated linguist and world traveler who had joined the ship to replace a "nice but helpless art professor," noted that it took him twenty minutes to get dressed—union suit, wool shirt, wool underpants and trousers, a sweater, leather jacket, watch coat, leather coat—and that he then could not move to get up to the bridge.

Although the raider managed to get through a cordon of British ships unseen, Rogge felt things had not gone the way they should have and therefore mustered his men. They had a lot to learn, he said; one idiot had rushed out on deck in uniform to stare at a passing British plane; others had marched about at night playing with flashlights; the Russian flag had been hoisted upside down, and the crew of gun No. 6 on the poop had paraded in full view of a pretend enemy during a drill. That sort of indolence and indifference verged on the suicidal, he told them; Germany did not control the exits from the North Sea, and she controlled the high seas not at all, no matter what the propagandists in Berlin claimed. It was time to work, not play at war.

The work began on April 16 when Rogge was handed the decoded version of SKL's wireless message "1814/16/57." He did not like what he read one bit: *"Ship 16* speed up march to South Atlantic. Appear soonest on Cape-Freetown route to relieve the situation in the North Sea." The rest of the signal concerned *Orion, Schiff 36,* which had set out on the sixth of the month. *Orion* was to make her presence felt in

---

* The Germans gave numbers to all the raiders, as they did to their auxiliaries of all types. It was the ships' captains' privilege to name them. Thus, *Schiff* 16 was *Atlantis, Schiff* 36, *Orion.* The British lettered these vessels as their activities became known. *Orion* was A, *Atlantis,* C.

the North Atlantic, and she could do that by pretending to be an Allied ship under attack by a pocket battleship.

Rogge, of course, understood the reasons behind SKL's move. So far, during the war, the communiqués from the navy had been a mixed bag of success and failure, with the U-boats providing most of the action. And even though the pocket battleships had raised such hell with the Royal Navy that Churchill had complained of "the disproportion between the strength of the enemy and the countermeasures forced on us," the performances of *Spee* and *Deutschland* had been a tactical disappointment, the former having been scuttled at Montevideo and the latter having sunk only two ships. The rest of the fleet's units, though irritating to the Allies, had accomplished very little before the Norwegian campaign. And in the struggle for that hapless nation, Germany's losses would be three cruisers, ten destroyers, one torpedo boat, and nine U-boats.

Atlantis' captain knew he would have to act to relieve the strain at home. He had intended to approach Cape Agulhas at a steady ten knots to lay ninety-two mines during the new-moon night of May 7, then take up raiding. Now he would have to speed up—that was costly (at twelve knots his expenditure of fuel rose 44 percent and at fourteen knots it jumped a full 90 percent)—and the British would be alerted to his approach if a ship he attacked radioed. And it was pointless, he realized, to cause a disturbance down south if *Orion* succeeded in convincing the Royal Navy that there was a pocket battleship loose up north; it would only make it harder for both raiders. He would compromise, taking a ship if possible without its getting off a distress message so that it would merely be reported overdue some days later. That was not what SKL had had in mind, of course, but he was only taking Raeder at his word: If orders from home conflict with the local tactical situation, the admiral had said, "Just carry on with your own plans."

Atlantis, most of her men thought, fed well; everyone—captain, officers, and crew (later, the prisoners, too)—shared the same menu, and they were all restricted to a few quarts of fresh water each. They crossed the Line on a "milksoup with noodles" day, but could not celebrate: too risky to have people running about the ship in the narrowest part of the Atlantic. April 24, it was pork chops, potato salad, and pudding for lunch; boisterous equator crossing ceremony with much pointed kidding about the captain's exactitude and "Papa" Kühn's ability to shout. Kühn used that capacity just a few days later when he hounded his men from truck to boot topping as they painted over the drab *Kim* with the bright white, red, and black of Japan's *Kasii Maru* (Kokusai Steamship Company, Ltd.), one of the twenty-six ships thought passable as a likely disguise in those waters. On May 2 they got a chance to stand to in full regalia to test the new disguise. Mohr, who had escaped a mine-sweeping job to become Rogge's maid-of-all-work as adjutant, was draped in a kimono; pilot Bulla, sporting flannels and accompanied by a small, fragile lad—his "wife"—was pushing a baby carriage (which had not been forgotten). On deck, there were only a few of the shortest, darkest men who might have passed as Japanese from a distance. Everyone else was at his battle station, hidden in deckhouses, behind bulwarks and the raider's collapsible sides. They were passing a big gray armed British liner, the *City of Exeter,* which was on a reciprocal course and just a few miles off to port. Rogge did not attack (he did not wish to burden himself with the 230 or so passengers the ship might have been carrying), but *Atlantis'* disguise did not hold. The liner reported having passed "a suspicious ship," and though the Germans were not to know that until mid-July, it was to affect their operations almost immediately.

Rogge's men were disappointed that he had let the big ship go because they seemed to have been trapped into a dull routine of drills, painting, repairs, or a movie now and then. The barber still charged 30 Pfennige (about 6¢) for a haircut, the shoemaker Mark 1.50 for a new pair of heels and soles, and the shoes did wear down in that big war. Even the wardroom below the bridge had settled into a stereotyped mechanical performance. The "Oberhaus" (House of Lords) did not like the radio blaring at mealtimes; the "Commons" did, and loud, too, for it was not at their end of the table. Conversations rambled widely from the war to overeating, red-bearded mining officer Johann Heinrich Fehler's smutty remarks, or a cutting jibe by one of the doctors. But shortly after 1400 on May 3, there was a shrilling of the alarm bells and the clatter of hundreds of feet trampling up and down, and along the steel ladders, decks, and alleyways in the helter-skelter disorganized organization of a warship going to battle stations. One officer tore by Mohr's cabin yelling, "They've got one, they've got one, just ahead and to port!!!" Clearly the man had buck fever, Mohr thought, as he picked up his binoculars and bounded for the bridge.

Within three minutes all the men were at their posts with the ship buttoned up for battle and the deadly quiet that had come over the raider broken only by the throbbing of the diesels and the swish of the water rushing alongside. Down below, the engineers, electricians, ammo handlers, and damage-control teams, all the men who never saw anything of an action and could only suffer its consequences, stood by their motors, generators, hoists, steering engines, and fire extinguishers waiting and hoping for the best. Up on the forecastle the lads in their white denims crouched by the 3-inch and 20-mm guns. Further aft, the gunners at the four 5.9s under the false shelter deck waited for the command to release the levers that would let the heavy hinged sides go clanging up. Amidships torpedo men fumbled with their bulky tubes while Bulla ambled about on the boat deck above them with his "wife" and "baby." Aft, on the poop and aftercastle the 5.9 and 37-mm gun crews were ready to send their house-of-cards disguises crashing at the single word *"Enttarnen!"* (drop the disguises). On the bridge there were only two men visible, Rogge and Mohr, as would be normal for a merchantman. Except for an occasional mumbled exchange, an order from Rogge, and the monotonous singsong of the seaman calling off the ranges from gunnery officer Lieutenant (s.g.) Lorenz Kasch's range finder hidden in a water tank above the wheelhouse, there was not a sound. Time seemed to have stopped as the other ship slowly, ever so slowly, rose over the horizon and grew in size, its masts, stack, ventilators, and boats gradually becoming distinguishable. It seemed almost unreal that this was what they had all prepared for for so long. At 1417, when only the rim of the vessel's funnel could be seen, Rogge ordered hard left to course 40° to close, and it was soon evident that they would meet in a crossing situation. By 1436 it was clear that the ship was a modern freighter, carried a gun in a tub on her stern, and was therefore without any doubt an enemy. At 1455 the German war ensign fluttered out and the flag signal "OL," "LNU," "LUL," meaning "Heave to or I will fire; you are prohibited from radioing," was hoisted. Nothing happened. 1456: "Starboard forward 5.9s 'Enttarnen!' 37mm and 3-inch permission to fire." The automatic 37-mm could not open up because its arc of fire was limited by the superstructure, but the 3-incher on the bow cracked out two warning shots. Still nothing happened. The other ship simply continued on its course and hoisted the red-white-red answering pennant that meant "I see your signal."

"To make our intentions more clear," Rogge ordered the two big starboard 5.9s to fire one additional warning shot each. That invitation apparently *was* a bit more clear; the Englishman hoisted his answering pennant close up, meaning "I understand your signal." He blew off some steam and it appeared that he was slowing down. Instead, he heeled over in a sharp turn to his starboard and rushed off. The handles of Rogge's engine room annunciators slid to full ahead. He then fired off one salvo of two 100-pound shells with his 5.9s (one hit the ship's stern) and then, when it became evident that the enemy had no intention of stopping, another salvo into the vessel's side under the port bridge. "Cease fire!" It was enough, Rogge hoped.

Two minutes later, at 1505, *Scientist,* ignoring the risk, started to radio a "QQQQ" message.* *Atlantis* replied with four more salvos, three of which went wide due to a faulty electrical converter. One lucky shell, however, struck a stay and the resulting explosion smashed the ship's sandbagged radio shack to splinters. A fourth salvo registered amidships, and minutes later the enemy again blew off steam and this time quickly lost way. Her men took to the boats. At 1526 *Atlantis'* boarding party, Mohr, a prize officer, and nine men, all in Roggian tidy uniform carrying a machine gun, pistols, grenades, seabags, tools, first-aid kit, signal flags, and Very pistol, and looking much like a landing party at Gallipoli, lowered their motorboat. Nine minutes later they scrambled up the 6,199-ton *Scientist's* ladder to be met by T. and J. Harrison Company's Captain Windsor and his chief officer, Watson, the only men who had remained aboard the now burning ship. The meeting was punctiliously courteous, reserved, and correct. No, Windsor said, he had no secret papers; he had thrown them overboard in a weighted sack; standard procedure.

The Germans gave the two officers fifteen minutes to pack, then fanned out to predetermined parts of the ship to investigate and collect whatever items might be useful, and an eerie business it was—that first time. It took one back to the tingling fears of children investigating a deserted house; an empty ship, footsteps reverberating, doors swinging to and fro with the swell, and the mementos of the former crew staring accusingly at the intruders. And who could tell but that the enemy had planted explosives which might then be ticking, undiscovered, ready to blow? Mohr dumped every scrap of paper and mail he could find into his bags for later evaluation; others collected binoculars, sextants, charts, and the like and ordnance men went below to attach their scuttling charges.

There was need for hurrying, too. *Scientist* was burning furiously by then and the fire could have been seen fifty miles away. Anxious to get away, Rogge ordered a torpedo fired to send the ship down just a few hours after she had first been sighted. She would be considered overdue at Sierra Leone on May 10.

Back on the raider, the two doctors, Georg Reil and Surgeon Sprung, carefully removed wooden splinters from the *Scientist's* radio-man while the rest of the seventy-seven prisoners were searched for knives, money, and matches (receipts were given and later honored). After a check for communicable diseases, they were sent below to their respective quarters, senior officers into a small section equipped with

---

* "QQQQ" meant a merchant raider; "RRRR" a warship; "SSSS" a submarine. In this case the brave message, sent out at great risk, was not picked up by any station except the raider's.

bunks, and the rest separated as was the custom on their own ships, whites into one room with hammocks, blacks into another. They were given blankets, eating utensils, soap, and shaving equipment. The whites would draw forty pfennigs per day for use at the canteen, they were told, and the blacks would get twenty pfennigs for working in various parts of the ship.

Once the curiosity about the prisoners wore off, and only hours after the action, everything was back to normal. Gunnery officer Kasch, who had ordered book No. 452, was sore at the library, which sent him No. 453 with a note saying that 452, while available, was a scholarly work. The ward room now had its long-wished-for "boy," a swarthy fellow named Kaloo who was handy with ashtrays, and Captain Windsor, when invited for a drink, insisted that he would have recognized *Atlantis* as non-Japanese immediately if his second officer had only wakened him when she came into sight.

Hitler's troops jumped off into Holland and Belgium and Luxembourg on May 10 for a startling campaign that eclipsed the British landing on Iceland and all but overshadowed the election of Winston Churchill as Prime Minister. On that night, a velvety black one with thousands of stars sparkling above, *Atlantis* laid her mines inside the 120-fathom line between five and twenty-six miles off Cape Agulhas light, whose bright beam flickered over the raider at regular and uncomfortable intervals. It was a dangerous venture, and one not worth the risk of losing a valuable ship and crew, Rogge thought, noting that such a job should be carried out by a captured vessel—one that could easily get by without being noticed and needed but a few men to man her.*

Rogge, rid of the mines, headed east to scour the Durban-Australia track between 25°S and 28°S but found nothing despite the use of his fragile plane whose engine finally gave out. He found nothing because of the vigilance of the *City of Exeter*'s captain whose warning about a suspicious vessel had been relayed to the commander in chief East Indies at Colombo who then diverted traffic to the north. A message sent out on the tenth and a warning that a German raider might be disguised as a Japanese and might be loose in the Indian Ocean was intercepted by *Atlantis,* which then changed her masquerade once more to become the Dutch *Abbekerk,* which she closely resembled. Lacking success, Rogge moved his operations north to intersect both the Durban-Batavia and the Mauritius-Australia shipping lanes. But it was not until June 10, the day after hostilities ceased in Norway, and the same day

* The operation was a failure despite Berlin's claims. The Agulhas light keeper reported an explosion May 15 and mine warnings were broadcast, sweepers readied at Capetown and East London. Eighty-one mines were swept up and the rest presumably blew up as they were supposed to when their moorings broke.

Italy entered the war, that he came up with another ship, the 7,230-ton Norwegian *Tirranna*.

Capt. E. H. Gundersen had seen the raider, which he mistook for the real *Abbekerk,* coming up on him on a slightly converging course, and he had been damned if was going to let the "Dutchman" pass him, not *his* new, two-year-old and fast ship. Rogge chased him for nearly three hours until exactly at noon, fearing he might not ever get any closer, he went into action. The Norwegians did not see the German ensign nor the flag hoist ordering them to stop because the sun was in their eyes. Since they kept on going and had ignored a few warning shots, which fell short and had had no effect, another warning salvo was fired. It was over, and its tall fountains could not be overlooked. *Tirranna* turned, showed her stern, and opened up with her wireless. *Atlantis'* radiomen jammed the message, but the Norwegians, zigzagging wildly, kept running, and they fought back with their 4.7-inch gun.* It took thirty-nine salvos and 150 shells to stop her. When *Atlantis* finally came alongside *Tirranna,* it was the second time in less than a year that the two ships had lain together. The first had been in Bombay the previous July when *Tirranna* and ex-*Goldenfels'* crews had played soccer. The scores were even found in the diary of the Norwegian's third officer, Svenn Bjørneby. By the thirteenth the raider was moving toward the Aden-Australia and Sunda Strait–Durban crossroads redisguised as the Dutch *Tariffa*—typically dark brown like many of the Allied vessels sailing under Admiralty orders—because it had been learned that the real *Abbekerk* had been sunk. But the change of venue and colors brought the raider no luck for nearly another four weeks. During that time *Orion* had made herself known to the world when the large liner *Niagara* ran into one of her mines off Auckland on June 18. A week later, even more portentous communiqués from the other side of the world, where France had capitulated, sent corks popping in the messes. Bets were made when the ship could enter some port and when the war would finally be over. The only agreement was that it would either last a very long time or be very short. Some thought a few weeks, others, and mostly those who knew the British, opted for that many years.

MUCKING ABOUT IN A BLOODY MESS

"Nothing sighted," "Nothing sighted," "Nothing sighted." It was the same entry in the log every noon on every day: "Nothing sighted," even

---

* *Tirranna*'s signal was heard by an American, *Eastern Guide,* which asked "shelled by whom?" Her suspicions allayed by *Atlantis'* reply and another far-off station which advised her that there was nothing for her, *Eastern Guide* did not relay the message.

in the new operation area roughly bounded by 0°S, 84°E, and 2°S, 87°E, which was terribly hot and uncomfortable. Practically not to be believed by the bored men was the huge black smoke cloud (bad Natal coal) sighted at 0643 on July 11. A ship! A ship! This time the men really welcomed the bells and tooting horns that urged them to quarters. Unsuspecting, 7,506-ton *City of Bagdad,* a World War I reparations prize then en route from England to Penang, came into easy range, did not use her Japanese-made 4.7-inch gun, and was stopped by a signal and four 3-inch warning shots. But then she radioed and that earned her both recognition onshore where her signals were heard and a shelling that smashed her radio room and parts of her upper works. Mohr puttered over to the wayless ship in his launch and rushed up to her bridge, where he found the slender white-haired captain kneeling in his demolished cabin by a safe and about to destroy some documents. "What a bloody mess," the German adjutant said in his perfect, slightly American-accented English as Armstrong White turned to face him. The British officer thought so, too, but there was not much that he could have done about it.

Mohr fished about the ill-kept ship while its twenty-one Europeans and sixty Lascars packed their belongings. He found some things he needed—convoy routing instructions, the captain's log and merchant codes, the latter among some winter clothing—and pounds of dusty bills, letters, pamphlets, and prospectuses that he did not. There was so much literature, he thought, that even the Kriegsmarine's bureaucrats would have been astonished. He also discovered a dirty piece of paper that neatly described *Atlantis* and showed a picture of one of her sister ships, courtesy of the *City of Exeter.* When he spotted White's personal RCA Victor radio, he commented that it was a pity a magnificent set like that should be lost. Armstrong White, realizing that he himself had little further use for it, and the fish none at all, said, "Why not take it?" then helped his captor "muck about dismantling it." That courtesy was rapidly repaid in the nightly invitations to Mohr's cabin in *Atlantis* where the British skipper was served drinks, met the raider's officers, and was allowed to listen to BBC.

Very welcome to the Germans were hundreds of pounds of fresh potatoes the *City* carried and the rice that would feed the many native captives (there were then already more than one hundred). Having taken what was needed, the old ship was sunk by Lieutenant Johann Heinrich Fehler in an experiment that netted him a few fatherly remarks from Rogge and a permanent place in the log. Fehler loved explosives, and he was aware that the forty pounds taken along to send the *Scientist* down had not been enough. This time he was prepared with seven times that amount and he was going to stay on board just to see what happened. The big bang was so effective that Fehler, his arm cut in the process, barely had time to escape to his boat as the ship rushed down within seven minutes. His captain thought the test noteworthy, but a repetition inadvisable.

During a careful debriefing after the action, the guns cleaned, the prisoners sent below, and the brass cartridge cases collected, Rogge emphasized several points. The crew had worked well even during the unexpected crisis when steering control was lost. (It took only one hundred seconds before it was regained.) Warning shots with the 3-incher he had asked for explicitly for that purpose were not apparently impressive enough. Henceforth, the 5.9s would do the job and at the same time give the gunnery officer a few ranging shots. Drifting rafts must be secured so that everyone clinging to them could be saved. The dead and dying should be bedded below, out of sight of the hustle and bustle of the boarding party's activity. The session was a bit depressing, for it foreshadowed a harder war. Not only were the Allied ships making every effort to comply with Admiralty orders regardless of the rules of war by radioing and fighting back, but their petrified crews took to the boats even when ordered not to. It was quite obvious even at that early stage of the war that a ship could not be stopped or silenced without the use of overwhelming firepower which caused panic and, much to Rogge's sorrow, destruction and death.

"Noon; 13.7; Friday; Nothing sighted." Everything was the same again, from the stiff white uniform coats and black ties on the bridge to the oily hands of the sweating greasers below. But the harder war started for *Atlantis* within twenty-four hours when she came across *Kemmendine* and her 147 people, many of them women and children. The sixteen-year-old 7,769-ton liner, steaming from Glasgow to Rangoon with piece goods, beer, and whiskey, showed no concern at the raider's approach, and was a very welcome sight because Rogge hoped he could use her to rid himself of his more than 200 prisoners. When wireless tuning sounds were intercepted by the main radio room on the bridge and erroneously thought to be coming from the British ship (they later turned out to be those of the raider's own auxiliary station down below), Rogge decided to nip the resistance in the bud. Ordering the ship to stop, he cut loose with his 5.9s which immediately set *Kemmendine* on fire. The British stopped, signaled that they were surrendering, and did not radio. Then, as the raider, her guns already trained inboard and covered again, worked in closer to pick up the numerous boats and their survivors, a shot was fired by a single man from the nearly deserted liner's 12-pounder (3-inch) gun and whistled past *Atlantis*. The boats pulled out of the line of fire frantically and Rogge's normal outward calm and self-discipline broke down. "Open fire!" His guns responded, causing the lonely figure across the water to hastily leave his exposed post. "Cease fire!"

An investigation by Rogge, two of his officers, Capt. R. B. Reid, master of *Kemmendine,* and Capt. Armstrong White, disclosed that the plucky gunner had acted in good faith:

> I can only say that owing to steampipe bursts no orders could be given through the telephone and no order was given to the gun or to use it. The orders that I gave was to stop immediately after we recognized your signals and we answered it with flag "K." Then I ordered all hands to take to the boats and get the boats away from the ship as quickly as possible. I was not aware that our gun had been fired until I was informed by the commander of the German warship.
>
> Signed: Reid, Master

Nothing was done about the matter which could have caused serious consequences and death to many people (luckily, no one was killed in *Kemmendine*). After all, how could a gentleman and officer like Rogge really, on reflection, bother to have a man who had been a London window cleaner punished?

For a while after the excitement was over, the raider looked and sounded like a bazaar. Most of the people had brought very little with them in the boats, and *Kemmendine*'s fire had spread so rapidly that the boarding party had been able to come back with little more than a few garments and a forgotten teddy bear. Clothing had to be distributed and the crying, jumpy mass of prisoners lodged. One lady and her two children were given the cabin of Ensign (S) Kurt Waldmann who was off running the prize *Tirranna*.* The rest of the European women passengers were assigned to the room belonging to the quartermasters' mates, who naturally resented the intrusion. The Indian passengers were sent aft to the contagious disease ward, which was empty, and the native crew went down to be sardined into the former mine room.

Rogge then had 327 prisoners on board, had traveled 23,000

---

* The German Navy, like most others, made a distinction between professional officers, reservists, and others in designating their ranks. "S" (*Sonderführer:* special leader) applied to merchant marine captains and officers given naval rank to perform certain duties, usually as watch, or prize officers, in which capacity they were most efficient. "R" stood for reservists. The various differentiations proved to be an endless source of irritation and dispute. The regular German Navy ranks compared to those of the United States Navy: Leutnant (Ensign); Oberleutnant (Lieutenant); Kapitänleutnant (Lieutenant S. G.); Korvettenkapitän (Lt. Commander); Fregattenkapitän (Commander); Kapitän zur See (Captain).

miles, and had captured four ships. And in his four months behind the enemy's lines, he had learned the lessons badly needed by SKL for their appraisal of the entire effort and the guidance of the other raider captains. Since he had kept radio silence despite their repeated requests for information, they had been dependent on enemy intercepts just to guess at his approximate whereabouts and doings. On July 11 and 12, their patience worn thin, SKL strongly urged him to pass on his acquired knowledge, adding that the chances of the British getting a fix on his transmission, and thereby his bearings, were slim, indeed. Once, Rogge again compromised: "6°S, 77°E; able to keep at sea for more than 85 days; have sunk up to 30,000 tons." Berlin's premise had been wrong; the alert British stations did get a fix on the message but, for them, unfortunately it was of no use, for it showed only latitude and that with an error of three degrees.

Atlantis' own radio officer, Lt. Adolf Wenzel, and mate Heinrich Wesemann, on the other hand, had achieved a grand coup during those days. Wesemann, an excellent operator whose competence had kept him on shore duty as an instructor, had volunteered for the job on the raider—of whose proposed employment he had heard from a friend despite all the hush-hush that had had Rogge and many of his men in mufti during her outfitting. The young mate picked out two British messages, one en clair on six hundred meters, the other in code on thirty-six meters, but both with the same dateline and an identical number of letters. With some help from Berlin, and some outdated superencipherment tables found in *City of Bagdad,* he then reconstructed nearly one half of the British merchant code, later kept up with its constant changes by employing newer tables captured from other vessels. Not so commendable, Rogge thought, was the work done by all but one man of the prize crew assigned to *Tirranna* which the raider had joined again on July 29.

Finding the mail and packages on that ship irresistible, Waldmann's men had helped themselves shamelessly until the hold, Mohr noted, was a dump, knee-deep in ripped paper, trampled cakes, mateless socks, and crumpled cookies. Waldmann had told them that they could have three pairs of socks, two shirts, and one sweater each, but Rogge's investigators inspected the men's bags and found themselves, much to their dismay, confronted by a pack of petty thieves. One man had squirreled away a watch, silverware, tea, forty-six pairs of socks, twenty shirts, and nine sets of pajamas. Actually, the stuff did not belong to anyone anymore and it might be sent to the bottom of the sea, but to Rogge the plundering was a serious breach of discipline. Worse yet was the theft of Captain Armstrong White's binoculars. A thorough search was made, but the thief was not discovered before he had thrown the glasses overboard. Though the British master intervened in the wretch's favor, a three-man court, Mohr, Bulla, and a senior boatswain's mate handed down a ruling, and that stood: two years.

During those late July, early August days, *Atlantis* was drifting alongside *Tirranna,* her men painting, shifting supplies, and getting the prize ready for her trip to Europe. On August 2 *Tirranna* raised the alarm. A ship! It was coming right at the two stopped Germans through the mist. It was also soon in their hands, and Rogge's men took what they needed—fresh provisions, blankets, instruments, tools, an excellent motorboat, and oil—before using the 6,732-ton *Talleyrand,* another Wilhelmsen liner like *Tirranna,* as a target for their plane, which practiced bombing and tearing out aerials with a trailing hook. The Norwegian's crew were taken over to *Tirranna,* where many of them found friends and relatives, and the third officer of *Talleyrand,* Finn Bjørneby, met his younger brother, Svenn, who had held down the same rank in the prize and whom he had not seen in three years. The captains, too, were friends and seem to have shared each other's tastes. Matias Foyn, of *Talleyrand,* greeted *Tirranna*'s Gundersen, who, he knew, had been missing, by asking whether he was still afraid of crossing the Indian Ocean unescorted. How did Foyn know about the company's other captain's worries? Well, that little gal back there in Melbourne had mentioned them.

On August 5 *Tirranna,* with Ensign (S) Waldmann still in charge, and assisted by *Goldenfels'* former first officer, now Ensign (S) Louis Mund, along with a sixteen-man prize crew composed mostly of personnel already under punishment, parted company with the raider and took along 273 of its prisoners. She was off to a very uncertain future—the blockade and France.

To *Atlantis'* crew life lost some of its flavor when all that colorful crowd was gone. While they had not been allowed much contact with the prisoners, the average sailor did have sympathy for them. The children, of course, had been a delight. The Germans had made them toys and a sandbox, gave them candies, and the hoppy little ones, probably as content as at home, had climbed all over. Rogge's officers did have a closer association with their opposite numbers who were allowed the use of the pool and could attend movies. Armstrong White particularly liked one actress in *Love Letters from the Engadine;* Mohr did not; she was not his type. "What, after this much time at sea, you're still talking about type," the Briton asked. They partied, too, either down in the captured captains' crude but somewhat comfortable quarters or in the Germans' cabins.

At midnight August 24, Mohr stood down tired from the first watch. With little desire for joining Kasch or Chief Engineer Wilhelm Kielhorn, a Bavarian, who was as competent in handling steins of beer as he was in getting the best out of his machinery, the adjutant drifted off to his cabin to read awhile before going to sleep. He did not hear the alarms rattling but he could not mistake Fehler's "Damn!" Back to the bridge it was at 0245 for many disconsolate hours of following a strange ship through alternating periods of showers, which blotted out everything, and sharp bright moonlight, which shone more on the raider than it did its opponent. No one could make out what it was—freighter, flattop, cruiser? Its speed, originally estimated at five knots, dropped to one and then nothing, and the Germans feared they were running into a trap. Q-boat? Had they been seen? Just before dawn, by which time it was clear that the vessel was a merchant type, Rogge had only one choice: attack without warning before the other ship, Q-boat, AMC, or not, took the initiative. A torpedo missed; Kash's first salvo did not. Three shells hit, immediately setting the vessel on fire. Its bridge structure collapsed within minutes. Sickened by what they had had to do for their own preservation, the Germans closed in and dropped two motorboats to lend assistance. Thirty-one men were saved; four young cadets died, trapped in their burning cabin, another was missing, and a sixth man succumbed to his wounds on *Atlantis'* operating table, victims of one of the many misunderstandings in many horrible wars—a tragedy to Rogge and his men no matter what they personally felt about the conflict at large. The twelve-year-old 4,744-ton *King City's* peculiar movements had been due to engine trouble, and her stopping to the failure of her boiler room ventilators.

It was grievous, indeed, the Germans felt, that so much could depend on so little. But then the whole war seemed to have gotten a firm hold on the men who waged it, could not stop it, and therefore let it spread without any resolution in sight. Göring's "Blitz," unsteadily shifting from target to target, was not showing any results and its failure led to constant on-again, off-again invasion crises that wasted both sides' energies and frayed their nerves. A few cruiser brushes in the Mediterranean showed Britain that the Italians were not about to take advantage of the initiative their numbers gave them, and the latter were turning their eyes on Greece, their ill-equipped soldiers in slow motion against Abyssinia, British Somaliland, and Egypt. In the Atlantic, to be sure, it was different. The U-boats alone were having a "happy time," sinking upwards of fifty ships per month, leaving the British desperately short of escorts and unable to do much about the wolves' far-flung depredations. But those few boats (the number of those operational had dwindled from an original forty-nine to thirty) were not going to win the war very quickly, Rogge and many of his men thought, and the United States, having traded British bases for fifty flush-deck four-stacked destroyers, was clearly not willing to stand aside if the Germans did show signs of winning. With America behind Britain, the latter could possibly last forever, and many of *Atlantis'* officers who had made their bets back in June over a few glasses of champagne had already lost. Gone, too, were the romantic dreams in which the raider, her ensign and pennant snapping, slid majestically into some neutral port—or even an Allied one, for that matter—to give her men some liberty, gentle, perfumed companionship, and a swim at a white sandy beach. The war was not going to be won at sea, the young crew feared; under it, possibly, but never on it, not with most of Germany's remaining fleet bottled up in port or undergoing repairs or alterations. Their commander had intimated this in his cautious appraisals of the loud and stupid propaganda whistling out from darkened Berlin, which had already been bombed.

Rogge had worries of his very own, some shared with his men, some not. Everyone realized that it had taken one month of "half ahead," "slow," or just drifting for each vessel captured or sunk so far—tiresome work. Understood, too, was the fact that the Admiralty never slept. Whitehall must by then have identified—even if not by name—at least three or four of the other raiders out prowling at sea, and Her Lordships would have realized that it was they who had been responsible for the loss of twenty-three ships. *Atlantis'* minefield had been discovered, and another, laid by *Orion* off New Zealand, had already claimed a large vessel. The two fields might have been attributed to one raider, but in August *Orion* had fought a vicious battle in the Tasman Sea—too far away to serve as an alibi for Rogge whose victims had gone missing in the Indian Ocean. In the Atlantic, where many Allied ships were long overdue, the situation was more confused, but certainly not enough to keep London's intelligence officers guessing overly long. *Widder* had injudiciously let some captives go in the Caribbean; *Thor* had successfully battled an AMC off Brazil; and *Pinguin,* en route to the Indian Ocean, had also made her presence felt. (Sixth raider *Komet,* outbound for the Pacific via the dreaded, mostly impassable Northeast Passage around Russia, had not yet done any damage, and could therefore not have been discovered.) Obviously, Britain's countermeasures would harden, no matter how preoccupied the Royal Navy was in standing off defeat around the world.

With few to confide in, and little to go on strategically, Rogge's most immediate problems revolved around his own immediate tactics, and these would be upset the day *Pinguin* rounded the Cape and came near to his operational area. He could not quarrel with SKL's decision to send a long-ranged ship like her, with little need for provisioning, to a distant ocean. But *Pinguin, ex-Kandelfels,* was a sistership of *Atlantis,* and Rogge deplored the employment of two identical ships, neither of which knew under which disguise the other was sailing, in the same general area. It cramped his style and would make his hunting more difficult. More galling, still, were the indications that the other commander, Captain Ernst-Felix Krüder, seemed to be poaching. An intercepted signal, "QQ 2937 S 4550E stopped by unknown vessel BRITISH COMMANDER . . . vessel now shelling us," which had also been picked up by the British, proved that *Pinguin* was way behind schedule. She should have been 2,000 miles to the east by then (east of 80°E) and Rogge fretted lest a chance meeting between the two tonnage-hungry raiders, especially at night, might end in disaster.

His other most pressing worries concerned *Tirranna* and his own communications system. Back at home, postal and telegraph experts had advised him that his wireless equipment was fine, as good, say, as the liner *Scharnhorst's.* But Rogge, Wenzel, and Wesemann knew that their two 125-watt shortwave and one 200-watt low-frequency sets were not the *Scharnhorst's* (1,000 watt) and that atmospheric conditions often made their use questionable. That is why *Tirranna,* which boasted a more powerful installation, had been ordered to advise SKL of her own release and expected time of arrival in Europe. But not one *dit-daah* had been heard from her, and it was imperative that SKL be forewarned so that the ship and its 292 people could be safely brought through the final desperate stretch to safety. There was only one thing Rogge could do: radio himself. Since he could not do that where he was without disclosing his position and possibly his intentions, he had to move some five hundred miles south to get off a signal. For some reason even that was not understood by Germany. He then ran another few hundred miles to the east and, though he did make contact that time, he was exasperated, complaining bitterly that "experts" at home should cause men at the front additional burdens.

His run to get off his message netted him two more ships, tanker *Athelking* and freighter *Benarty,* both of which were badly shot up because *Atlantis'* operators mistook the origin of some wireless messages. The two vessels had radioed as was expected of them by the Admiralty, but they had ceased transmitting once actually attacked, the former by the raider, the latter by its plane as well as the barking 5.9s. *Athelking* had asked for medical assistance and was about to receive it when she was thought to be signaling again. The raider renewed its shelling of the fourteen-year-old motor tanker to silence her, and three men of her complement of forty were killed, including her captain.*

Rogge had hoped to operate against the normally heavy concentration of shipping off Sunda Strait, but had to give up that plan because anyone drawing a line through the positions given by his last quarries could easily deduce his intentions. Not wanting to commit the same error *Spee*'s captain had in the South Atlantic, he decided to lay low for a while in the south, perhaps picking up a ship or two on the Australian route while diverting attention from the mid-Indian Ocean area. To get anything down there, he would need some luck, he knew, for the chances were stacked against him. They had worked it out once in the chart house and had come to the conclusion that it was definitely very difficult to find a ship on a big ocean. If, for example, there are thirty vessels on passage between Australia and Africa, traveling within an eight-degree belt, they would have a strip 480 miles by roughly 4,000 miles in which to search. A good part of every twenty-four hours is dark, some of it moonless, and during the hours of light average visibility is only approximately 30 miles. Quite difficult, and even more so if your weakly built Heinkel happened to have its motor drop out in a landing. But they did run across a ship late September 19 and Rogge was delighted at the opportunity of getting rid of his 230 prisoners. For a few moments it even looked as if he might. *Atlantis*' blinker clapped: "Do not radio." The stranger instantly replied: "Understood." "Stop or I will shoot." "Understood." "What ship?" *"Commissaire Ramel."* "Wait for my boat." *Commissaire Ramel* blew off steam and set its lights as the raider closed for an inspection. Then the French ship radioed. Rogge hesitated for a moment before ordering his guns into action. A damned shame, he thought, as the vessel burst into flames, its hull red or white hot with streams of molten glass running down its sides and hissing into the sea like lava. Down she slid over her stern and out went the rosy glow reflected from the clouds above. Sixty-three more prisoners were added to *Atlantis*' holds.

Friday September 27 was a black day for *Atlantis*, which was by then off Sunda Strait. During the morning the first part of a wireless indicating that *Tirranna* had arrived in France brought about much satisfaction. But the cheer lasted only until a continuation was decoded that afternoon. *Tirranna* had made her offing all right forty-seven days after separating from the raider in the Indian Ocean, but that was all.

---

* The British ship had, in fact, not radioed again, but her original message had been repeated by a nearby ship whose signals the Germans believed to be coming from the supposedly surrendered tanker. Both signals were received by the East Indies Station at Colombo, which immediately sent AMCs *Arawa* and *Westralia* and light cruisers *Capetown* and *Neptune* out searching for the raider.

Though in sight and contact with shore (Ensign Mund had been landed near Cape Ferret to phone the authorities), she never made port. Due to a failure of radio communications en route and poor preparations by the officials on land, the prize ended up a target for H.M.S. *Tuna,* which torpedoed her without warning and sank her within two minutes. Petrified Indians were crushed trying to escape the holds, others mashed as the shifting deck cargo of cars pinned them down. Recriminations over the loss of life (seventy-one Indians, nine British, six Norwegians and one German, according to Finn Bjørneby; sixty prisoners, one German, the latter's records state) and ship were severe amongst the Germans, many of whom still harbor bitter resentments.

Back in the Indian Ocean, Rogge's wearisome stay off Sumatra brought no results except the twenty-seven-year-old Yugoslav *Durmitor,* which, though a neutral, was declared a legal prize because her pajama-clad captain (the Germans observed that that outfit seemed to serve as his night, day, and battle dress) foolishly radioed asking *Atlantis* who she was (he should have communicated by visual means), and admitted that he was headed for enemy-held Batavia "for orders." He was carrying only a cargo of salt and nothing else worth taking, but his engineers said they had enough coal to reach Japan. That decided the vessel's fate—prison ship.

"CLASSICAL STUFF"; BEANS; SAMURAI SWORD

Rogge had to get rid of his captives. They were a millstone around his neck, even though the Arabians proved handy as wipers for Kielhorn's black gang, the Indians for chipping the rust "Papa" Kühn hated so much, and the Chinese—at least those who were not afflicted with syphilis—in the mess where Lung, Chan, and Fong soon became known as Krischnan, Franz, and Willi. The curry and rice Rogge liked so well seemed to get more exotic each Wednesday when it appeared on the menu, but all rations had already been curtailed to keep the raider at sea longer. That, of course, affected the prisoners, Europeans and natives alike, and though they spent up to six hours on deck, had access to the ship's large library of captured English books, beer while it lasted and many a bottle of harder stuff (for the senior officers), their lot was not getting any better. They quarreled among themselves and many of the ratings were bitter that the Germans always supported what vestiges of authority the captive officers still had left. Actually, many of the Germans themselves were not in the best form those days; much grumbling and bulkheading about their officers who seemed to party a lot ("too

much Monday" one Chinese called it surveying the empty places at the
mess) but were always pressing the men in what seemed useless disciplines, the monotonous diet, tactics, and their own role in an endless
war. Sometimes the cheerful music that was constantly piped through
the rooms even got on the simplest men's nerves. "Always that classical
stuff like Kant," one fellow groused. It was hot and humid and difficult to
sleep, but that was no excuse as far as Rogge was concerned. He read
them off quietly and firmly at a muster. They were on a warship and at
war, and their duty to Germany was to fight that war as the SKL and he
best saw fit; their obligation to their shipmates was grin and bear it.
Then he told them that henceforth four men in turn from each division
would be given a week off. They would live aft in the empty contagious
disease ward on the poop and could do anything they liked, or nothing
at all. Battle stations, yes, but no reveille and no saluting.

The men responded with a will, right the next day, October 26, to
prepare and provision the *Durmitor* as a prison van. She was not much
else—and should not have been that—a filthy, ill-found ship infested
with rats and roaches. Her crew had had little to eat or drink and they
had not had the wherewithal to keep her painted. Rogge could not afford
to give her any but the most essential provisions, and all the prisoners,
except the eldest, wounded, and senior officers, would have to sleep on
tarpaulins on top of the clammy salt in the holds. He was sorry he had
to treat them that badly, but he had no choice; his ship, his country,
came first, he told them. Cheers!—everyone wanted to get off the highly
vulnerable raider regardless of comfort. The officers were given their
choice: Stay or go. Bloody well go, it was, they said over a good-bye
sherry with Rogge, who then asked them to promise not to make
trouble. They did, and they thanked him for his courtesies and, as
Armstrong White put it, the "decent spirit of the German rank and
file."

Many of the 299 prisoners in *Durmitor* did get to hate the
Germans, though, for the voyage to the Italian Somaliland became a
nightmare of heat, hunger, thirst, and near mutiny. To keep order, prize
Commander Ensign Emil (S) Dehnel had only twelve men plus an officer who had been courtmartialed for a homosexual attempt, and he had
determined that he had 15.8 tons of fresh water—approximately three
cups per day for both drinking and cooking—just enough to last until
they arrived at the nearest Italian base. But it soon became evident that
the ship's Yugoslavs had overestimated the amount of coal in her
bunkers and that meant less speed, no reserves for condensing water,
and, in turn, fewer rations per man per day. Dehnel put his men to work
cutting up anything that would burn, mixing oil, paint, and cinders to

augment their fuel, and he had a sail that netted him another half knot in speed rigged between the mast and stack. After eight days, the restive prisoners, thinking themselves deliberately deprived and badly used, gathered in an ugly, shouting, mass, threatening to take the ship. Dehnel stepped down among them, then took a delegation to the depleted larders explaining that he could not and would not give up the ship under any circumstances. Cowed by his determination and finally apprised of the circumstances, the captives shuffled off to their discomforts, which were to last until the verminous ship grounded at a tiny port on November 22 with no water at all and only 661 pounds of beans and 441 pounds of coal. Pestered by a series of tragicomedy adventures with the local Italian administration, the harried prize officer continued on to Chisimaio, where he found a number of German ships, in one of which, *Tannenfels,* he was later to return to *Atlantis.*

Without any more fortunes steaming her way, the raider had meanwhile moved its operations into the Gulf of Bengal, where she was favored with three ships. *Teddy,* a 6,748-ton Norwegian tanker, was taken intact with a ruse on the night of November 8/9 by the Germans who pretended to be a British AMC, the ex-Holt liner *Antenor.* The next night, Rogge used the same ploy to capture the modern 1939-built *Ole Jacob,* another Norwegian tanker whose officers, having had doubts about *Atlantis'* true identity, managed to get off a signal or two, then guilelessly asked the raider to stop following them. *Ole* finally lost way but kept her radio humming to tell the world what was going on. Rogge did not shell her, though, because he needed a tanker with Diesel fuel (*Teddy's* ten thousand tons of oil were of no use to him) and he still hoped to get her undamaged. His boarding party tuckered over with only three men, Mohr, navigator Paul Kamenz, an ex-Lloyd captain, and a helmsman visible, and they were disguised as British. Ten other men, all armed to the teeth, were hidden under a tarpaulin. Cutting in alongside, the two German officers clambered up the Jacob's ladder and stripped off their disguises to face the startled Norwegians with a "Hands up!" The rest of the Germans, entangled in the tarp, some pushing, some pulling in the best circus tradition, took awhile to join up, but they soon had a fine new ship in their hands—it was down to its marks with ten thousand tons of aviation gas. Her signals had been heard, though, and commander in chief East Indies immediately organized a hunting group composed of His Majesty's light cruisers *Capetown* and *Durban,* heavy cruiser *Canberra,* and AMC *Westralia.* The hunt had no success, but Rogge did next day when he bagged *Automedon,* a ship that had heard *Ole's* last dramatic signal: "Being stopped by an unknown vessel."

For some reason, that ship's master made no move to avoid *Atlantis,* which was approaching in a crossing situation from port and would have passed close behind his stern. But the raider turned to a parallel course, unmasked her battery at 0904, and fired a warning shot with her 5.9s. *Automedon* radioed, got off her name, an "RRRR" (it should have been "QQQQ"), and part of her position before *Atlantis'* operators jammed her calls. Rogge ordered salvo fire to break the resistance, and his gunners did not miss. They hardly could. Their hapless target was only 2,300 yards distant on a glassy sea. Four salvos went crashing through the ship's thin metal superstructure before her radioman quit trying. The raider then instantly ceased fire, only to resume the shooting when a man was seen running to the Englishman's gun. Three more salvos, and that was it—twenty-eight rounds, nearly half of which were hits. Twenty minutes after the opening shot, the German boarding party sheered in alongside to be met by Second Officer D. Stewart, who showed them around his shredded vessel. The captain had been killed along with all the other officers stationed on or near the bridge.

When the captain's safe was broken open, it yielded a bit of cash and conversion tables for the merchant code. From the strong room, the Germans took 120 sacks of mail and 15 bags of secret official correspondence—"Safe hand, British Master Only"—which the unfortunate officers had been unable to destroy. The mail was transshipped to the raider along with whatever foodstuffs, beer, whiskey (Johnnie Walker Black Label) the Germans could find. The remainder of the extremely valuable cargo of cars, bicycles, medicine, sewing machines, oranges, and copper plates, had to be sunk with the ship, whose crippled steering gear made it impossible for her to be dispatched to a meeting place as had *Teddy* and *Ole Jacob*. That night, *Atlantis'* radio room overheard another Holt liner, *Helenus,* repeating *Automedon's* distress message, but they forgot to alert Rogge and thus inadvertently saved the nearby ship.

Since Rogge still needed diesel fuel, he took what *Teddy* had, then sent the vessel and its huge cargo of heating oil down in a funeral pyre so hot that it created rain clouds and showers. When SKL later heard about the waste, they rapped the captain's knuckles sharply. But to Rogge, self-preservation came first, and he had no way of knowing that *Pinguin* had captured a tanker fully laden with diesel fuel. The German short-signal code then still lacked the sentence structure necessary to get such information across, and Krüder had merely signaled that he himself was fully topped off.

The secret material found in *Automedon* was extraordinarily valuable. Rogge and Mohr discovered plans and maps, intelligence appraisals, new code tables, top-secret mail for the High Command Far East, secret notices to mariners, and a War Cabinet report giving a full summary of the defenses in the Far East. It was so important that the German captain felt he had to get it home as quickly as possible, and the easiest way of doing that would be to send *Ole,* with which he had rendezvoused again on November 16, to Japan. At Kobe, the German naval attaché, Admiral Paul Wenneker (*Lützow* ex-*Deutschland*'s former commander), parlayed her cargo into an equal amount of oil—one third of the total available to the Germans in the East—and an excellent Japanese seaplane, both of which were later useful to *Orion.* The top-secret dispatches were evaluated and some time later—after the fall of Singapore—Rogge received a samurai sword from the Japanese Emperor, one of three awarded to Germany (the other recipients being Hermann Göring and Field Marshal Erwin Rommel).

While *Ole* was running toward the Tenno's domain, *Atlantis* was working southward, her officers occasionally enjoying the fruits of their war—soap, records, socks and shirts, magazines, and captured liquor. But there were annoyances as well. Rogge could not agree with SKL's constant redispositions which had the various raiders shuttling back and forth over the vast ocean as if they were amusement boats headed for the beaches of Heligoland, and he said so in no uncertain terms, the nicest blaming Berlin's "torpedo boat perspective" on the Versailles-imposed shortage of skilled officers and enlisted cadre.

Rogge did not, however, object to an SKL-sponsored meet with raider *Pinguin* and her prize, *Storstad,* December 8, the first German-manned vessels he had encountered since early April, for two good reasons: he could top off his fuel tanks from the prize and he was able to rid himself of 124 burdensome prisoners in the latter.

ROCKS

The Kerguelen Islands are a bleak, isolated, treeless group lying just on 50°S. There had once been a whaling station there but it had been abandoned. A Frenchman named Boissière had tried to raise sheep and had failed. Rats, hares, penguins, and sea lions loved the place because no one ever came there, and very few people—except those suffering from scurvy—had ever appreciated its major foodstuff, Kerguelen cabbage, edible raw, but with a dreadful stench when cooked.

Atlantis, her crew shivering in the unaccustomed cold, raised the islands on December 14. The excitement on board as the anchor chains rattled out under a cloud of rusty dust just outside Gazelle Bay cannot be imagined by anyone who had not been at sea facing destruction for 259 days. Land, land, and some form of security, it was to those who thought peace meant switching on their navigation lights. A party was sent ashore disguised as whalers to investigate, and though they found only the remarkably preserved remains of the former settlement, they enjoyed themselves immensely just exploring and poking about in the deserted bedroom, stalls, and tryworks. Rogge had the narrow entrance channel buoyed before risking a passage, and he then cautiously maneuvered his ship in past fields of kelp that usually marked rock formations and buoy No. 1. He was close to No. 2; "thirteen meters," the man at the fathometer sang out, "thirteen meters, ten meters." "Stop engines!" Rogge ordered, but it was too late. *Atlantis* carried into an unmarked pinnacle rock, rose up on it, and jolted to a stop. *"Prost!"* (actually "Cheers," but "We've had it," in this usage) Mohr said to himself. Everyone shared the same thought; marooned, eleven thousand miles from home behind the enemy's line; most embarrassing, too. "Full astern!" No luck. The first reports started coming in: double bottom cells damaged, collision bulkhead torn in by the antimine spur, oil tanks undamaged, ship taking some water. Nothing too serious yet, but *Atlantis* would not come off. The men's spirits drooped, but they were not given much time to ponder their fate.

Rogge ordered and they slaved; worked till they thought their backs would break, their legs collapse. Five hundred and forty tons of oil were pumped to tanks near the stern, as were fifty tons of fresh water. Thirty tons of sand were removed from the forepeak, and another thirty tons from the hold—all bagged and carried aft. Thirty tons of ammunition followed, as did ten tons of provisions, five tons of fixtures, and both anchors and their chains (sixty tons). Shells and cartridges were trundled to the living quarters from the after ammo room which was flooded with two hundred tons of seawater. Another four hundred fifty tons were let into the former mine-prisoner room and fifty tons into the well deck. Those labors netted an 8½° trim by the stern, but *Atlantis* still could not be budged from the pinnacle that held her fast, and despite the changing tides. They tried rocking her by rushing the men back and forth between the railings to the shrill of the boatswains' pipes. They set both bowers and the stern anchor and took a heave. No one could envision staying there, they could not face the taunts if they had to be rescued by another German, and they certainly did not want to be taken prisoner. Thirty-eight hours the toil and worry lasted before they were able to tear loose from the needle-sharp rock that steepled upward from the deep water on all sides of it.

Once safely anchored inside the bay, divers were sent down but could not agree on anything except that the ship's bottom looked in bad shape. Finally, Rogge and Kielhorn descended. The damage was extensive and it would take days to fix in a fully equipped dry dock. But they were going to have to do it right there themselves; there was no dry dock—there was no dock. It was terrible work. Underwater cutting torches would not function and the torn plates had to be drilled by hand, ripped clear with the ship's winches, piece by piece. A watertight, airtight cofferdam had to be built, the forepeak cemented, all gear, ballast, and ammunition dragged back to where it had been, and the flooded rooms dried out.

Meanwhile shore parties rigged up a nine-hundred-yard firehose line to an inland waterfall. It was good for four hundred tons per day and let them open the taps on board freely for the first time. Gunners marked off range scales on the rocks so that the ship could fire over the hills if necessary. Deck details redisguised the ship as the Norwegian *Tamesis,* and Kielhorn's gang pulled their diesels, generators, and fittings apart. No one had a minute off until Christmas Eve, which was celebrated in the traditional German manner, all the rooms decorated, fake trees, *Lebkuchen,* and presents—ties, socks, tobacco, wallets taken from the enemy's military shipments—for all. Rogge read St. Luke's Christmas story, there were peas and smoked chops for dinner, and punch—nine hundred liters—later on.

Some men wanted to be left alone, others stared at the bleak hills about them. They had had no mail from home, and there were many of them who felt sorry for themselves, longed for their loved ones. Loosened tongues wagged. "Do you think, Herr Leutnant, that I would go through with this crap willingly?" one trusting man told Mohr. "If a steamer comes along, all right, I'll do my job then, but otherwise . . . you get shot if you don't." Enthusiasm was waning, the adjutant feared, and there seemed to be those who hoped the damage would force them home.

Finally, the men got onshore in turns. There was not much to do or see, but the land smelled good. Hunting parties brought back ducks and hares. Rogge's scottie, Ferry, found no hydrants, but bushes are better than stanchions, and the doctor tried to ride a walrus.

Preparations for New Year's Eve were overshadowed by the death of a second of their numbers (the man had fallen off the stack where he was working; the previous casualty had died of a stroke) and his burial ashore, but their lives had to go on and they had a job to do. *Atlantis'* war was far from over.

Germany's navy had done well during the year, and the Royal

Navy, though no longer kept in anxiety about the homeland's shores, was faced by a slow, insidious, and deadly danger—the continuous loss of shipping. U-boats had sunk 471 vessels (mines and aircraft had accounted for very nearly as many), and the 43 million tons of imports Britain needed each year to keep up her resistance had been whittled down to an insufficient 38-million-ton rate by October. That was not enough, Churchill warned Roosevelt. "The decision for 1941 lies upon the seas," he wrote, adding, "unless we can establish our ability to feed this island, to import the munitions of all kinds which we need, unless we can move our armies to the various theaters . . . we may fall by the way."*

Admiral Raeder's surface fleet, recovered from its injuries and mechanical difficulties, was stirring. *Scheer* had sailed in the latter part of October, had attacked convoy H.X. 84 in November, and had sunk a number of ships in the South Atlantic. She was an enormous threat to the Royal Navy, which could no longer afford the large hunting groups that had brought *Spee* to bay a year earlier. Cruiser *Hipper* had been out again, too, prowling in the North Atlantic. And though she accomplished nothing, had been driven off by convoy W.S. 5a's heavy escort of three cruisers and a carrier on Christmas day, her arrival in Brest as the first major fleet unit in occupied French ports portended uglier things to come. *Gneisenau* and *Scharnhorst,* their Norwegian campaign damages now fully repaired, were being prepared to debauch, and there had been six raiders loose on the oceans. Those weakly armed ships had sunk fifty-four vessels of 366,644 tons (fully 17 percent of the tonnage attributable to the U-boats). Their "well conceived tactics," Britain's Prime Minister said, had caused "us both injury and embarrassment."†

* Winston S. Churchill, *Their Finest Hour* (Boston: Houghton Mifflin Company, 1949).
 † Ibid.

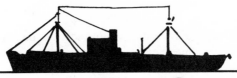

CHAPTER 3

The Other Raiders Sail, 1940

ORION: FIRST TO STRIKE   Signal "1814/16/57," which had inconvenienced Rogge so much back in April 1940, did not affect the plans made by *Orion*'s short, wiry, and energetic captain, Lt. Comdr. Kurt Weyher, except that it meant he would be fighting sooner than anticipated. And that was all right with him; he had, after all, a long way to go before carrying out the first part of his original orders—mining the ports of New Zealand. Still just off Newfoundland on April 16, and sleeping in a deck chair in the chart room behind the wheelhouse, Weyher had had an even rougher time than Rogge in the eighteen days since he had ordered his steel cables unshackled and had backed off from buoy "7A" in Kiel harbor disguised as a two-funneled naval auxiliary. On the way out to the Süderpiep, *Orion*'s men had dismantled her dummy wooden guns and taken down the fake second stack in which seaman Paul Schmidt had puffed cigarettes contentedly for many days— even while on duty. His job had been to toss oily wastes and rags into a forge to produce some real smoke. Then the raider's 377 men slaved away for three days until the dull gray auxiliary was changed into Holland America Line's *Beemsterdijk,* complete with green-and-white funnel bands, yellow hull strip, white upper works, and black topsides. On April 6 they had gotten the impatiently awaited order: *"Schiff 36* start loading today," that is, in decoded parlance, "Clear to sail."

It was an unpropitious time to set out, and it seemed more and more so to Weyher as he headed north, unescorted, past mines and smack into the fight for Norway in which battleships, carriers, cruisers, destroyers, submarines, and minelayers of both sides were shuttling up and down, east and west, through the North Sea like so many Hamburg ferryboats during commuting hours. Weyher quickly ran into trouble. First, on April 8, it was a steamer running northeast with a destroyer. "Evaded," his log read. Seven hours later another steamer, escorted by four destroyers. That force was probably Britain's *Teviot Bank* steering for home from mining operation "Wilfred" off the Norwegian coast. "Shit!" Weyher exclaimed, worrying that someone would start fooling around with his disguises and give his game away before he was ready to fight. He did not understand why the British (who steamed up very close to investigate) turned away.

Once safely north of the Arctic Circle, the raider was repainted to become the Russian *Soviet,* because the real *Beemsterdijk,* judging by radio chatter, seemed to be somewhere in West Indian waters. Furthermore, there was hardly any reason why a Holland America liner should be that far north. Driven hard by the executive officer Lt. Comdr. Adalbert von Blanc, the crew finished the job in jig time, but not without a lot of physical discomfort. It was bitter-cold work and the ship's steam heat had been turned off to conserve as much energy as possible for her decrepit machinery. Unventilated, dark, and cold, the crew's quarters stank like a badly kept zoo. Von Blanc sympathized with the men, but there was not much that he could do about their discomfort.

By late April, *Orion* was down on the crossroads linking Britain with Panama and the Azores with the Gulf of Mexico, masquerading as the Greek *Rocos.* Her crewmen, no longer cold or wet, were anxious to get into action, and wondered just as anxiously how they would react when the bells rang. A slight foretaste on the twenty-second, which had them at battle stations and ready to drop heavy black tarpaulins over their false neutrality markings the second their captain decided to attack, had been a teaser. Visible to the hundreds of eyes peering from their concealed positions at the guns on deck (*Schiff 36*'s weapons were all topdecks disguised as deckhouses, cargo, or a crane), a tall blue-stacked British vessel had been permitted to pass rushing by only two miles away. Their commander was tough, but he was no daredevil, the men decided. The other ship was too fast.

Weyher, son of an educator, had joined the Imperial Navy on April 1, 1918, and was the Kaiser's youngest cadet when the armistice was signed in November of that year. For a spell, during the chaos following the First War, he elected to fight with the right-wing Free-Korps in the east, then rejoined the navy to become an ensign in 1922. A well-rounded training period in torpedo boats, as the commander of a small U-boat, watch officer in cruiser *Königsberg* and training ship *Niobe,* torpedo boat skipper, executive officer of the *Gorch Fock,* subsequently captain of the *Horst Wessel* (now the U. S. Coast Guard's gleaming white *Eagle*), and author of a 1939 study on the potentials of cruiser warfare against Britain's shipping, he was a good candidate for selection as a raider captain. Though himself not intellectually or emotionally prepared for war with Britain—Admiral Raeder had told him

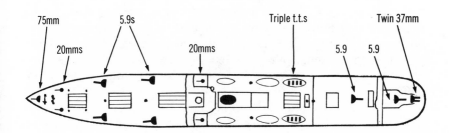

75mm   5.9s   Triple t.t.s   Twin 37mm

20mms   20mms   5.9   5.9

ORION, SHIP 36, ex-KURMARK

Built:	1930, Blohm & Voss, Hamburg
Tonnage:	7,021
Length:	463.5 feet, Lloyds Register
Beam:	61.1
Depth:	27.0
Speed:	14.8
Armament:	Six 5.9-inch; one 75mm; one twin 37mm; four 20mm; six 21-inch torpedo tubes; 228 mines*
Planes:	One Arado 196; later, one Nakajima 90-11
Complement	356 (varied due to prize crews and new drafts)
	*Shaded guns and tubes indicate a mounting below deck
Ships sunk or taken:	8 (including one prize) = 48,477 tons HAXBY, TROPIC SEA, NOTOU, TURAKINA, RINGWOOD, TRIADIC, TRIASTER, CHAUCER Plus one half of 21,125 tons, TRIONA and RANGITANE sunk during operations with raider KOMET = 10,562½-tons Plus 14, 342 tons, NIAGARA and H.M.N.Z.S. PURIRI sunk by mines = a total of 73,576½-tons**
Length of cruise:	510 days, 4.6.40-8.23.41
Fate:	Returned to Europe
	**½-ton in deference to extensive literature on tonnage claims during combined operations

only that summer that he had been assured on that score by Hitler—
Weyher was, just as that war did begin, pleased to receive his mobilization orders directing him to take over *Schiff 36*.

On April 24, 1940, he executed his "1814/16/57" order, striking the 5,207-ton *Haxby* so hard that she suffered sixteen killed in an
action that lasted but six minutes. Weyher had warned her to stop but
she did not; and he had forbidden her to radio, which she did. Much of
the signal was blotted out by the raider's interference, and her station
was soon silenced by its guns. *Orion* lowered two boats to pick up
twenty-four survivors, including the master, Capt. Cornelius Arundel.
Given dry clothes and some tea with rum to revive them, the dazed
prisoners were then taken down three decks to await their first ration of
unaccustomed German food—sticky black bread, sausages, and ersatz
coffee.

The morning after first setting foot on the raider's planks, the
prisoners were surprised to see that they were aboard not *Rocos* but
Mandu. They would have been even more astonished if they had known
what *Orion*'s radiomen were tapping out: "RRRR 3020 . . . by pocket
battleship . . . ," another deliberately garbled message in merchant
code. The Germans were just not certain that *Haxby*'s original signals
had been heard by anyone, and they wanted to be certain—as per SKL's
instructions—that the Allies would think a "pocket" out. The ruse did
not work because no one apparently picked up either call.

His interim task thought accomplished, Weyher steamed south
for a meeting with the ancient (1913-built) German tanker *Winnetou,*
which had been caught at Las Palmas by the war and which on April 9
had set out, festooned with marine growths, to replenish the raider. The
vessels rendezvoused on May 14, and *Orion* took on 1,720 tons of oil
before sending the supply ship to a waiting position some three hundred
miles west of the Maria Theresa Reefs in the South Pacific.

The fueling procedure was a beastly job involving some two
hundred men wrestling with greasy, snaking hoses, slippery lines, and
oily pumps, and it helped prove that steamships were basically ill-suited
as raiders. *Schiff 36* used up an average of forty tons of oil per day
compared with the seven or nine tons burned by a motorship, and she
always had to keep her engines going. A diesel-powered vessel could
stop, start, or speed up at will, but it took thirty minutes before oil-fired
boilers could turn out the power to increase speed only two or three
knots to thirteen knots—a distinct technical disadvantage that was to
embitter the hard-driving Weyher during most of his 510 days at sea. On
May 21 he rounded Cape Horn and on the thirtieth he lay stopped for a
while as he did several days later, to effect the first of hundreds of engine

repairs that were to plague his ship for the rest of the voyage. The geared steam turbines had already driven one ship, the Hamburg-Amerika Line's 7,021-ton *Kurmark,* for a good ten years, and they had seen service before that in pushing the company's 22,000-ton passenger liner *New York* across the Atlantic. They were not up to the task of endless, no-time-in-port steaming. In fact, SKL later admitted that the ship should never have been employed as a raider. Weyher, of course, knew that from the start. He had been quite disappointed when he first saw the ship and the plans for its conversion, the former hardly better than the World War I *Wolf* and the latter not much of an improvement over those made a quarter of a century earlier. His relatively low rank had not helped either. When he insisted on alterations or additions to his ship, the *Silberlinge* told him that he had better ask his commanding officer to authorize the changes.

WIDDER (RAM): A WILD ONE, INDEED

If the athletic thirty-nine-year-old regular navy officer Weyher had been irritated at first sight of his ship, his frame of mind could not be compared with the aggravation felt by Reserve Lt. Commander Hellmuth von Ruckteschell, forty-nine, after he took over command of *Widder (Schiff 21)* on January 18, 1940. Putting the blame squarely on the navy and the Blohm and Voss yard (which had also rebuilt *Orion*), Ruckteschell officially reported that his raider was a "dubious proposition," and so it was to be. But whatever the material condition of his ship, he would never have turned the appointment down: He was the only reservist to be offered responsibility for such a ship.

Son of a protestant pastor and of Baltic extraction, Ruckteschell was an interesting personality. Highly cultured, he was an artist at heart, as were many of his brothers and sisters. In World War I he had served at Jutland and had then joined the U-boat service to which he applied himself so aggressively that he became one of the several dozen commanders to be blacklisted by the Allies for real or imagined "breeches of the customs of war." Not wishing to be judged by his foes, he fled to Sweden, then to Lapland, where he worked as a lumberjack and surveyor before returning to Germany. He read a lot, loved classical music, enjoyed wood carving and glass painting, and, being quite religious, he took up the postulates of Rudolf Steiner's anthroposophy. Though physically tough, he showed the symptoms shared by many overstrained U-boat officers: a nervous stomach and severe migraine headaches. At times irritable and temperamental, he was under a cloud at headquarters, according to the scuttlebut one admiral and some of his peers remember, for having kicked an enlisted man, and he was deemed by some of his associates to be unfit emotionally to command a raider.

Recalled to the colors in 1939, he had first been assigned to an auxiliary minelayer and then *Widder* with orders to raid in one of the most dangerous and proscribed areas of all, the Central North Atlantic. He cast off at Kiel on May 5, 1940. Only seven hours and twenty-nine minutes later, he was attacked by a British submarine whose torpedoes he was able to avoid. His escort of S-boats (motor patrol boats) fought off another sub the next day, and on May 13 a third, H.M.S. *Clyde,* chased the slow raider and forced her to unmask her hidden stern gun in self-defense. Troubled by a high consumption of oil, *Widder* fueled twice from *Nordmark* (ex-*Westerwald,* which had accompanied *Deutschland* at the beginning of the war) and *Königsberg,* a 6,466-ton North German Lloyd freighter, before settling down on the Trinidad-Azores track to snare her first victim, *British Petrol.* The empty tanker was roughly gunned into submission without warning because ex-U-boat officer Ruckteschell, still wary of Q-boats, thought she would certainly radio and fight back. Twelve days later, he caught up with the Norwegian *Krossfonn,* which did not run, radio, or fight and which was not shelled.

T. J. Harrison's *Davisian* did not radio and her men did not put their 4-inch gun to any more use than had the Norwegians, but that was because they could not. The first of *Widder*'s eight 5.9-inch salvos tore down their antenna and the crew quickly started to lower the boats. Seeing that, the Germans ceased fire. A few British seamen, however, were observed making aft for the gun and the raider's 37-mm and 20-mm cannon started hammering away. Result: three dead in *Davisian* and the first of several charges to be made against the German captain in a still controversial war crimes trial after the war.

After *Davisian*'s destruction, the gaunt commander (he had been promoted) had one hundred prisoners aboard and that was one of the reasons he committed himself to a deliberate action that was to create tremendous repercussions both among the Allies and in the other German raiders. Ruckteschell had no one he felt he could confide in, and, being a reservist long unaccustomed to the navy's ways, he was not too sure of himself. The younger line officers like Lt. Konrad Hoppe had quite some difficulty appreciating his philosophizing in higher transcendental spheres and he, in turn, though endowed with an uncanny intuition in dangerous combat situations, lacked the flair for a closer association with his men. He liked them—as long as they were not stupid or useless dabblers—and they eventually learned to appreciate him as a being apart. But even his executive officer, Günter Heinicke, "much to his regret," could not bridge the gap as he should have in the "marital" relationship demanded of captains and their top staff officers. To Heinicke, who was eighteen years younger, a regular "Prussian" line officer, World War II U-boat skipper, and the antithesis of Ruckteschell, the latter seemed like the director of an orchestra who had not had time to learn the entire score and was forced to conduct a premiere without any rehearsal at all. His captain, he thought, was a strong-willed intellectual with all the traits of a highly bred racehorse.

When they sighted *King John* on July 13, Ruckteschell decided to take her with all means at his disposal to prevent her from signaling. And that he did, but without being able to silence her. When she radioed, he shelled her into submission and then sent his doctors out with the boarding party to assist the survivors and report on the crew. Their findings were unsatisfactory: three dead, six injured, and fifty-nine new prisoners, Yugoslavs, Portuguese, Maltesians, and Spaniards, twenty-one of them survivors of a ship sunk by a U-boat, "a dirty, lousy folk," Ruckteschell needlessly observed. The captain of the 5,228-ton freighter, George E. Smith, who had tried to escape with a boat, but had been caught, quickly noticed that Ruckteschell lost his temper readily. Watching the vessel sink, Ruckteschell noted that it was taking a long time. "Naturally, made in Britain," Smith retorted, infuriating the German.

The German did not want all the extra prisoners; he hoped he would be making some more, soon, and he wanted to make his presence known to the enemy quickly before moving off to another area. Smith, his chief engineer, and all the wounded, he decreed, would stay in the raider; the rest, and the forty men of *Davisian,* would be let go to make their way to the Lesser Antilles only 240 miles away.

When the first of them landed on St. Barthélemy on the seventeenth in two boats with their tales of a murderous foe and the first accurate description of any raiders, Adm. Sir Charles Kennedy-Purvis, commander in chief America and West Indies Station, stopped all independent sailings, rerouted his convoys, and sent his entire force of cruisers and sloops out searching. The Admiralty in London, aware that nearly a dozen ships had disappeared and many of them in the Atlantic, were certain that several raiders were out on the prowl, but most of their forces were by then tied up in fighting elsewhere and it was out of the question for Whitehall to reconstitute the powerful hunting groups of yesteryear. It would have been inadvisable, moreover, as the chances of finding one of the raiders were as good as locating a toy boat on the Great Lakes.

THOR: WIELDING A HEAVY HAMMER

"Heil, Hitler, heil, Hitler!" they shouted as one, their skinny arms outstretched in the straight-arm salute. That reaction to his speech should have surprised Ensign (S) Werner Sander. He had just told the fifty-nine men and nine passengers of the freighter *Kertosono,* then on its way from Curaçao to African and Indian ports, that they would be well treated, but that any resistance would be broken by force and that the ship would be scuttled if intercepted. It was not the sort of address that called for such hearty cheering, but then the fifteen meek oilers and wipers who were trying to ingratiate themselves with their new masters were Chinese. If their action amazed the German, it did not so their Dutch captain, D. de Boer, or their third officer, K. C. van der Lingen. The Chinese, they knew, were still on board only because United States immigration officials had hustled them back to the freighter when they had tried to jump ship in New York to avoid wartime duty.

    Kertosono had been stopped on July 1 by a ship thought to be Dutch but which was actually a German posing as a Yugoslav. De Boer had not fought back because his armament had consisted of only two revolvers. Now, *Kertosono* was a German prize heading for Europe. Sander was pleasant, even courteous, and one of his sailors confided to Van der Lingen that he was glad he had not had to shoot him when they had first boarded the Hollander. So was Van der Lingen. The latter was even happier when they got safely to Lorient on the twelfth, and happiest of all when he and his mates stepped out on the platform of Rotterdam's main station that September—free men. The name of the ship that had captured them was *Vir,* they told their friends.

    On July 17 Rear Adm. Henry Harwood, victor over *Spee* and now off the La Plata in His Majesty's light cruiser *Hawkins,* studied the accumulating evidence—German wireless traffic, *Widder*'s released prisoners, several ships reported overdue—and it all seemed to indicate that a raider might be southbound near Brazil. The admiral ordered AMC *Alcantara* to patrol the Pernambuco-Trinidade Island area where the Germans had lurked in the First War. Eleven days later, the former 22,209-ton, nineteen-knot liner (Capt. J. G. P. Ingham, DSO, R.N., commanding), one of the make-shift, make-do conversions that were as unpopular with their mostly reservist crews as they were with the Germans, was on station at 24°14′S, 32°08′W. She had lost one funnel in being rebuilt, and she was armed with eight 6-inch and two 3-inch guns.

    Close by, in a fast (eighteen knots) former fruit carrier (once the *Santa Cruz* of the Oldenburg-Portugiesische Line), were 195

British, Belgian, Dutch, and Arabian officers and seamen. But those people could not enjoy the lovely sunny Sunday morning and the light northeast breezes. They were prisoners from five ships, *Delambre, Bruges, Gracefield, Wendover,* and *Tela,* and they were locked below in cramped quarters in the small (3,862-ton) ex-banana boat they knew as *Vir,* home port Split, Yugoslavia. They had been wakened as usual at 0600, cleaned their quarters, washed, breakfasted, stood roll call at 0900, and they were waiting to be allowed on deck for the few cherished minutes the German commander, Otto Kähler, permitted them.

On the bridge of *Vir,* which in actuality was *Thor (Schiff 10),* ex-*Santa Cruz,* the square-built, square-faced forty-six-year-old Kähler chomped on a cigar. He did not know who the large steamer they had first sighted at 0900 was. By 1006, however, it was painfully clear that whoever she was, innocent liner or AMC (Kähler was confused by the missing funnel), she was definitely following in the raider's wake. Always conscious of the opinion and morale of his 349 men, and being himself a cool and practical man, Kähler had lunch served to half of the crew at a time, and he even pretended to enjoy his own. But no matter what course he steered, the other ship followed suit. And she was faster, too.

Kähler, son of a merchant captain, had already made his First Officer's "ticket" when he chose the navy as a career prior to World War I in which he served in U-boats. Alternate peacetime staff and sea-going appointments led him to the captaincy of *Gorch Fock* and in 1939 to the command of the Kriegsmarine's fleet of patrol boats. A practical man without frills, he was a superb navigator and seaman. He was well acquainted, of course, with Chapter F, Paragraph 4 of the top-secret operational orders handed him on his departure from Kiel on June 6. "Engagements with enemy warships, even auxiliary cruisers, must be avoided." A raider's job was to hit and run, appear and confuse, to create the widest dispersal of the Allied might. It was not their business to do battle; they were too valuable as a strategic-economic weapon for that. Though those instructions were very reasonable, there was no way in which *Schiff 10* could comply that July 28. Whoever the ship following the raider was, it would be its actions that would determine the near future. At 1200 the other vessel, which had been closing steadily from astern, centimeter by centimeter, began to radio a coded message, part of which went out before the rest was jammed by *Thor's* operators.

In *Thor* they could not understand the message, but Kähler knew that all British warships were being alerted and that his only chance lay in fighting and, if lucky, in making good his escape. At 1258 he turned sharply right to 175° and stepped up his speed to fifteen knots.

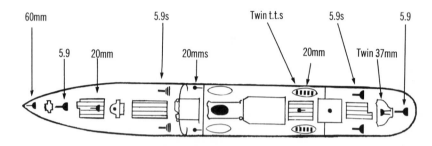

THOR, SHIP 10, ex-SANTA CRUZ
(First Voyage)

Built: 1938, Deutsche Werft AG Hamburg-Finkenwärder
Tonnage: 3,862
Length: 379.7 feet, Lloyds Register
Beam: 54.8
Draft: 26.5
Speed: 17
Armament: Six 5.9-inch; one 60mm; one twin 37mm; four 20mm; two twin 21-inch torpedo tubes*
Plane: One Arado 196
Complement: 347 (varied, due to prize crews and new drafts)
*Shaded guns and tubes indicate a mounting below deck
Ships sunk or taken: 12 (including one prize) =96,602 tons
KERTOSONO, DELAMBRE, BRUGES, GRACEFIELD, WENDOVER, TELA, KOSMOS, NATIA, TROLLENHOLM, BRITANNIA, H.M.S. AMC VOLTAIRE, SIR ERNEST CASSEL
Length of cruise: 329 days, 6.6.40-4.30.41
Fate: Returned to Germany

(Second Voyage)

Ships sunk or taken: 10 (including 3 prizes) = 56,037 tons
PAGASITIKOS, WELLPARK, WILLESDEN, AUST, KIRKPOOL, NANKIN, OLIVIA, HERBORG, MADRONO, INDUS
Length of cruise: 324 days, 11.20.41-10.10.42
Fate: Put into Yokohama; destroyed 11.30.42 by an accidental explosion in a tanker tied up alongside

"1259," Quartermaster Henry Militzer, formerly First Officer of *Santa Cruz,* jotted in the log, "war flag raised at main top." That was Leading Signalman Hans Baasch's job. He hauled the bundled ensign up and gave the halyard a quick jerk to break the stops and set it flying. Theo Müller, boatswain and gun captain of No. 1 5.9-inch, was already at his post on the forecastle, his trainer and pointer at their hand wheels, the hot case and projectile men virtually immobile, just balancing to the heel of the ship. The more than man-high gun was loaded, its electrical and manual firing circuits and mechanisms set, its metal disguises down. It was going to be a fight to the finish, they all knew. At 1300 the salvo gong rang for a four-gun, 15,000-yard shoot at *Alcantara* whose searchlight was then blinking "What ship?"

R.N. Captain Ingham had the answer he needed. As soon as he had closed the range enough (five minutes) for his own old guns (vintage 1913) he replied with a 6-inch salvo of his own. His shooting, the Germans regretted, was good, indeed.

Thor's ancient weapons, already obsolete in World War I and now incapable of shooting close patterns, were handled with calm expertise by forty-year-old Werner Koppen-Boehnke. At 1308 the Germans observed the first hits striking home behind the AMC's bridge and on his stern. *Thor*'s men could not repress relieved smiles. Two minutes later, however, the raider itself shuddered under the impact of two 6-inch shell hits. The first screeched and clanged right through the ship from starboard to port without exploding, doing only minor damage to electrical cables, pipes, and the forward ammunition hoist. The second smashed the starboard motorboat and sent splinters buzzing down the decks and the torpedo flat below, where they killed three men and injured four. Damage control teams and medics jumped to their jobs. At 1321, with the enemy apparently stopped and rapidly falling behind, and his own guns spewing out shells unpredictably, Kähler ordered smoke, and at 1335 he ceased fire to break off the engagement. He, his gunners, and the engineers headed by Reserve Lt. Heinrich Hille had done well.

Alcantara was crippled. She had been hit several times in her massive superstructure, her wireless cabin had been wrecked, and a three-foot-by-one-foot hole had been punched into her starboard engine room. That hit, though only a glancing blow that did not go off, was enough to cause her to lose the only real advantage she had—speed. Water rushed in, stopping the vital pumps, and the ship lost way and had to be heeled to port by the transfer of oil to keep the dangerous hole clear of the seas. Kähler would have "gladly finished her off," for a glorious feather in his cap, but he realized that in reengaging he would expose his command to the risk of taking another hit that might easily end his own usefulness. Calm and collected throughout the running fight, he now appraised the situation correctly and fought off temptation. It was time to disappear, before the AMC's messages brought a pack of warships on his trail. While he buried his dead—the "worst part of the voyage," to Koppen-Boehnke—and repaired his damage, Britain's heavy cruisers *Dorsetshire* and *Cumberland* steamed out from Freetown and Simonstown to intercept him, and *Alcantara,* built in pleasanter times (1926) for more genial purposes, committed her own two dead, treated seven wounded, and then stood into Rio de Janeiro, scarred, holed, and listing.

Thor fled south to nearly 40°S and then east with her men hoping that *Alcantara*'s somewhat inaccurate description of their ship might be applied to *Widder* by the Allies. They were also pleased to hear that the British ship *Domingo de Larrinaga* had been sunk far away, across the Atlantic (presumably by raider *Pinguin*).

PINGUIN: A TOUGH BIRD

The raider that put *Larrinaga* down was a beauty named *Pinguin, Schiff 33*. She was a sister of *Atlantis* and had also been converted by the same yard. She sailed from Gotenhaven on June 15 with 300 mines for her own use and 25 torpedos and 80 mines for U-boats. Her orders were for the Indian Ocean with the waters to be mined left pretty much to Captain Ernst-Felix Krüder's discretion. The Antarctic, SKL added, would be of particular operational importance during the December whaling season. *Pinguin* brushed by a British submarine off Norway, then marched undetected through the Denmark Strait and down to a rendezvous on July 18 with U-A in mid-Atlantic between Bélem and Dakar. Lack of proper equipment and bad weather caused the transfer of 15 torpedos and oil to stretch out a whole week, and the U-boat then had to be towed all the way to her station off African ports.

On the thirty-first *Pinguin* caught up with the *Larrinaga,* which had her gun trained and immediately radioed. It did her no good, however, for she sank about three hours after first being sighted, and the raider's skipper had the first thirty-two of some hundreds of prisoners he would take on board.

KOMET: INTO ORBIT

On the day that *Pinguin* sank *Larrinaga, Komet* (*Schiff 45*), last of the first wave of raiders, was lying at anchor off Novaya Zemlya, and her

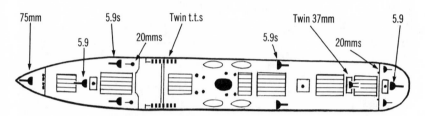

75mm 5.9s Twin t.t.s Twin 37mm 5.9
5.9 20mms 5.9s 20mms

PINGUIN, SHIP 33, ex-KANDELFELS

Built:	1936, Deschimag, Werk Weser, Bremen
Tonnage:	7,766
Length:	485.6 feet, Lloyds Register
Beam:	61.3
Draft:	31.1
Speed	17
Armament:	Six 5.9-inch; one 75mm; one twin 37mm; four 20mm; two twin 21-inch torpedo tubes*; 300 mines
Planes:	Two Heinkel 114, spare fuselage and wings, later one Arado 196
Complement:	345 (varied, due to prize crews and new drafts)
	*Shaded guns and tubes indicate a mounting below deck

Ships sunk
or taken: 28 (including 16 prizes) = 136,551 tons
DOMINGO de LARRINAGA, FILEFJELL, BRITISH COMMANDER,
MORVIKEN, BENAVON, NORDVARD, STORSTAD, NOWSHERA,
MAIOMA, PORT BRISBANE, PORT WELLINGTON, OLE WEGGER,
POL VIII, POL IX, POL X, THORLYN, SOLGLIMT, PELAGOS, STAR XIV,
STAR XIX, STAR XX, STAR XXI, STAR XXII, STAR XXIII, STAR XXIV,
EMPIRE LIGHT, CLAN BUCHANAN, BRITISH EMPEROR
Plus 18,068 tons sunk by mines MILLIMULMUL, NIMBIN, CAMBRIDGE,
CITY OF RAYVILLE laid in cooperation with PASSAT, ex-STORSTAD
= a total of 158,256 tons

Length of
cruise: 328 days, 6.15.40-5.8.41
Fate: Sunk by H.M.S. CORNWALL

officers and chiefs were having one of those many parties their corpulent commander, Capt. Robert Eyssen, enjoyed so well. Eyssen went to bed at 0130, the rest guzzled and mumbled on until around 0400. They were waiting for the Russians to give them the go-ahead for their journey through the ice-blocked Northwest Passage to the Pacific, a most risky undertaking, and the first of its kind for a western European warship. The timing was right. The dour Russians were still testing their ill-found friendship with the Germans, and they had agreed to provide navigational and icebreaker assistance. Eyssen was going to need the help. The possibility of circumnavigating northern Russia had first been explored by scientist Adolf Erik Nordenskjöld in *Vega,* and it had taken both the summers of 1878 and 1879 to break through the heavy ice and slim leads. The first ship to complete the perilous transit without wintering over had been the Russian icebreaker *Sibiriakoff,* and that had been in 1932. Five years later, more than twenty Russian ships, led by highly experienced ice pilots, had been forced to spend the winter drifting in and with the pack ice.

Eyssen, forty-eight, and abundantly confident in himself and his ship handling, had chosen the route himself despite the reservations held by some of the rightly dubious naval staff. Son of a Guatemalan coffee plantation owner, he had been posted as an ensign to S.M.S. *Karlsruhe* in World War I. The cruiser, having sunk or captured seventeen ships of 76,609 tons, blew up on November 4, 1914, in an unexplained explosion. She took down 263 of her men, but Eyssen and nearly 150 others made it home on the supply ship *Rio Negro* to fight again. Between the wars, he had served in staff duties and had commanded the trim white surveying vessel *Meteor.* When World War II broke out, he volunteered for duty on a raider and had picked the tiny 3,287-ton North German Lloyd *Ems,* smallest of all the German raiders. *Komet,* as he was to call her, had to be small (she drew only twenty-one and a half feet fully laden) in order to be able to pass through the relatively shallow Laptev Sea, and she had to be strengthened for navigating in ice. Eyssen knew and got just what he wanted.

When *Komet* left Gotenhaven's slip No. 5 on July 3, she was chock-a-block full of, among other things, 2,180 tons of oil, fueling hoses, and a fast 11.5-ton aluminum motor minelayer, LS-2, called *Metiorit.* Her hold had been jam-packed with freon gas cylinders, acetylene torches, spare heating units and piston rings, 35.6 tons of meats, 30 tons of potatoes, 60 tons of flour, 38.1 tons of vegetables, 12.3 tons of fats, 3 tons of coffee, 5 tons of marmalade, 12,000 cans of milk, 10,000 eggs, 1.2 million cigarettes, 46,000 cigars, 100,000 liters of beer, 5,000 bottles of liquor, 25,000 bars of chocolate, 6,000 packages of cookies,

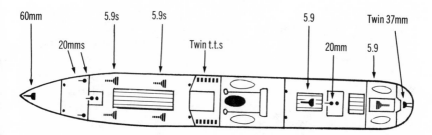

Diagram labels:
- 60mm
- 20mms
- 5.9s
- 5.9s
- Twin t.t.s
- 5.9
- 20mm
- 5.9
- Twin 37mm

KOMET, SHIP 45, ex-EMS
(First Voyage)

Built:	1937, Deschimag, Werk Weser, Bremen
Tonnage:	3,287
Length:	358.8 feet, Lloyds Register, not overall
Beam:	50.2
Depth:	19.9
Speed:	14.5
Armament:	Six 5.9 inch; one 60mm; one twin 37mm; four 20mm; four twin torpedo tubes (above water), two single torpedo tubes (submerged)*; 30 mines; one motor mine-laying launch
Plane:	One Arado 196
Complement:	270 (varied, due to prize crews and new drafts)
	*Shaded guns and tubes indicate a mounting below deck
Ships sunk or taken:	6 (including one prize) = 31,005 tons
	HOLMWOOD, VINNI, KOMATA, AUSTRALIND, KOTA NOPAN, DEVON
	Plus two, 21,125 tons, RANGITANE and TRIONA with raider ORION; Total 41,567½-tons**
Length of cruise:	516 days, 7.3.40-11.30.41
Fate:	Returned to Germany
	**½-ton deference to extensive literature on tonnage claims during combined operations

KOMET
(Second Voyage)

Length of cruise:	8 days, 6.10.42-14.10.42
Fate:	Sunk by H.M.S. M T B 236

99 movies, 540 records, sports equipment, 569 books, tents, skis, and reindeer sleds. In addition, there were 1,850 5.9-inch shells, cartridges, 250 rounds of 60 mm, 5,000 37 mm, and 14,000 20 mm, torpedoes, pistols, and machine guns.

Eyssen had to wait an entire month far north of the Arctic Circle drifting or anchored because the Soviets reported that ice conditions made any passage impossible. Though this waiting period was seemingly endless (some of the youthfully exuberant officers feared the war would be over before they ever got into it), it was well spent in training to perfection. There were no "Irish pennants" in *Komet*. If something was adrift, there was *"Krach"* (noise, trouble). Eyssen expected things to function properly.

Finally, on August 13, after the thirteenth change of anchorage, *Komet* was off through the Matochkin Strait and into the Kara Sea, where two Russian pilots were signed on to conn the raider through the ice—lots of it, mushy ice, pack ice, solid ice—most of it able to stop the ship and much of it capable of crushing her like a plastic toy. To the Russians, who were used to the ice but could not help wondering what sort of ship they were in, and to the Germans, who had never seen such hopelessly bleak seascapes, the threatening rumbling, screeching, and groaning of the ice, the strained working of the ship, its constantly tinkling engine room telegraphs, and the hum of the steering engine were trying, tiring, and alarming.

After twenty-three days, having covered 3,300 miles, 720 of them in very heavy ice, *Komet* passed through the Bering Strait. It had been a rough trip with the raider iced in solidly at times, her rudder damaged, and dependent on icebreakers *Lenin, Stalin,* and *Kaganovitch.* Bon vivant Eyssen had even had to appear at a vodka-soaked party in *Stalin* when his watch told him it was really only 0600 German time. Though interesting, the food, toasts, and particularly the potato liquor had been almost as rough as the ice. The last part of the epic voyage—a unique naval event—was made without the leather-coated, tough-faced Russian experts because Moscow, realizing that the war was by no means over despite the spectacular German victories in the west, got cold diplomatic feet. *Komet* was ordered about, but Eyssen refused to comply with any foreign demands and accepted full responsibility for his ship and any complications that might arise. The Russians shrugged, then socked the Germans with a $130,000 bill for services rendered. For September 5, Eyssen's personal war diary, which was published after his death with a foreword by the competent Adjutant Wilfried Karsten, reads: "I passed the Bering Strait between 0200 and 0230 this morning. This trip has been enough for me; I would not do it voluntarily a second time."*

Once safely in the Pacific, the captain battered through a typhoon on his way south to the Japanese-mandated and former German colony Lamotrek, where on October 14 he met *Kulmerland,* out from Japan with supplies, and then waited for the arrival of *Regensburg* and raider *Orion.*

* Robert Eyssen, *Komet* (Jugenheim: Koehlers Verlagsgesellschaft, 1960).

CHAPTER 4

The Great Pacific Basin, 1940

MINES AND FLAMES To any seaman, the 70-million-square-mile Pacific Ocean and its various arms have never lived up to what that name implies. Its typhoons are murderous and its tsunami waves killers. Men have fought on its waters and for its bordering lands and lush islands as long as either were inhabited. In 1940 another struggle was going on, between unevenly matched protagonists: on the one side, a still mighty array of British, Australian, and New Zealand cruisers, destroyers, sloops, AMCs, and other auxiliaries, all wearing the white ensign; on the other side, two German raiders.

One of the raiders, *Orion,* had crept across the Pacific undisturbed to bring the ugly face of war at close hand to the Commonwealth islands that had basked securely in its arm's-length absence since their discovery. On the night of June 13 the raider had arrived at the approaches to Auckland's Hauraki Gulf blacked out, sinister and silent, *"Klar zum Minenwerfen,"* they called it—clear for mine-laying. While *Haxby*'s worried prisoners in the lower hold ticked off the drops (they lost count at 168), Weyher laid 228 mines in three fields between Couvier Island and the mainland in a nervy operation that lasted seven hours and ten minutes and was always in sight of land. As the seconds of those hours elapsed and the horny, heavy mines dropped into the inky black water, the German watch on deck stared quietly at four steamers passing close-by and narrowly missed inbound H.M.N.Z.S. *Achilles,* a light cruiser, and AMC *Hector,* which slipped by unnoticed in the dark. Five days passed before the ugly eggs connected to give New Zealanders a taste of what had become commonplace in the mother country's shallower seas, an ŞOS from a ship named *Niagara.* The big (13,415-ton) liner was going to the bottom with $10 million in bullion (which by an extraordinary feat lasting nearly two years was later raised). The waves had hardly splashed together over the big hulk before the New Zealand Naval Board canceled all merchant sailings, switched off its

60

coastal navigation lights and stopped its weather broadcasts. Air searches were vectored out and *Achilles* and *Hector* steamed out for long fruitless searches. Australia Station, too, responded to the crisis with precautionary sweeps, aircraft reconnaissance, and extensive patrolling led by H.M.A.S. *Perth.*

But Weyher slipped clean away, and on the nineteenth, when some eight hundred miles east of the Kermadec Islands, he halted the Norwegian *Tropic Sea,* whose crew of forty-eight (complete with captain's wife) surrendered without a fight and were taken along to a rendezvous with the old tanker *Winnetou,* Capt. Fritz Steinkrauss, commanding. Provisioning and fueling lasted until the thirtieth, when the prize was released to France with twenty-eight Germans and fifty-five prisoners under the command of Fritz Steinkrauss, whose old tanker was sent to Japan.* For Weyher and his men the next seven weeks in the vicinity of the Fijis were to be a foretaste of hell without fresh foods, with rationed refreshments, and with sleep impossible in the humid heat of improperly ventilated and dripping holds (120°). Lack of success (the British Phosphate Commissioner's fast *Triona* escaped before an attack could be mounted, and only a small [2,489-ton] French ship, *Notou,* fell into their hands on August 16) turned their moods as sour as their sweat-glistening skins. Disappointed, Weyher turned southwest into the dangerous confines of the Tasman Sea, where, four days later, he was to demonstrate his tactical ability and teach the unwritten laws of the sea that to him applied to frightened friends and fearless foes alike.

Only one day's run from Cape Egmont, steaming west through rain squalls, *Orion*'s lookouts caught a glimpse of the New Zealand Shipping Company's seventeen-year-old refrigerated cargo ship *Turakina* out from Sydney with a load of foodstuffs for Britain and rolling heavily in high seas. Weyher came about on a converging course to intercept. At 1750, though still out of range, he took the chance that the ship would surrender when ordered to do so by blinker. But that was not what his opponent, Capt. J. B. Laird, who had vowed that he would fight if brought to bay as had the company's Captain Bisset Smith when waylaid in the First War by *Möwe,* was about to do meekly. *Orion*'s challenge was all he needed to order his men aft to their 4.7-inch gun, his stern to the raider, and his radio officer, S. K. Jones, to work. Jones did work, too, and with good results, for his frantic messages alerted the

* *Tropic Sea* reached the Bay of Biscay safely but was there intercepted by H.M.S. *Truant,* whose commander, H. A. V. Haggard, jammed the Norwegian captain, his wife, and the British into the submarine, leaving Steinkrauss, his Germans, and some Norwegians to make their way to Spain. The rest of the Norwegians were taken to Gibraltar by flying boats.

area and sent *Achilles* and *Perth* out again from Wellington and Sydney as soon as they had steam up to box the raider in. (The Germans, however, overheard the shore stations recalling the crews from liberty and could thereby estimate the cruisers' positions.)

At 1756 *Orion* opened fire and obtained a hit with the third salvo. Within minutes *Turakina* was in flames and her foremast came crashing down along with the lookout posted there. She was still fighting, however, and her shells, some over, some short, lay uncomfortably close to the raider. At 1808, when she was virtually stopped and her men were going into the boats, *Orion* ceased fire, coming to within 2,300 yards to lend assistance. Two minutes later Laird's tenacious lads opened up again, denting *Orion*'s hull plates in close misses. Weyher was forced to reply in deadly kind and he then sent two torpedoes crashing into the battered wreck on which Laird ran aft, ordering his gunners to "have another shot at the . . . !" Third Officer J. R. Mallett had to regretfully report, however, that only the muzzle of his gun was still above water. At 1822 it, too, and all the rest of the valiant ship and thirty-five of her crew were gone.

Weyher had fourteen men from one boat picked up and he then spent another five hours (during which he lost sixty miles in distance and ability to escape) maneuvering from one little life-belt light to another, his men outboard in rubber boats to fetch the last twenty-one survivors from the high seas. On his bridge he could hear his men mumbling in stage whispers about the risk he was taking. Testily he snapped at them, explaining what war was and then what one seaman's duty to another was. It was sad, he said, to sink ships, and horrible to kill. Once that was over, one fought man's common enemy, the seas, to save as many souls as possible.*

Making good her escape despite dawdling over rescue work and *Achilles*' and *Perth*'s efforts to catch her, *Orion* steamed clear around Tasmania to molest whatever traffic she could find in the Great Australian Bight. Since there was none to be found, Weyher had some fake mines prepared for dropping off Albany on September 3. The mischief cost him one dead and several wounded—the only casualties suffered during his entire cruise—as one of the contraptions went off prematurely. He was spotted and identified the next day by a Lockheed Hudson bomber and barely managed to elude others sent out in search

---

* *Turakina*'s lookout died and was committed by Weyher. Laird, who was killed fighting, was only "commended for good service" by his government and that (the official history, *The Royal New Zealand Navy*, S. D. Waters, Wellington, 1956) "indicated a lack of imagination and appreciation . . ." by the authorities in 1940 because Captain Bisset had been awarded a posthumous Victoria Cross for his equally gallant fight in 1917. Weyher concurs.

in the bad weather. With nothing but trouble around, he then made off to patrol the Australia–South Africa route before returning to the Pacific, where he was to meet supply ship *Regensburg* at the Marshall Island atoll Ailinglapalap. He arrived there on October 10 after another morale-deadening period of no success, and his dulled sailors were immediately put to work taking on oil (3,000 tons), fresh apples, eggs, and potatoes and painting the ship. Two days later, *Orion* and *Regensburg* sailed in consort, the latter with orders to dress ship (with flags) in case she spotted anything—an eventuality few but the aggressive Weyher believed in any more than they could visualize a day without engine repairs. Much to their surprise, they did catch someone lit up as innocently as in peacetime on the night of October 13. Weyher switched on his own running lights to dim and then gradually brightened them to make his approach seem slower. At 0255 he blinked the standard demands and had the guileless *Ringwood,* home port Oslo, in his hands without any trouble at all.*

Five days later at 0445, *Orion*'s alarm buzzers sounded again, three long, three long, three long. *Schiff 36,* disguised as *Maebasi Maru,* was chasing a vessel she could not catch. *Regensburg,* also in Japanese disguise, tried to waylay the stranger. The latter, however, turned into the lagoon at Lamotrek and, as she did so, her Japanese neutrality markings became visible. It was an awkward situation, for inside the palm-fringed atoll there were two other "Japanese" ships, raider *Komet* and supply ship *Kulmerland.* Loaded with camera-toting passengers and curious officials, *Palao Maru* made inquiries but was fobbed off by *Komet*'s Eyssen with an appeal to the newly signed Tripartite Pact and authentic Japanese clearing papers held by the two German supply ships which had come from Japan.

"FAR EAST SQUADRON"

On the twentieth, Eyssen, as senior officer present, took command of the "Far East Squadron" (the first since Graf Maximilian von Spee's time in World War I), and set off in line abreast with three of the redisguised ships (*Regensburg* was to return to Japan for more supplies) for the

---

* *Ringwood*'s white-haired Captain Parker, who later gave Weyher a lovely carved camphor chest in appreciation for the good treatment he had received, and his thirty-five men joined *Notu*'s and *Turakina*'s crews in the raider, but his seventy-year-old carpenter could not be appeased until he was assured that his equally old and ornery cat would be taken care of. Since his fellow prisoners apparently objected to the critter's stench, the Germans had to solve the problem diplomatically, saying that the beast might be useful catching rats elsewhere in the ship.

southern seas to interdict the Panama Canal and America's traffic east of New Zealand. The area of operations was a good choice for thirty ships transited there during the search, but luck was not with the Germans, whose *Orion* was barely limping along in constant need of boiler repairs, her crew without water for days and more than one hundred of them down with ptomaine poisoning due to a spoiled potato salad. The captains met on November 24 and decided to start back north for a landing on the Australian trust island of Nauru, which exported nearly a million tons of phosphates annually. The next morning *Komet* snared her first victim, not a very big one, to be sure (all of 546 tons), but Eyssen's first success in six months at sea. The little *Holmwood* was taken without a fight and her twenty-nine crew and passengers (including four women and five children) were taken off along with several hundred live sheep. If the little inter-islander had only radioed, another ship, *Rangitane,* which, with 16,712 tons, was the largest ship ever to be sunk by a raider would have been saved.*

Rangitane left Rangitoto on the morning of the day *Holmwood* was captured and would have been diverted had the routing officers ashore been given any advance warning. That not being the case, she was allowed to proceed on a course that led her right under the guns of the German squadron. At 0252 of the twenty-seventh, Capt. H. L. Upton, DSC, R.N.R., flung a coat over his pajamas when his second officer called him to the bridge to report suspicious vessels on either side, and he immediately ordered a warning message to be made. Eyssen, too, was on his bridge in pajamas, slippers, housecoat, and, naturally, white cap. He and Weyher soon had *Rangitane* in a cross fire that forced Upton to stop and abandon his valuable vessel even though he could have outrun both of them. Boarding parties from both raiders vied with each other in being the first to arrive on the large liner, and what they found made their eyes bulge and their mouths water. The two-stacker had been loaded with 124,881 cases of butter, 33,255 cases of meat, and 23,646 cases of cheese among other products. The butter alone, by Eyssen's tabulations, would have sufficed for 15,610,125 weekly wartime rations at home; the cheese, 2,955,750; and the meat

---

* "We are fully aware that any attempt to send the message would have brought about the shelling of *Holmwood,* and that this might have meant heavy loss of life, including the lives of women and children. . . ." That "must be faced in an effort to locate and destroy raiders. This should be realized by persons who travel by sea, and the parents of children who travel by sea; and lest the cool prompt judgement of masters be hampered at critical moments, there should, we suggest, be no unnecessary passenger traffic," the New Zealand Commission of Inquiry on the Loss of Certain Vessels and alleged Leakage of Information, found. (Waters, *Royal New Zealand Navy).*

3,494,300. But there was no time for shopping. The ship was sinking and time was uppermost in Eyssen's mind because *Rangitane's* signals had gotten through clearly. (The Navy Office in Wellington promptly ordered a number of warships, *Achilles* and AMC *Monowai* among them, to find the raiders. Some flying boats were also dispatched and one of them flew over the Germans but failed to spot them. On the twenty-eighth *Achilles* arrived on the scene of the sinking, which was marked by a long oil slick, but she found only a red and white life buoy—the kind starlets and tourists pose with—and a number of cases of butter, two of which were retrieved.*

Two days after their capture Eyssen ordered the prisoners to be exchanged between the squadron with *Kulmerland,* the noncombatant and therefore safer vessel getting all thirty-nine women, except one wounded lady, and five children, to each of whom the benign skipper personally handed a bar of chocolate. Most of the military ex-passengers and former ships' companies were transferred to Eyssen's *Komet,* which they found palatial compared to *Orion* or *Kulmerland,* in which they had albeit been treated courteously. In *Komet* they were handed toothbrushes, paste, soap and towels, tobacco and four cigars each, and were allowed to keep their sextants, watches, and typewriters. Meals were served by their former stewards and they were provided with books, cards, chess sets, and deck chairs—for senior officers—by a guard who, according to one captive, saluted each time he entered their quarters in what was certainly "no hell ship." They were treated not so much as prisoners but as "unwanted guests."

On December 5 Eyssen had Weyher called over to *Komet* to receive instructions for the proposed landing on Nauru. It was to take place in three days and would be led by the flagship's executive officer,

---

* As with so many sinkings it is difficult to tell exactly how many people were involved. *Rangitane's* chief steward told Weyher that there had been 113 passengers and 191 crew on board. The company's history, *Ordeal by Sea* (S. D. Waters, The New Zealand Shipping Company, London, 1949), has 111 and "about 200." Germany's official evaluation of *Orion's* cruise, *Operationen und Taktik, Heft 15"* (Berlin, October 1944), states that 303 survivors (of which 3 died) were taken on board the various German ships, and that 2 had been killed on the liner during the action, while another 1 or 2 presumably drowned. Eyssen's figures show that 303 were saved (36 women), 1 woman was killed in *Rangitane,* 1 corpse left in a boat, presumably drowned, 1 or 2 men and 3 persons (2 brothers, 1 woman) succumbed to their injuries while under treatment on the raiders. New Zealand's history (op. cit.) agrees with the company's history by the same author in the number killed: 5 passengers, 5 crew, and the Official Australian history (Hermon G. Gill, *Royal Australian Navy,* Australian War Memorial, Canberra, 1957) says 11 passengers and crew died, while Lloyd's publication, which unfortunately is at times erroneous (Charles Hocking, *Dictionary of Disasters at Sea during the Age of Steam,* Vols. I, II; Lloyd's Register of Shipping, London, 1969), has 16 killed.

Joseph Huschenbeth, whom many of the men found to be the antithesis of the cosmopolitan, tolerant, and internationally minded skipper. *Schiff 45* would provide eighty-six men and *Orion,* ninety-nine; prisoners and private mail, Eyssen chivalrously declared, would be let off ashore. Weyher, who always found his senior difficult to get along with, did not complain about the landing party but he was not about to let any of his white and savvy captives go close to an area where he would be conducting operations for a while longer. St. Nicholas Day (December 6), when many German kids get little pre-Christmas gifts, the squadron ran across *Triona* again and finally cornered her after a confused chase lasting nine hours and seventeen minutes during which three of the running, radioing clipper-bowed vessel's sixty-four-man complement were killed. Eyssen let *Orion* handle the disposal of the ship while he sailed away with his faster, more reliable raider to reconnoiter Nauru, off whose coast the three Germans were to rendezvous early on the eighth for an assault on the phosphate ships usually found drifting near the island waiting to go under the giant cantilevered loading platforms. He made his offing on the evening of the seventh, then closed to within three miles of shore. At 1833 he stopped the Norwegian *Vinni,* took her thirty-two men on board, and then scuttled the 5,181-ton motor ship, which had been waiting for a whole week for the westerlies to abate and make loading possible. Capt. H. Hendricksen and his first officer, A. Jensen, met Eyssen in the raider and were delighted to hear that they would already be released on the morrow. When asked if they were willing to part with any intelligence, which they refused to do, he bombastically told them, laughing, "It is not necessary, either. I have all the information I need. It is five ships [including *Triona,* which should have arrived that evening] and I will get them within twenty-four hours." He did not tell them that he had gleaned that accurate appraisal of the shipping situation from captured documents, but he did get the rest of the ships in a razzle-dazzle shoot-'em-up that lasted less than twenty-four hours, utterly baffled the residents and radio operators on shore, and even confused the Germans themselves.

Weyher and Eyssen met as planned on the morning of the eighth and conferred for two hours, after which *Komet* turned to round the island from the north while *Orion* searched to the south where she soon sighted the running lights of a ship. When approached and signaled to stop, *Triadic*'s master, who had not observed the blinker message but who had seen the strange ship, switched off his lights and steamed away until his radio gear and steering engine were smashed and one of his men killed by gunfire. He then stopped, dumped the Phosphate Commissioner motor ship's papers, and lowered two boats, which then crawled for nearby Nauru. Weyher, with no time to pick up survivors—he had spotted another vessel to the eastward—ordered *Kulmerland* to do so.

Komet, having observed the shooting and not wanting to accidentally tangle with *Orion,* rounded the island once more, then picked up one of *Triadic's* boats which carried First Officer Low and some passengers, such as Mr. and Mrs. G. W. Dillon and the family G. R. Ferguson, all still in their nightclothes. Once helped aboard by the Germans, Low asked Eyssen, "What the hell did you want to fire without warning for?" Miffed, Eyssen, who could not have known anything about the New Zealand Commission's opinions about fighting raiders and the foolhardiness of passengers venturing to sea in wartime (see footnote p. 64), had not done the shooting in the first place and was sure that Weyher would have given the vessel a chance to surrender, snapped back: "You were on an armed ship and I treat you as a warship. Why do you carry passengers on your ship with a gun on?" (*sic*) He then left the other boat to *Kulmerland,* from whom he heard that *Orion* was off stalking still another ship. That was *Triaster* (also the Phosphate Commissioner's), also new and nearly as large as the 6,378-ton *Triadic,* commanded by Capt. A. Rhoades, who did not get off a warning and who along with sixty-three shipmates was aboard *Orion* a prisoner by 1154. Less than two hours before that, *Komet,* then finished with *Triadic's* boats, had tangled with yet another, a clipper-bowed and four-masted ship. It was the 3,900-ton steamer *Komata,* whose master, W. W. Fish, had seized up his predicament when called to the bridge by telling his engineers to "give her all she's got!" He could not read *Komet's* signal and "all she's got" was not enough to escape the raider, whose guns silenced his radio, blew his first officer to pieces along with the port wing of the bridge, and mortally injured the second officer.

By midafternoon of that hectic December 8 the German squadron had been all squared away again, and the landing on Nauru had been called off because of the prevailing seas which made boat work impossible.

But what of Nauru? Most of the frantic activity had taken place within sight of shore where all lights had been lit as if the place were having a carnival. The burning *Triadic* had been seen early in the morning and so had *Komet* and *Kulmerland,* but the bad, rainy weather had made any closer observation impossible. Nauru's radio operators had asked nearby Ocean Island whether they had heard any distress messages but had received a negative reply. Later, *Komata's* signals were heard and understood by Ocean Island but not on Nauru, where a clever ruse by *Komet's* radioman, who had transposed the stricken ship's call for help into an innocent commercial communication with a far-off station, drowned out the signal. Ocean Island did try to pass on *Komata*'s anxious message, but the Nauru operators' fears were allayed by *Komet*'s interference.

Nauru's administrator did advise Australia's Naval Board of some strange happenings offshore: Two unexpected Japanese vessels [*Komet* and *Kulmerland*] were apparently standing by a burning ship [*Triadic*]. "Other British and Allied Vessels which are drifting on account of weather and which should be in vicinity of *Triadic* but which have not been sighted and which have not communicated anything untoward are *Triaster, Komata, Vinni, Triona* due Nauru 8th December,"* the rest of the advisory said. Time of sending: 1048 December 8, hours and days after those 25,900 tons of shipping were no longer bound anywhere. The board, guessing what might have happened, ordered all ships headed for Nauru to disperse. There was little else they could do, for the only man-of-war, AMC *Manoora,* was then 2,400 miles away at Darwin.

The "Far East Squadron" had meanwhile also dispersed with *Komet* and *Kulmerland* headed for an oiling at Ailinglapalap and *Orion* out raiding off Ponape. They met once more for another Eyssen try at Nauru, but the attempted landing again failed because of continuing high seas. By that time Eyssen was getting somewhat sick of his *müden* (tired, slang for sad) task force, one of whose ships was constantly in need of repairs. But before he would disband the formation, he ordered it to Emirau Island in the Bismarck Archipelago to release the 675 prisoners, of which 153 were in his own ship, 265 in *Orion,* and 257 in *Kulmerland.*

They had all been treated well, they agreed: They had had books to read and games to play (bridge and solitaire gave way to simpler games like snap and sevens as the tedious days wore on); they had listened to blaring German records, martial music, symphonies, Christmas carols, and one obviously captured disk, "Adolf, you've bitten off more than you can chew," wondering whether their captors did not get the lines, whether they too thought it was funny, or whether it was simply a matter of noblesse oblige.

December 20 was a big day for everyone. Eyssen joined the prisoners—whom he had provisioned with radios, kerosene, foodstuffs, cigarettes, and even four rifles—on deck and, pointing to a nearby palmy island, said, "Well, tomorrow you will be drinking whiskey and soda over there." Debarkation began the next morning and by midafternoon 343 Europeans and 171 natives had reached the neat little island, which was inhabited by two white planters, their wives, and a number of

---

* Gill, *Royal Australian Navy.*

natives. The various ships' companies set up primitive camps while some of the officers set off in a local motor launch to circumvent Eyssen's twenty-four-hour restrictions and effect their own transferral to Australia. Their arrival there at Townsville on New Year's Day not only set the press pecking away with the wildest nonsense—the old daredevil Luckner had been at it again, there were three squadrons of raiders, etc.—but official inquiries as well. There must have been spies afoot, it was thought; worse yet, possibly traitors. Even Australia's Navy Minister, W. M. Hughes, lent credit to the spy scare in a public statement. The rumors were quickly squelched, however, by simultaneous investigations in Australia and New Zealand, whose Commission of Inquiry rightly conjectured that the Germans had been correlating intercepted radio messages, captured documents, and occasional loose chatter to surmise where those ships might be found. "The statements attributed to him [Eyssen]," the commission decided, "seem to us to be more likely a part of an attempt to impress his captives and through them to disseminate uneasiness and distrust in New Zealand, or they may have been manifestations of boastfulness and of a taste for melodrama."

Finally rid of the prisoners (except for 150 that Weyher retained for security reasons), the "Far East Squadron" broke up, *Komet* back toward Nauru, *Kulmerland* to reload in Japan, and *Orion* for a long-delayed refit at Lamotrek where, on the last day of the year, she met *Regensburg* and *Ole Jacob,* now under the command of Captain Steinkrauss who had tried to take *Orion*'s prize *Tropic Sea* to France.* Weyher was delighted to see his compatriot again and to get some oil and food, but he was aware of the ramifications of the release of the prisoners—a godsend to British intelligence—and furious that the men had been let go by Eyssen over his own protest.† But Weyher had other worries as well and those went to the very heart of his exasperation with his decrepit ship. SKL, apprised of his difficulties and constant need for oil (roughly fifty-four tons per day by then), had resolved to recall the raider once its overhaul had been completed and supply ships had been redisposed to meet his demands. Weyher would be returning via the Indian Ocean, they said. That was a bitter blow to his ambitions. In following SKL's orders, he would be steaming through areas already worked over by other raiders (they had sunk forty-two ships by then) and thus be deprived of success.

Komet's captain, for his part, refuted SKL's stand. Of course, the

---

* *Ole Jacob* was *Atlantis*' prize which had exchanged her cargo of gasoline for oil in Japan. Steinkrauss, having landed in Spain after his encounter with H.M.S. *Truant,* had made his way to the Orient via the Trans-Siberian Railway.

† SKL shared Weyher's opinion regarding the mass release and radioed so in a coolly-worded message pointed at *Komet* but addressed to all raiders.

prisoners talked but the raiders' previous operating area had been compromised anyway and he would have had to feed the lot of them for quite a while. And that, with provisions limited, would not have been an easy thing to accomplish, he reasoned. Depressed by a holiday season alone without his wife and their two children, suffering from the heat (he spent part of Christmas Day luxuriating in a tub of freshly caught rainwater and cakes of ice), and still intending an island shoot, he sailed back to undefended Nauru. Eyssen arrived there at 0300 of the twenty-seventh—this time the lights were out—and at 0545 he spoke the signal station to warn the residents to stay clear of the oil tanks and phosphate works and not to wireless. His gentlemanly message was understood: He had to fire a warning shot to drive the many, curious, chattering natives off the beach. Judging by the ensuing pell-mell rush for the bush, that was understood, too. Then he shelled the island's tanks, cantilevered cranes, storage bins, boats, and mooring buoys for an hour and eighteen minutes, expending 126 rounds of 5.9-inch, 360 37-mm, and 719 20-mm ammunition. As the only attack made by any raider on a land target (Rogge and Detmers entertained similar plans), it was an outstanding success. The damage done to the plant was extensive; 13,000 tons of oil were burned and the resulting fire collapsed several large storage bins. The vital phosphate shipments were interrupted for ten weeks and were never brought back to full scale until long after the war.

As an event, it caused repercussions far and wide. The world's press waxed hysterical; Royal and Dominion naval officers went back to their plotting-room boards in haste. Trans-Tasman convoys were initiated, troopers were to be escorted as far as Honolulu, phosphate ships to Nauru and Ocean Island. Even the Japanese were annoyed because everyone was saying that the raiders had been outfitted under the auspices of the Imperial Chrysantheum. In Germany, SKL, unable to decide whether the phosphate shoot had been in the overall interest, sent Eyssen coolly guarded congratulations but warned all its raiders that henceforth such independent actions should be avoided. Eyssen was riled by all the fuss but by New Year's Day he was again mollified—he had not been passed over. Wearing the black and two-balled standard of a rear admiral at his truck, he was headed for the Indian Ocean where *Atlantis* and *Pinguin* had been so successful.

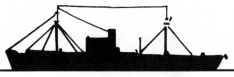

CHAPTER 5

The Indian Ocean, 1940

"STOPPING HERE"   The Indian Ocean covers an area 28,-356,276 miles square to an average depth of 2,147 fathoms. In 1940 its inshore waters were mostly patrolled by aircraft and an assortment of naval vessels that were meant to make them safe for Allied cargo vessels and dangerous for German raiders. In the enormous open spaces starting just a few hundred miles from shore, however, the former took a risk when traveling alone, and the latter, though always alone and vulnerable, found good hunting.

During the latter part of 1940, there were two of those ships, *Atlantis* and *Pinguin,* marauding above and below the equator and almost at will, it seemed. British and Commonwealth stations heard their victims' messages of distress, planes and ships were sent out to secure the seas, but the vastness of the ocean defeated their purposes. By the time *Pinguin* brought her first ship to on August 26 only some 250 miles from Madagascar, *Atlantis* had already sunk four and captured another. *Schiff 33*'s Krüder used his aircraft that day to take Norway's 7,616-ton motor tanker *Filefjell* and the gamble paid off. The Heinkel dropped a weighted bag containing a message in atrocious English on the ship: "On account of vicinity of enemy raider alter course to 180° [toward *Pinguin*] distance 140 miles. From that point take up course direct to 31°N 37°E. Thence you get further informations. Do not use wireless." Later the plane ripped out the ship's wireless with a grapple and rattled off a few rounds with its machine gun as a warning. Then it landed, signaling, "Remain stopping here. Cruiser *Cumberland* will go with you" (*sic*). But the unarmed, edgy Norwegian did not need much of a warning. They were standing on ten thousand tons of gasoline and were quite willing to surrender.

The next two days were busy ones for Krüder. Between 0418 and 0615 of the twenty-seventh he stopped, shelled, and picked up the forty-six-man crew of *British Commander,* whose signals, proving *Pinguin* to be behind schedule, disturbed Rogge in *Atlantis* and aroused

71

the Royal Navy into a prompt and multi-gunned reaction with H.M.S. *Neptune,* light cruiser *Colombo,* and AMCs *Arawa* and *Kanimbla* (The latter discovered only a patch of oil at the scene of the attack.) Four hours after dispatching the "noisy ship," *Pinguin* took *Morviken* and its thirty-five men in classic, old-style raider form—signals, shot across the bow, no gunfire, no damage, no injuries.

His battle with *Benavon* on September 12 was a brutal affair quite in keeping with the style of warfare so prevalent in World War II. The raider had come in so close (little over a mile) that the Ben liner first tried to comply with the rules of the road by maneuvering around its stern, then sent her seamen running to their 4-inch gun and 3-inch flak. At 0728 Krüder opened fire. So did his opponent, Captain A. Thomson, who, though still in his pajamas, got his licks in first with a ricochet that penetrated the raider's port side and ended up in the crew's quarters, hot, dented, and menacing. It did not explode and was thrown overboard, but had it gone off near the mine compartment very little of *Pinguin* and her 325 men would have remained. Krüder's eighth salvo took effect, putting the spunky British 4-inch gun crew out of action, and in the next eight minutes, Thomson and twenty-three officers and hands were killed, most of *Benavon's* lifeboats shattered and blown away, her aerial cut, the bridge blasted, and metal and glass sent flying about the engine room, one end of which was filled with smoke, the other with scalding steam. Chief Engineer R. C. Porteus, in charge of twenty-five survivors, was hauled aboard the raider to be joined the next day by the entire crew of *Nordvard,* a fine Norwegian motor ship which had been taken without any struggle and sent off with 179 prisoners to France, where she arrived November 22.

Pinguin's slender, strong-faced captain had volunteered for the Navy in World War I, had served at Jutland and in the Black Sea. After the armistice he had fought with the rightist brigades in the political battles for Berlin, then rejoined the service in which he was posted to a training cruiser and the educational and construction bureaus ashore. He was a clear thinker, imaginative, and at forty-two quite willful. His branch speciality had been mines and, contrary to most commanders, he appeared to like working with the beastly spheres.

As he marched eastward to his assigned station off Australia two months behind schedule and came much too close—ninety miles—to *Atlantis* the day she sank *Commissaire Ramel,* he and his coolly-reasoning navigator, Lieutenant (S) Wilhelm Michaelsen, formerly captain of the 14,700-ton liner *Steuben,* sat down for a study of some charts showing Australian and Tasmanian coastal waters. Painstakingly the two men laid out a plan that would block at least six channels with the least number of mines possible, in the shortest time possible, and without having a vessel strike the mines prematurely and thereby give away the operation before it had been completed. Dividers in hand, they walked off the distances, only to find that it could not be done by one ship alone even with delayed-action mines. Two ships? That was it, the enthusiastic captain and reserved lieutenant navigator declared; a fabulous idea. The next problem was to catch a ship without half blowing it apart before it stopped. On October 7 they had the ship they wanted and she was unharmed. It was *Storstad,* an ideal vessel and, being a tanker, wholly inconspicuous. Most useful then and in the future, too, was the Norwegian's cargo of twelve thousand tons of diesel fuel. For two days the Germans burned and tore out the partitions in the vessel's after mess hall and engineers' quarters and by the third, 110 mines—each gingerly transported over to the prize on matresses laid in a boat—had been stowed away. On the twelfth Krüder said good-bye and God-speed to Erich Warning, staff captain of the 51,700-ton North German Lloyd liner *Bremen* during its blockade-running dash from New York in 1939, whom he had appointed in command of the auxiliary minelayer *Passat,* ex-*Storstad,* and whom he was not to see again for a whole month. Warning's orders were precise, nice in their simplicity, as was the entire program the exuberant Krüder and his perfect counterpoise, Michaelsen, had worked out for the two ships. Its schema was beguilingly plain. (See page 74.)

Steaming in heavily traveled waters, close enough inshore to see the streetlights of Upright Point and St. Catherine's Hill, and ignoring all other vessels and inquiries from land, the two skippers accomplished their missions exactly as outlined. Themselves silent and blacked out, sometimes showing running lights if that seemed the local practice, they marveled at the heedlessness of the Australians whose lighthouses at such places like Stephens Point, Baranja Head, South Neptune, and Cape Barda still flashed brightly, serving the Germans as accurate navigational fixes. Just as *Pinguin* was laying her last field in Spencer Gulf during the night of November 7/8, the 10,846-ton *Cambridge* struck one of *Passat*'s mines and went down with the loss of one man just two and a half miles off South East Point. Within twenty-four hours of her loss, *City of Rayville* hit another mine at the western entrance to Bass Strait (again with one man killed) to become the first United States vessel to be sunk in the war. The Royal Australian Navy closed ·off Bass Strait and the Port of Melbourne; planes lifted into the air and seamen started sweeping mines, an activity that caused the youngsters until then accustomed to playing sailor in waters considered safe to become "green about the gills," as their commander in auxiliary *Orara*

	PINGUIN		PASSAT	
DATE	EXERCISE: NO. PLACE TO BE MINED	NUMBER OF MINES	EXERCISE: NO. PLACE TO BE MINED	NUMBER OF MINES
Night of 28/29 October	Exercise I Sydney-Newcastle	40 with 48 hrs. delayed action	—	—
29/30 October	—	—	Exercise I Banks Strait	30 with 48 hrs. delayed action
30/31 October	—	—	Exercise II Eastern Entrance Bass Strait	40 with 48 hrs. delayed action
31 October/ 1 November	Exercise II Hobart	40	Exercise III Western Entrance Bass Strait	40
Further, and if at all possible:				
6/7 November	Exercise III Spencer Gulf	40	—	—
	Total No. Mines	120		110

observed. Ashore there was talk of U-boats, but the Navy Office in Canberra knew better, though a short search for the intruders by a light cruiser, H.M.A.S. *Adelaide,* was fruitless. It had to be because Krüder and Warning were then already moving at their best speeds southwest of the mainland toward a rendezvous that, on November 15, brought to a close an operation SKL rightly deemed "outstanding in its planning, preparation and execution."*

The British *Nowshera* complied peacefully with all of Krüder's demands on November 18 and that was too bad, for not only were all her 113 ship's company taken prisoner and the vessel itself sacked, but any signal from her would have warned *Maioma* and *Port Brisbane,* then steaming westward toward the same area, and would also have alerted H.M.A.S. *Canberra,* then inbound from the Indian Ocean after a search triggered by *Atlantis'* capture of *Ole Jacob.*

Maioma was plodding along harmlessly at around eleven knots on

---

* *Pinguin's* fields had less effect than *Passat's,* damaging only the 10,923-ton *Hertford* (back in service a year later), sinking the 1,052-ton coaster *Nimbin,* the 287-ton trawler *Millimulmul,* and indirectly causing the loss of minesweeper *Goorangai,* which collided with steamer *Duntroon* and went down with all hands.

November 20 with a cargo of butter, steel, and frozen meats, but her captain, H. S. Cox, was not too happy. He was concerned, he confided to Second Steward Alfred R. Nash, when the latter appeared on the bridge early that morning, about a ship that had been sighted on the horizon. Just as Nash was finishing with the first sitting of lunch at 1343, the ship's siren blew and the steward left his tables for his post at the ammo hoist of the 4-incher, grumbling all the while about the damned drills. They could at least let a man get lunch served and the silverware cleared, he groused. Once on deck, he saw a plane ripping out their steamer's aerial as it thundered by overhead. It then banked to drop a message: "Stop your engines immediately. Do not wireless, in case of disobedience you will be bombed and shelled." Two warning bombs fell harmlessly in the sea. Neither Cox nor his crew, composed largely of Stornowaymen, were about to be intimidated by a plane, however. With watches double-banked in the firerooms, the stokers managed to get up to thirteen and a half knots. As the 8,011-ton ship turned and made smoke, her fourth engineer, Ernest Howlett, was fighting a private war with the aircraft. Exposed out on deck, service rifle in hand, he was vainly trying to pick off the pilot while Nash watched their gunner handling his Lewis gun in a "ding-dong battle with the plane." Meanwhile, a spare aerial had been rigged and the ship was on the air only twenty minutes after the first attack. And it continued sending *Maioma*'s position, plane attack, and description of the approaching raider, for nearly three hours until Cox had to lower his red ensign to surrender. All eighty-seven men were then transferred to the raider as Krüder prepared to retrieve his plane, which had been forced down out of fuel, its floats punctured by machine-gun bullets. Just as he was leaving the area to avoid the countermeasures he felt sure would be—and indeed were—made (*Canberra* then refueling at Freemantle, sallied forth as soon as she had steam up, and *Perth,* held up by convoy duty, followed two days later), Krüder's regular steaming watch reported another ship, and the captain, conscious through intercepts that the Aussies were on his trail and not wishing to take another risk with his only remaining plane (the first Heinkel had been demolished back in September), decided to take on the vessel by surprise after nightfall to prevent its radioing. He stalked all of the twenty-first, and in his quarry, *Port Brisbane,* the men worried all day.

"OVERTIME"

They had been only some sixty miles to the north when they heard *Maioma*'s signaling and saw a suspicious tanker (*Storstad*). Cautiously,

Capt. H. Steele had detoured still farther north coming back to his original course only at night. The ship's company had been standing double watches until 2100 of that evening when Steele dismissed them and himself left the bridge for a short rest.

By that time, Krüder's men were going to action stations, and their preparations alarmed their latest captives no end. Nash, who had been distressed that his overtime records, "the first I had really earned," had gone down when *Maioma* was scuttled, wondered whether he'd ever need any money again. The first day in captivity had gone by passably and he had been surprised to see the raider's pilot come down to their quarters in the hold to shake hands with their gunner, both congratulating each other on their survival. Nash had crawled into his bunk that evening ready to sack out when he heard a tinkling sound coming from a large ventilator trunk running up through his compartment. At the third bell, the steward was thoroughly perplexed and alarmed as a "clackety-bang, bang" started up in the mysterious trunk.

The racket that frightened Nash was, of course, one of the raider's ammo hoists. At 2230 *Pinguin*'s searchlight gripped *Port Brisbane* in an icy stare, but the warning shot that followed had no effect. Krüder tried blinker signals. Across the black water, Steele responded with a radio message, then dumped his secret materials and, knowing that resistance would be useless, recalled the men who had gathered at one of the two 6-inchers aft. Krüder, however, lacking the immediate submission he expected, opened fire with his main battery and the 37 mm, and that was when Nash really saw "tough men in a state of terror, banging on the steel for Germans to let us out."

For those in *Port Brisbane* it was far worse. Her hull and radio shack were holed, the bridge demolished, one engine room telegraph jammed full ahead, the other full astern. The man taking verbal instructions to the engineers was killed, and Steele had to lower his boats. Krüder picked up two of them with sixty men but told the British captain that he could not spend time looking for the remaining one because he knew that a cruiser (*Canberra*) was out searching for him and that it would have heard *Port Brisbane*'s calls. He then torpedoed Steele's command along with its badly needed cargo of meat, butter, and cheese, none of which he could touch for the same reason he could not go after Second Officer Dingle and the twenty-seven men in the missing boat.* Krüder's knowledge of the old-fashioned-looking warship's movements was the result of Australia's lax censorship. The heavy cruiser's departure had been announced in the House of Representatives by Navy Minister Hughes, and since ministerial statements were ex-

---

* Dingle was picked up by three-stacked *Canberra* twenty hours later.

empted from censorship, the Australian Broadcasting Commission innocently spotted the information on the evening's news program.

Krüder fled, cutting south, then some thirteen hundred miles west, during which time he overhauled his engines and found time to chat with Steele, who considered the treatment of captives in *Pinguin* "as one seaman would another, both doing their duty to their country. Krüder, in fact, did what he could for us—it was not much as there seemed to be several Nazi officers amongst his men—but he showed no bitterness toward us saying that his time would come someday. And it did." On the thirtieth, Steele says, the German captain called for him and, pointing to a ship on the horizon, said he would be sinking it that night. It was *Port Wellington,* and the British captain hoped that if things went well, depending on the point of view, he would soon see his brother-in-law, F. W. Bailey, the vessel's first officer, safe and sound.

Storstad had reported the ship in the morning and Krüder had crept up on her until he was less than a mile off, intending to overwhelm her by surprise and strike her dumb before she could radio. And that he accomplished with his shells bursting in the smoking room and the wireless office, which caught fire. Actually the shooting appeared terribly inaccurate to Second Officer P. Beeham but it did kill *Port Wellington*'s radio officer at his post and injured the captain so severely that he later died in the raider. Next in command, Bailey took over, had the boats launched, but was soon back on board collecting clothing for the ship's seven women survivors who had by then been quartered in *Pinguin*'s officer country. They brought Krüder's unwanted guests to an unsupportable 405 in number, and since he had to get rid of them somehow, he wirelessed SKL that he was about to send *Storstad* home with them and all the diesel oil she still had in her tanks.

That, as noted, led to the meeting with *Atlantis* on December 8, after which the prize was released with 524 prisoners. If any of them had known what Rogge and Mohr thought of conditions in *Storstad* ("terrible"), they could only have agreed, and those who had considered the food in *Atlantis* or *Pinguin* poor and the quarters cramped soon ran out of adjectives to describe the tanker's rations and accommodations. "Cooking facilities looked poor" to Bailey, "the sanitary conditions appalling." Steward Nash thought the smells and crowding "unbelievable and hard to describe." Time on deck was limited by the great numbers to half an hour every second day. The rest of the hours they stared up at the hatch waiting for either food or water to be lowered. When the water came down one day, Nash remembers, "I presented the first man his, only to be met with the remark 'That tastes awful.' The second man likewise expressing his distaste and saying *how* it tasted;

and the third man said, 'Yes, it does taste like *it!*' Some Chinese had mixed up the latrine buckets with those the Germans intended for water.

Between January 6 and 8, the prison ship was lying in the South Atlantic at a point the Germans knew as "F" (27°S, 12°W) of waiting area "Andalusia," and with her was an impressive armada of Admiral Raeder's ships: raider *Thor, Scheer,* naval tanker *Nordmark,* and a British reefer, *Sheer*'s prize *Duquesa. Storstad* received thousands of eggs from the prize and she pumped the remaining 6,500 tons of diesel oil into *Nordmark* for use by *Scheer,* prizes or raiders like *Kormoran,* the first of a second wave, then rolling past Norway's clefted coasts for a run through the Denmark Strait.

By this time, the prisoners were beginning to dead-reckon their position accurately. *Port Wellington*'s Beeham and some others had collected what things they could, a string, knife, pin, map, a table of sines and tangents to integral degrees, a watch, pencil, toilet paper, and a paper compass rose, which they pasted on some cardboard with honey and which was used to get the angle of the sun. With those primitive means and a masterly application of all they had learned for their Board of Trade Certificates and the practical knowledge gained in years at sea, they soon had their calculations down to a precise science. When they announced their findings, they were met with mild skepticism, but that was soon allayed one hot day when the Germans allowed the canvas bridge dodger to sag a bit as they stood in line to take the meridian altitude. They were watched with a keen interest by the prisoners, for it was reasoned that the second their caps dipped down as they bent over to read their sextants it would be apparent noon. Down went the caps and the British had exact Greenwich mean time. Beeham found his observations only fourteen to fifteen minutes (or that many miles) out in latitude. He also contrived to make a signaling lamp, which he and his companions hoped to use if they came on a friendly cruiser.

Storstad entered the Gironde early in the morning of February 4, 1941. Beeham's calculations had shown that they would be in the approaches to the river at dawn. From Bordeaux he and the others were sent to Germany, but four of them, *Maioma*'s Howlett, who had fired at *Pinguin*'s plane with an Enfield, his shipmate, Fifth Engineer Dunshea, *Nowshera*'s Fifth Engineer R. Bellew, and *Automedon*'s S. E. Harper (caught by *Atlantis*), never got there. With four francs between them they jumped from the train as it slowed for a bend not far from Blois, from which they journeyed to Spain and finally reached home. The rest, like Nash, eventually reached camp Marlag and Milag Nord near Bremen and there they hungered, raised gardens, read, gambled, organized concerts, plays, and sports events, went on work details—mostly picking potatoes—and tried to find ways of annoying the camp commandant, a tough disciplinarian they called "sour Kraut." They were finally released in the spring of 1945 by elements of General Montgomery's 21st Army Group.

"ONE HUNDRED ICEBERGS, SIR!"

After leaving *Storstad* and *Atlantis,* Krüder made his way to the Bouvet–South Georgia region to seek out the British–Norwegian whaling fleets. By December 20 *Pinguin* was in among the drifting ice, some of whose table bergs measured 150 feet high by some 3,000 feet long. Young adjutant Ensign Hans-Karl Hemmer had the watch; visibility was poor (less than half a mile and hardly enough to bring a ship with way on to a stop). Suddenly the water temperature dropped—a sure indication of a berg nearby. Hemmer had the captain called and was ringing down for less speed just as Krüder appeared with a long drippy nose to see what was wrong. Nothing really; they were close to a berg and the junior officer had acted quite correctly. Capricious and always irritable when disturbed after lunch, Krüder nonchalantly shrugged, "Oh, well, I am going back to my cabin. Report again when you have one hundred icebergs in sight." Hemmer, who liked and admired the captain, felt small but remembered the orders well. A few days later he again had the watch while Krüder napped and all had to be still on the bridge like the night before Christmas. There were so many bergs about by then that it would have been silly to count them and Hemmer felt the time ripe for revenge. Off went the bridge messenger to tell the captain that there were one hundred bergs in sight. The sailor came back without Krüder but reported that the latter seemed to have been rather awesomely angry at first, thoughtful next, and smiling at last.

On the twenty-third the man with the long nose had a Ritterkreuz to add to his decorations and three days later a bad scare. His plane, its fuel consumption suddenly rising by 40 percent, had been forced down at sea. Luckily it was found after a three-hour search. By New Year's Eve Krüder was close enough to the whaling fleet he was seeking to overhear their exchanges over TBS (talk between ships) and he knew that he would soon meet up with the factory ships *Ole Wegger* and *Pelagos* and their thirteen catchers. Their capture was to be a one-time stunt hardly ever outclassed by his compatriots Kähler and Ruckteschell, who had been fighting their raiders *Thor* and *Widder* far to the north in the same Atlantic but in a more bitterly contested arena for most of 1940.

CHAPTER 6

The Atlantic, 1940

COURT-MARTIAL Traditionally, in modern times, the Atlantic, North and South, has been by far the most heavily traveled of all oceans, and in 1940 it inevitably became the fundamental factor on which Britain's survival rested. The sea lanes crossing it led to Africa, the Americas, Australia, India, and New Zealand, and while the Royal Navy could never hope to achieve absolute dominion over all the United Kingdom's sea communications, it endeavored with tenacity and skill to establish zones of maritime control. The most harshly contested and heavily defended were those in the Atlantic, and it was there that Britain maintained most of its fleet. It was there, too, that *Widder* and *Thor* fought their agonizing war; the former always in the northern hemisphere, the latter on both sides of the equator. Their operational zones were clearly defined and limited by zones reserved for U-boats, warship raiders like *Scheer, Hipper, Scharnhorst,* and *Gneisenau,* and the vast United States–proclaimed Pan-American Neutrality Belt that lay mostly west of 20°W.

On July 18, 1940, the day *Widder*'s prisoners from *Davisian* and *King John* arrived on a Caribbean Island to give the world its first accurate description of a modern raider and its operating methods, the small twenty-one-year-old German tanker *Rekum,* its bottom a tangled mess of slimy marine growths and encrusted with barnacles from its long stay in the Canaries, steamed unobtrusively out of Tenerife. She was westbound with a load of oil for *Widder* and she met up with the raider ten days later. Having no fresh vegetables, she was a disappointment, but she did deliver 1,465 tons of oil and was then released to a rendezvous with *Schiff 10* (*Thor*), which was at the time fleeing south after her July 28 engagement with AMC *Alcantara* off Trinidade Island.

One week after the meet, *Widder*'s lookouts sighted an empty tanker running west. Ruckteschell opted for a night attack which, though risky, was most likely to bring results in the least time with a minimum expenditure of ammunition and the least opportunity for the quarry to radio. All it took was accurate navigational plotting, nerves, and a willingness to expose a raider to return gunfire at close ranges. Tracking the vessel all day, he closed in for the kill after dark guided by a beam of light from a carelessly opened door and poorly blacked-out portholes. He came so close on a reciprocal course (thereby diminishing the other ship's chances of escaping) that the tanker, itself fearing an imminent collision, set its running lights seconds before being smothered by a shower of thirty 5.9-inch shells. The terrified Norwegians in the motor tanker *Beaulieu,* 6,114 tons, call letters LDOG, lowered two boats while Ruckteschell, harking back to a message from SKL which warned that the British had even ordered their masters to resort to small arms if necessary, sprayed the helpless ship, arguing that he did not wish to be picked off by rifle fire. He let the boats go but found that he had to explain both actions first to his own officers and men, many of whom could not be expected to understand such methods that easily, and later to a British court, which was even less inclined to find any justification for leaving seamen to their fate some twelve hundred miles from the nearest land. It is true that it might have taken hours to find the boats and that Ruckteschell had to be cautious. The bright flashes of his guns and the glare of the searchlight might easily have attracted any nearby enemy warship. It was also evident that many Allied seamen chose to escape with a maddening, propaganda-fed, irrationality that frustrated rescue work and led them to their own destruction. But that did not deter *Widder'*s Exec Heinicke, who often quarreled with his captain, from taking a strong stand. Ruckteschell had to stick around to pick up all possible survivors, he advised, for the men were clearly having difficulty in going along with some of their commander's sudden, and to them apparently ruthless, procedures. The older man listened. Actually, *Beaulieu'*s twenty-eight survivors (four men, including the captain, had been killed) were very fortunate. They were picked up on the ninth by tanker *Cymbeline,* which took them to Gibraltar. Just a day before their rescue, Ruckteschell did take time to save the entire complement of the Dutch *Oostplein,* which he had overhauled at night. He did not want any prisoners, he noted in his log, but the Netherlanders, headed by their captain, A. L. Lievense, had signaled an SOS from their boats and this time the German commander thought they had little chance of making shore despite the fact that they were closer to safety than had been the Norwegians.

Night attacks were very successful, Ruckteschell found, even though the long, tedious shadowing at his best speed cost nearly twice as much oil as would a shorter chase by day. He was presented with a bit of a puzzle on the eleventh: "something suspicious on the horizon. Probably a sailing ship," torpedo officer Malte von Schack, a dashing lieutenant ever ready for action or fun, reported. That meant it could be a naval vessel whose top hampers were often mistaken for the yards and canvas of square-riggers. It was a barque and it backed its main when ordered to stop. Though of Finnish registry, *Killoran*'s agent and the owner of her cargo were British, thus freeing the Germans to sink her under the prize rules after her eighteen-man crew had been taken over.

It almost seemed as if the sinking of the old windjammer brought misfortune in its wake, as superstition had it. Ruckteschell ran into a lot of trouble, mechanical, personal, and enemy. His problems with machinery were really nothing new, but he had to train seamen to relieve the engineers who, much like *Orion*'s, were fighting a steady but losing battle against the old and unreliable apparatuses. The fact that a propeller blade, already cracked at the outset, had hit ice and had been used by Ruckteschell to smash up a deserted lifeboat (he admitted that had not been too sensible) had not helped, but the main fault lay with the propulsion plant. It was "nonsense," he noted in his war diary (as had Weyher) to use a steamship as a raider. They took too much oil; their boilers could not be shut down and fired up again quickly thus making repairs for the men already busy with leaky condensers, burned-out tubes, and crumbling firebrick all the harder. As crippling and embarrassing as those deficiencies were and as much as he railed against them, he was even angrier at some of his men. The worst case—and it would have been so considered by any seaman—involved a junior officer. Ruckteschell, with his singular sense for danger aroused, had appeared on the bridge during the first watch one night to find the officer of the deck, an ensign, leaning on the rail, apparently dozing. That seemed unbelievable; not only did it place the entire ship in jeopardy but it was bad for morale. Ruckteschell called for a special court-martial with hopes of a death sentence, hardly to be expected in such a case. Indeed, when the court in *Widder* gave its verdict, it was three years demotion to seaman and loss of the man's civilian captain's papers. Ruckteschell's further efforts for more severe punishment were unsuccessful.

"HERE I AM *THOR*"

"I am in position as ordered," tanker *Rekum* radioed Sunday morning, August 25, telling Kähler something he expected and the British, if they were listening, that a German ship somewhere south of the equator was chatting with another Jerry in the same vicinity. Vexed, Kähler responded with an emergency transmitter set on very low volume, then took oil from *Rekum* and found that he himself would have to replenish some of the supply ship's stores. *Thor* had accomplished nothing during an entire month and with the exception of fighting a small fire accidentally set by Dutch prisoners from *Tela,* her bluejackets had had no excitement at all. And they could not have reported even that, for their contact with Germany had fizzled out. With none of her transmissions getting through and *Thor* dead to the world, unable to notify Berlin that *Rekum* was again available to *Widder,* SKL diverted *Eurofeld,* then on its way from Tenerife to France, to supply Ruckteschell with oil.

CLINKER-BUILT BOATS AND CURSES

Ruckteschell, meanwhile, had been refining his method of attack: track by day, fast approach by night; sudden smashing assault with the main battery and with the automatic cannon raking the enemy's deck to keep his gunners from their weapons. Risky for a vulnerable raider and very rough on merchantmen who might be the exception and not be armed or who might elect not to fight when challenged. But that was where the trouble lay. It was never certain what they would do, and Ruckteschell could readily argue that the Admiralty's orders to its masters could not be reconciled with international law, a hazy concept at best. Britain's most able naval historian, Capt. S. W. Roskill, DSC, R.N., remarks in the official history, *The War at Sea,* that "it is only fair to mention that the captains of German armed merchant raiders generally behaved with reasonable humanity towards the crew of intercepted ships, tried to avoid unnecessary loss of life and treated their prisoners tolerably." Ruckteschell, he adds, was the "only exception," his conduct being "so far contrary to the Hague Conventions that he was brought to trial and convicted as a war criminal in 1947." But, says the same Roskill in his excellent *A Merchant Fleet in War,* "under international law the immunity of a merchant ship from attack depended on her not 'resisting' capture. The Germans always held that to wireless constituted resistance, and so justified their action in shelling ships which acted in that manner. The issue has never been cleared up by the international lawyers. But it should be remarked that we ourselves have put forward the view that to sail merchant ships in escorted convoys was to offer 'resistance' to capture." (Running or shooting back naturally was considered "resistance" by all parties.)* Ruckteschell was not a lawyer and

* Compare *The War at Sea* with Roskill's *A Merchant Fleet in War* (London: Alfred Holt & Co., Collins, 1962).

some of their specious arguments were as much an anathema to him as were the "Rocks and Shoals" (uniform code of conduct) preached by black-shoe naval academy graduates around the world. On August 28 when his watchkeepers reported a ship, he did what he felt was right: "My tactics . . . [are going to be] the same as with the previous two [*Beaulieu* and *Oostplein*]. But I have only 20 minutes; at 2018 the moon will be up."

Anglo Saxon was the name of his ravine, an ordinary tramp and one of four similar ships owned by Britain's now defunct Nitrate Producers Steamship Company. Ruckteschell pounced on her and his first salvo landed on her gun, setting off its ready-use ammo. When she tried to radio, *Widder*'s flack started hammering away and was "making so much noise that it was hard to halt and the 'cease fire' came through much too late." Torpedoed moments later, the small 5,594-tonner went down hissing in a cloud of smoke that smelled of its cargo, coal. Only a few blinker signals were seen in the dark, and since no one seemed to be asking for help, Ruckteschell steamed off, noting that the Canaries were some eight hundred miles away and therefore reachable.

The forty fellows in *Anglo Saxon* would have had no more of a chance than if they had been attacked by a U-boat, and the subs usually used torpedoes and did not bother to rake ships' decks. Some of the crew, like Wilbert R. Widdicombe, had had premonitions when they signed on back in England. But then almost everyone could recall premonitions those days. Tall nineteen-year-old Robert Tapscott had had few worries; he was more the make-money-and-spend-it type, and on the night before the sinking he had been late for his trick on duty because he had wanted to finish a cribbage game. When the shooting started and instantly scored, they had little choice but to run, duck, and lower the boats, most of which were splintered and burning, and when their own ship and the raider were gone the next morning, First Officer C. B. Denny, Tapscott, Widdicombe, and four other men took stock. It was not much work, for all they had was a tattered sail, compass, sea anchor, ax, boat cover, flares, matches, a medical kit, six pairs of oars, one tin of biscuits, eleven tins of condensed milk, eighteen pounds of mutton, and four gallons of water. On September 2, the day one entry in *Widder*'s log read: "The *Anglo Saxon*'s people could have reached land by now," that ship's former radioman, R. H. Pilcher, whose gangrenous foot had become offensive and for which he apologized, told his mates that he would not be needing his half-dipper allotment of water. By sundown, he was dead.

That same evening *Widder* was close to the northern boundary of its operating area astride the Trinidad-Azores track and by 2145 she had sunk tanker *Cymbeline,* which had picked up *Beaulieu*'s crew the previous voyage. It had been a perfect attack and it even seemed that Heinicke's prodding had taken effect. Hearing cries for help, Ruckteschell dropped light buoys, then spent four hours searching for survivors. They were hard to find in the dark. It took his sea duty detail more than two hours of boat work to collect all twenty-six. He was decent in spending the time, but he had no way of knowing how risky his efforts had actually been. *Cymbeline* had seen him stalking her, and judging by her evasive movements he guessed that she might have. He did not realize, however, that she had actually contacted an AMC by radio—or so her second officer allowed. By morning there were three of the tanker's crew still missing, but they were far from dead. Perversely, as it seemed to the Germans when they heard about it, Capt. J. A. Chadwick, his first officer and third engineer had lain doggo in their boat to avoid capture and had then sailed off for the Azores. For fourteen days they sailed, the three of them, before they were saved by tanker *Yolanda,* which took them to Venezuela.

Since *Widder* was scheduled to meet *Rekum* again in the area where *Beaulieu* had disappeared and *Cymbeline* had radioed, Ruckteschell tried a dash south, hoping to catch a ship and attract attention elsewhere before returning to the rendezvous. Constant machinery breakdowns—"the engine is beginning to spit"—hampered his progress, cut his speed in half. But on September 9 he did get a ship, the *Antonios Chandris,* bound for Buenos Aires with British coal. A boarding party informed Capt. George Gafos to provision his boats. He was going to have to sail for it, he was told, because Ruckteschell wanted to be reported. Sailing conditions were good and there would be plenty of rain for water, Ruckteschell opined in his log. While Gafos and his men began their journey, Ruckteschell returned north to 26°N, 46°W as ordered to meet *Eurofeld,* which ran and ran and ran just like her Allied counterparts, until *Widder*'s signalers could convince her by blinker that they were friends. Ruckteschell, having meanwhile heard from *Rekum,* took *Eurofeld* along to meet the tanker, which supplied him with 1,645 tons of oil. Both ships were discharged on the twenty-first, the former to France, where she arrived on October 8 with prisoners who were eventually released to their homelands, and the latter to give further succor to either *Widder* or *Thor.* (See page 203 for a diagram of *Widder.*)

By the eighth Ruckteschell, too, was on his way home, his ship crippled by "spitting" engines, burned-out bearings, and a host of cumulative deficiencies. Having effected some repairs on September 28, he had tried eight knots, then twelve, just to see what would happen. The bearings burned out and the ship was unable to proceed at even five

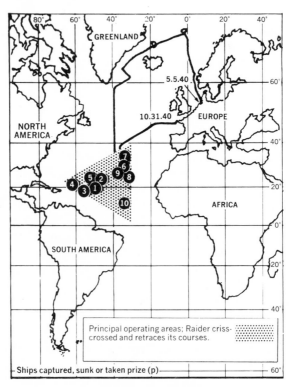

ROUTE OF WIDDER

1. BRITISH PETROL	6.13.40
2. KROSSFONN (p)	6.26.40
3. DAVISIAN	7.10.40
4. KING JOHN	7.13.40
5. BEAULIEU	8.04.40
6. OOSTPLEIN	8.08.40
7. KILLORAN	8.10.40
8. ANGLO SAXON	8.21.40
9. CYMBELINE	9.02.40
10. ANTONIOS CHANDRIS	9.09.40

knots until October 4. On the seventh Ruckteschell radioed SKL saying he would have to come home. His dilemma would have delighted Captain Gafos and his twenty-one men, who were rescued the next day by Portugal's *Serpa Pinto*, half dead, fourteen hundred miles from where they had been abandoned on September 9. But it hardly would have mattered to Tapscott and Widdicombe, who were by then *Anglo Saxon*'s only survivors and had been reduced to drinking urine and alcohol from their compass, eating seaweed and the tiny shrimp that clung to it.

PRISONERS AND BOOZE

On October 8, far to the south of those unfortunate men, Capt. J. W. Carr and his 8,715-ton reefer *Natia* were in serious trouble and would soon be victims of *Thor*. The raider had been working the South Atlantic for sixty days after her encounter with *Alcantara,* but it was not until September 26 when Kähler captured and sank the Norwegian whale oil tanker *Kosmos* without a fight that he had any success. When *Natia* was sighted at noon just sixty miles north of the equator, *Thor*'s men sprang to their stations delighted at the prospect of action. Kähler did not share Ruckteschell's preference for night attacks and in that he was right, his executive officer, Carl Jung, and Koppen-Boehnke thought. *Thor* was faster than *Widder* and her skipper could make his opening round and choose his range—a bit better than nine thousand yards was best as far as the gunnery officer was concerned—as he saw fit. *Thor* closed on *Natia* rapidly, unfurled her ensign, and opened fire at 1327. Half an hour later, having taken eight or nine hits (175 shells were fired at him) and realizing that he was only "risking people's lives in a hopeless struggle," *Natia*'s master gave in and abandoned ship. In the evening he slung his hammock next to *Gracefield*'s Captain Brimmer, went to sleep to the tune of "Good Night, Sweetheart," and was awakened the next morning by the loudspeaker broadcasting "Roll out the Barrel." That day he attended the funeral of one of his seaman who had been injured during the attack. Kähler, who was to become one of Carr's good friends after the war, was also present and offered his condolences.

    Kähler then had more than 350 prisoners. They were a distinct problem. It took some 20 men to guard them, and since they outnumbered his own crew and the ship always had to be ready for action, he could only let 60 or 70 of them out on deck at one time and then only in good weather and when his men were not working on the guns. Kähler was aware of their discomfort, but he shared Weyher's opinion that prisoners should not be released, and he could not rid himself of them until *Rio Grande,* which had been held up by the Brazilian authorities, arrived on November 9 to take them to the Gironde, which they would reach December 13. On the way, prisoner Charley Frame of the *Wendover* and some of his mates hatched an imaginary escape plot to trap a Dutch informer, but they were let off easily by the ship's captain, Heins, who liked traitors no better than they did, and later, while crossing France, *Natia's* fifth engineer, P. Harwood, and steward's boy Donald Beverly did escape. The rest (Kähler had kept four British officers, an injured sailor and two neutrals and the Dutch were released) spent the remainder of the war in Germany, their boredom broken only by Red Cross parcels and such minor incidents as the camp commandant's header from a bike into a snowbank.

"HEIL, HITLER!" SAYS WHO?

While Kähler was dealing with *Natia* and then marking time again, Ruckteschell was making for home not at all sure he would get there. He had finally won the affection of many of his men and had taken Heinicke, navigator Ludwig Rödel, and the doctor into his confidence and was on good speaking terms with men like Schack and twenty-three-year-old pilot Konrad Hoppe. The crew felt sorry for the old man, and their confidence in the ship's officers was high. That much Heinicke knew from his petty officers and the tone set by the ship's paper in which everyone was allowed to express his opinions without the risk built into many corporate suggestion boxes. His engines asthmatic and divisions at general quarters, watertight doors shut and extra lookouts posted as low as they could be gotten along the rails where they had a better chance of spotting an enemy submarine's tiny silhouette, he crawled for the Bay of Biscay to a rendezvous the night of October 29 with U-29, which cautiously exchanged recognition signals "L" for "X" but added an astonishing "Heil, Hitler."

Roughly 3,600 miles from where *Widder* was wheezing the last few miles to safety, two mahogany-brown men so skeletonized that they were almost indistinguishable guided their dun-colored gig ashore at Eleuthera's Alabaster Bay and stretched out under a bush. They were found on October 30 by a native farmer named Martin, and were taken to Nassau's Bahamas General Hospital, where they identified themselves as *Anglo Saxon's* Tapscott and Widdicombe. The two men, who looked like burned black mummies—"the only sign of life was their haunted eyes shifting from side to side," Sir Etienne Dupuch, editor-proprietor of

Nassau's *Tribune,* remembers. Their survival was incredible. Naturally enough, the Duke and Duchess of Windsor paid them a visit, but neither of the two men who had lived on that boat for seventy days and had suffered through each of them ever again received much attention—they were, after all, just what *Port Wellington*'s Beeham called "cogs in a vast machine."*

Another "cog," Ruckteschell, was home free the morning after the two dying men crawled over the hot Caribbean sand on their pinlike arms and legs. At 1135 on October 31, his starboard anchor rattled down eleven fathoms, leaving eighty-two fathoms of scope to swing around in the roadstead of Brest. That day, still a lieutenant commander, he became the first raider captain to be awarded the coveted Ritterkreuz. His tactics in a most dangerous area with an old, hard-to-disguise steamship that required constant fueling and endless hours of maintenance had been superb, SKL said. So good at raiding—and possibly so difficult a personality—they found him that he was immediately assigned to precommissioning duties in another raider then known only as *Schiff 28.* Widder's guns and installations followed him to the new ship, but the old raider, useless in that role, was decommissioned. She was to become one of the few German ships to survive the war.[1]

CHECKMATE

After *Thor* passed her prisoners to *Rio Grande,* the lot of the remaining four British captains improved no end. They were allowed many hours on deck, food and water rations increased, there were movies twice a week, and every Sunday night they received a bottle of whiskey. Nevertheless, life was monotonous as hell for them as well as for their captors, who were then vainly searching on the La Plata–Africa route. At dawn, December 5, the tedium was broken. Alarm! The Germans trampled to battle stations and *Natia*'s Carr got up to play a game of chess with Captain E. Winter of the *Wendover.* The game did not last long, for the raider's first salvo at they knew not what shook the knights and pawns off the board and acrid smoke started to penetrate into their chamber. They began to count the detonations; one got as far as 395, the other to 411 during the sixty-seven minutes as they sat nearly suffocating in their

* Widdicombe went to sea again and was lost in the sinking of *Siamese Prince* off Scotland on February 18, 1941. Tapscott took longer to recover, later signed an affidavit saying that a German raider had sunk *Anglo Saxon* and had then turned its guns on the men in the boats. It was an impression many frightened survivors in many wars, shocked by their ordeal, ducking from flying fragments of steel and deadly ricochets, retained even after much of their hatred had worn off, but it was usually one impossible to substantiate.

cabin. When they were released, Bernhard Meckmann, a former merchant officer and well-liked WWI veteran, told them that there had been a nasty fight with a Britisher, an AMC named *Carnarvon Castle,* in fact. One of *Thor*'s signalmen had sighted the large ship coming out of a bank of haze at 0531 when it was only four miles away, and it had immediately been recognized as an AMC, presumably the 20,122-ton *Carnarvon Castle,* which had earned a peacetime reputation as the fastest liner (nineteen knots) on the South Africa service. Kähler was not surprised at being brought to bay. SKL had informed him that battleship *Resolution* and ten cruisers were in African and South American waters, and he knew for certain that both AMCs *Queen of Bermuda* and *Carnarvon Castle* were close to his operating area, the latter having, in fact, just removed some German passengers from the Brazilian *Itape.* He had tried to avoid her.

Hoping that morning that he might vanish in the mist, Kähler turned to port, bringing the liner astern, and for a while it looked as if he might succeed in escaping. The other vessel at first remained on its original course, alternately visible, sometimes just a grayish shadow. But it soon turned to follow in *Thor*'s wake, rapidly closing the range. Kähler then knew he would have to fight, and having the only raider with three 5.9s aft, he decided to force his opponent into a stern chase.

Carnarvon Castle made "SC" (What is the name of your vessel?), then "K" (You should stop your vessel instantly), and followed up that order at 0701 with a six-inch shell that fell some 300 yards short. Up went Kähler's battle flag, down came his disguises, and the first two-gun salvo roared out at 1702, range 14,100 yards. The fourth salvo had the AMC covered, and Kähler, realizing she was the faster ship, bore off to the north, turning the chase into a circular fight in which he could engage his entire port battery. Making smoke at times to hinder the enemy's spotting, he continued in a gradual turn to starboard. He fired two torpedoes but missed. The shooting of *Carnarvon*'s starboard battery (four 6-inch guns; her total armament was eight 6-inch, two 3-inch, and six Lewis guns) was good in deflection, but at a range of only 8,000 yards, her shells were going over even though Capt. H. N. M. Hardy's tars thought they had hit and set the German on fire. Neither damaged nor burning, *Thor* was actually in control of the action, circling and firing at six-second intervals and beginning to register with some serious hits. More relaxed than he had been in the engagement with *Alcantara,* Kähler "nearly jumped for joy," one of his officers recalls, and well he might have because the AMC's electrical control system had been shot away, her guns had to be trained by hand, her funnel was holed, her superstructure riddled, and her shooting, though still accurate, was becoming erratic.

The German gunnery officer, too, was having trouble with his weapons; glycerine was leaking out of the recoil cylinders, the barrels would not go back in train, and their salvo patterns were badly scattered. The hungry, grimy, and exhausted gunners like Theo Müller— they were too busy to be scared—were doing their best, as were the Royal Navy men in *Carnarvon Castle,* some of whom were from South Africa where the squat-funneled liner had been armed and equipped only nine days after the war began. Suddenly at 0803, completely to Kähler's surprise, "the enemy, his speed undiminished, turned hard away to the north. *Carnarvon Castle* was fleeing."

Hardy was, indeed, showing his stern in the classic naval maneuver called "getting the hell out of there." The rationale: "The haze had increased and, as the enemy was continuously making smoke on and off and all spotting through the splashes of her shorts became extremely difficult and hitting a matter of luck." At 0805 Hardy dropped three smoke floats to cover his escape, and at 0806 his two after guns, the only ones still shooting, ceased fire. Three minutes later Kähler, having expended 593 rounds and with only 30 percent of his 5.9 ammunition remaining, also quit, undamaged, without casualties, free to go where he wished at his top eighteen knots.

London's communiqué about the action was most reserved and uncommunicative:

> The armed merchant cruiser H.M.S. *Carnarvon Castle* (Captain H. N. M. Hardy, DSO, R.N.) was in action yesterday with a fast and heavily-armed German raider disguised as a merchant ship in the South Atlantic. . . .
> There was heavy firing on both sides during the engagement and a considerable amount of ammunition was expended as H.M.S. *Carnarvon Castle* gave chase to the enemy.
> H.M.S. *Carnarvon Castle* received slight damage and there were some casualties. The next-of-kin will be informed as soon as possible. It is not yet known what damage was inflicted on the enemy raider and she was last reported steaming north at high speed away from the scene of the action."

The slippery wording led commentators and the press to wonder who had done what to whom and who had come out best. Berlin gloated that the British vessel "was severely damaged," and that was something the press could see for themselves on December 7 when *Carnarvon Castle* stood into Montevideo past the wreck of *Graf Spee* with a five-to-ten-degree list. She had taken more than twenty hits and the ugly rough-edged black scars showed clearly in her bridgework, the promenade deck and hull. Six of her men were dead and 32 injured. The British had to ask for an extension of the normal twenty-four-hour stay permitted warships in a neutral port to make the liner seaworthy again. While riveters patched her holes, the AMC's officers took shore leave, toasted the Battle of the Falklands (December 8, 1914), and said that they had hit the German, which some thought had armored decks, fair and square, putting his guns out of commission.

Their observations were as inaccurate as London's were transparent, but their enthusiasm was fair enough. Most AMCs held no advantage over a raider whatever except the psychological one of being able to call for help and steam into whatever port they wished. An AMC generally mounted more heavy guns, but those weapons were hardly any better than the raiders', and their broadsides (four guns) were the same. The British ships had no torpedo tubes. They were larger, to be sure, and could therefore theoretically absorb more punishment. Their very size, however, made them better targets—and bigger bonfires. Neither side really had the edge in speed (it depended on the ship) and both had to work with inadequate fire control and internal communications systems. Both types carried large crews and in those men lay the raiders' greatest supremacy. Not in their courage or morale, perhaps, but in the makeup of the complements. Most of the officers and ratings of the AMCs were reservists, many already on the retired list, and the sprinkling of regular officers and leading hands was scanty. In the German ships the proportion of highly trained men was vastly greater.

Relieved that his second AMC had not been more aggressive and not knowing how many warships his encounter would bring down on his neck (they were *Cumberland* and light cruisers *Enterprise* and *Newcastle*), Kähler cleared away to the south where he cruised until December 21, when he rendezvoused with the old tanker *Eurofeld* to top off his tanks with 1,358 tons of oil. He was freshly decorated with the Ritterkreuz for his truly outstanding performance and he was ready for a Christmas Day meet with *Scheer,* which had come down south after a two-month cruise in which she had sunk or captured eight ships.

On December 27 nearly 16,000 pounds of frozen meats and 52,000 eggs were taken from *Scheer*'s prize *Duquesa,* which had been nicknamed "Commissary Department Wilhelmshaven South" for her fantastic cargo of 15,000,000 eggs and 3,500 tons of meat. The large naval tanker *Nordmark* arrived the same day and from her Kähler received some of the supplies he had requested but noted that much had been forgotten or badly crated due to inattentiveness by bureaucrats in offices at home, undoubtedly more worried about ration stamps than their wards at sea.

New Year's Eve the assembled ships sang out the old year in a celebration that brought to close a year in which Germany's regular warships working as raiders had sunk seventeen merchant ships (96,986 tons) and the merchant raiders, fifty-four vessels of 366,644 tons. On the next morning, the pocket battleship's boat chugged over the water for the first pleasant surprise of the new year. Jammed into the craft was a band tooting a little serenade. Perhaps, everyone hoped, as did the men in *Atlantis, Orion, Pinguin, Komet,* and the new *Kormoran* far away on other seas, it would be another successful year and a short war.

NOTES

1. Only four of the strange ships survived the war, and one of them, *Schiff 5,* never fought as a raider. *Widder,* worst of the lot mechanically, became the British reparations prize *Ulysses* and was then reregistered German as *Fechenheim,* of the Unterweser Reederei, which purchased her for 2.4 million marks from the Ionian Steamship Company, spent another 1.6 million in 1951 getting her fit for classification. Three years later, on Germany's day of mourning, May 17, yard workers discovered that some loving engineer had placed a wreath on one of the old, uneconomical turbines which were being replaced by a diesel plant. At 1821, October 3, 1955, with two Norwegian pilots and her captain, Ludwig Lindner, unaware that a beacon had been moved but a few yards, the old veteran tore her sides open between hatches No. 1 and 3 while running into Maloy Sound with 11,306 tons of ore. Lindner managed to beach her, but she broke up the next day, becoming a total loss after everyone had taken off. No one on board was held responsible for the accident because relocation of the light had not been publicized.

CHAPTER 7

Atlantis:
Her Next Eleven Months at Sea

SICK OF THE SEA AND MEAT CLEAVERS   As the prospects for peace dimmed in the years before the war, Thomas and Jno. Brocklebank, Ltd., unique among shipping companies in wearing their blue and white house flag at the foremast peak, took a leading role in preparing for war. By mid-1938, 101 of the company's 105 deck officers had been trained in gunnery, and its ships' decks were being strengthened to carry the guns for them to use when the time came. Since 80 percent of their vessel's wheelhouse and bridge fronts were wooden, the Liverpudlian line took an active interest in sandbags, helmets, and steel pillboxes to be mounted in the bridge wings for the crew's protection. The very old and tried firm, which had actually started business in the colony of New York back in 1770, had received a Letter of Marque from King George III in 1779 authorizing them to outfit their tiny 220-ton brig *Castor* and to "seize and destroy the ships and goods belonging to the King of Spain and his subjects." Today, there are some World War II records in the company's Cunard Building office that read in part: "On completion of loading for the United Kingdom the *Mandasor* (Captain A. Hill) sailed from Calcutta on the 13th of February, 1941. Eleven days later (February 24), a wireless message was picked up saying that she was being bombed, since which date the vessel is missing, and it is unfortunately presumed that she is lost with all hands."

The dates are wrong by exactly one month and so, fortunately, was the presumption that the entire eighty-two-man complement had perished. The firm found that out in the summer of 1941 when the ship's third officer, a Mr. Livingstone, arrived at Gibraltar after a roundabout journey from Calcutta via the Indian Ocean, France, and a Spanish prison, to report on "Voyage 62," mostly under German guard. Nearly four months of their company was too much for the good man, and when he was some forty miles from Libourne in the wine country of Bordeaux on May 12, 1941, he jumped out of one of the "40-and-8s," so well known to generations of soldiers, and made his way to freedom much as had some other British seamen from ships such as *Nowshera, Maioma,* and *Natia.* But the whole part of *Mandasor*'s story was not to be known until the end of the war, and even then some of the details in the firm's fine history were inaccurate, as was so often the case when anyone dealt with raiders. *Schiff 41,* for example, was not the same as *Schiff 16.**

Mandasor was en route on January 23 from Calcutta to Britain via the Mozambigue Channel and Durban, another roundabout way, but one thought safer than the direct route across the Indian Ocean where one of the German raiders was known to have been operating. The Seychelles were relatively near and so was the Chagos Archipelago and air cover. It was brutally hot at midday when Hill sighted a vessel apparently headed from Australia for the Gulf of Aden. The stranger was over ten miles away, but the British captain, heeding caution and his instructions, steamed off at a right angle to his westerly course until the other ship was hull down over the horizon and then gradually disappeared. The next day dawned bright, the horizon was clear. Shortly after eight bells, the freighter's claxons sounded, and when Hill reached the bridge he saw a small float plane plunging down between his masts to tear out his aerials. The aircraft wheeled, came in again, its machine guns and cannon snapping, with their projectiles buzzing through the engine room skylight and blowing off the 4-inch gun's sight. While Hill's third officer replied with a machine gun of his own and was himself hurt, and the wireless lads rerigged their antennae, a ship was seen coming up fast and with obviously hostile intentions. "QQQ GCXN 6.23S 61.36E chased by raider and bombed 6.23S 61.36E *Mandasor* chased and bombed by merchantship raider," the Brocklebanker said. "GCXN de FPB" (Colombo): "RRR" (Understood), the German answered, trying to confuse any listener; but Hill's boys kept on sending until sixty-one 5.9-inch shells (eight hit, killing four men and mortally injuring two) forced them to stop. The boarding party did not find much because of the fire amidships and Hill left his command for the last time, chugging over to the raider on a glassy sea in a launch. On board the German, Hill was taken below to quarters "well fitted with bunks and bedding, washrooms, a library, table tennis, dart boards and so on," and

---

* John Frederic Gibson, *Brocklebanks 1770–1950* (Liverpool: Henry Young & Sons, Ltd., 1953), Vol. II.

"well-cooked" food. Pretty soon he was asked up to meet "a tall, good-looking man with a soft voice and kindly attitude toward prisoners." His name was Rogge.

It all sounds simple: Find a ship, any ship—most of them were enemies and all of them either fit into that category or were neutrals presumably working for the enemy—catch it, and sink it. That, essentially, is what *Atlantis* did with *Mandasor,* but it took over a day of work and it cost Rogge his last plane. Pilot Bulla had sighted the ship in the morning of the twenty-third and Rogge had had to make a choice: try to capture her by day or kill her at night. The first was a doubtful matter by that time because the Allies' ships were far more cautious than they had been when he first took *Scientist* almost nine months earlier, and the latter always seemed to Rogge a dubious proposition. He chose the first proposition, but *Mandasor* turned away; then he had hung on to the Briton's smoke cloud, estimating his course and speed until dark—which came on with the suddenness that it does in the tropics. His navigator and quartermasters miscalculated by a few minutes during that weary night (or *Mandasor* made some slight unpredictable move), and by morning they were faced with the same predicament they had faced the day before. Bulla started his plane, and found the ship only some twenty miles away, Rogge dropped a work boat supplied with fuel and ammunition for the plane, and told the pilot to stop and silence the vessel until the raider could get into range. Bulla tried and failed; Rogge tried and succeeded only too well. With the noise and vibrations caused by the shooting, Rogge, like Ruckteschell had in *Widder,* found his communications unreliable and had to use his typhon to silence the guns. But that was only after the ship had radioed a warning which resulted in the British on the Seychelles ordering another nearby ship, *Tantalus,* to alter its course, and a renewed search by heavy cruiser *Canberra* and light cruisers *Colombo, Leander,* and *Sydney.* Bulla set down near *Atlantis'* boat but one of his floats was leaking and the plane capsized, leaving its crew and the four men in the boat nearly helplessly seasick twenty-five miles from where the action was.

That incident, coming just thirteen days after their departure from the Kerguelens, was just another example of the "endless anxieties" that gripped *Atlantis'* men just hours after they left the shelter of those cold and barren islands. It was not fear of action—they welcomed any fight as a change in routine—it was more the inescapable tension of a man on the lam, always in cop country with no friends to rely on and never sure he was not being tailed.

And they could not be sure how long that life would have to go on, for the war was definitely dragging. Battle cruisers *Gneisenau* and

Scharnhorst had finally put out from Kiel, *Scheer* was about to come east, newcomer *Kormoran*, with two ships already to its credit, was about to replace the pocket battleship in the South Atlantic, and Gen. Albert Kesselring's Fliegerkorps X had landed on Sicily to show the Italians how to handle the Royal Navy. That was okay, but Roosevelt's "Four Freedoms" message, which proposed weapons for the Allies and the Lend Lease Bill, was not.

On the evening of the thirty-first *Atlantis* was farther southwest astride the Gulf of Aden–South Africa route. Her captain was on the bridge again with Mohr, his messengers, the navigator, the quartermasters, and signalmen. Dr. Georg Reil and his assistant, Dr. Sprung, were watching their gleaming sharp instruments being boiled. The raider was at battle stations, blacked out, silent except for the engines and the whirring blowers, stalking. Most of the men like Wesemann felt sorry for the fellows out across the water who were about to be shocked out of their senses even if they were not killed outright. Be they enemy or not, it was an awful feeling standing there knowing that someone, some guy like yourself, was about to get it.

Wesemann was normally stationed in the hot, cramped wireless room by the bridge. If something important came in over his sets, all he had to do was knock on the thin wooden partition separating him from Rogge's beautiful, polished cabin. When the ship was in a fight, and he had to speak to the commander, he just opened a little window that led into the chart house. He did not have anything to do that night, nor did the doctors need their shiny scalpels, forceps, or saws. Rogge was passing orders calmly and quietly as he always did; the gunners had trained on a dark shadow of a target, fired when told to, stood back to load again; the searchlight crew had flicked their switches to set the big beam glowing, and the signalmen had flapped their wrists, making the little metal venetian blinds on their blinkers clatter "Stop!" "What ship?" Reading off the reply was simple: *"Speybank."* No one was hurt, and it was a beautiful ship, loaded with teak, ilemite, manganese, and monazite. She was as British as boiled potatoes and kippers—a natural prize and, being one of seventeen nearly identical sister ships, a natural candidate for an auxiliary in the German Navy.

The 5,154-ton *Speybank,* with a prize crew on board, was released for a new meeting place, and the very next day another ship was sighted heading westward. Her master, R. S. Braddon, was sharp, his lookout unusually watchful. When the raider was still sixteen miles distant, Braddon turned away. Then, nine times, *Troilus* signaled "0326S 5235E *Troilus* suspicious," causing *Colombo* to send out a warning to all vessels and alerting His Majesty's carrier *Formidable* and cruiser *Hawkins,* then steaming off Somaliland in support of British ground operations. That night, Mohr did not get to finish *Lady Chatterley's Lover,* for he was back on the bridge preparing for another "ungentlemanly" night attack. It was not much of a brawl, and by the morning of February 3 the wild panic that had broken out among the Chinese in the Norwegian *Ketty Brövig*—the first unarmed vessel *Atlantis* had ever come across—had been stilled and the ship's boilers relit after some difficulty attributable to an awkward design. The old tanker, built in 1918, was a handy catch for the Germans. She had only two men injured, and was carrying 6,370 tons of oil and 4,125 tons of diesel fuel. *Ketty* was sent off to await events, and *Atlantis* left the Seychelles region for a renewed rendezvous with *Speybank* on February 8. Two days later the 7,480-ton *Tannenfels,* which had left Chisimaio just fourteen days before the British captured the port (along with fifteen of the sixteen Axis ships which had been stupidly left there) and on which *Atlantis'* Ensign Dehnel and his *Durmitor* prize crew were embarked, joined up, and on the ninth *Ketty* reappeared. Several days of uninterrupted work, exchange of fuel, charts, logs, provisions, crews, and the transfer of forty-two British and sixty-one native prisoners from *Atlantis* to *Tannenfels* followed before the four-ship convoy steamed south to meet *Scheer,* which had entered the Indian Ocean on February 3. Rogge and Theodor Kranke, the pocket's captain, conferred, and it was surprising, the former felt, how comforting it was for the loneliest man on a lonely ship, the commander, to have a good chat and exchange views with another person burdened with the same responsibilities. *Scheer* oiled from *Ketty,* Ceylon tea was traded for eggs from *Duquesa,* meat for rice, wine for whiskey, and magazines for news.

The lack of touch with home was actually the hardest thing to bear—far harder than any of the other deprivations. Wesemann, for example, had three brothers in service. One had fought at Narvik; had he returned? The oldest, who had foreseen that they would never meet again, fell at Sedan on May 14, 1940. Wesemann heard about his death from *Scheer.* The youngest was to be killed that summer in Russia, but, again, the brilliant young code-breaker would not discover that tragic loss until after Christmas.

On the seventeenth the ships separated, *Scheer* going toward Madagascar, *Atlantis,* with *Speybank* in train, toward Chagos, *Ketty* to a waiting area, and *Tannenfels,* taking Hill and his crew along with escapee-to-be Livingstone in her tween decks, to France.

Speybank immediately proved her worth in extending the raider's line of vision. At noon on February 20 she reported a ship. Rogge trailed and Mohr in his obligatory black bow tie fumed under his pith helmet. *"Carambe, carambe, carambe,"* the multilingual officer mumbled to himself as the lookouts announced bearings to the other ship. Seven hours of effort; the medical instruments checked again, the torpedoes regulated and the Zeiss glasses wiped; then the vessel switched on her lights. She was the Vichy French supply ship *Lot* escorting submarines *Pegase* and *Monge*. Had she seen any ships? *"Non." "Merci, bon voyage,"* *Atlantis* signaled, adding, *"Vive la France."* The gunports slid down again and the instruments were put away as the raider's officers turned "to the evening's business of a whiskey and soda." On February 21, another ship courtesy of *Speybank*'s lookouts. Nine hours and reams of graph paper with plotted course later, they had it where they wanted it. Out went the guns, and the covers were whipped off the cannon. They were not needed; the ship was *Africa Maru*. "Good practice," Rogge noted sourly.

And bittersweet was his late February chore of handling another small squadron consisting of *Ketty, Speybank,* and a *Scheer* prize, *British Advocate,* which the pocket battleship had left behind in her haste to evade an impressive East Indian Command armada—no less than one carrier, five cruisers, and an AMC—arrayed against her off Madagascar.* It turned out that *Ketty* had something unusual to report: Ching You, a weak little fellow, had gone after the Norwegian chief with a meat cleaver because the latter had reprimanded him for dumping garbage out his porthole. *British Advocate*'s problem was different. To Mohr it appeared that *Scheer* (not unlike *Atlantis*) had dumped its most unreliable personnel on the prize. Leaning on the British crew to run the ship, wasting fresh water in showers, and incapable of reading signals, they were a "catastrophe" to the adjutant who had gone over to inspect the ship. "So what," their mate allowed himself to counter, "it doesn't bother the oak one bit if pigs rub themselves against it." That bon mot brought him three days arrest from Rogge, who did not think the man's classical quotation apropos.

Fueled and provisioned by February 27, *British Advocate* sailed off unlamented for France. *Ketty* went to meet *Coburg,* which had escaped from Eritrea, but the two ships were intercepted and sunk by H.M.A.S. *Canberra* and *Leander,* which were presumed to have had intelligence of *Coburg*'s routing from the careless Italians at Massawa. That left *Speybank,* which Rogge kept hanging around for another rendezvous on March 21, whereafter he dispatched her to France under

---

* *Scheer* escaped the dragnet, slipped away for Kiel, where she reported in as the most successful warship raider (seventeen ships and 113,233 tons taken) on April 1, 1941.

the command of *Tannenfels'* ex-first officer, Paul Schneidewind, an excellent choice.*

.

MOODS

"Still no ship, still no ship, still no ship," one of *Atlantis'* officers confided to a diary he was not to supposed to keep for security reasons. "The sun burns the decks and the same clouds hang in the sky. When 14 days go by without sighting a ship everyone starts to get nervous." The raider was cruising along the previously so heavily laden Durban-Australia-New Zealand track waiting to catch one of the beautiful ships laden with apples and frozen meat and to supply the Italian submarine *Perla,* which had been ousted from its Red Sea base by the British Army's advance. The Germans had not been in action since capturing *Ketty* on February 2; the water was clear blue, the horizon clear blue, and there was not a smudge of smoke on it. Generally, morale was excellent, but with little activity to keep the men in high spirits, trifling matters became important, even personal. Petty disputes arose yet never seemed to get to the point. Even Rogge appeared to be getting irritable and his and Kühn's concepts of running a raider as if it were a training ship led to mumbling in the mess and a troublesome discordance among the habitual malcontents found in any such situation.

Censoring the hundreds of letters that went out with *Speybank,* the division officers discovered a healthy optimism and concern only for those at home. One letter, and only one, was different. It was defeatist and vicious, complaining about the food, a lack of faith in the officers, and their lack of confidence in the men. An investigation showed that the man was speaking for a group which had chosen that peculiar and most unmilitary way to draw attention to alleged grievances. They got a hearing and their beefs were soon found to be of flimsy material woven during twelve months of searching for something wrong. One man had not received the ship's crest which he had been promised; the gunnery officer, they said, acted with the airs of one of the Kaiser's boys; the petty officers had fried eggs for breakfast; the officers' coffee had more beans in it; whiskey was more expensive in the canteen than in the mess; no one was ever apprised of the command's intentions; the exec treated the men with no respect; and Rogge, whose return to Germany had been

* The thirty-eight-year-old skipper made fast in Basin 19, Bordeaux, May 12, and before a year was over was out again with the same ship on a mission Rogge had realistically considered a foolhardy risk for his own valuable raider, reasonable for an expendable vessel—mine-laying.

approved by Berlin, was merely abusing the crew by hanging around until he could claim to have made the longest raiding cruise ever. Not one of the rumors held water; most of the men making them had long lists of previous misdemeanors in their dossiers, and since many of them were Nazi party or affiliate members, it was not at all surprising, Mohr, now Oberleutnant, thought, that they were inclined to show a socialist bent. Actually the investigation would not have been necessary under normal circumstances, for the majority of the crew were in fine fettle. But on a raider then a full year at sea with prospects of many more months of cruising in store, the slightest discordant note could become a serious matter.

Submarine *Perla* was a day late in meeting *Atlantis* at the end of March. Her crew was in a good mood, but they had only one homemade chart and did not seem to be too warlike. They needed oil and wanted a lot of liquor, sugar, and so forth, which Rogge, always the gentleman, would have gladly supplied them if their requests had not stirred up a tempest in a teapot in his own wardroom. Oil the Italians got, but they received only twenty-five liters of rum instead of twenty-five bottles of cognac and they were handed less sugar and fewer cigarettes than they had asked for. Both "Houses" of Rogge's "Parliament" calmed down while their chastened skipper tried to talk the Italians into operating with him in South African waters where the appearance of a submarine would have created quite a stir. *Sí,* they would try, they said. It is too bad that they did not, as far as the Germans were concerned, for Britain's dauntless white ensign was being tattered and frayed, stretched to the tearing point by the ever-widening war, and even the slightest additional pressure would have brought it dismay.*

Atlantis left the Indian Ocean for the Atlantic on April 8 and met *Dresden* (out of Santos with little but water, wood, and some grease due to a snafu) on the sixteenth. Only eight hours after the freighter and its captain, Walter Jäger, were released the next morning with orders to stand by for the time when *Schiff 16* or *Kormoran* might have some prisoners to transfer, the punctilious and tidy Rogge had what amounted to a human zoo—all manner of nationalities, convictions, temperaments, and sexes, young and old, traipsing about on his immaculate decks. Though his crew welcomed the crowd and enjoyed the spectacle it made, Rogge could not; to him it was a nightmare.

* The Kriegsmarine's six merchant raiders had sunk twenty-five ships during the first quarter of the year, its warship raiders thirty-seven in nasty assaults that had bought success even to the chronically misfortunate *Hipper* and completely dislocated Britain's convoy cycles for a time.

   The happening really started back with the Coronation of King
George VI at which Rogge, a guest, saw some distinctive four-masted
Bibby liners and was told that they were regularly employed by the
empire as troopers. On April 17, 1941, he saw such a four-master,
blacked out but brightly illuminated by the moon down in the horse
latitudes of the South Atlantic at 27°41'S, 08°10'W. As a man with
strong ethical convictions, he had compunctions about taking her on
without warning, but he knew that he would have to do the job "silently"
and as quickly as possible if he ever hoped to remain with his ship in
those relatively constricted waters. The other vessel was behaving errati-
cally, zigging as no zigzag clock would have allowed (poor helmsmanship
it later turned out), and her radio operator asked *Atlantis* just as stupidly
as had *Durmitor*'s, "What station is that?" Having apparently seen the
raider, the ship raised a flag but its colors could not be made out in the
predawn murk. Under the circumstances, Rogge was justified in opening
fire; six salvos went off, and six shells hit; one the radio room, one the
engine, two along the waterline and the rest in the superstructure. The
vessel stopped and lowered its boats, and that is when the trouble and
the wailing and the disagreeabilities started.
   She was an Egyptian, the *Zamzam*, ex-Bibby liner *Leicestershire*,
belonging to the Société Misr de Navigation Maritime, and, if the pun
can be excused, a misery she was. Built in 1909, she had indeed once
been a trooper but had then carried pilgrims bound for Mecca. Some
voyages, even in wartime, can be enjoyable; *Zamzam*'s last one definitely was not. She had left New York late in March bound for Cape
Town and other African ports with a mixed cargo of lubricating oil, tin
plate, trucks, and ambulances, steel bars, Coca-Cola, batteries, and
girdles. She carried 202 passengers, 138 of them American, 26 Canadian, 25 British, the rest South African, Italian, Norwegian, and Greek,
who were served by a crew that was Egyptian, Sudanese, Greek, Turk,
Czech, and French. The passengers had written home from various ports
saying that they did not expect to be treated as neutrals (which Egypt
nominally was but actually was not) if apprehended because of the strict
blackout and their zigzagging. They did not like the prices of the liquor
served at the bar—some of them frowned at the booze itself—and they
appreciated each other's company even less. There were too many
cliques; missionaries—Catholic, Adventist, Baptist, Lutheran—who
sometimes joined each other to sing "Lead, Kindly Light" and for
cookies and tea in the saloon. But they generally disapproved of some of
the twenty-four volunteer American ambulance drivers and a group of
tobacco buyers who frequented the bar and bellowed bawdy songs.

When *Fortune* magazine's editor Charles J. V. Murphy and *Life* photographer David E. Sherman joined the filthy ship at Recife, they found hordes of people shouting rudely, "clamoring to be let off."

And off they got that morning of April 17, the wildly screaming crew being in such a hurry that they left passengers swimming and found themselves shaken off *Atlantis'* lines so that the Germans could help seventy-seven women and thirty-two children aboard and hoist up three seriously wounded in stretchers. Everyone was saved but even then the various groups quarreled over the reason for their miraculous luck or the misfortune of being sunk. It was either God's goodwill or wrath, the arguments ran. Conscious of the repercussions very likely to ensue over the taking of so many Americans, Rogge and Mohr singled out the two Time-Life men for special VIP attention, even helping Sherman take pictures.

And those were grand; everyone milling about in whatever they happened to have gotten together; the Germans grinning, busy getting what clothes, mattresses, and food they could from the sinking ship. They brought back a little girl who had become lost, a golden chalice for the priests, and a tricycle for someone small and deserving. But none of the bewildered captives even ventured to guess what would happen next. Since that remained to be seen, or simply because the whole event had been beyond their comprehension, two ladies quickly recovered their sangfroid to ask Mohr for some orange juice. He was sorry, he said, he had not tasted any of the stuff in a year.

Down in the sick bay amidships on the starboard side of the main deck, Drs. Reil and Sprung stretched on their rubber gloves under the glowing lights to operate on New Yorker Frank Vicovari, an architect and leader of the ambulance boys, and Ned Laughinghouse, one of the tobacco men. They could not pull the latter through, but they saved Vicovari's leg, which was so badly injured that he could not be moved to *Dresden* with his fellow prisoners the next day.

None of them was as happy to get off the raider as Rogge was to see them on their way. If it had not been for *Dresden,* they might have crippled his ship by reducing his larder almost as effectively as an enemy shell hit. He intended that *Dresden* should pass on the Americans and all the women and children to a neutral ship or, if that was not possible, to put into Tenerife to effect their release. But Berlin said no. France it was for all the 328 prisoners, and the barrel-chested Jäger was to have them on his hands for thirty-three days. Trunks and suitcases were opened to clothe those in need, the ladies first, and Murphy found it "astonishing how much the raider crew had carried off the *Zamzam*"—and then again to *Dresden.* For some, they had saved nearly everything, but accommodating as Jäger was, the trip was no pleasure cruise. When they arrived at St.-Jean-de-Luz on May 10, officious German guards confiscated the pictures Mohr had deliberately permitted Sherman to snap (the photographer smuggled a roll of others past the fools in a tube of toothpaste), and the Americans were taken to Biarritz from whence they were repatriated that summer.

SHIPS IN THE NIGHT

Between April 19 and 25 *Atlantis* lay with *Schiff 41, Kormoran* (which had sunk seven vessels, and sent one as a prize to France, but was suffering from faulty bearings), ubiquitous naval tanker *Nordmark* (consort to *Scheer, Thor,* and *Kormoran*), and *Alsterufer,* which had come from Germany with mail (the first), planes, and ammunition. *Atlantis* took enough oil, water, coal, and provisions to extend her seakeeping ability to the end of the year. The three Arado 196s were most welcome planes, as they were sturdier than the Heinkels. Welcome, too, were most of the replacements for the fifty-odd men previously sent off in prizes. One of the new officers, though a nice old gentleman, was not well received, and he went home again, to both his and the raider captain's satisfaction. The good fellow had not been to sea for eight years and was oblivious to etiquette: one does not wear slippers to lunch in a warship's officer's mess.

A few days later supply ship *Babitonga* arrived from South America to be dispatched to a waiting area, and on May 7 Rogge gave chase to a ship that turned out to be a Frenchman. On the fourteenth inside the Cape-Freetown track and almost on the same position where *Scientist* had been brought to over a year earlier, *Atlantis* signaled a ship for ten minutes, vainly trying to stop her peacefully. The ship continued on its way. *Atlantis'* guns spat for four minutes. Seven men were killed and fifty-one rescued from the old, 5,618-ton British *Rabaul,* whose sixty-five-year old second officer had indeed seen the raider's signals. Unable to read code, however, he had simply ignored the blinker, hoping the stranger would go away.

The night of April 17/18 was hazy, warm with a bright quarter moon shining through cumulous clouds to stipple the water in alternate patches of silver and black. *Atlantis* was drifting, all but the watch asleep. Shortly after midnight a vessel was made out, and then another, steaming in line astern and bearing down on the stopped raider. Alarm! *Atlantis'* engines were started up slowly so that her diesel exhausts would not spark, but before she had made much headway, the other ship's bow waves and sharp, staggered bow-on silhouettes were clearly distinguishable. They were warships, British, the unmistakable battleship *Nelson* and carrier *Eagle,* both plowing along at fourteen knots heading north. Slowly, ever so slowly, Rogge turned, all the while showing his stern, always hoping his funnel would not flare up, always conscious that his ship and the entire crew's lives were at stake. *"Prost,"* Mohr thought once again; Kielhorn's gang down below were aware that a ship had been sighted. What was going on? they wanted to know. When informed by the bridge, they were rigidly silent as was every soul on board; there was nothing to say. This time it was their own lives that were on the block. Slowly the seconds passed as the two enemy men-of-war passed astern by only an estimated seven thousand yards to gradually become indistinct in the dark.

Later in the day, a Sunday, Rogge spoke a few words of thanks for the raider's deliverance. After three days he stopped a ship which was let go when it turned out to be a Greek under charter to Switzerland, and on the twenty-third he stalked an American whose poorly illuminated neutrality markings nearly cost him his neutrality privileges. On the twenty-fourth the new Arado spotted still another vessel which was shadowed all day and then battered into burning scrap, its funnel burst and blown aside, a mast down, and her rudder jammed by five salvos in a very short action which left twelve of her men dead, the rest in boats and life jackets on the water. With the ship on fire, abandoned and circling for an imminent collision with *Atlantis,* Rogge had a torpedo fired to get her out of the way. The "eel" broached, flipped to another course, turning about the raider to foam toward it from the other side. "A most unpleasant situation" to Rogge for the short time it lasted. A second torpedo also missed and he had to expend a third before the vessel's treacherous fires were washed out by the sea. Rescue operations were difficult and took a long time because the boats showed no lights, and the 4,530-ton *Trafalgar's* thirty-three survivors would never have been found but for the little red flashlights pinned to their life jackets.

The twenty-fourth was another vexing day, at least to architect-ambulanceman Frank Vicovari whose left leg was still in traction and his right in a cast. He could not forgive the Germans for attacking *Zamzam* without warning nor for the death of Laughinghouse; he thought Rogge, who had come down with champagne one day to say hello, too smug; he did not like surgeon Sprung, though Dr. Reil seemed to be a genial clubman; and he did appreciate a pantryman named Teddy who always managed to sneak him a few goodies to nibble on.

Vicovari vainly wondered how he could do damage to the raider. The day *Trafalgar* went down, he found the Germans in an excellent mood. Their biggest and only available battleship, the *Bismarck,* had blown up Britain's *Hood,* long believed to be the most powerful ship afloat. Vicovari was shocked, but Britain's Admiralty rose to the crisis, efficiently marshaling every ship they had nearby to draw on—six battleships, two battle cruisers, two carriers, dozens of cruisers and destroyers. Three days after *Hood* had broken apart under a cloud of smoke, the German battleship was gone, too, having been crippled by aircraft and torpedoes and pummeled for hours by heavy guns in what U. S. Fleet Adm. Chester Nimitz called a *Bismarckdämmerung,* and what was indeed the last effective sally by any major German fleet unit.

The Kriegsmarine's defeat pleased Vicovari and he asked every German who came near whether they had heard the news. They had. But what neither they nor he could know was that the British were following up their victory with a systematic scouring of the Atlantic in which they intercepted nine German supply ships within one month, two of which were captured (one apparently with its secret papers intact) and three sunk.

In *Atlantis* they were aware, of course, of some of the Royal Navy's activities and Rogge wondered whether it would not be wise for him to disappear for a while, particularly since he had been advised that *Orion* would be in the Atlantic by July and *Komet* not much later. Three was a crowd, he thought, and the area had been thoroughly stirred up already. For the time being, though, he headed northeast where his pilots brought him another ship, the fifth they had located since the cruise began. Rogge followed her and at nightfall he attacked. The first indication *Tottenham*'s second officer, D. V. Cameron, had of the attack "was the raider firing a shot across our bow and we realized this was not the action of a friendly vessel, so the usual 'RRR' message was transmitted. It was dark and the only target we could see was the flash of the guns. We did fire one shot from our four-inch anti-submarine gun but obviously, as we could not pick out a target, this was only a gesture." *Atlantis*' men saw the shot fall short, and she, the Ascension Island's and the Walvis Bay's stations heard the British ship's wireless. Rogge sent thirty-nine 5.9-inch and eleven 7.5-mm shells her way for two hits and *Tottenham*'s Captain Woodcock abandoned while way was still on the ship, thereby swamping two boats as they hit the water and their excessive weights collapsed the davits.

With his position known to the British, Rogge was in a hurry to be off. He picked up twenty-nine men including Woodcock and Chief

Engineer Edward Nolan, but could not find any more in the darkness. For that Captain Woodcock berated him, saying that seventeen of his freighter's men were missing (published material that has five men killed in the action is incorrect; only one was injured), and that he should search for them. The German replied that *Tottenham* had radioed and that he could risk his own ship in that locale no longer. The prisoners were then escorted below by tall Lieutenant Mohr, who appeared to Nolan "most helpful and friendly and a perfect gentleman." So much so, in fact, that the adjutant and Rogge later visited the British in Marlag, Milag Nord, and after the war, when both Woodcock and Nolan were in Hamburg with M/V *Wanstead,* Rogge, then a vice-admiral, presented them with a bottle of wine and a copy of his superb book about *Atlantis.** But the Germans' chivalrous attitude did not help the seventeen men missing from *Tottenham,* whose starboard boat, all reports and literature on the subject say, drifted ashore in Brazil on August 22—awash and empty.

It was awash because its plug had been pulled, and it was empty because Cameron and the sixteen others had abandoned it. When the boat was being lowered and then rapidly filled with water because of the speed the *Tottenham* was still making, Cameron and the eleven men then in it, unanimously deciding to avoid capture, just sat there ducking and hoping not to be discovered. They bailed, and in the morning found another five men who had escaped on rafts. Provisions were taken off the rafts and a deserted portside boat, but, consisting only of water, condensed milk, and hard tack, they "were very meager indeed." Being on the fringe of the southeasterly trade winds and the equatorial current, Cameron knew they would have to try for Brazil, eleven hundred miles distant.

Their rescue of the eleventh day by *Mahronda* was most fortunate: Their binnacle light had been seen during the night and the ship's master, thinking it might be a U-boat's, had stood off until dawn. Naturally, seaman Cameron pulled the boat's plug once everyone was off; as a good officer, you do not leave wreckage floating about where it might damage someone's propeller.

Just at dawn five days before Cameron hauled himself aboard, Rogge was carefully approaching another ship and playing innocent and incautious. The vessel steered away for a while and then, when nothing happened, she returned to her course, letting the raider come within 9,600 yards before reconsidering, showing her stern, and transmitting.

* Wolfgang Frank, working with Bernhard Rogge, *Schiff 16,* 4th ed. (Oldenburg, Hamburg: Gerhard Stalling Verlag, 1955).

Her message was smothered by *Atlantis,* which sent off a series of personal messages like "am happy our pet waits for dad, many kisses, Gerty." Rogge opened fire, but the 5,372-ton British *Balzac* skillfully zigged and zagged, slaloming between shell splashes until 192 5.9-inch and 53 3-inch rounds, the most the raider had ever fired, had been expended and she was hit four times. After the fortieth salvo *Atlantis'* forward battery broke down as the old guns overheated, and their barrels expanded and the recoil mechanism refused to function. Soon No. 5 gun on the poop followed suit. Rogge's gunners, bathed in sweat, greased the slides, hosed down the guns to cool them, and manhandled the blistered barrels back into firing position, and the captain, with only one gun left bearing to port, was about to bring his starboard battery into action when *Balzac* lowered her boats. Fifty-one prisoners were taken (three men had been killed and the third officer was wounded so badly that he died in the raider).

The arduous one-sided fight brought Rogge's take to twenty-one ships, which had mounted twenty-seven guns and registered 139,591 tons, the last five falling into his hands in the South Atlantic, an area he believed was becoming too hot. The release of *Zamzam* neutrals, the freeing of the prisoners in *Alstertor,* and the presumed approach of *Komet* and *Orion* decided him on the Pacific, which he would have to himself while *Kormoran* worked the Indian Ocean. SKL had ordered him to meet *Orion,* which, unable to fuel from *Ketty Brövig* (sunk in March) or from any of the ships the British had rounded up in the Atlantic, would be desperately in need of oil, and he was on his way to the rendezvous when he had to muster his men for a special announcement: Hitler had attacked Russia. Wesemann remembers his big captain mumbling something like "What sort of nonsense is he up to now?" and in the lower decks the news was received with undisguised pessimism. It was a bitter blow to men who, though intellectually and physically far removed from the events in Europe, knew that now all bets on the war's end were off.

On July 1, some three hundred miles north of Tristan da Cunha, *Atlantis'* and *Orion*'s men manned their rails for a cheery hip, hip, hurrah. It was the first time the two ships had been in touch since their gunnery exercises seventeen months earlier, and the meeting was a break for both, far greater for Weyher's men, who had not seen any action in 210 days. Weyher was understandably disappointed and disgruntled and Rogge did not blame him. The man had had bad luck, and *Orion* was a stinker. Rogge would give him provisions, ammunition (150 rounds), but he was not about to part with more than five hundred and eighty-one tons of oil. *Schiff 36,* he told his colleague, used up as much oil in one week as *Atlantis* did in two months, and clearly the latter was in better shape to serve the war effort. Furthermore, he was not about to stick around in the Atlantic until August waiting for *Anneliese Essberger* to replenish the additional five hundred tons of oil *Orion* wanted in order to extend her cruise a few days. SKL agreed, and the unfortunate Weyher had to bow out. On the sixth they separated, *Orion* bound for home, *Atlantis* for a journey around the world.

LEADERSHIP

In *Atlantis,* though never safe and always confined to a few decks with less space than a small inn, Rogge's men were human beings, not numbers. Rogge was a formal disciplinarian, to be sure, but he did not believe that a man's will had to be broken by drill and harshness to make him obey and follow. "You can not ever bellow obedience into a dog," was his theory. An instant response to orders, even some heel clicking, ties and coats, were necessary, he believed, to avoid emotional and military disasters, but it was just as important that a subordinate carrying out those orders did so cheerfully, knowing why they were given. That implied confidence in the officers and good communications between all ranks, a concept Rogge had instilled in his officer corps. The men responded, found the great majority of their superiors, starting with Rogge, readily accessible for whatever problems—even the most personal—that might arise. And how or why did morale—Rogge's "greatest worry"—stay as high as it did over so many months?

To a twenty-two-year-old like Wesemann, it was simple and he could tick off the reasons succinctly: (1) Everyone shared the same risks; (2) pride in accomplishment; (3) reliance on each other; (4) regularity of duty; (5) orderliness of the command; (6) constant and thorough information concerning tactics and plans; (7) respect for the individual regardless of rank; (8) well-planned entertainment—sports, movies, plays, hobbies, lectures on any conceivable subject, an excellent library, records; (9) good contact between the bridge and the lower decks, tolerance and freedom for each individual; (10) an unclouded trust in the command and Rogge's art of leadership which worked its way down through the ranks.

Keeping up the mood, the willingness to respond, the discipline, "actually took up more of my time—especially during the second year—than did the planning for our operations," Rogge says. And it was well that he had given it so much thought for the month-long, storm-battered

haul through the Indian Ocean and the first weeks in the Pacific brought
him no success, just tedium for all.

Up in the officers' country, one of the "House of Commons"
observed that their conversations had gotten duller with consequently
less friction; "the whole intellectual niveau was not very exciting. While
the petty officers play chess, study English or Spanish and are busy with
all sorts of educational matter, the height of our life is 'Doppelkopf' (a
simple card game) or a brief banter over some whiskey," one junior
officer remembers. They still kidded and joked, enlisting the radio room
to provide the meteorologist with false data; typhoons to starboard, high
pressure to port, heavy seas astern, hail ahead. Rogge feigned annoy-
ance at the man's incompetence. And for Kamenz, the ex-Lloyd officer
who had taken *Ole Jacob* to Japan and had then returned to *Atlantis* via
the Trans-Siberian railroad, Germany, and a supply ship, and was
known for his antipathy to freemasons and the like, they prepared
something special. Knowing that he would have to be innoculated again
against typhus and cholera, the doctors, cloaked in white hoods and
vestments, met him with their sharp needles in a room lit only by a
single candle.

The enlisted men, too, enjoyed their sport; angling for shark as
seamen always do. One of the many-toothed beasts, when cut open,
disclosed a can marked *"Rindfleisch"* (beef). What a surprise if some
British tar had caught it. They had their parties, and good ones they
were, it seems, for one man, a supply department mate named Christ-
mann, decided one night at 0200 that they needed another bottle. Being
a brave sailor of the Reich and amply fortified, he marched off and up
the ladders to the officers' country to pound on the almighty exec's door
with what he thought was a legitimate request. Kühn expansively allowed that it was not. And yet the days were dull, and so repetitive the
rehashed tales that anyone, Wesemann remembers, coming in the middle
of a yarn could easily take over from the raconteur.

On September 10, eighty days after their last catch, they captured
a vessel quite by chance. The officers had been playing with a medicine
ball in an unfavorable wind. Rogge ordered the bridge to change course
and the raider then stayed on the new heading, moving slowly about
halfway between the Kermadec and Tubuai islands. After dark, they
suddenly spotted a vessel coming out of a rain squall, and though it
radioed, it was stopped without damage or injury to personnel. It was
the Henry Tschudis Tankreederei's 4,793-ton *Silvaplana* with a very
valuable cargo of rubber, sago, tin, copper, coffee, and spices, and
Rogge decided to keep her as a prize.

Ten days later they uncovered a 20 mm. to fire the salute required for *Komet's* Rear Admiral Eyssen who was at a meeting place arranged by SKL for both raiders, *Komet's* prize *Kota Nopan* and supply ship *Münsterland*. The first discussions between Eyssen and Rogge went off well, but when *Münsterland* arrived the next day with fresh provisions and it was time to divvy up, the admiral became ruffled despite the courtesies *Atlantis'* skipper, a mere captain, showed him. Rogge "most obediently" suggested this or that, but he had been out so long—eighteen months—that he was damned if he would permit even a superior officer to get away with the best of the rations, especially when "Herr Admiral" was already homeward-bound. Eyssen wanted part of the beer and fresh food assigned to *Atlantis*, but Rogge insisted on his rights. Notes were carefully prepared and compared. *Atlantis'* men, Rogge said, had not had any fresh vegetables in 540 days; *Komet* had enjoyed them at least five times in only 430 days. After Rogge's original load of potatoes gave out, his ship had had only thirty-five meals at which they were served (the last one four months previously) while *Komet's* gang had gobbled up spuds fifty-seven times (the last, three days earlier). The recitation showed that records are always good for something, and Eyssen had to back down, insisting only on a share of the beer. But he then supplied *Atlantis* with ammunition, aircraft gas (for which he had no more use, having lost his plane), an X-ray machine, nails, and clothing, in exchange for which he took on some rice for the prisoners of three ships he had taken in the Pacific. He also took along some of Rogge's sixty-four remaining prisoners such as *Tottenham's* Woodcock and Nolan, the officers going to *Komet* and the natives to *Kota Nopan*.

The four ships then separated, *Kota Nopan* and *Komet* Europe-bound, *Atlantis* and *Münsterland* to *Silvaplana*, which Rogge had left behind so there would not be too many German ships in one spot. The Norwegian prize was outfitted by the twenty-seventh for her journey to France, where she arrived November 17, and *Münsterland* was sent back to Japan.

Amply provisioned and bunkered, Rogge could then theoretically have remained at sea until March 1942, but the captain planned for the following reasons to arrive at a French port by December 1941: His engines would soon need a major overhaul; his crew, though in "excellent spirits," would find the strain ever harder to bear; there were no immediate prospects of a change in Germany's fortunes at sea; it was obvious that the United States attitude, which was fast changing from "short of war" to a de facto involvement, would make operations in the Atlantic far more difficult in the future. *Atlantis* would remain in the Pacific until October 19 and then head for home.

"THE ENEMY MUST BE GIVEN FULL CREDIT"

Rogge visited Vana Vana (one of the Tuamotu Group) on October 9, and some of his men got ashore for the first time since the Kerguelens nine months earlier. Though a "tropical paradise" with fine beaches and tender coconuts, the atoll's resident girls were not the Hollywood type. A stop was also made at Henderson Island where a sign saying "This island belongs to King George V" was found and by the twenty-ninth *Atlantis* was sixty-five miles below Cape Horn, bound for a meeting south of St. Helena with U-68, which Rogge had volunteered to supply "in the common interest."

He met the boat, one of those gradually working their way down in African waters for their first appearance south of the equator, on November 15, and supplied her with oil, water, food, and soap, and then departed on a supply mission ordered by SKL. He was to tend to the needs of U-126 northeast of Ascension Island in nearly the narrowest part of the Atlantic and he was not at all in sympathy with the instructions. It was not the job of a raider to waste time and risk itself when it was well known that supply ship *Python* would be available to the submarine. Rogge's colleague, Weyher, then already home with *Orion* and temporarily serving at SKL, could not believe it. Rogge had been out too long for his own good; no one in his right mind would acquiesce to such an assignment, he mused, telling the planners that it was folly to risk a big crew for a mission like that. When he checked back in a few days later to see how the meeting had come off, he was told, "Never mind asking, it has already happened."

On November 22, the day U-126 took the raider's lines, Mohr found the tension on board "nerve-wracking." Lieutenant Ernst Bauer and seven other men from the U-boat boarded *Atlantis* for some decent food and coffee, Bauer's served on white linen by a former Lloyd steward. Fueling connections were made and oil was soon throbbing through the snaking hose to the U-boat, toward which the raider's launch was chugging with supplies. It was partially cloudy, the sea calm and the German ships rose and fell rhythmically in long gentle swells. All seemed well and might have been so, had not Rogge been having a streak of bad luck of the kind a raider captain can ill afford. His plane had been damaged the day before and was therefore unable to provide air cover, and his engineers had the port diesel apart to replace a piston in No. 3 cylinder.

At 0815 a steamer with three stacks was reported and three minutes later, as *Atlantis'* men rushed to their stations, it was recognized as a *London*-class heavy cruiser. The U-boat's lines were cast off, the fuel hose cut, and the raider turned to port to show her stern and thus an indistinguishable silhouette. Though "it was evident right from the start that our own chances were extraordinarily slim," Rogge did what he could to get the Britisher—H.M.S. *Devonshire* (eight 8-inch; eight 4-inch, eight 21-inch torpedo tubes and numerous automatic weapons; speed: thirty-two knots)—within range or at least over the U-boat which had crash-dived without its exasperated commander.

But the cruiser's skipper, Capt. R. D. Oliver, R.N., confident in the superior range of his turret guns, stayed out of *Atlantis'* reach, maneuvering at twenty-six knots and some 17,500 yards off with "frequent alterations of course to frustrate a torpedo attack." Oliver's Walrus plane had spotted a merchant ship during its dawn reconnaissance, and from its description it seemed that the vessel closely resembled the raider described in ex-prisoner Murphy's *Life* magazine article of June 23, 1941, and the Admiralty's *Weekly Intelligence Report No. 64.* He headed for the stranger and sighted her at 0809, catapulted his plane again, and then at 0837 fired two salvos "spread to right and left." "My object was," Oliver reported, "(a) to provoke a return fire and so establish her identity without doubt or (b) to induce her to abandon ship in order to avoid bloodshed, particularly as she might have a number of British prisoners on board."

Rogge knew the game was up. He was outranged, and with only one engine operating unable to speed up enough to draw *Devonshire* across U-126's path, even if the fast cruiser had been willing to be forced into that trap. There was nothing he could do to engage, and he could only try to save as many lives as possible. He stopped, and so told *Devonshire* in flag hoist "MT."

Bauer's exec, mistaking the opening salvos for a depth-charge attack by the plane, went deep, and lost whatever chance he had of torpedoing the cruiser, and Rogge, clinging to a last strategem and bit of hope, radioed "RRR *Polyphemus,*" pretending to be the Dutchman he was disguised as. It did not work. Oliver's wireless room reported that only three instead of four "RRRRs" had been used and that the ship had forgotten to add its call letters. Just to be sure, though, he signaled his base asking whether *Polyphemus* was "genuine." "No, repetition, No," they said and at 0935 *Devonshire* opened fire "to destroy the enemy raider."*

"The first salvo lay short, the second questionably left but covering, the third was a hit through the battery deck and into the aircraft's hold," which immediately caught fire, Rogge's log shows. He abandoned

---

* Supplement to the official London *Gazette,* July 9, 1948.

while *Devonshire's* double turrets pumped thirty salvos at the helpless ship, killing seven men on board and in the water and wounding a score of others (including Kühn), two of whom died later.

Frank Vicovari was still in *Atlantis,* then, his leg wounds needing the attention Rogge's doctors thought lacking in another ship. He was reading Conrad's *The Rescue* as the action began and, with a fine flare for the dramatic, he later told *Collier's* (July 29, 1944) that he had planned to kill as many Germans as he could with his cane while everyone else was busy fighting fires, setting scuttling charges, provisioning the boats, and caring for the wounded. But he could not bring himself to kill Dr. Reil, who came in to shake hands and advise him to make for a boat. So he smashed a clock, found the tinkling of glass "soothing," and was soon in a lifeboat with the men from the raider— the only one, he told the writer (or the editors found it more interesting that way) that always attacked without warning.

Atlantis was taking hits in hatches No. 4 and 5, the torpedo room, the aft control position, and her bridge, which was already untenable due to the fire forward. All communications were dead. The forward magazine, abreast the foremast and two decks down, blew up at 0958, and Lieutenant H. J. Fehler was told off to trigger the scuttling charges at 1016. The raider went down without her battle flag flying. It had not been hoisted because Rogge could not fire a shot in self-defense, and he did not wish to disclose the true nature of his vessel. The men in the boats and life belts gave her a last three cheers.

Devonshire sped off to recover her plane, whose reports had made it clear that there was a submarine about, and U-126's exec soon surfaced cautiously to find both the British and *Atlantis* gone and a flotilla of boats and rafts that looked much like a Sunday at the park all waiting for him to do something. At 1458 he picked up the first survivor and at 1500 he turned over command to his shipwrecked commander Bauer again.

"The tragic sinking of the HK *Atlantis* was all the more a bitter pill because the ship had to be abandoned without a fight," Rogge later penned in the U-boat. But he did not let sentiments get the best of him while his men still needed attention. Fifty-five men were jammed down through the U-boat's narrow conning tower, needing the skill of an eel to find a place to sit or stand in the overcrowded boat's torpedo rooms and officers' quarters. Fifty-two remained on deck with their life jackets on and their rubber floats handy; 201, in four lifeboats and two motor launches, were taken in tow toward Brazil. And a difficult tow it was with the boats shearing out in following seas and their lines constantly chafing through, necessitating repairs and slowdowns. But on the third

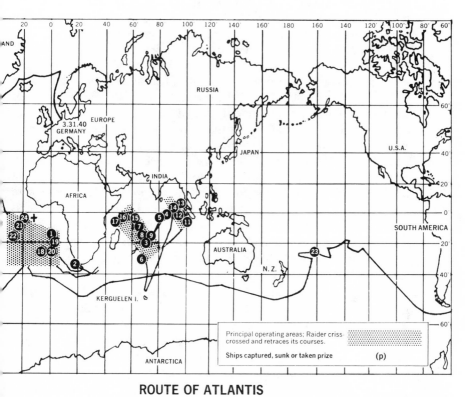

ROUTE OF ATLANTIS

day, they were able to trade their places on and in *U-126* and their pounding, dancing wet boats for the hard planks and some bedding down in the hold of *Python,* whose cooks filled them and Vicovari with coffee, schnapps, and stew. It was "paradise" to Mohr, who had found a place in one of the freighter's luxurious cabins. *Atlantis'* boats were hoisted aboard and immediately reprovisioned.

With nothing to do but eat, sleep, and help stand watch, the raider's crew relaxed, played cards, and watched *Python's* men go about their business, while Rogge, sitting in the same cabin he had once occupied as a passenger, mulled over their sinking and wondered if he had done enough to avoid it. (The Germans still think that treachery may have played a part or that the British had broken the U-boat code which was simpler than that of the surface ships. They may be right, for the United Kingdom had, indeed, gained an insight into their military and naval communications with the help of a stolen cypher machine.) What Rogge did not know then was that the very U-boats that he had supplied—and others like U-111, U-67, and U-A, some of them with sinkings as far south as Walvis Bay, to their credit—had attracted a lot of attention and it had not been difficult for the South Atlantic Station to come to the conclusion that "the appearance of U-Boats as far south as St. Helena suggested that there must be supply ships operating in the calm area south of St. Helena." Cruisers *Dorsetshire* and *Dunedin,* AMC *Canton* and auxiliaries *Koningin Emma* and *Prinsess Beatrix,* acting on an erroneous raider report had been at sea conducting a search, and the Americans, already convoying ships of all nationalities in cooperation with the Royal Navy, and patrolling in the South Atlantic with Task Force 3, had captured blockade runner *Odenwald* earlier in the month saying, as they were not sure of the legality of their act, that they suspected the German ship to be a slaver. After *Atlantis* had been sunk, His Majesty's corvettes *Aster* and *Marguerite* went out to make prisoners of her survivors but found nothing, and at 1300 Wednesday November 26 H.M.S. *Dorsetshire* (with the same speed and armament as *Devonshire;* Capt. A. W. S. Agar, R.N., commanding), which had spent over one hundred days at sea during the previous four months, mostly just searching, steamed out from Freeport to patrol an area some 720 miles south and west of St. Helena. And that is just where the 3,664-ton *Python* was going with orders to supply U-68 and U-A.

U-68 was in position on time on November 30, but U-A arrived a day later and was taking on fuel from *Python* at 1530 when *Atlantis'* trained lookouts sighted a ship with three stacks. Cursing horribly, more than four hundred Germans scrambled about the U-boats, *Python,* its launch and rubber rafts, packing away provisions, dogging hatches, letting go lines and fuel hoses, and, with not much foresight necessary under the circumstances, preparing the boats for lowering. U-68, her deck hatches wide open and taking on torpedoes, could not dive right away. U-A was in a better position, and she spun off to intercept the enemy cruiser, which was *Dorsetshire*.

Python's master started up fast, too fast for the ship's exhausts emitted a big puff of smoke, much to the *Atlantis* veterans' dismay. That did not matter much, though, because Captain Agar had already seen them and was coming up at twenty-five knots, his crew closed up at stations. *Python*'s smoke just confirmed his suspicion that the ship had been lying stopped when first sighted. As he steamed up in pursuit, patches of oil were seen along with the supply ship's rafts and launch. Though most doubtful, it was just possible, Agar thought, that the ship was an Allied vessel having stopped to pick up survivors of a U-boat sinking, and then, steaming off in full flight from what she presumed to be a German warship. To be certain, he signaled. Getting no response, he fired two warning shots which caused the suspicious vessel to stop and make smoke—a foolish move on *Python*'s part because it might have caused the British to fire in earnest. Agar, worried about U-boats, stayed eight miles off, steaming at high speed as he watched the German being abandoned and set on fire. It was well he did, too, because U-A sent five torpedoes his way, all of which missed, because the skipper had underestimated *Dorsetshire*'s speed.

Atlantis' men threw everything they could into the boats, food from the pantry, and provisions intended for the U-boats, then sat about in eleven boats and seven rafts with *Python*'s men and Vicovari, who had by then become a mascot of sorts, waiting for the U-boats to reappear. U-68, totally out of trim due to the weight of additional supplies, oil, and torpedoes, had been unable to mount an attack on the British cruiser and U-A had missed; both had to dive again when *Dorsetshire*'s plane flew over for a final check, but they were then available for precisely the type of operation U-boats are most unsuited for—rescue.

When Agar wisely left the scene, sorry "that this encounter did not fulfill our expected desire of an action with the enemy," there were 414 of *Atlantis*' and *Python*'s men waiting to be picked up.* Roughly 100 men crawled into each of the cramped U-boats; the rest were distributed among ten boats and one motor launch, which, running under its own power, served as a communications boat, mess barge (with hot food from the U-boats), and shepherded the rest of the boats

* Ibid.

whose lines continued to break, leaving first one, then several, adrift and far behind.

The whole rescue operation was galling to the submarine officers who wanted to get on with the war and who knew that Adm. Karl Dönitz would have to recall them now that they were disabled by overcrowding and orphaned for lack of a supply ship. U-A's Hans Eckermann, huffy about his chore and annoyed by the 105 *Atlantis* men jammed in with his own 55-man complement, took off one day in a vain assault on a tanker, leaving Karl-Friedrich Merten (U-68) with Rogge and Mohr on board, cursing his luck, the additional five lifeboats cast loose by his ambitious colleague, and the incredibly slow progress— never more than six knots when the boats were towing well. Two other U-boats, U-124 and U-129, had been told off by Dönitz for a rendez-vous and to bring the survivors to France. The latter was met on December 3, her arrival alleviating the crowding a bit, but not enough for Mohr. He had found a spot under the wardroom table preferable to a bunk that had to be vacated every ninety minutes under a "hot sack" system to make room for someone else. Mohr's new bed was hard, but it would have suited him well if it had not originally been the hideout of scotty Ferry, who resented the intrusion and could be accommodated only when the adjutant consented to his sleeping on his stomach. U-124, commanded by one of Germany's highly independent breed of aces, Jochen Mohr, had not manned her "Afrika" wavelength, had not there-fore paid any attention to Dönitz's orders, and had then been delayed by sinking His Majesty's cruiser *Dunedin* and a steamer. She did not show up until the fifth, an exasperating period for the survivors and the other skippers, and one that might have placed the entire operation in jeop-ardy. Berated by Rogge for his lack of cooperation, the U-boat captain acknowledged his fault, sort of, with a "Yes, Sir."

Between December 14 and 18, four Italian submarines were met and these took from fifty-five to seventy men each from their German counterparts, *Luigi Torelli* from U-A, *Enrico Tazolli* (U-68),*Giuseppe Finzi* (U-129), and *Pietro Calvi* (U-124). *Atlantis'* Mohr was one of those who enjoyed the increased comforts of *Tazolli*, where he marveled as much at the officers' comfortable quarters and excellent mess as he did at the social distinctions rank made among the Italians—even in a submarine. He enjoyed the company of *Tazolli*'s slight, charming, boy-ish-faced skipper, Carlo Fescia Di Cossata, one of Italy's top-notch naval officers, and he whiled his time away with Cossata's mildly erotic library until their safe arrival at St. Nazaire on Christmas Day. By the twenty-ninth all eight submarines had arrived, ending an extraordinary rescue effort "for which," Roskill notes, "the enemy must be given full credit."*

Atlantis' men spent hours eating, quaffing beer, sitting in hot tubs of fresh water in a requisitioned hotel in Nantes, where they finally received mountains of mail, much of it very welcome, some of it most sad. Together with Rogge, who as the modern world's most successful raider captain had collected an oak leaf cluster for his Ritterkreuz, they marched to the cathedral where they sang the song of thanksgiving for their deliverance after 655 days at sea. Never, their commander remarks, had the chaplain heard men sing that song so well. They had sunk sixteen ships and taken six prizes for a total bag of 145,697 tons. They had sailed 110,000 miles, 5,000 of them since the sinking, and never, since March 1940, had they heard the clip-clop of a horse cart, sniffed a Konditorei, or stepped on cobblestoned streets. It seemed incredible to be on land where there were newspaper vendors, sparrows, women, and children. By New Year's Day, when Vicovari was on his way to the rigors of imprisonment and eventual repatriation, the Germans were rolling toward Berlin where they arrived for a formal reception by Admiral Raeder at the Hotel Kaiserhof. From there it was home for leave and thousands of mind years from the cruel sea that had, to them, at least, been generous.[1]

NOTES

1. Rogge, a well-furnished gentleman, lives with his second wife Elsbeth, in a lovely home beside a pond in the Hamburg suburb Reinbek. If anyone is representative of the finest stereotype former naval officer, it is he, and his balanced attitudes and sophistication have done much for Germany. Returning from his epic voyage, he was awarded the Oak Leaves to the Ritterkreuz and was appointed chief of staff of the Naval Educational Inspectorate. Promoted rear admiral in 1943, he became responsible for the selection and training of officer candidates of all service branches. C-in-C, Fleet training formations in 1944, he advanced to Vice Admiral and took command of Task Group III, wearing his flag in *Prinz Eugen*, then bombarding Russian positions (March 1945) near Danzig. After the capitulation he served a short stint as a Schleswig official, then turned to private business, and in 1955 he formed his own industrial consulting firm. Recalled to the colors in 1957 by the re-born Bundesmarine as Rear Admiral commanding the Schleswig-Holstein-Hamburg district, his duties between 1958 and his retirement in 1962 included command of all Nato forces in Schleswig Holstein. Since then,

* Roskill *The War at Sea.*

he has busied himself with corporate directorships and the promotion of a group devoted to sailing. Running *Atlantis* was his most responsible command, he says, adding with a smile, "once you are an Admiral you are nothing; you are already out of it." How does one exert leadership? "Well, with a Christian respect for the human qualities of others, conviction and trust in oneself."

Atlantis *six days before her end* COURTESY DR. ULRICH MOHR

Atlantis *torpedo and gunports open* COURTESY DR. ULRICH MOHR

Momentary peace:
Atlantis *in the Kerguelen Islands*
COURTESY DR. ULRICH MOHR

Bernhard Rogge,
Captain of Atlantis
COURTESY DR. ULRICH MOHR

Atlantis *survivors*
homeward-bound on U-boat
COURTESY DR. ULRICH MOHR

Kurt Weyher (right), captain of Orion, *with Fritz Steinkrauss* COURTESY KURT WEYHER

Orion 5.9-inch *(top) and 37 mm; sketches by Weyher* COURTESY KURT WEYHER

Orion No. 6 gun
under false skylight;
lifeboats collapse in action
COURTESY ADALBERT VON BLANC

Orion's *much-used plane in hatch*
COURTESY ADALBERT VON BLANC

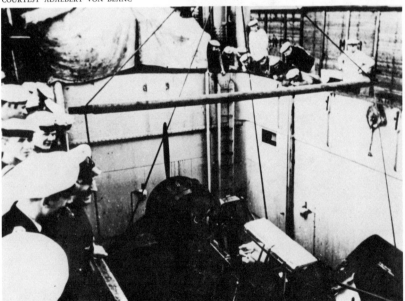

Orion *with her plane*
COURTESY KURT WEYHER

Orion *going into action;*
bulwarks dropping outboard
COURTESY ADALBERT VON BLANC

Widder *as* Ulysses

Thor *as* Santa Cruz

AMC Voltaire *in happier times on maiden voyage*

AMC Carnarvon Castle *standing into Montevideo for repairs*
COURTESY UNION-CASTLE LINES

Otto Kähler, captain of Thor
COURTESY MRS. URSULA KÄHLER-VON FRIEDEBURG

Robert Eyssen, captain of Komet
COURTESY WILFRIED KARSTEN

Different types
of prisoners
on Komet
COURTESY KARL AUGUST BALSER

Komet *gunports No. 2 and No. 4 open*
COURTESY WILFRIED KARSTEN

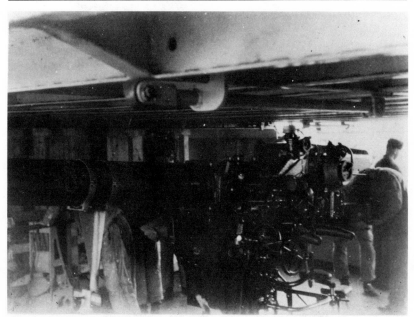

Komet; *a 5.9-inch under deck*   COURTESY KARL AUGUST BALSER

H.M.S. Devonshire *sank* Atlantis; *her "County" class sisters*   COURTESY ROYAL NAVY,
destroyed Python *and* Pinguin   MINISTRY OF DEFENCE

Whale catcher Adjutant

Pinguin

Kormoran

H.M.A.S. Sydney

Ernst-Felix Krüder,
captain of Pinguin
COURTESY MRS. KRÜDER

Hellmuth von Ruckteschell (right),
captain of Widder *and* Michel,
with his navigator Ludwig Rödel
COURTESY JÜRGEN HERR

Horst Gerlach,
captain of Stier
COURTESY MRS. GERLACH

Theodor Detmers
(second from right,
sitting) with officers of Kormoran
in Australian prison camp
COURTESY AUSTRALIAN WAR MEMORIAL

Stier *being repainted just before her end*

Stier (*left*), Dalhousie *sinking; taken from* Michel

Michel's *lookouts on main mast*
COURTESY JÜRGEN HERR

Michel

Michel's *MTB* Esau *being lowered*

Günther Gumprich (*left*), *captain of* Thor *and* Michel,
on Thor's *bridge with Lt. Bernhard Meckmann* (*center*),
and unidentified officer

Uckermark *and* Thor *after the explosion in* Yokohama COURTESY DR.HERMANN KANDELER

U.S.S. Tarpon

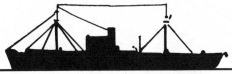

CHAPTER 8

The Atlantic, January—June 1941

"A QUESTION OF PEOPLE" The multi-hued, foam-streaked, and explosion-torn waters of the Atlantic that were to be by turns so unkind and so kind to Rogge were by any standards, cruelest of all during 1941. In the first half of that year, German U-boats sank 263 ships (of the 432 they were credited with for the entire twelve months). Warship raiders accounted for 37 vessels—all they ever did get in the outer oceans for the rest of the war. The Hilfskreuzer wiped out 46 Allied merchantmen in all of 1941, of which they took 31 of them in their first six months in the Atlantic—even though there were never more than three of them in that vast theater, which stretched from the ice of the Arctic to the ice of the Antarctic.

The first to strike in the new year was the newcomer *Kormoran, Schiff 41,* which at 8,736 tons was the largest of the raiders. Her captain was Lt. Comdr. Theodor Detmers and a tough, lean, and practical man he was. Born the son of a merchant in the Ruhr August 22, 1902, he had joined the navy in 1921 to seek a career as an officer. He served on tours of duty overseas in light cruiser *Köln,* at home in Berlin, and in torpedo boats. In 1938 he became skipper of the large new destroyer *Hermann Schoemann.* His experience with her experimental engines, which had to be treated as gently as raw eggs, taught him that there were "no impossible situations; it is just a question of people"; either people master situations or they are mastered by them. By this axiom he commanded and fought.

Back on June 17, 1940, having just returned to Wilhelmshaven from a sortie off Norway with *Hipper, Scharnhorst,* and *Gneisenau* and having sent half his crew off on leave, Detmers got orders to pack immediately to take over command of *Schiff 41.* He had no idea what

137

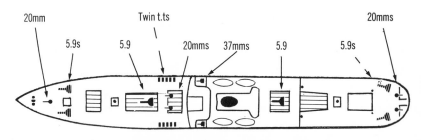

KORMORAN, SHIP 41, ex-STEIERMARK

Built:	1938, Krupp-Germania Werft, Kiel
Tonnage:	8,736
Length:	515.1 feet, Lloyds Register
Beam:	66.3
Draft:	30.5
Speed:	18
Armament:	Six 5.9-inch; two 37mm; five 20mm; two twin 21-inch torpedo tubes (above water); two single 21-inch tubes (submerged); 360 mines*; one motor mine-laying launch
Planes:	Two Arado 196
Complement:	397 (varied, due to prize crews and new drafts)
	*Shaded guns and tubes indicate a mounting below deck
Ships sunk or taken:	11 (including one prize)=68,274
	ANTONIS, BRITISH UNION, AFRIC STAR, EURYLOCHUS, AGNITA CANADOLITE, CRAFTSMAN, NICOLAOS D. L., VELEBIT, MAREEBA, STAMATIOS G. EMBIRICOS
	Plus H.M.A.S. SYDNEY, 6,830 tons (displacement)
Length of cruise:	352 days, 12.3.40-11.19.41
Fate:	Sunk by H.M.A.S. SYDNEY

sort of vessel she was, but the appointment spared him an agonizing choice: whether to take his furlough at a beach like Norderney or in the Tyrolian Alps. Detmers was in Hamburg the very next day to find himself captain of a raider, "a childhood dream come true." He had the job he had once asked for even though he knew that by the book he was too young and too junior an officer to be considered. Now that he had it, he knew he would be burdened with responsibilities he had not encountered before except in the numerous World War I raider books he had once read so eagerly. Not only would he have to master technical and operational difficulties, but he would find himself responsible for more than four hundred men. And it would be those men who would work and fight his ship well or poorly, according to the manner in which he cared for their needs and exercised his leadership.

Schiff 41, ex-Steiermark of the Hamburg-Amerika Line, was so new when the Kriegsmarine requisitioned her in 1939 that she had only just completed her builders' trials; the bugs that were to plague her later had not yet shown up. She had been designed for the Hapag's Far East service. Her diesel-electric power plant could push her along at a respectable eighteen knots and at ten knots she had an endurance of 70,000 miles. Joiners, welders, and shipfitters had torn her apart again at the Deutsche Werft and had fitted her out with much the same equipment as all the rest of the raiders except for a fast motor minelayer, LS 3—which was never used—and a radar set, the first on any raider—which did not work. Reconstruction and working up exercises, interrupted by the preparations for the invasion of England, took such a long time that Detmers, impatient to get into action and fearing that any major alterations might delay his departure by months if not forever, simply accepted many of the things already done improperly or overlooked entirely. He did fight for a gyro compass, but could get only four repeaters, one for the helm, two in the bridge wings, one for the steering engine, but none for the guns and torpedo stations. Of his officers and crew he knew only one quartermaster but he made no special requests of the personnel bureau. At 1405 on December 3, the self-confident Detmers ordered "Leinen los" (cast off) for the last time in Gotenhaven's Slip No. 5. Loaded down with provisions for 420 men, ammunition, 5,200 tons of fuel, three separate cargoes of stores, three hundred mines, twenty torpedoes, and another thirty mines for U-boats, Kormoran, though an excellently handling ship of Maierform construction, soon rolled so badly in the first heavy seas that she was dubbed "Rollmoran."

During the night of December 13 she broke through the Denmark Strait, undetected, and by the twenty-ninth she was far enough down in the Atlantic for Detmers to fill up a pool he had had cemented between the bridgeworks and hatch No. 3. There was a movie every afternoon and those who thought one viewing belowdecks in the tropics in a room that could hold 120 men would be close to Dante's Inferno seemed to be in the minority. The hellhole was full every day.

On January 6 Detmers signaled and stopped the Greek *Antonis,* then sank it in the middle of the Atlantic between Brazil and Dakar with her 4,800 tons of coal. The Greek's twenty-eight-man crew and one blind passenger were sent below where they had their own galley and heads but where they would have to sleep in hammocks rather than the bunks provided the raider's men. Detmers asked the captain to stay with his crew even though there were especially built cabins for captains and women prisoners. It was a policy he always maintained even with British officers who, the Germans were surprised to find, mostly preferred to keep their distance from the ratings. Detmers thought his practice of keeping the officers and men together paid off because the former could act as go-betweens and would thereby retain control over the ranks. But it was an unusual procedure for most of the raiders whose captains conformed to custom and preferred keeping the captive crews separated from their leaders who might incite them to mutiny or sabotage. He pitied the prisoners but felt that they "had their own disciplines," and that their contact with his own men had best be limited to the mild-mannered, genial Lt. Joachim Greter, *Kormoran*'s torpedo officer, who spoke excellent English. Detmers differed from his peers, too, in that he always ate in the mess. Accustomed to the "close familiarity bred in torpedo boats and destroyers," he wanted "closer contact with the officers," and thought that his joining them at mealtime would not restrict their social freedom. It probably did, however, cut down the banter and certainly on any ill-considered mouthings about the ship's management. To Detmers "critique and a little frolic were all right as long as they did not get out of hand," and the officers such as the slim twenty-three-year-old Greter, who liked the "old man" immensely, felt his presence constituted no imposition—certainly no more of one than his ban on hard liquor.

WHALE OIL

In mid-Atlantic just north of the Tropic of Capricorn, on January 6, the day *Kormoran* sank *Antonis,* raider *Thor* was at a final meeting with *Scheer, Storstad,* and *Nordmark* (see p. 104) before heading southeast for the Cape–South America tracks. And much farther south at 55°19'S, 00°47'W, not far from Bouvet Island, Captain Krüder, his *Pinguin* surrounded by ice, was still stalking the Norwegian whaling fleet—factory ships *Ole Wegger* and *Pelagos* and supply vessel *Solglimt*—whose radio traffic he was by then monitoring. Tension had soared to one of the apexes of *Schiff 33*'s cruise during that three-week hunt through fog and ice, his adjutant, Hans Karl Hemmer says, and some of the ready-to-pounce thrill can still be sensed in the unemotional language of Krüder's log:

13 January 41: 1200 hours: 56°29'S; 06°26'W, WNW 1-2, sea 1, cloudy, snow, good to fair visibility, icebergs. *Solglimt* will, as can be seen from their conversations, be alongside *Ole Wegger* at 0530. Judging by radio bearings so far, I am about 70 miles away. At noon ran off to southeast to get a western fix.
2200: Start westerly run in.
2315: White lights in sight 2° to port. A bit later many lights of the two ships lying side-by-side and several catchers can be made out. Shortly thereafter everything lost in a snow cloud and remained so for about 45 minutes. We can approach unseen.
14 January 41: 1200: 57°45'S; 02°30'W, W 2, sea 1, cloudy, snow, mostly good visibility, icebergs.
0015 clearing. *Pinguin* is right on top of the ships.
0020: Searchlight on, boats put over.
The two ships, lying side-by-side with several whales between them and lit up by innumerable deck lights and cargo lights, are swept by our searchlight to document the presence of a warship. Will not fire a warning shot for the present so as not to alarm the men working as if in the deepest peace and to prevent the catchers from being scared up.
Several times blinker signal: "Do not use wireless or telephone, we are sending a boat."
Meanwhile two prize commandos go alongside.
Engine reports that motor unclear after stopping; one cylinder making water. Crack in the cylinder.
0045: Blinker message [from prize crew] "ships in our hands."
1. *Ole Wegger,* Norwegian, 12,201 tons with 7000 tons whale oil and 5500 tons fuel. Crew about 190 men . . .
2. *Solglimt,* Norwegian, 12246 tons, 4000 tons whale oil, 4000 tons fuel, Crew 60 men . . .
3. The nearby catcher boats, some of them with whales alongside, are being boarded. They are the boats:

Pol VIII	298 gross tons	
Pol IX	354 "	"
Pol X	354 "	"
Thorlyn	247 "	"

Former Lloyd captain Erich Warning was the man who took the factory ship *Ole* and the *Solglimt,* both armed with a 4.1-inch gun and both insured by Lloyd's of London for £324,424 each. The whale oil they carried was worth £ 440,000. He captured them completely by surprise, climbing aboard from his boat. He ordered the crews into the messes while he conferred with Captains Evensen and Normann Andersen, telling them to remain calm and to continue with their work, for which they would be paid by Germany.

Less spectacular but just as stirring was Adjutant Hemmer's adventure. He had been detailed, he remembers, with eighteen men to secure the catchers. "I was naturally excited and since my English was limited to what I had learned in school, I scribbled 'I am Ensign Hemmer, Officer of the German Navy. Your Boat is Captured. Do not offer resistance, let your crew stand to attention.' on a piece of cardboard and hung that around my neck. It was a black night, misty with visibility 1,000 yards. We motored up to the first boat, naturally the slowest one. I rushed on board and up the ladder to the captain's room, pulled my pistol and flashlight, and was met by the sight of a man sleeping in his woolly underwear snoring in a fug you cut cut. I shook the man by the shoulders and rasped out my ditty in a broken voice. The result was staggering. He grunted and turned over. That nearly disarmed me. Just imagine how surprised that captain should have been at suddenly seeing a German officer (especially one with a cardboard sign hung around his neck) fumbling about by his bunk 10,000 miles down in the Antarctic." But both Hemmer and the woolly Norwegian quickly recovered: Signed by Krog Andersen, the Dagbok (log) of *Pol IX* (which Hemmer still has), says, "14 January 41, German officer and men came on board." That officer's men soon had four catchers in their hands, but another three escaped as a result of *Pinguin*'s inoperative engine.

The raider left the scene at 0400 the same morning to capture the nearby *Pelagos,* and at 2209 that evening Krüder sighted one of her catchers. The brightly lit mother ship came into view forty-four minutes later. At midnight the raider was stopped only 219 yards from her unsuspecting victim, which had been warned by radio and was seized along with her 210 men as effortlessly as had been her consorts. *Pelagos* had worked out 9,500 tons of whale oil, and her seven catchers, which were also bagged, grossed 2,064 tons, thus giving Krüder a marvelous one-day haul of 39,847 tons of shipping and some 20,500 tons of whale oil with a value of about $4.1 million.

It took Krüder nearly two weeks to straighten out and man his fifteen-ship squadron and make adequate provisions for its trek to France. *Pelagos* and *Solglimt* were released on the twenty-fifth (they arrived at the Gironde on March 11 and 16, and on February 2 *Pinguin* steamed off with *Ole* under Warning and a flotilla of eleven catchers commanded by Hemmer, who hoisted a pennant Krüder had given him in the newest of the lot, *Pol IX*. The Europe-bound boats would need refueling before they got to France, and since their German crews were not all trained navigators and were too few in numbers to boot—Krüder could not spare more of his own crew—they would need additional men to get them home safely. SKL promised both, setting up a meet with *Kormoran* and *Duquesa* in the South Atlantic.

CLOSE CALL

Kormoran had meanwhile suffered her first teething problems. Three bearings had burned out and it seemed to Chief Engineer Hermann Stehr that the white metal alloy used in their manufacture was too weak and that there would be more mechanical trouble to come. Fortunately, Detmer's power plant did not let him down on the evening of January 18, when he was following the British tanker *British Union* into the red ball of the setting sun on a level with the Canaries. The tanker's captain, L. Atthill, radioed and had the raider's gunfire returned, but without success, and at 1944 his ship was burning and his crew lowering the boats. Atthill and 27 men, a monkey and a bird were picked up, and Detmers, notified that the ship had radioed, sailed off, reluctantly leaving behind seventeen missing tankermen. He knew that his raider, laden as it was with mines, "could come out of an encounter [with a warship responding to Atthill's call] only with luck," but he did not realize how fortunate he had been that night. H.M.A.S. *Arawa,* an Australian AMC armed with seven 6-inch and two 3-inch guns, had received that tanker's message, had seen *Kormoran*'s searchlight and the flashes of her guns, and had narrowly missed engaging the raider. Happily, the AMC did save eight of the seventeen missing men from one boat.

PERSONNEL

Down below the equator and some one hundred days since her last success (*Natia*), *Thor* was still without luck. All Kähler got for his endless searching was an order from SKL directing him to join *Scheer* in giving up a number of men as prize commandos for *Pinguin*'s whaling fleet at a meeting that would draw in *Scheer, Eurofeld, Nordmark,* and *Duquesa* and take place between January 22 and 25. When the involved transfer of provisions, prisoners such as Carr and Winter, experienced officers like the pocket battleship's Ensign Ludolf Petersen, a group of middies who had to be given last-minute refresher courses on how to find Europe, *Thor*'s tall big-fisted Bernhard Meckmann and twelve enlisted men, had been accomplished, Kähler started off for Europe, planning to be home by the end of April. On the twenty-ninth his radiomen intercepted a raider message from *Eurylochus* and correctly assumed that the British vessel's distress was the result of an action taken by *Kormoran*.

WARNING SHOT

January 29 was a brooding hot day, with a heavy haze close to the surface obscuring the horizon, and in that heat just nine degrees north of the equator Detmer's crew was busy until late that night. Their work started at 1316 with the alarm bells clanging. Detmers had just gotten up from lunch. When he arrived on the bridge, all he could see through the glaring haze was the bow wave of a ship whose outlines were just barely visible seconds at a time. He made for it, sent an "obligatory" shot across her bow, and ordered her to stop. He preferred warning shots for several reasons: (1) "the enemy would know he was about to be stopped"; (2) "it saved ammunition if he did stop"; and (3) to be practical, which he was, "it did not matter much if the ship did ignore the warning because by then she could not get away anymore anyway." *Afric Star*'s captain, C. R. Cooper, did ignore the shot, increased speed, and ordered a "QQQQ" call sent out. It was smothered by interference from the raider, which then shelled the ship for four minutes to stop and silence her. Cooper, carrying passengers, two of them women, made no use of his 4.7-inch gun and he and the rest of the seventy-five people on board were over in *Kormoran* by 1518, the men down in the 'tween decks under the forward guns, the women in a spare ward next to the hospital. "It was then," Torpedo Officer Greter remembers, "that we noticed that the vaunted German efficiency had broken down. We had forgotten to take along clothes for the captured ladies."

The *Kormoran* watch officer who had first sighted *Afric Star* had hardly had time to enjoy his prize of a bottle of champagne when, at 1825, another vessel, blacked out and (judging by its tall stack) a Blue Funnel liner, was reported. Three minutes later, Detmers' men had uncovered their guns and fired a star shell which hung over the 1912-built 5,723-ton ship with an all-exposing glare. Below it, the Briton's captain, A. M. Caird, ordered more speed, his gunner F. Laskier trained the cannon, Third Officer George W. Povey gathered his fire parties, and the radio officer tapped out a "RRRR" message giving his position and call letters. At 1831 *Kormoran* opened fire with one of her guns shooting star shells. Detmers had his searchlight switched on and off, not to illuminate but to confuse the enemy gunners into underestimating the range—which they presumably did, because the Germans never did see the fall of Laskier's shot, four rounds, against sixty-seven for *Kormoran.* *Eurylochus'* Chinese firemen deserted their posts, her steering was gone, and Caird reluctantly ordered his boats away only nine minutes after the action began.

Detmers ceased fire when the British abandoned—two of the boats were in pieces, his opponent Povey observed—only to resume shooting with the 5.9s and 20 mms when his radio room insisted that *Eurylochus* was sending again. Her signals caused such commotion at British stations, whose messages the Germans could read thanks to code tables found in *Afric Star,* that Detmers ordered a torpedo fired so that he might be finished with the ship. Povey and forty-two others were fetched out of two awash boats and questioned about the fate of their captain: He and some of the thirty-eight men still missing must still be in rafts, they said. The next morning, when towels, soap, razors, and tobacco were being issued, Povey took the opportunity to ask the Germans why they had turned their automatic weapons on his ship and why they had not troubled to look for Caird. The machine-gunning was intended to stop their radio, Greter responded, and no attempt had been made to collect all the survivors because that same radio had compromised Detmers' position and there was no telling how close an enemy cruiser might be.*

Caird was far from gone, however, even though he passed a night very uncomfortably with twenty-seven others (eleven men were killed in the action) in some rafts whose emergency rations, being under water, they could not and, luckily, did not need to reach. They were rescued next morning by the Spanish *Monte Teide,* which transferred the wounded and eight Europeans to AMC *Bulolo* on the thirty-first.

GOOD ORDERS

Going in the opposite direction with instructions prohibiting any offensive action between 10°N and 10°S during the February 1 to 5 period, *Thor* was to operate south of 30°N, leaving the rest of the North Atlantic to the U-boats and fleet units. Kähler was to terminate his cruise before the end of April, after which the raider would be refitted for another voyage. His men, he thought, were downright cheerful when

* Cruisers *Norfolk* and *Devonshire* responded to *Eurylochus'* call but discovered nothing.

they heard the news. He wondered, himself, if he could bring *Thor* back safely to Germany.

"KISMET"

Tying up was the last thing on his colleague Detmer's mind. *Kormoran's* master's axiom about people mastering situations reflected his confidence in the worth of Germany's raider program. But, already bedeviled by a shortage of white metal of sufficient strength to replace his crumbling bearings, how was he to comply with SKL's plans? He had asked Berlin for the material, but had not told them how serious his situation was for fear that he might be ordered in for repairs. That was the kind of psychological mistake he was prone to and it left SKL unaware of the extent of his problem. To avoid dampening any enthusiasm, too, he refrained from mentioning his qualms about the names of *Kormoran's* victims his officers had had neatly painted on the forward bulkhead of the wardroom under the clock. That clock, Detmers mused, might well be ticking away the time for his own command. "Every wisp of smoke, every mast top could have spelled the end," he later explained, "and though a raider captain soon learned to live with that concept, it was still a fact that could not be escaped." Relative youngsters like Greter paid that no heed; it was "kismet," they figured—once, that is, they were past the first few days during which they felt they could never go to sleep for fear that "something might happen."

"JUST A BIT MUCH"

On February 7 *Schiff 41* rendezvoused with *Nordmark* and *Duquesa*, which had been in tow since early January to preserve the last of the ship's coal for her reefers. *Nordmark* had no white metal but she pumped 1,339 tons of oil into the raider. *Kormoran,* in turn, took one hundred sides of beef and 216,000 eggs from *Duquesa* and shipped 170 prisoners over to the naval tanker, which departed two days later. Detmers had thanked the captured officers for their cooperation and he had had his one and only drink—a bottle of beer—with them in a token of farewell.

"Drinks and games didn't enter into the game of war," *Afric Star's* second officer, G. T. King, remembers, "but we were glad we had been decently treated, receiving the same food as the Germans." *Eurylochus'* Povey, too, felt that aside from the cramped quarters and monotonous diet, over which the Germans had little control, they had been "well treated," and he attributed that in part "to the fact that the Jerries were themselves subject to capture at any time," in part to a "certain fraternity among seamen."

In *Nordmark,* Povey was sent down a small hatch forward into low decks "packed with men, all wearing only underpants and running with sweat," and King found the smell of the bodies "just a bit much by morning." They were allowed on deck from 0830 until 1830 except during meals, which had to be taken below where the diners left puddles of sweat wherever they sat. A few days of that and they were again transferred, this time to *Portland,* a ship making its way home from Chile. King found the guard in her "first-class bastards."

There was talk of taking the ship, and after the Germans discovered clubs hidden away in the hold they entered the prisoners quarters with pistols drawn. Frustrated, a small group of men led by *Afric Star*'s able seaman Arthur E. Fry broke through to an adjoining hold where they set fire to the cargo just before their arrival in France— an act for which they might have faced certain death and one that netted Fry the British Empire Medal after the war.* While fire parties extinguished the flames and armed guards were sent below to herd the sullen crowd forward to keep it in check, a fuse blew, lights went out, and an edgy guard fired three shots, either to draw attention to his own plight, as the Germans say, or in panic, as the British felt. The shots killed two men, one of them the husband of a passenger from *Afric Star.*

On March 16 the captives were on shore at Bordeaux and they soon wound up in the same place where Nash, Carr, Frame, Nolan, and all the rest were too. King complained of a leaky roof, was told that that was better than fighting in Russia, and *Tottenham*'s Nolan found the facilities, chapels, and library ample, the cricket and football, orchestras, comedy shows, and crap tables fun, the radio sets which had been smuggled in, interesting. There was a major trade in eggs, pork, and chickens, for cigarettes, chocolate, coffee, and soap from the Red Cross parcels—which were envied but never touched by the strictly rationed but disciplined Germans. A tunnel was dug but the escapees-to-be were caught. Caught, too, was one seaman returning from a working party, which was always searched. To avoid such a search, the men would throw bags over the fence to their pals inside. One day an old German lady told the prisoners something for which she herself could have lost her freedom: the local Gestapo, or whatever they were, were going to be inside instead of the prisoners. Over came a bag, and its owner was apprehended. When opened, the sack was seen to be full of manure.

* Fry was found out and sentenced to death but he was reprieved and later repatriated in an exchange of prisoners.

THE BUSINESS OF A WAR

That was the kind of a trick *Pinguin*'s Krüder might have appreciated had it been played on him, but he was working, not fighting, not fooling. He and his whaling fleet joined *Nordmark* and *Duquesa* between February 15 and 18 to be provisioned. On the eighteenth, *Duquesa,* then completely out of anything that would burn to keep the reefers going, had to be sunk. *Ole Wegger* and ten of the catchers were dispatched in groups of two to France, with another fueling planned for the latter up in the North Atlantic, where they would meet *Spichern* (*Widder*'s ex-prize *Krossfonn*) and *Thor.* The eleventh whale catcher was to be used as a scout. Nicely named *Adjutant* and placed under the command of the proud adjutant Hemmer, she was sent on ahead with supply ship *Alstertor* (which had joined up) to the Indian Ocean, where Krüder planned to meet them again. First, however, on the twenty-fifth, he rendezvoused with *Kormoran,* to which he handed some white metal. The latter's crew were by then beginning to learn what it took in restraint to master the endless weeks at sea, particularly those days when Detmers shut down the pool because too many of them had ignored his warnings about sunburn. And they had nothing to show for their acquired patience but a meet with U-124 and *Scheer* on March 15 and 16. On the twenty-second Detmers' officers did have another name, *Agnita,* painted under the ticking clock. Though a small (3,552-ton) British tanker, her surrender (she did wireless) and subsequent sinking, happily without injury to any of her 38-man crew, was a welcome change.

Three days later, Detmers had the Canadian *Canadolite* in hand, undamaged, her forty-four men unharmed despite their attempt to run and radio. No sooner than he finished with *Canadolite* he was informed of a raider message sent out in haste by a ship called *Britannia,* which, he correctly guessed, his colleague Kähler was engaging.

LIFEBOAT NO. 7

Thor's Kähler had spent most of February and March in a fruitless hunt, the monotony broken only by meetings with *Eurofeld* and a new supplier, *Alsterufer,* and the chore of supervising the provisioning of *Pinguin*'s ten whale catchers from *Spichern,* which was then released for France along with the prizes.*

At one minute before 0700 on Monday, March 25, *Thor* swung

* The tanker and all the boats except *Star XIX* and *XXIV*, which were scuttled when intercepted by H.M. sloop *Scarborough* on March 13, reached Europe by March 20, where they were then employed as submarine chasers.

suddenly to a course thirty degrees NNE ½ E as her watch officer rang down for fifteen knots to close a vessel belching black smoke and steaming on a southerly course. It was large and had a gun. When Kähler got within eleven thousand yards, the ship turned north, making away at high speed behind a curtain of oil and chemical smoke. The German war flag jerked up on *Thor*'s main, and Koppen-Boehnke's gunners cut loose. The enemy was fast and she radioed "RRRR *Britannia,* RRRR 0724N 2434W gunned . . ." then switched to "QQQQ" signals with a powerful station the raider's operators tried to jam. For *Thor* the shooting was difficult because of the smoke and the prey's skillful, evasive helmsmanship, but after 159 shells had been fired and several hits were seen to flare up, the vessel stopped, her signal flags "OMR" (I am surrendering) flying. *Thor* made "Leave your ship" just as her radio room reported to Kähler that a British unit had signaled a group of numbers to the 8,799-ton *Britannia.* Decoded, they read "help 72° 112," and were understood to mean that some vessel, presumably a warship, was telling the stricken liner that assistance was coming up from 112 miles away (less than five hours steaming for a cruiser) on a bearing of 72°. That was bad news for Kähler. He fished Deck Machinist Edwin M. Falconar off a raft and then waited until *Britannia* had been evacuated before sinking her. Reluctantly he left the survivors to sail off in their numerous boats, for reasons of his own self-preservation. The people in the boats, he reasoned (and so advised his crew) would be picked up in a few hours. At first, neither he nor his men had many qualms about deserting the British, and those that they did have had to take second place that afternoon when Müller's anxious pals were startled back to general quarters by the sighting of another ship. It was not the British cruiser come to aid *Britannia* as so many feared, and Kähler stopped her with just a shot across the bow. All thirty-one men of the Swedish *Trollenholm,* bound from Newcastle to Port Said with English coal, were taken prisoner and the ship sunk—all within ninety-four minutes.

That should have made the twenty-fifth a day for celebration, but the messes were rather quiet, remembering the burning oil and sharks left above the bubbling, roiled water where *Britannia* had gone down. Thinking it helpful to Berlin's code-breakers, the survivors, and even good for propaganda, Kähler had advised SKL to broadcast that there were some five hundred people adrift and his reasons for leaving them. Nothing was done about the message, however, until April 5 when Dr. Goebbels had more rousing news about the Hilfskreuzer. By then it was too late for those in the boats.

By one count, there were nine boats, some already making sail, and a number of rafts amid the flotsam as *Britannia,* her shrieking siren gurgling a last time in the burning oily sludge, went down almost vertically over her bow. Some boats, like No. 4, were splintered; others, namely port No. 6 and starboard Nos. 1, 3, 5, and 7, were overcrowded. And in them, judging by the reports of those who eventually survived— the only way to arrive at any figures—were at least 317 souls, with another 14 known to have found very temporary security on the slippery gratings of the rafts. How many others there were hanging on to the boats' hard lifelines and seine floats and clinging to boxes, hatch covers, or tabletops—as Lt. A. H. Rowlandson, R.N., did for a while—will never be known. Sharks leave no traces, and the sea wipes out all misery. But there must have been many more, floundering for a while, then hanging limp in the harnesses of their sodden life belts.*

The eighty-two men jammed with standing room only in No. 7, a clinker-built, 28′ x 10′ x 3.9′ boat with a Board of Trade capacity of fifty-six persons, broke down, according to its commander, *Britannia*'s third officer, William MacVicar, into eighteen Europeans, twenty-five Indian passengers, and thirty-nine Goanese and lascar crew. And it was against those men that MacVicar had to take stern measures right from the start. The unruly crew were forced forward; the rank-conscious Indian passengers, who refused to bail or work, were separated amidships by lashed oars to keep them from the Europeans; and the latter retained control of the tiller and the pathetically inadequate provisions. In the four days since the sinking they saw, but were ignored by, three ships, and they were then already vainly trying to beat sanitary measures into the natives, one of whom had urinated on the head of a man bent over bailing.

On that day, the twenty-ninth, only three of the ten men who had joined Lieutenant Commander Rowlandson on a raft and some planks were still alive. One of the dead had been killed by a shark, some had swum away seeking a boat, one fellow "to shore to buy a newspaper." That evening, the remaining survivors were lifted aboard the Spanish *Cabo de Hornos,* which then searched the area to pick up four more men from two rafts, one boat containing seven and another with sixty-five, and so wirelessed to all ships at 2000 asking their assistance.†

---

* Originally, when *Britannia* left Liverpool on a dull, cheerless March 11, there were approximately 327 passengers (R.N., R.A.F., Army, Indians, and twelve women) plus about 200 (mostly natives) crew on board. Quotes and estimates are from correspondence with MacVicar, the company, MacVicar's log for No. 7, a report filed by MacVicar and Sublieutenant L. S. McIntosh, and survivors' accounts such as Frank West, *Lifeboat Number Seven* (London: William Kimber & Co., Ltd., 1960).

† In *Thor,* they heard that message. As a master seaman, professionally concerned, and a human being, Kähler was shocked, surprised that the warship he had presumed coming up had not been able to find the people from *Britannia*

April 4 was another horrible day for the survivors in Lifeboat No. 7, their skins cracked, limbs swollen and covered by salt sores, unable to munch biscuits due to their thirst. MacVicar had taken the natives' knives at great risk, working alone among them, unable to ask for help for fear of losing prestige. He had sent one of them crashing down, eyes protruding, frothing and lips drawn back in a snarl, but all that that professional seaman did note in the boat's log which he kept was, "Natives quarreled badly during the night."

FINISHING HIM OFF

The fourth was also a terrible day, the last for 72 of the 269 British naval personnel manning a thin-stemmed, tall-stacked old 13,245-ton liner that had been employed almost exclusively in cruising before the war and that had just five days previously departed from Trinidad on a patrol. The day was a frightening one, too, for 300-odd officers and ratings in *Thor*. Precisely at 0615, ten minutes after the sun rose over moderate wavelets and scattered whitecaps some nine hundred miles west of the Cape Verdes, the raider's lookout spotted a smoke cloud and under it two masts and one funnel. Kähler, his ship disguised as a Greek, turned toward the vessel and observed that she was making a series of "AAAs" (call to an unknown ship). At 1645 his ensign fluttered out and he gave her a shot across the bow. To his dismay, he instantly recognized her then for an ex-liner with two guns visible on her foredeck alone and therefore unmistakably an AMC, the third he had encountered and apparently attracted like a magnet. "This time," his log predicts, "I have to finish him off."

Koppen-Boehnke's first 5.9-inch salvos smashed the AMC's generator and radio station, and by 1649 his shells had set the old paneling and layered paint amidships of the eighteen-year-old liner into a blazing inferno. *Voltaire* (Capt. J.A.P. Blackburn commanding), without electricity, and only a few of her eight 6-inch and two 3-inch guns firing irregularly, was soon out of control, turning in circles at twelve to thirteen knots, taking on water, the fire raging from her bridge to the mainmast, truly "an Admiralty-made coffin" to her men. By 0715 most of her guns were out of action, the crew of one 6-inch aft turned to ashes. But she was still firing with one gun forward and one aft, the latter led by Blackburn. Kähler's ancient guns seized up again as they had in both previous battles, and he was forced to cease fire and rely on

---

whose radioed position had been off only sixty miles in longitude and even less in latitude.

a torpedo which he intended to fire at 1806. Luckily for all the silent tars crowded onto *Voltaire*'s poop, busy moving the wounded from one side to another to provide them with some shelter, it never came to that. Kähler had seen the white flags they were waving.

Fearing an explosion in the AMC, he lay off four thousand yards to pick up the many men who had jumped and were struggling in the water, but once *Voltaire,* listing badly to port, had slid down by her stern, he spent five hours in rescue work, his men motoring from one clutch of bodies, some dead, some nearly so, and all covered with oil, to save whom they could. Once on board the raider, the survivors' valuables were collected, receipts given, and they were searched. Roger Coward, a radioman who later wrote a book about his experiences, remembers that search well, if only for a happening that now seems far removed from what he had just lived through.* One British lad, Bob Wilton by name, in skivvies like most of them, had his backside padded like the proverbial kid expecting a spanking. Naturally, the Germans wanted to know what he had there. Wilton was determined to protect whatever he had in his pants, the Germans equally insistent on finding out what it could be that the defenseless, nearly naked, and oil-soaked man was defending. After much protesting, Wilton owned up: It was a book—*Principles of Mercantile Law.*

Dr. Jürgen Harms and his assistant, Knorr, soon realized that their hospital was too small and their provisions inadequate to have all the wounded carried to it. Enlisting the help of *Voltaire*'s surgeon, they opted for the torpedo deck, where the survivors were cleansed of the stinging and clinging oil and then treated as necessary. With every second or third *Voltaire* man wounded, forty-two of them seriously, the three professionals and *Thor*'s medics were busy until well into the night. Two men, a cadet and a fireman, could not be saved, and they were committed under their own ensign with *Thor* stopped and both Blackburn and Kähler attending.

Though Kähler could be generous with his time because he knew that the AMC had been unable to wireless, it was fortunate for Blackburn and 196 other officers and men that the Germans did stay around to pick them up, because the Admiralty had no idea of what had happened to *Voltaire*. It was only on the fifth that a foolish and clumsy German communiqué advised them that a raider had sunk both *Britannia* and the AMC, and it took another two days before the Canadian AMC *Prince David* located the wreckage and patches of oil covering an area of three square miles where *Voltaire* had gone down. Still, it had been a risk for the Germans, and Blackburn thanked Kähler, who

* Roger V. Coward, *Sailors in Cages;* London: Macdonald, 1967.

responded by expressing his admiration for the British crew's valiant fight and their subsequent unbowed bearing, an impression that found its way into *Thor*'s log: "As a soldier, I expressed my admiration for the courage and heroism the captain and his men displayed during the fight and later in the water. The behavior of that crew, which faced certain destruction, was truly exemplary."

It had taken 724 rounds, more than half of *Thor*'s total ammunition, to bring them to their knees, and though the raider had suffered no hits other than a severed aerial and superficial damage caused by its own gun blasts, it had been a vicious fight. It showed, Kähler noted, that a raider is always in enemy waters, and that any battle meant risking everything, the operation, the ship, and everyone's life. When he asked Blackburn why he had not been showing his battle flags during the engagement, the tall British captain said that they had meant to raise them, naturally, but that the halyards had been burned through before they could do so.

CALCULATED RISK

Roughly fifteen hundred miles to the southeast of *Voltaire*'s last stand and on the other side of the St. Peter and Paul Rocks, Theodor Detmers, three days a full commander on April 12, was playing an innocent tramp, going through twenty-two course changes in a patient game he finally won by capturing *Nicholas D.L.* and her thirty-eight-man crew. The Greek was the sixth vessel *Kormoran* had been in contact with since taking *Canadolite* on March 25. The first three, met on March 27, had been the German Navy's U-105, U-106, and *Nordmark,* on the last of which the raider unloaded forty-two prisoners; the fourth, merchantman *Rudolf Albrecht,* from whose holds a welcome assortment of vegetables, cigarettes, and newspapers appeared; the last, a Britisher named *Craftsman* ignored the rules on April 9, radioing, stopping, and radioing again (Detmers had both signaled and sent a shot across her bow) with the result that five of her fifty-one-man complement were killed, her captain blinded by sand bagged as protection for the bridge. Having settled with the 8,022-ton ship and the easily fooled Greek, the new Fregatten-kapitän steered south for a talk on the twenty-fourth with *Atlantis'* Rogge, who had just sunk the multi-national *Zamzam,* and had *Alster-ufer* in tow. *Kormoran* was munitioned and relieved of a new batch of seventy-seven prisoners while Detmers consulted with Chief Engineer Stehr about the advisability of sallying forth into the Indian Ocean without a resupply of white metal. He took the risk. During the night of

May 1/2 he rounded the Cape to join *Pinguin, Orion,* and *Komet* in a new theater, and thus left the Atlantic to Rogge and *Thor*'s Captain Kähler.

SECURITY

Kähler, fearing that the disappearance of AMC *Voltaire* and Berlin's premature April 5 announcement of her destruction by a Hilfskreuzer would bring swift retribution, had left the battle waters on April 14 for the northwest to meet tanker *Ill,* to which he handed 170 prisoners along with *Voltaire*'s doctor to take care of those with minor injuries. Two days later, he took his twelfth ship, after indicating to the Swedish ore carrier *Sir Ernest Cassel,* with two warning shots, that he wished her to stop and ordering her captain by loudspeaker not to radio.

Only a week later, his watertight doors shut, flack uncovered, and his men standing heel-to-toe watches, Kähler was pressing for the English Channel. At 0645 April 23 he exchanged recognition signals with a pair of Heinkel 115s and at 0838 did the same with three destroyers of the 5th Flotilla, which would, he hoped, escort him to Germany. Rather it was to Cherbourg that he was ordered due to a severe storm which made it impossible for the requisite number of minesweepers to join him during his transit of the channel. He did not want to go in for fear that *Thor* would be photographed by the British, who would then know that one raider, at least, was no longer haunting the Atlantic. But in he went on April 24 past Fort de Querqueville to drop his starboard anchor at 2055 for the first time in ten months, during which he had steamed nearly 57,000 miles and had accounted for 96,602 tons of shipping.

Disguised as *Sperrbrecher X,* he continued his voyage on the twenty-eighth with a heavy escort of a dozen minesweepers and motor gunboats, and at 1327 of that day he fell in with the real 1,360-ton *Sperrbrecher 60,* which was to guide him into Hamburg. They missed picking up the Elbe pilot and that was unfortunate, because the approaches to Cuxhaven and Hamburg are treacherous, with strong currents and ever-shifting sandbanks. What was worse, though, and what made Kähler's final hours on board a nightmare only a sailor can understand, was their not having been able to keep their charts up to date. It was a black night; the *Sperrbrecher* disappeared, buoys sharply canted with the viscous black current were seen, flashing lights passed with no one able to understand what they marked. To Kähler it was the worst experience he had had during the entire cruise. Later in the day, when the harbor pilot was being picked up at Blankenese just a few miles from Hamburg, the security-conscious captain got a surprise. On the pilot's boat were the families of some of the raider's men, and one lady had come all the way from Bremen for the joyous reunion. At 1700 the last lines were ashore at the Deutsche Werft (which had originally rebuilt *Thor*) shed No. 60, and after a giant *Bierfest* on board, the raider was taken in hand by the yard to be refurbished. Her crew went on leave, and though warned about talking, they soon found out that their return was nearly an open secret despite the security measures taken by the Kriegsmarine to keep everyone guessing about the raiders. (*Atlantis'* owners, for example, were paid for the use of their ship for months after she had been sunk). Everyone, it seemed, knew who they were and naturally that they had sunk *Voltaire* and *Britannia*.[1]

WILL TO LIVE

Only 195 of *Britannia*'s passengers and crew had been accounted for by April 15 when Kähler snared his last victim, *Sir Ernest Cassel*. *Cabo de Hornos* had rescued 77, Shaw Savill's *Raranga* had picked up another 67, and 51 had been found by the 3,100-ton Spanish *Bachi* after having spent only five and a half days in Lifeboat No. 5. And in No. 7, MacVicar penned his second-to-last entry that day: "Considerable excitement at dawn this morning for when breeze came up it brought an 'earthy' land smell and the water appeared dirty shore green and we saw some driftwood. Land was sighted at 1400 . . . unable to land owing to surf. . . ."

Maddeningly close, they watched the long, flat beaches, peered helplessly during the night at a lighthouse flashing two white, one red at fifteen-second intervals. The last of the Europeans to die (five did out of eighteen) did so the next morning, as did two more Indians (forty-four out of sixty-four), only hours before the boats grounded at 1600 "and we all waded ashore. Made camp on beach." Written by a man whose badly injured foot had turned gangrenous, MacVicar tells only a very small part of the ordeal during which he estimated his position to within 120 miles after twenty-three days and navigated some 1,500 miles without any instruments except a compass that was off by twenty degrees. Nor does it say what they suffered; the stench of excrement in the bilges, where some of them appear to have drowned; the horror of bodies bumping alongside the boat when it was becalmed and unable to sail. Nor does it say that for every man dead there was more room, more buoyancy, more rations. When he stumbled ashore near Curupu Island and not far from São Luís, Brazil, the grand total of those who came

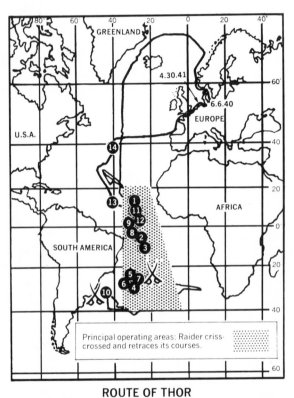

ROUTE OF THOR

1. KERTOSONO	7.01.40
2. DELAMBRE	7.07.40
3. BRUGES	7.09.40
4. GRACEFIELD	7.14.40
5. WENDOVER	7.16.40
6. TELA	7.17.40
7. Fight with H.M.S. AMC ALCANTARA	7.28.40
8. KOSMOS	9.26.40
9. NATIA	10.08.40
10. Fight with H.M.S. AMC CARNARVON CASTLE	12.05.40
11. TROLLENHOLM	3.25.41
12. BRITANNIA	3.25.41
13. Fight with H.M.S. AMC VOLTAIRE	4.04.41
14. SIR ERNEST CASSEL	4.16.41

through *Britannia*'s battle alive was 331. Of the 153 Europeans known to have gotten into boats or on rafts, 81 percent came through, but only a third of the Indians had the strength to survive. MacVicar and—thanks to him—his boat's crew did, too.

Notes

1. Seaman Kähler, much to his disappointment, did not enjoy another shipboard command. Working in Berlin, he made rear admiral in 1943. His naval career ended September 1944 in the vicious fighting and final capitulation of Brest where he was Naval Commandant Brittany. Quickly back on his feet after the war as a shipping consultant, he married the gracious widow of General Admiral von Friedeburg who had committed suicide after signing the surrender instrument in the schoolhouse at Reims. He died, age 73, shortly before a planned trip to England, where he was to visit former prisoners. His gravestone in Kiel reflects what he considered most important in life: "Kommandant Hilfskreuzer THOR," the chiseled inscription reads.

CHAPTER 9

Decline in the Outer Oceans, 1941

Whether immediately *in extremis* like MacVicar in the Atlantic or not, the moral fiber of Germany's raider captains was being severely tested those days in good times and bad. The good, of course, meant captures or sinkings, but there were only eight of those during the first six-month period of 1941, and these were spread out as widely as the positions where they took place in the outer oceans. Just eight ships to be chalked up to five raiders: a paltry bag for 182 days of steaming.*

But though the tonnage figures did not add up to much more than 42,000, the dearth of shipping available for destruction showed that Berlin's strategic aims had at least partially been met. The raiders' previous go at disruption of the Allies' sea lanes had forced the latter to reroute or convoy their traffic and that meant hundreds of extra days en route for the heavily laden freighters and tankers, whose precious cargoes were delayed by that many days and whose masters could thus only make perhaps half as many voyages as they could have if the seas had been safe. The fewer passages, the less food, steel, oil, men, and machines of war for the hotly disputed Mediterranean and the embattled home islands of Great Britain.

The poor hunting was to be the biggest drag for Weyher and his men, who had taken to calling themselves "overseas transport workers" for the endless labors endured in reprovisioning their floating sauna *Orion* and keeping her engines turning over. Weyher had been forced, by Eyssen's operation off Nauru, to move to crater-formed Maug, and there, from January 12 to February 5, he brooded in the wind-still heat and clouds of mosquitoes with *Ole Jacob,* repairing defects and hustling supplies from *Regensburg* and *Münsterland,* which brought him a

* *Atlantis* accounted for three; *Pinguin,* three; *Kormoran,* two. In the Atlantic the tally was far more impressive—eighteen ships and eleven whale catchers—with three ships credited to *Atlantis;* eight to *Kormoran;* three and the eleven catchers to *Pinguin.*

sturdy Nakajima 90-11 seaplane that was to prove far better suited to conditions met than its German-built counterparts.

Weyher's orders were for the Indian Ocean, which, much to his distaste, he would have to share with three other raiders after mid-March. To get there, he plotted a course through the Coral and Tasman seas, round Australia along 30°S, hoping to pick up a ship or two on the way. There were none. Worse still, *Orion* and *Ole* were overflown and circled February 16 not far from Bougainville by an R.A.A.F. Short Sunderland, which was thought to have reported them. The sighting forced Weyher off course and far to the east and it created new hardships for the crew, who had to remain below in the steaming holds for fear they might be caught on deck by another aircraft. At last, on March 20–21, *Orion* reached her station in the Indian Ocean 9,700 miles from Maug, fueled again from *Ole,* and sent her off to point "Theodor" (26°S, 80°E), where it was to meet *Schiff 45.*

ADMIRAL BYRD CALLING

Having left the burning Nauru behind at the end of 1940, *Komet*'s Admiral Eyssen had roamed the farthest south (72°36′S) of any raider, well below the Antarctic Circle among the bergs near Cape Adare and Scott Island, in the hopes of tackling some Allied whalers. No luck; all his somewhat surprising detour netted him was a friendly exchange of some German wine for whale meat and acetylene gas from the Japanese factory ship *Nisshin Maru* on February 22. Disappointed—the only English transmissions heard were those presumed to be emanating from an Admiral Richard E. Byrd expedition—Eyssen headed for the bleak Kerguelens, where he anchored March 7 and spent the next three days exploring the deserted settlement Jeanne d'Arc, Accessible Bay, and Foundry Branch. On the eleventh *Komet* stood out for a meeting with *Pinguin* and *Alstertor.*

MATTER OF LUCK

Pinguin had parted company with *Kormoran* in the South Atlantic on February 26 and had then rounded the Cape into the Indian Ocean, to catch up with *Alstertor* and Hemmer's tiny command, the whaler *Adjutant.* Raiders *Komet* and *Pinguin* and the *Alstertor* met at 1050 on March 12, some 120 miles east of the treeless Kerguelens, while Hemmer proceeded independently to sound the entrances of the various bays so that Krüder could avoid a grounding such as the one that nearly wrecked *Atlantis*. *Komet* left on March 14 for a rendezvous with *Ole Jacob*, and subsequent operations south of 20°S and east of 80°E in the area adjacent to that of *Orion*.

Krüder, for his part, remained in *Atlantis'* Gazelle Bay for eleven days, during which he kept his men refurbishing, painting ship with their oxtail-sized brushes, and hauling largely ruined provisions from *Alstertor*. Fitters and welders prepared *Adjutant* for an intended mine-laying mission (at Karachi), and since *Pinguin*'s hoses could not stretch all the way to the waterfall (as had *Atlantis'*), the ship's boats were scrubbed out to turn them into carriers capable of returning with some 150 to 200 tons of water per day. On the twenty-fifth Krüder released *Alstertor* to "George" (23°S, 80°E), where she was to supply *Orion* and receive oil from *Ole*. He himself took *Pinguin* (now disguised as Norway's *Tamerlane*) out in company with *Adjutant* for a rendezvous with *Atlantis'* prize *Ketty Brövig*.

What Krüder did not know was that *Ketty* had already been sunk on March 4 near the Saya de Malha Bank, under suspicious circumstances and not far from where the Italian *Ramb I* had been destroyed. He waited for her in vain, chancing instead on April 4 on *Ole*, which had just oiled *Komet* and which was herself expecting *Ketty*. Krüder, taking the possible loss of *Ketty* into account, topped off from *Ole* (ordered back to "George" for *Orion*) and then headed for a short search of shipping near the Malha Bank, where, after April 23, he stood to the north to crisscross the Mozambique track.

April 24 was very nearly disastrous for *Pinguin*. Hemmer, in *Adjutant,* was rolling along in the swells of his own search sector to the north of Mahé Island, when suddenly a large steamer was sighted, already fully above the horizon only ten miles away and on a reciprocal course. *Adjutant*'s lookouts had failed for once, and all Hemmer could do was turn away. "What in hell," he worried, "would a British captain think on seeing a whaler in that part of the Indian Ocean?" He reported the course and speed of the ship to Krüder, then hung on just below the horizon, thinking himself out of sight. *Pinguin* did not appear until 0200 the next morning, and at 0515 she fired the first and only salvo, cutting *Empire Light*'s mast and antenna, and crippling the British vessel's steering. At 0600 Krüder signaled to his whaler: *"Adjutant* has carried out its job superbly. Success á conto [sic] *Adjutant."* Hemmer "burst with pride" until he motored over to the raider to discuss future operations with Krüder's alter ego, Michaelsen. The navigator casually mentioned that the British captain who had been captured with his seventy-man crew had seen the whaler, and had debated all day whether or not he should report it by radio. "Krüder," Hemmer remembers, "did not add a word; that was his way; but it had all been just a matter of luck, not success."

The Kapitän zur See was at the time being most stubborn, desirous of capturing a tanker to be used, as had *Storstad,* as an auxiliary minelayer in an operation planned for Bombay. Since he had been unable to employ the lost *Ketty* for that purpose, he had requested *Ole.* SKL said no (the ship was needed to keep *Orion* going); it was up to him to find his own tanker. On the twenty-eighth, three ships were sighted, and the last unfortunate one, *Clan Buchanan,* was attacked next morning. Her first officer, S. S. Davison, reported to his company from Durban three months later that he had had the watch at 0515 that morning but had seen nothing, only the flash of guns whose second salvo hurled the 7,266-ton liner's 4.7-inch gun into the engine room. Some attempt was made to destroy codes and mail, but *Adjutant* managed to fish several sacks containing codes, mail, and the war diary of His Majesty's cruiser *Hawkins* out of the water.

"GO TO VIOLET"

But everyone can make wrong assumptions. The Germans sank the crippled ship early on April 28 some three hundred miles north of the Malha Bank, took its 110 men prisoner, and then continued on with their search for a tanker as if nothing at all had happened. Krüder's radio officer, Charlie Brunke, was quite certain that *Clan Buchanan*'s call had not been received by any station. Unapprehensive, Krüder asked SKL to order *Alstertor* to "Veilchen" ("Violet," 14°S, 73°E) to receive prisoners, and was informed that the supply ship would be there on May 8. With quite a few days left before the meet, he decided to cover the Persian Gulf–Mozambique track for a likely tanker, and he gave Hemmer some explicit orders before doing so. Just suppose, he reasoned, that *Clan Buchanan*'s signal had been heard and properly evaluated. Well, to be safe, *Adjutant* was to steam for Veilchen independently at the slightest indication that the Royal Navy had been aroused. That precaution arranged, he left the whaler to press into the lion's mouth between five major enemy bases. At 2030 on April 29 the salt-encrusted and not-so-military gang in *Adjutant* received a signal from *Pinguin:* "Go to Veilchen."

Clan Buchanan's terse message had been heard by two British stations, contrary to what Brunke had thought, and the lion was moving to shut its jaws. Urgent signals passed between Royal Navy bases, and the Admiral in command of the East Indies Station ordered the New Zealand light cruiser *Leander* out from Colombo and "Force V"—His Majesty's heavy cruiser *Cornwall,* light cruiser *Hawkins,* and carrier *Eagle*—from Mombasay.

Adjutant escaped the net while her men, in bathing suits, fished for sharks and waited at Veilchen for *Alstertor,* which duly arrived on May 8. Hemmer's boss, still obsessed with his tanker-minelayer plan, eluded the British, too, but following his belief that it was safest where the enemy least expected you, he had headed northwest and still farther into danger, closer to Africa and Aden, farther away from the wide-open seas and cooler breezes that might at least have made living more bearable. On the seventh he fell in with the tiny (3,663-ton) tanker *British Emperor* three hundred miles southeast of Socotra. It was to be a melancholy encounter for the crews of both vessels.

Krüder tackled *British Emperor,* which he had been shadowing, at dawn on May 7, planning to silence and take her intact. He could not. Though quickly aflame and going down, the tanker managed a wireless "QQQQ de *British Emperor* 0830N 5625E." Loud and clear, it was intercepted not only far across the globe in Germany but also close-by where it mattered most and where reaction was immediate.

One recipient of the alarm was Capt. P.C.W. Manwaring then steaming some five hundred miles to the south in H.M.S. *Cornwall.* Manwaring bent on twenty knots, then twenty-five, to cover the gap between the Seychelles and Chagos Archipelago with his planes. At Colombo they picked up the message, too, and the station ordered heavy cruiser *Liverpool* and light cruiser *Glasgow* into the hunt from the north while AMC *Hector* was directed to cover shipping. *Leander,* which had left Colombo for Suez with Anzac replacements for the hard-pressed Middle East Command on May 6, was told to turn her charges over to H.M.A.S. *Canberra* to join the chase.

"GONE IN FIVE SECONDS"

Pinguin's lookouts spotted a shadow at 0330 on May 8. Once again, good training and Zeiss glasses had paid off. It was *Cornwall* they had seen off their starboard bow silhouetted against a setting moon. At daybreak the seas were calm, the horizon clear. By that time Manwaring had flown off both his stubby, biwinged seaplanes, and at 0707 one of them sighted *Tamerlane,* ex-*Pinguin,* only some sixty-five miles from the cruiser. The plane was seen on the raider, too, but neither Krüder nor the pilot took any action. With a plane overhead, it would not have mattered which way the former turned, but the man at the controls of the aircraft could have spared *Cornwall* an hour's steaming in the wrong direction if he had reported by radio before landing at 0800. As it was, Manwaring did not recover both planes until 0825 and it was only then that he bore off sharply in pursuit of the sighted ship. He had not yet brought all his boilers to immediate notice when he received the pilot's report and he did not notify the Admiralty of the sighting. His failure to do so was criticized by London and attributed to excessive concern "with the possibility of her wireless being intercepted." Since London could have advised him that there were no friendly merchant ships in the area, Manwaring's omission also caused him unnecessary anxiety later in the day.

At 1015 he catapulted another plane which flew over the raider. The ship seemed innocent enough, was flying the Norwegian flag and signal flags that showed her to be *Tamerlane,* which she certainly resembled. Krüder had decided there was nothing for it but to brazen it out, then fight if he must—even with 130 mines still on board. When the plane returned to the cruiser with the information, *Cornwall* stepped up her speed to twenty-six knots, then twenty-eight, and at 1345 she again launched one of the aircraft to keep in touch with the stranger. At 1530 *Cornwall's* tars went to battle stations. *Tamerlane* came into sight at 1607. When challenged, Krüder had a raider report flashed out over a captured British merchant ship radio set just as any Allied ship might. Twice Manwaring, still not certain he did not have a genuine Norwegian under his guns, challenged, and twice he fired warning shots. With the second, and when *Cornwall* was 10,500 yards away, *Pinguin* turned to port, hoisted her ensign, unmasked her guns, and opened fire, quickly straddling the cruiser with 5.9-inch shells. Manwaring could not respond immediately because the training circuits of his 8-inch turrets had failed. By the time the four forward guns of "A" and "B" turrets had been brought under manual control, *Cornwall's* steering system was disabled by a hit, and for some minutes, until the controls aft could be cut in, the cruiser was unmanageable. By 1718 all of the three-stacker's four turrets were in action, but because she was taking hits and splinters from near misses she opened the range. Krüder let go two torpedoes with his ancient brass tubes but they missed, and at 1726 the raider shuddered under a four-gun salvo, one of whose shells struck forward, another under the bridge, and a third in the engine room. The fourth detonated her mines in an awesome explosion that tore her to fragments and sent a cloud of smoke thousands of feet into the air.

Clan Buchanan's men had been told that morning, First Officer Davison says, that the prisoners would be permitted to stay in an alleyway on deck to allow them to escape if anything serious happened. During the afternoon, there was "great activity" topsides and the guns opened up over the prisoners' deck, shooting for about ten minutes. Then a "terrific blast swept all in our cell off their feet and hurled them into a corner." When Davison came to, he found the cell door open— A German officer had unlocked it, he heard later—and they rushed up to the shelter deck to look out through the open gunports. The Germans, who seemed well organized, showed no panic. But there was no time to launch any boats. Davison saw that half of the ship was already underwater, and as she heeled to starboard, sliding under over her stern, he jumped. When he surfaced, *Pinguin*'s bow was up in the air. "She was gone in five seconds."

The few Germans, British, and a handful of Indians who had not been killed paddled in pools of oil, clinging to a shattered raft, some beams, pieces of furniture, counting their numbers, anxiously waiting for someone to pick them up. An hour and a half they hung on, some despairing, others reassuring and convinced that the cruiser would come back. She took so long, Davison thought, for fear that *Pinguin* had dropped mines. The Germans, knowing they had not, feared the worst, but the real trouble lay in *Cornwall*'s engine room. Electric power had failed, the fans had stopped, and the temperature below rose to two hundred degrees, causing the death of one officer from heat stroke and the abandonment of the engineering spaces.

When she reappeared, the survivors were hoisted aboard for medical attention, a wash, and cigarettes. There were not many to care for, though, for not all the prisoners had been as lucky as Davison and *Clan Buchanan*'s crew, of whom only eight Europeans and five natives were saved. Krüder, seeing the hopelessness of further resistance against the heavy cruiser, had, by one account, just ordered the prisoners freed and his ship scuttled when the explosion tore him to pieces. As a result, only some 22 of the 225 men taken with the last three of thirty-two ships captured, sunk, or mined, had come out of the calamity alive. Of the Germans, only Dr. Hasselmann, Dr. Roll, one prize officer, and 57 ratings survived. Krüder, 18 officers, and 323 enlisted men perished.

The action was a singular success of the Royal Navy, and it provided the Allies with strategic and tactical lessons. It was obvious that a raider was difficult to corner and that once snared he would be hard to unmask. In part to facilitate that work Whitehall was fashioning—and would have completed by May 1943—a complex, worldwide "check-mate" system under which the name and location of any Allied vessel could be determined at any time. The close-in tactics bore scrutiny, too, for it was manifest that such a German fighting machine could prove hard to handle once it had shed its mask of innocence. Extreme

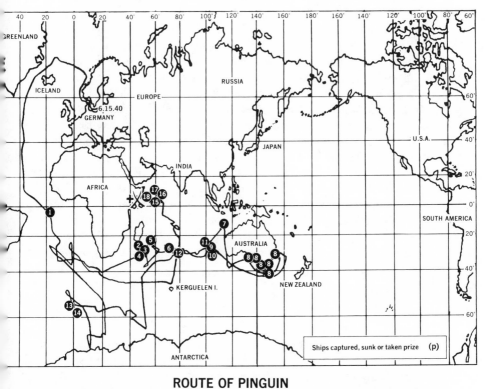

ROUTE OF PINGUIN

caution was the only answer. But not all aspects of the battle with *Pinguin* were to filter through to be properly evaluated and digested by all the white ensign's commanders. Had they, the Royal Navy could have avoided a disaster later in the year.

The Kriegsmarine surmised what had happened the moment *"Tamerlane's"* message was intercepted, and their fears did not lack confirmation for long. On May 9 the Admiralty announced the sinking of a commerce raider in the Indian Ocean, and the press the world over picked up the story, some, like the New York *Mirror* mistaking the 8,000-ton *Pinguin* for the 22,000-ton Hamburg-Amerika liner *Hansa* (which was in Germany for all neutral correspondents to see), others sagely pronouncing that "the problem of catching and sinking these potential dangers to ships operating on routes to Britain is being solved." To the Germans, the gratuitous broadcast came as a surprise. Why, Weyher, for one, wondered, would the British disclose a secret that might have kept SKL and its raiders waiting anxiously for days, impotent in their ability to make plans? Was it bluster like Berlin's, lack of other good news to spot in communiqués, intention, or innocence?

To Hemmer, waiting at Veilchen, it was just very sad. He called his crew together and with "three hurrahs and the record 'Good-bye, Johnny' we said adieu to our comrades." He soon had other things than his friends of 328 days at sea to worry about. Namely his future. SKL had ordered *Kormoran,* which had left the Atlantic after her meet with *Atlantis* on April 20 to rendezvous with *Alstertor* and *Adjutant,* to service the latter and either take her over as an escort or send her on to *Schiff 45.*

STANDING FROM UNDER

Detmers had entered the Indian Ocean complaining of a lack of vitamins. The only fresh vegetables he had left were onions; served with practically every meal in any manner conceivable, they made his ship "stink like the Balkans." *Kormoran* arrived at Veilchen on May 14 to inform Hemmer that she had no need for a "second eye" and that *Adjutant* was therefore to be subordinated to Eyssen, whom Hemmer had met at the Kerguelens and for whom he had little use. Detmers refueled the whaler and *Alstertor,* noting that that was really not the proper job for a raider, then sent the former off to *Schiff 45* and the latter home on the fifteenth.*

---

* His signal to that effect was to cause serious consequences for *Orion.* *Alstertor* was one of the supply ships intercepted by the British in the Atlantic

As ordered, Hemmer steamed reluctantly toward the middle of the Indian Ocean (90°11′E, 25°53′S) to meet *Komet,* which had had no luck since she had left *Pinguin* in March and had accomplished nothing since her Nauru shoot in December. She had fueled from *Ole Jacob* on March 24 and was, by late May, prepared to leave for the Pacific again. Delayed by heavy seas and worried that he might run out of oil, Hemmer arrived for the meet early on May 21, a day or so later than Eyssen had expected him. Hemmer, pleased to have made it, signaled "K to K" (commander to commander), he says, respectfully reporting his arrival. Eyssen replied, "Your report to read 'K to A' (commander to admiral). Where have you been so long? Come alongside immediately." To the youthful skipper of *Adjutant* that was a psychological blow, though most likely it was not intended as such. Eyssen's log simply says, "welcomed *Adjutant,* ordered him to come alongside to starboard."

ROACHES AND THE ROYAL NAVY

Following the release of *Ole Jacob* on March 21, *Orion* covered thousands of miles of the southwestern Indian Ocean east of Madagascar to no avail. On April 10 she joined *Ole* again and *Alstertor,* then cruised fruitlessly until the twenty-fifth, when the supply ship was released for Bordeaux (she was recalled three days later to take *Pinguin*'s prisoners; see p. 161). There were no enemy ships; only neutrals. There was not even much opportunity for sport, Weyher recalls; "the men were always working and unless you call running up to the bridge and wandering back and forth there a professional sport, I did not engage in any either."

> Sunday 30.3: Coffee, cakes; fruit soup, Rouladen, creamed potatoes, mixed vegetables, pudding with sauces; boiled ham, sausage, butter, bread, coffee.

Their menus read well, but the potatoes smelled musty and tasted bad; the butter was rancid; the vegetables, unless canned, were as tasteless as the milk. The frozen meat had hung too long and no one liked the mutton; all pastries, noodles, etc., contained cockroaches and these ringed a finicky man's plate after lunch. To top it all off, it became

---

after the *Bismarck* was sunk. She was scuttled when caught by aircraft and a destroyer on June 23.

known that the cooks had accidentally dumped a whole litter of young rats which were nested in some dried fruit into a kettle and steamed them until they were quite delicate.

The mail brought by *Alstertor,* too, was somewhat of a disappointment. Only four of the fifty-eight bags contained news from home; the rest, all addressed to Navy Post Office Number M 11809, contained among even less interesting material pen-pal letters from Bund Deutscher Mädchen (Hitler Youth Girls) anxious to be pleasant to some soldier of the Reich. No, it was not all a great adventure, and Weyher, who could indeed be patient, was right in crawling around the ship, stopping in spaces the skipper was not ordinarily expected to visit, to chat, listen, and give some cheer. As a result, and due to von Blanc's "exemplary management," Captain's Mast was held only three times during the entire cruise, and generally punishment was light with offenses written into a man's record with a pencil so that they could be erased at a later time.

On May 7 *Orion* topped off her tanks with 970 tons of *Ole*'s oil, giving her a total of 3,855 tons and enough to last her until the beginning of August, by which time she was expected to be in the Atlantic. On the seventh, also, *British Emperor*'s call for help was heard and the following day those of *"Tamerlane,"* which was taken to be another catch of *Schiff 33.* That night a British message indicating *Pinguin* had been sunk was decoded. Quite close to the Seychelles on the seventeenth, *Orion*'s flak crews stood by their weapons while unhappy engineers once again worked on their machinery. The ship's speed dropped from thirteen to ten knots, which really was not too bad for that raider, whose skipper cannot remember how many "days and miles we covered at speeds of only four to five knots." Chief Erwin Kolsch reported all clear that evening, and the next day, when *Orion* was 340 miles northeast of the islands, dawned overcast but with a visibility of between twenty and twenty-five miles.

At 0652 the Arado was lowered for one of the eighty-five flights Lt. Klaus von Winterfeld was to make. Just ten minutes after buzzing off, the plane was seen to climb, apparently seeking cloud cover. Weyher, assuming that a ship had been sighted, pressed forward for an interception. At 0802 Winterfeld returned from an unexpected quarter, fired off two red flares (danger), and was hastily hoisted aboard. What he had to say was most alarming: "0744 heavy cruiser approximately 45 miles off bearing 312°. Course 60°, medium speed. Plane probably not seen." A hastily drawn plot showed that *Orion* and what the pilot described as a three-stack cruiser were on a collision course. (The 8-inch-gunned warship was victor-over-*Pinguin Cornwall,* which had sailed from Mauritius on May 17 with H.M.S. *Glasgow* on reports of a radio fix indicating a German unit around two hundred miles from Diego Garcia; the signal had been *Kormoran*'s stating she had released *Alstertor*.) It being a hot Sunday, church service and all that, the only thing Weyher could hope for was that his plane had indeed not been seen and that the British did not have a radar set switched on. Turning away to the southeast, he told Kolsch to open her up. The chief, he noticed, "must have been sitting on the safety valve," for *Orion* trembled and shook, and for once, without breakdown or making smoke, managed a top thirteen knots. And that it did for an hour and a half while the best anyone could do was to appear unconvincingly unconcerned. Lt. v. d. Decken, who had replaced the regular lookout on the forward mast, reported smoke puffs, apparently from three funnels at 1000, then masts. *Orion* quivered, pushing the warm waters aside as if she were doing twenty knots, but everyone tensed for that last minute when the battle flag would be hoisted, the one minute that would tell. Within half an hour the masts and smoke thinned, then just as the last of the latter had hazed out of binoculars and range finders, the ship's alarm sounded "..-. ..-. ..-." signaling an aircraft warning. At that, one of Weyher's reserve officers quietly advised the "old man," "I'm going to lunch. If I have to climb overboard, I might as well have eaten something." He could have done so in good conscience for the reported "plane" was soon seen flapping its wings.

Weyher informed SKL of the incident and was told to quit the hot area for the Atlantic. On the way there, the handy Japanese plane sank, the men had to go without water again for days because of condenser trouble, and the chief brought some bad news to the bridge. The lignum vitae bearings of the stuffing box were wearing out, leaving the propeller shaft flailing around, a danger to the ship. Repairs were urgent, but they could be done only in a dry dock. *Orion* sailed on, tanked for the last time from Steinkrauss' *Ole* and released him June 6 to France, where he safely arrived on July 19. On June 20 Weyher rounded the Cape, steaming against increasingly heavier seas, virtually unable to gain headway and in imminent danger of foundering.

"Q" MESSAGE

While *Orion* was fighting for her life, the clock on the messroom bulkhead of *Schiff 41* was still ticking away. To Detmers, his Gunnery Officer, Lt. Fritz Skeries, and 1st Lt. Joachim von Gösseln it seemed that *Nicholas D.L.,* sunk on April 4 in the South Atlantic, stood for

Nicholas der Letzte (the last). They had not taken a ship since that Greek went down, and though a change from routine, their visit with *Adjutant* and *Alstertor* had not contributed to their score. SKL suggested that *Schiff 41* like *Pinguin* and *Orion,* try the Seychelles area, but Detmers was not about to stick his neck into a noose. He therefore spent a few weeks cruising in a gigantic triangle bounded roughly by 80°E, Ceylon, and the Chagos Archipelago. On June 13, a week before Hitler began his disastrous attack on Russia, an American was sighted and on the fifteenth the raider stalked a vessel which not unreasonably made off in some haste when a faulty valve in *Kormoran*'s bow smoke generators suddenly vented clouds of white smoke.

An attempt to mine Madras fell through on June 24 because of an encounter with a vessel that acted suspiciously like an AMC. Two days later, however, Skeries' guns made short shrift of the old Yugoslav *Velebit,* which had betrayed herself at 0224 that morning with a glimmer of light shining through a poorly blacked-out port. The ship's second officer, who could not read Morse, did not respond to the raider's many, repeated signals, and Detmers consequently had the 4,153-tonner gunned. Twenty-nine 5.9-inch shells were expended over a seven-minute period during which *Velebit* was repeatedly ordered to stop. She did not, and was so quickly engulfed in flames that Detmers did not bother to waste further ammunition on her. He rightly guessed that she would either founder or eventually fetch up on the Andaman Islands, which is what did happen. Only nine of her thirty-four-man crew could be rescued, but a few others were later reported as having reached the islands in their burning hulk.

At 1730 the same day *Velebit* was attacked, an Allied vessel was heard reporting the interception of an incomplete "Q" message stemming from some ship steaming somewhere along the 88°16′E meridian. That signal was from the Australian United Steam Navigation Company's 3,472-ton *Mareeba,* home port Melbourne and at the time en route from Batavia to Colombo with a cargo of sugar. It was Capt. M. B. Skinner's seventh year at sea in two world wars and he was considered a superb seaman. At around 0600 that morning, according to his diary, he had spoken the Australian light cruiser *Sydney.* But neither her proximity nor his wartime experiences stood Skinner in good stead, for he had been so skillfully stalked by Detmers that he had taken no notice of the raider. Startled at 1728 by a ship whose flag hoist was ordering him to stop, Skinner ordered his operator to get off a raider warning. Twelve minutes later, he and his entire crew of forty-seven (one died later in *Kormoran*) went into their boats and captivity. (On July 1, "Force T," composed of carrier *Hermes* and light cruiser *Enterprise,* steamed out of Tricomalee for a search between Sumatra and Ceylon, the area vacated by *Kormoran* just the day before.)

ADJUTANTS

July 1 was a long day as far as Hemmer was concerned. He had been in a pretty bad mood for the forty days since he had joined *Komet* west of Australia, and that was a long time for anyone to have the blues. That day, he was called to Eyssen's quarters and it was not for a commendation. His troubles, it seemed to him, had all started on May 21, when he had come under the admiral's jurisdiction. By June 1, *Komet* was headed back to the Pacific and her skipper intended to employ Hemmer's whaler as a minelayer off New Zealand. Mounts for a 20-mm and a 60-mm cannon were built into the little ship, and its machinery was overhauled by the raider's engineers. *Adjutant*'s crew had been given a few days' rest, but Hemmer complained that his men had poor quarters and that he had to share a cabin with one of *Komet*'s officers. What was worse was that he would no longer be skipper of *Adjutant*. Eyssen had ordered that his own adjutant and mine specialist, Karsten, would take over as captain of the whaler during the proposed operation. Hemmer would go along as navigator. There were other matters, too, that galled the young man, some petty, some not so, but they all seemed important. Hemmer's old crew, subjected to the big-ship discipline of the raider's stiff executive officer Josef Huschenbeth, sought redress in looking down on their new companions as upstarts who had managed to sink or capture only five vessels, two of them jointly with *Orion,* in about the same number of days it had taken their *Pinguin* to strike seventeen big ships and eleven whalers from the Allies' roster.

On June 11, at 0900, Karsten took command of *Adjutant,* hoisting his own pennant with orders to lay ten magnetic mines off both Lyttelton and Wellington, New Zealand. To Karsten, who nicely chose to sleep in the radio shack, leaving the captain's cuddy to Hemmer, the operation was to remain his fondest memory. Not so to some of the more querulous of *Pinguin*'s old crew, one of whom wanted to throw the new skipper overboard, nor Hemmer, who could not reconcile himself to losing his command to an outsider.

Adjutant was in sight of Auckland on the twentieth, Goodly Head light at the northern entrance to Port Lyttelton was seen shining bright and clear. The whaler was prepared for scuttling, just in case, but all of the first ten mines were laid without any interruption. By 0200 the next morning, the little ship was on its way north to enter the strait between

New Zealand's North and South Islands, for a far riskier operation. All navigational aides were again found to be lit as they always had been before the war. At 2100 the Germans had a good fix on Boring Head, and an hour later on Pencarrow Head. Their pennant and war flag ready to be hoisted, they pressed into the narrows at a top fourteen knots, soon found themselves in close proximity to some patrol craft and between the beams of two searchlights. Spoken from shore, they made smoke, laid a double row of mines less than one mile off Pencarrow and approximately the same distance from Palmer Head without arousing any countermeasures. Karsten and Hemmer thought they had been detected but nothing would ever be known about the daring intrusion until more than four years later when the R.N.Z.N. had access to the Kriegsmarine's records. And for all the anxieties the two adjutants went through that night, no ship ever came to grief on the mines, which were exposed to thousands of crossings and routine sweeps but were "probably defective."

By 0130 of the twenty-sixth *Adjutant* was steaming at her best toward the east, but three and a quarter hours later and still only seventy miles from Wellington her engine broke down. Karsten made sail with a tarpaulin which pushed his ship in strong winds at one and a half to two knots, hardly enough for steerage way. Once the engine was patched, the little ship wallowed toward its rendezvous with *Komet* east of Chatham Island, where it finally arrived on July 1. Eyssen, hearing that its machinery had become virtually useless, had everything of value removed from the whaler (Hemmer took the wheel and bell) and then had her scuttled. As she was settling, *Komet*'s gunners pumped a few rounds into her for practice. Hemmer watched sadly and was then called to Eyssen's office to be debriefed.

He was, but only in a sense. Other than the admiral, only Huschenbeth, Chief Engineer W. Alms, and Karsten were there. The admiral was having Hemmer up for a report, which was duly noted in the log: "Ensign Hemmer had unfortunately become rather self-assured by the fine success of *Pinguin* and his independence as commander of *Adjutant* and both he and the whole crew of *Adjutant* believed that they could look down condescendingly and with exaggerated pride on *Komet*!" That attitude would not do, the admiral said, ordering the young officer confined to his quarters for five days. Embarrassed and yet convinced that he as navigator and actual boss of the whaler had assured the success of the mine-laying, Hemmer says he aged considerably during those days—ten, he remembers. On July 3, Eyssen, who was anything but mean, handed out four of the five Iron Crosses First Class allotted to *Komet*. One went to his executive officer, one to Alms, and another to Karsten. One was kept in reserve, and the fourth pinned on Hemmer "in recognition for his earlier activities as a member of *Pinguin*'s crew and subsequent commander of *Adjutant*."

"DIRECTLY FROM KIEL"

By July 1, the jaunty Weyher, captain of *Schiff 36,* was no more lighthearted than the downcast ex-skipper of *Adjutant,* but his mood was governed by an entirely different set of circumstances. Going west in hurricane-force weather, the badly working *Orion* sprang leaks, took rolls of thirty degrees to each side. Camouflage plates were wrenched loose or bashed in. Worst of all, and a near catastrophe for the ship, was the wild pitching, which alternately had the propeller thrashing uselessly in the air or biting deep into the sea. Because of the oscillations of its shaft, the main bearing casings broke from their foundations and had to be wedged down to hold the shaft in place and save the ship, which was close to foundering. Fifteen hundred tons of water ballast were pumped into the holds, to stabilize her. Whether or not it would seemed questionable. Weyher took the risk, he says, against the advice of his most seasoned officers because "the ship was about to go over anyway."

News that Germany had invaded Russia made little impression on many of the men who had been away from home so long that even major events in Europe seemed remote, but Weyher had a good idea what fate was in store for Germany. "Well, Captain," one of his reserve officers who had fought in World War I mumbled, "if we ever come out of this in a draw, we'll have been damned lucky." That, Weyher now says, "was a unanimous impression, but we kept it to ourselves." Besides, they had more immediate matters demanding attention. Weyher had the option of operating in the Atlantic and timing his return to Europe for the new-moon period of late September or of steaming straight for France. He would need oil in either case and more of it if he were to last through September. SKL deemed an earlier breakthrough advisable because of the Royal Navy's post-Bismarck-sortie sinking spree, and it was feared that the German naval dispositions had been compromised with the capture of the papers of one of the supply vessels, *Gedania.* Codes had to be changed and new arrangements made to feed and fuel the raiders.* It was decided to order Weyher to Rogge's *Atlantis,* which could provide him with nine hundred tons of oil and would,

---

* *Orion* was to have oiled from *Egerland.* The tanker was sunk by His Majesty's light cruiser *London* and destroyer *Brilliant* on June 5. SKL substituted *Lothringen,* and then that ship was brought to by aircraft from H.M.S. *Eagle* and the guns of cruiser *Dunedin.*

in turn, be compensated with fuel from *Anneliese Essberger*, which was then, however, still only ten days out from Dairen. But Rogge, as mentioned earlier (p. 109), having no intention of waiting for *Anneliese* to show up—if she were not intercepted—would not give *Orion* more than 581 tons. That meant that Weyher, with only 2,732 tons of oil remaining, could last only until the beginning of September, and from his discussions with Rogge it was clear that he would once again be cruising in an area that had already been "grazed."

The two raiders separated July 7. As to be expected, *Orion*'s lookouts failed to find any new victims in the same square miles of ocean *Atlantis* had just relinquished after sinking five ships. Instead, her engineers had ceaseless trouble: more water had to be pumped aboard and the Arado was smashed during a rough landing. SKL rightly advised Weyher not to engage an enemy unless a favorable outcome could be guaranteed. How one gauged that, they did not say.

These conditions seemed to have been met by 2046 of July 29 when a spread of torpedoes hissed out of her tubes toward a freighter the raider had been following for seven hours. Nothing happened for eight minutes and then *Orion*'s 5.9s cut loose at a range of less than four miles. The other ship radioed "SSS 1646N 3801W *Chaucer* gunned," which indicated that they thought they had been attacked by a sub- marine and that their wireless operator had been given the wrong position. That was indeed what had happened. *Chaucer*'s "sparks" had felt a "sharp thump" against his ship's side at the same time *Orion*'s guns had opened up. He assumed they had been hit by a U-boat, and in his haste to get a message off he grabbed the wrong chit which showed a position 235 miles from the present one. *Chaucer* repeated her message, adding "torpedoed" and at 2059, finally realizing he was not up against a sub, her operator sent out an "RRRR" that apparently was never heard by any other station. The erroneous "SSS," however, much to Weyher's satisfaction, had been relayed by a nearby ship and later by Freetown. Sub warnings, he knew, caused alarm, but were never fol- lowed up by any heavy units that could be dangerous to a raider.

Orion blasted away at the ballasted ship with both her 5.9s and flak. At 2107 *Chaucer*, Capt. Charles Bradley commanding, gamely replied with her 4-inch and 40-mm Bofors, whose shells burst above the raider's deck, showering splinters down on the exposed personnel but inflicting no injuries. The only damage suffered by *Orion* was caused by the concussion and blast of her own guns. Pipes burst, electrical circuits sputtered, the main shaft's gyrations became more irregular, and one of the "sea lords" was left wondering whether he was eligible for the oval, black wound medal third class because a popped rivet had cut his leg.

At 2125 Torpedo Officer Klaus Thomsen sent another spread swishing out of his starboard triple mount. One of the "eels" was seen to hit, and though it did not detonate it was enough to make *Chaucer,* bathed in the inescapable glare of Weyher's searchlight, stop.

What followed was typical of *Orion.* Ordered to lower the starboard motorboat, the sea duty detail reported they could not because the rheostats for the deck winches had fallen out during the engagement. It took eight minutes for the port boat to get under way but then all forty-eight of *Chaucer*'s establishment (thirteen wounded) were made prisoner, just as had Captain Bradley's father by *Möwe* in World War I.

Once more the plane was wrecked and twice more Weyher had to let ships go because of his inadequate speed, and once more, for the twentieth time, the men were put to work on a new disguise—this time the Spanish auxiliary *Contramaestre Casado. Orion,* shaking and groaning at all of her best twelve and a half knots, was heading for the barn, her crew standing watch-on-watch, alert and worried that something might still prevent their homecoming. They were a splendid lot, all of them, Weyher mused, from von Blanc in the wheelhouse to the lad locked down between watertight doors in the constantly flooding shaft tunnel where he was to make sure that the wedges holding the bearings .down were tight. How wildly they had cheered down in the South Atlantic when their captain (who, like all raider commanders, had SKL's permission to intern his ship if need be) told them France it was. And now they were nearly there, savoring the thoughts of home and furlough. Two escorting U-boats, U-75 and U-205, were picked up west of the Azores August 16 and 17 but the former had to drop behind because of engine trouble. Short of oil, Weyher suffered through three "nerve-wracking days" worried whether he could pass east safely into the Bay of Biscay ahead of convoy OG-71. If he could not, he would be in trouble, for the convoy had been attacked by U-boats and there was no telling how much naval activity there would be in its train. They were bad nights, he vividly remembers after thirty years. He just barely made it the night of August 21 but at 0350 the next morning the terrifying alarm "dit dit daah dit" clanged through the ship sending its men to antiaircraft stations. The plane disappeared and the tense sailors stood down. At 0505 the bells rang again. The planes were German Condors. The men stood down again, wishing to get the next few days over with, pack their kit, and walk ashore. At 0553 "dit dit daah dit." Heinkel 115s. Recognition signals were exchanged and one of the fliers blinked "Bravo Tommy from Tommy." He was Klaus Thomsen's brother. By evening four new Narvik Class destroyers took over the escort which they passed on to a minesweeper flotilla the next day. "Where are you from?" queried the flotilla commander. "Directly from Kiel," the last port *Orion* had cleared one and a third years before. Weyher's signal light shutters clattered back. Land was sighted at 0728 that morning and by 1044 the raider was anchored in the dirty brown waters off Royan, where a tug brought out fruit, vegetables, eggs, and most important of all, mail. During the afternoon, while the tough commander conned his ship past good old friends, *Regensburg, Ermland,* and *Ole Jacob,* his white-clad crew gaped at the long-forgotten sights along the shore. Some of them cried. They had sunk 73,477½ tons of shipping (counting the mines off Auckland and credit for half of *Triona* and *Rangitane*), had been away for 510 days, and logged the longest run of all raiders, 127,337 miles. They had not done too much physical damage to the enemy but he would be the first to recognize their achievement. As Roskill records in Britain's official history: *"Orion* was an old ship and, although not a very successful raider, had performed a remarkable feat in maintaining herself in seagoing condition for so long a period away from a proper base."* "I led my ship with common sense and luck, my men with my heart," Weyher, who was deservedly awarded the Ritterkreuz, says. "We did our duty."[1]

HOME TO BERTHA

By the time Weyher had furloughed his crew and finished with all the tiresome paper work attendant to all big business, be it war or martini couchy, Eyssen had managed to show his men and the dissident *Pinguinites* some success. Crawling east, then northeast around Australia and New Zealand after sending Karsten off with *Adjutant,* he celebrated his wedding anniversary on July 23 hoping that he would embrace his wife and two children in a peacetime Germany the next time it came around. Thereafter nothing much happened until *Adjutant* returned and was scuttled. On July 14 he met *Anneliese Essberger* (out of Japan on a blockade running trip to Europe) not far, as distances go in the Pacific, from the Tubuai Islands. She had enough oil—692 tons—to permit his economical raider to operate until January 1942. But the rest of the stuff she brought did not have much value. The twenty-two toothbrushes, thirty-nine combs, and twenty-four garters, for example, were a "joke" if they were seriously intended for a crew of nearly three hundred men who had been at sea for over a year. *Anneliese* was released on the twenty-fifth and Eyssen made off for the Galápagos Islands, where SKL had finally allowed him to operate (they had fretted over United States sensibilities) and where he hoped to snatch away some of the traffic that

---

* *War at Sea.*

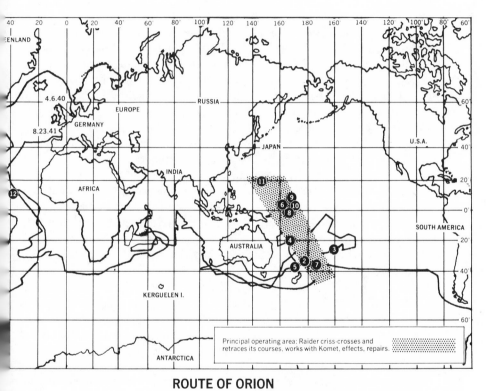

ROUTE OF ORION

	4.24.40	7. RANGITANE (with Komet)	11.27.40
	6.13-6.14.40	8. TRIONA (with Komet)	12.06.40
C SEA	6.19.40	9. TRIADIC (at Nauru)	12.08.40
J	8.16.40	10. TRIASTER (at Nauru)	12.08.40
INA	8.20.40	11. MAUG ISLAND	7.02.41
OOD	10.13.40	12. CHAUCER	7.30.41

had been diverted from the Cape Town to the Panama Canal route. On the way to the land of the giant tortoises he was advised to have his ship home by the end of October so that it could be refurbished for another sortie which was to begin before the long winter nights ended, making a new breakthrough more difficult. Since it was roughly 13,500 miles from the Galápagos to Bordeaux, Eyssen figured he could operate on the Panama-Australia track until the end of August. On the third of that month he told the men: home by Christmas. (See *Komet*'s route, page 244.)

Capt. W. J. Steven, of the 5,019-ton *Australind,* ran unerringly on a collision course into Eyssen's hand and to his death at 1537 on August 14 just south of the Galápagos. He thought he could safely pass the oncoming, small "Japanese" ship port to port and even told his watch officer so. At a bit over five thousand yards Eyssen hoisted his ensign and the black cross and two-balled admiral's standard and then sent a warning shot across the British ship's bow. A second warning shot followed. Steven ordered a radio message gotten out and he sent his gunners to their four-incher on the poop. At some three thousand yards Eyssen fired seven salvos, thirty shells. The second salvo hit, setting the bridge on fire and killing Steven. *Australind*'s radioing stopped and so did the shooting, one minute after it had commenced. Karsten went over to take mail, radios, foodstuffs, tools, and forty-three prisoners (one engineer had suffered Steven's fate and another died in *Komet*) from the flaming ship. Bombs and scuttling charges were set off at hatches 1 through 4 while Karsten rushed from the blazing superstructure just as it collapsed.

August 17 was a Sunday. In ten-year-old *Kota Nopan* the Javanese boys were just going through the alleyways banging gongs to call the crew to the church service Capt. W. J. Hatenboer was going to deliver. But the skipper received a note asking him to come to the bridge. There was a ship dead ahead and she was wearing Japanese colors. The Japanese were, of course, neutrals, but Hatenboer had his orders to be careful. He turned away, making for the shelter of the Galápagos only around forty miles away. The Japanese followed. At 1045 the German war flag replaced the Emperor's meat ball, and canvas covers painted with swastikas dropped down over the neutrality markings on the ship's sides. Black smoke poured from *Kota*'s stack as her engineers went to full ahead. A warning shot. Hatenboer's radioman tapped his keys and Hatenboer himself replied to Eyssen's warning with two 4-inch shells that fell short by some one thousand yards but were good in train. That was too much for the German admiral: *"Feuererlaubnis!"* *Kota*'s secret documents splashed into the sea and she set her Netherlands flag, stopping to lower her boats. Hatenboer, Fourth Officer Siebren Tuinhout, and several others were gathered on the raider's deck. And there they stood, dazed, like cows in small circles, and since the Germans could not get them to line up, they just left them until they were sent shuffling below under the guardianship of ex-North German Lloyd officer Ensign Albert Ulrichsen.

Since *Kota*'s cargo of tin, manganese, gum, and kapok was immensely valuable—United States insurers alone lost an estimated $1 million when she went missing—Eyssen decided to send her home as a prize with twenty-four Germans for whom the Dutch and Javanese would work and by whom they would be paid. Just to make sure some of the cargo got to Europe in case one of the ships was lost or enough fuel could not be found for *Kota,* some of the latter's goods were transferred to the raider. To make room, *Komet*'s men dumped empty barrels and other expendables, including Karsten's 11.5-ton motor mine-layer, into the sea. For two days the reloading job went on until another vessel was sighted in the distance, presumably steaming for New Zealand. *Komet* gathered in her boats and started up her engines, taking twenty-five minutes before she could take up with the gray stranger. By 1655 *Devon* was lying stopped, undamaged and her 144 men (113 Indians), including Capt. R. Redwood, none of whom had paid *Komet* the slightest heed, unhurt. She was scuttled.

A month of uninspiring workaday chores followed. Eyssen needed oil for *Kota* and was advised by SKL that he could rendezvous with his old friend *Münsterland* (out of Yokohama on August 25) not far from where he had met *Anneliese.* A colleague, Rogge, who was then standing east after having captured *Silvaplana,* would be there, too. Some six hundred tons of *Kota*'s cargo were transshipped and electric heaters were built into the Dutch ship's holds for the natives, many of whom were already sick when captured. Foreign radio stations were heard discussing the missing *Australind* and *Kota,* and United States officials seemed upset by their disappearance. Britain warned shipping to stay clear of the Galápagos. Hemmer still harbored grudges and was taken aback by Eyssen's cocktail and dinner parties, not the sort of privilege the other raider captains allowed themselves. Naturally, the list of guests was small, for Eyssen's crew only numbered 270 and most of them were enlisted men.

TICKING CLOCK

With Weyher running for home and *Komet* in the Pacific, *Kormoran* had the Indian Ocean to herself during August. Detmers had been lucky in avoiding H.M.S. *Hermes* and *Enterprise* by the Bay of Bengal, but it seemed that his good fortune was over. Back and forth he went across the equator to the west of the East Indies, south as far as the Australian Sea. He had his bright, colorful Japanese disguise painted over with a drab gray and brown to turn his ship into the Dutch *Straat Malakka,* which she closely resembled. He would be sent to the Pacific, SKL had advised, once he could be relieved in the Indian Ocean, but he did not think it would ever come to that. German ships were having a rough time in the Atlantic and it seemed doubtful that any more raiders could ever be gotten out again. His own lot and that of his crew were getting a bit harder to bear, too: "We lived from one newscast to another . . . nothing but water and sometimes we felt quite useless." It was not until September 23 that he came up with the coal burner *Stamatios G. Embricos,* which was steaming with her lights on because the captain did not wish to be gunned down by a raider. Detmers scuttled the Greek, picked up five men and the captain from one boat. The other, with twenty-four men, vanished in the dark but was discovered the next day by the raider's plane, which was making one of its few flights (seven vs. eighty-five for *Orion*'s).

The Greek had not radioed but when she went overdue at Colombo not many days later, East Indies Station had H.M.A.S. *Australia* out for a long search which took her all the way down to the Kerguelens where the "wallabies" found evidence that the islands had been used by the Germans. It was not much, some brushes, a can of shoe polish, and straw wine-bottle covers. Nor did the Australians have any idea that five German ships had anchored in the various bights. But just to prevent a recurrence, the heavy cruiser dropped a few magnetic mines before steaming off.

By that time, *Kormoran* was west of Australia, and Detmers, somewhat tired of his unrewarding "police" activity, was planning to lay a minefield off Perth. He had rendezvoused with *Orion* and *Komet*'s old supplier *Kulmerland* between October 16 and 25 but could not lay the mines because SKL had advised that a convoy escorted by H.M.S. *Cornwall* would be in the area. On November 19, when *Kormoran* was plowing along on a northerly course roughly two hundred miles west of Sharks Bay and Carnarvon, Australia, two of her roaring diesels on line to generate electricity for the humming motors, her wardroom clock above the eleven neatly painted ships' names that represented 68,285 tons of Allied merchantmen was still ticking. Its hands, moving with the deliberate jerks of all such timepieces, indicated 1515, and all had been well.

ROLLING HOME

That same day, clear across the globe, relatively close to the Azores and Hamburg-bound, *Komet* was making a comfortable eleven knots, pushed along by six-to-seven-knot westerlies and escorted by U-516 and U-652, which had been met during the previous two days. Now disguised as the Portuguese *S. Thome,* she had been a long time and had come a long way since parting from *Atlantis* in the Pacific: Around the Cape, through the November 4 anniversary when Eyssen had been an ensign and his WWI *Karlsruhe* had blown up nearby, and past the Atlantic narrows through which SKL was then funneling five other German ships (prizes *Silvaplana, Kota Nopan,* blockade runners *Odenwald* and *Portland,* and supply ship *Python*)—pressing their luck, the admiral thought with much justification. She had come a long, long way.* Eyssen was pleased by his new disguise—the real *S. Thome* had been heard signaling nearby and her presence would therefore presumably be expected by the Allies—and under normal circumstances he could anticipate being in Hamburg in not too many days.

SECOND TIME OUT

Not even a hundred kilometers from that great city, a tall, good-looking, regular navy captain, standing on *Thor*'s bridge that evening of the nineteenth next to the pilot who was to guide him through the Kiel Canal to Brunsbüttel, was worried about his ship and future. It was obvious to some of his officers and the forty-three other men who had served under Otto Kähler on the raider's first cruise and who had agreed to go again that the vessel was in all respects ready for sea. The shore gang at the Kiel naval base knew it too, for they had all been through the disorderly rhythm of building, training, and provisioning before, and many of them with the same ship. Hardly anyone, not even the Brunsbüttel signal station, the canal lockkeeper, or the teletype operators, believed that Fleet Post Office No. 13395 was just a lowly Sperrbrecher. And since so many authorized or unauthorized personnel were aware of *Schiff 10*'s identity, there was good reason to believe that Lt. Cmdr. Patrick Beesly's Section 19 of His Majesty's Operational Intelligence Centre across the Channel would be in the know, too. The forty-one-year-old Capt. Günther Gumprich, who was to take *Thor* out, was not

---

* *Odenwald* was captured on November 6 by U. S. Task Group 3.6 (light cruiser *Omaha,* destroyer *Somers*) whose ingenious commander claimed he had suspected the German of being a slaver. When Eyssen overheard *Odenwald* reporting her seizure at 01°N, 28°W, he was only 187 miles from the scene.

far from guessing the truth when he penned his doubts about security in his war diary.

His raiding campaign started off with a bang right the next evening at 2139 when *Thor*'s canted bow crunched into the improperly lit Swedish *Bothnia,* which had been anchored in the fairway. The Swede, his foreship opened like a can, and loaded with ore, sank like a rock; no one was hurt but it was back to Kiel and dry-docking for Gumprich, and it would be a long time before he ever reached the Indian Ocean to replace *Kormoran,* which by then needed a replacement.

QUESTION OF SURVIVAL

It was a clear hot day that November 19 and *Kormoran* was rising and falling rhythmically to gentle swells on a course set for twenty degrees. Detmers had left the bridge to join some officers like Joachim von Gösseln, who had just lazed up from a nap, down in the wardroom for a cup of coffee. Shortly before 1600 the bridge messenger appeared to call the captain. Ship in sight, he said, adding that it might be a sailing vessel. Gösseln, who was battle deck officer, gulped his coffee and ran to his cabin for his cap while Detmers bounded up the ladders for the bridge. From there he could not see much more than a slight speck on the horizon. The foretop lookout kept up a running commentary; one sail, he cried out, two sail, several ships, smoke. Detmers did not like it a bit and with a fine feel for the probabilities he ordered general quarters, came to course 260, and rang down to have all engines on line for full ahead. By 1602 the engineers had reported all clear and Detmers was peering through the gunnery glasses to make out the vessel that was taking shape in the flimmering heat on the horizon. It did not take him long to decide that that clear, sunny Wednesday was going to be a big day and, to be realistic, possibly his last. The whitish speck grew quickly, its color turned to gray, and its boxy bridge, tall masts, and even-sized stacks soon developed into a light cruiser of Australia's *Perth* class. Detmers did not give the question of survival any thought; "I just knew that I had to do my best, make every effort to increase our chances."

TOUCHING GROUND

Admiral Eyssen had meanwhile vastly improved his own chances. He sighted German aircraft on November 21 and at 0605 of the twenty-third he was abeam of Cape Ortegal, preparing to disguise his ship as *Sperrbrecher 52*. By 1050 he had air cover and at 0650 of the twenty-fourth he was in the good hands of some German minesweepers. Two days later, his men in life jackets, the flack manned, boats outboard for instant lowering and floats cut loose in case of need, Eyssen stood into Cherbourg, to anchor behind the inner mole. At 0915 of the twenty-seventh his lines were fast at Le Havre's Quai Oblique from which he cast off again eight and a quarter hours later with an escort of six R-boats, five M-boats, and three torpedo boats, which were to prove useful in warding off the Dover coastal forces that engaged the Germans in an inconclusive but noisy action between Boulogne and Dunkirk during the early hours of the twenty-eighth. Eyssen's escort claimed several MTBs damaged, but suffered three dead and eleven wounded in turn. Only one man was hurt in *Komet,* but his slight injury seemed a token of things to come, for his had been the first surface fight for any raider coming from or going to Germany. Eyssen holed up in Dunkirk during that day, then set out for the final lap late that evening in poor visibility. Passing Holland, he let the Dutch prisoners listen to a radio program from their homeland, but Tuinhout remembers it to have been a disappointment. The station was featuring the same woman they had heard when they last left Rotterdam; she was still giving knitting instructions. At 1520 of the twenty-ninth the ship's alarm system broke down and a low-flying Bristol Blenheim managed to surprise the flack crews by dropping four bombs. Three of them splashed into the sea harmlessly but the fourth came down on *Komet*'s bridge deck not three yards from where Lieutenant Hemmer—he had been promoted—was standing watch. He ducked, and the bomb passed through the railing, leaving its tail piece on board. Taking note of the damaged stanchion, Eyssen logged: "I had enormous luck." At 0310 of the thirtieth *Komet* passed *Elbe 1* and at 0715 the ship was anchored off Cuxhaven to send *Tottenham*'s Nolan (he had been transferred from *Atlantis*), Tuinhout, and another 107 of their fellow prisoners ashore to "Sauerkraut's" Marlag and Milag Nord and the Dutch home. At 1117 Eyssen dropped his hook at Brunsbüttel to confer with the once more outbound Gumprich, of *Thor,* and at 1800 that evening he made fast at Hamburg's Schuppe 80, home "in peace" after 515 days of raider warfare. The night proved to be the most moving China-born gunnery officer Karl August Balser had ever experienced. He had the watch and no one was yet allowed ashore. With measured steps he walked down the gangplank in the rain, checked the ship's lines, and then stooped to touch the basalt paving stones, just to feel the land. *Komet*'s crew would get a forty-five day furlough, Eyssen the Ritterkreuz, and the ship, modern though slow thing that she was, would be sent out again. It was clear to the admiral that the work of refurbishing her would take a long time even though only three months had been scheduled. She did not leave until ten months later, and then, it seemed even to die-hard Huschenbeth, it was too late.[2]

THE QUICK AND THE DEAD

Bradley's Head is one of the most prominent landmarks in the lovely harbor of Sydney, Australia. It juts out into Port Jackson from the north and its park is open to all. The people go there weekends to watch the busy shipping and the sailboat races from beneath the conspicuous fighting top of H.M.A.S. *Sydney* installed there to commemorate a World War I action in which the Australian-manned Town class cruiser had pounded Germany's famous *Emden* (see Chapter 1) into a hulk of jagged metal on North Keeling Island. A few steps from the old masts stands a magnificent Port Jackson fig tree dedicated to the 645 officers and men of another H.M.A.S. *Sydney* sunk in another war without trace or survivors.

Sydney had left Freemantle on November 11, 1941, to escort the 6,683-ton coastal steamer *Zeelandia,* packed with troops and bound for Malaya, where the brooding Japanese were expected to create mischief at any moment. On the seventeenth, as expected, she handed her charge over to His Majesty's cruiser *Durban* and two days later signaled to confirm her return for the twentieth. It was the last anyone ever heard of her. On the twenty-first she was overdue but there was no immediate concern. By the twenty-third the worrying and agonizing had started. One day later all of the Commonwealth's high-powered radio stations were ordered to call on her to report. There was no reply. An aerial search from Pearce produced no results nor did another launched by the Royal Netherlands Navy, which had been asked to help. On the evening of the twenty-fourth, the British tanker *Trocas* broke radio silence with some startling news; she had picked up twenty-five German sailors from a rubber raft two hundred miles west of Carnarvon. It was clear from their statements that their ship had been in action with *Sydney.* They did not know what had happened to her, but in all probability the cruiser no longer existed. More air searches were vectored out and Australian naval vessels, the Dutch cruiser *Tromp,* and six merchantmen were directed to the area reported by *Trocas.* On the twenty-fifth the government, without reference to its naval board, ordered its censors to forbid "any reference press or radio, to H.M.A.S. *Sydney.*" That implied a defeat or worse and the rumors that spread rapidly across the land caused a great deal of anguish and disbelief.

The *Sydney* of World War II was completed at Portsmouth on September 24, 1935. She was of 6,830 tons displacement, mounted eight 6-inch guns in twin turrets "A," "B," "X," and "Y," evenly distributed fore and aft; eight 4-inch; and numerous smaller automatic weapons as well as eight 21-inch torpedo tubes. Low-slung and with her funnels nicely spaced amidships, she was a graceful ship, and her complement were proud of her fighting record in the Mediterranean where she had bent on her full 32.5 knots and proudly flew her white ensign in several engagements with the Italians, whose cruiser, *Bartolomeo Colleoni,* she sank. Since February 1941 she had been principally engaged in patrolling and escort duties for the Australia station. On May 15 a new officer had taken command. A professional from the time he entered the naval college in 1913, J. Burnett was the third Australian graduate to be promoted captain (1938). He had done his tours with the "kipper" navy (R.N.) and, being considered an excellent staff officer, had been appointed assistant chief of Naval Staff on his return from Britain in 1939.

Burnett took *Sydney* out from Freemantle on November 11, 1941, with *Zeelandia.* On her return trip eight days later close to tea time, with nightfall due in about three hours, the cruiser was steaming south-southeast some 150 miles southwest of Carnarvon in a gentle southwest swell and at moderate speed. Close to 1600 her lookouts probably sang out: "Ship bearing about 50°, some 12 miles distant." Someone, presumably Burnett, ordered a change of course to west-southwest on a gradually converging course with the stranger most likely thought to be an inbound merchantman.

It was *Kormoran,* and to the Germans in the raider, the Australian's change of course meant only one thing. They had been spotted. Detmers had always known that once stopped by a warship there was nothing left but to fight, and there was nothing he could do then but to stall for the time needed to start his last engagement at the most opportune moment. Disregarding the 360 mines still in the hold, he sent his men to battle stations, had the lookout called down from the masthead and his conspicuous seat lowered. The ship's heading was changed from north-northeast to southwest, stern to the cruiser. At 1628 a cylinder of No. 4 diesel ran hot and had to be blocked off. This reduced *Kormoran*'s speed to fourteen knots, and it took half an hour before the engine could be brought on line again. During that time *Sydney,* overhauling on starboard, flashed a series of "NNJs" to which Detmers had no reply because he did not know what it meant. When the cruiser had come within seven miles, she ordered *Kormoran* to show her call letters. Stall, Detmers said, and his men did a grand job of expertly playing the inexpert merchant signalers. Messages were received but not understood, flag hoists were incomplete, twisted. The whole thing was a mess; and why not? As far as the Allied navies were concerned, it seemed that the only flag hoists most merchantmen knew were "Q" (request free quarantine pratique), "G" (I require a pilot), or "P" (the vessel is about to depart). Detmers showed Dutch colors, and finally his flags fluttered out so that they could be read "PKQI" for *Straat Malakka,* just as she was listed in Lloyd's.

Sydney slowly edged in closer, her turrets and port torpedo tubes trained on the lubbers, her plane warming up on its catapult. At 1700 *Kormoran* broadcast a "QQQQ" in the Dutchman's name. *Sydney* said nothing. She did not use her wireless and apparently made no effort to contact land to establish the *Straat Malakka*'s bona fides. Surprisingly, her secondary armament seemed to be unmanned and some of the crew were seen leaning on the rail gawking. That was as unwise as it was almost suicidal for Burnett to come within less than a mile of a strange ship. "Where bound?" the Australian asked the Germans, who could not believe their enemy's lack of precaution. Batavia, they said, as Greter's torpedomen made the last adjustment to their cumbersome weapons. Over half an hour of creeping uncertainty had passed since the first sighting. *Sydney*'s signalmen hoisted "IK" and once more the Germans, not knowing those were part of *Straat Malakka*'s secret letters, could not reply. Tired of fooling around with the Dutchman, who seemed just as inefficient as other merchantmen were, Burnett flashed in clear asking for the vessel's secret letters. He was right abeam of the German, steaming at the same fourteen to fifteen knots and only a little over sixteen hundred yards away—well within rifle range.

Since Detmers could not answer the last query, up went the German battle flag, down went the disguises, and out came Greter's torpedo tubes and Skeries' 5.9-inchers while the 20 mms rose into position. Within six seconds one ranging shot was on its way. It was short at a bit over fourteen hundred yards. A second was over, but within two more seconds a three-shell salvo smashed into the cruiser's bridge and forward control tower. *Sydney* replied with a full eight-gun salvo but missed. Then, almost instantly, both her "A" and "B" turrets were out of action, her plane blown off the catapult between the funnels by the German 5.9-inch guns, which were turning her into a blazing punctured mass of metal, while the raider's 37 mm concentrated on her bridge and the 20 mms hammered away at anything that moved on deck. Greter got off two torpedoes, one of which missed. The other struck *Sydney* in the vicinity of the forward turret. The cruiser shook under the explosion, its bow dipped down to the base of the jack staff and it lost way. Greter, at his station behind the bridge, had entertained little hope of surviving that unequal encounter. He knew from his experience in cruiser *Leipzig* when it was torpedoed by H.M.S. *Salmon* on December 13, 1940, what an "eel" could do. He did not get any particular kudos for his hit—there was no time for rejoicing—but he and everyone else were mightily pleased by the success, hopeful then that they had a prayer of a chance.

But the fight had not been a one-way affair. *Sydney*'s two after turrets, "X" and "Y," were shooting back, the former registering hits on *Kormoran*'s funnel and engine room, where burning oil squirted out of ruptured lines to set the engineering spaces on fire. The main fire-fighting system was soon punctured and useless and by 1745 the raider's motors were dead as the result of an explosion among the sensitive transformers. Hardly anyone stationed in the burning compartments, and only one man in the glass-enclosed control room, managed to escape.

The crippled *Sydney* had in the meantime turned sharply though cumbersomely toward the raider as if to ram at about 1740, when the top of "B" turret was blown off like a popped plastic toy. She missed, slowly steaming past the raider's stern, all her turrets by then disabled and pointing to leeward. Somehow she got off four torpedoes but they had swirled harmlessly past behind the German. Detmers brought his port guns to bear for the first time and he hoped to follow the Australian to send him down. Just as he was about to, his engines cut out and it soon became evident that they could never be repaired. Greter had another try with a torpedo but it failed to hit, and at 1825, the German guns, having fired some 450 shells, fell silent on a command from the bridge. Immobilized, and unable to get at the raging fires below, Detmers helplessly watched Burnett's command, shattered by some fifty hits and drifting rather than steaming, vanish into the dusk in the direction of Australia. The glare from her fires could be seen until about 2000; after that, nothing.

Unable to comprehend their fortune, knees weak from excitement and exertion, the Germans went about securing their ship and checking the damage. There really was not much that could be done with her. They probably could have somehow subdued the inferno below, say by flooding, but they would never have been able to get the motors going again. Detmers' raider was not a raider anymore; she was ready for a salvage tug but there was no one to whom he could turn for assistance. Besides, the *Sydney* must have reported them and the hunt was most likely already on. Literally a sitting duck, Detmers, though "hardly believing what had happened," was determined not to be taken. He gave "the hardest command" in his life. Scuttle; *"Aussteigen"* (get out).

"THAT'S WAR"

Some of *Kormoran*'s boats were damaged, others stored below out of sight, and since there was no electric power for the winches, two of the big steel boats—one of them Greter's—had to be lifted out of No. 1 hold with block and tackle by hand. By 2100, three boats and a number of rubber rafts had been provisioned, lowered, and manned, but one of the rafts apparently sprang a leak which capsized it, drowning some forty men, mostly wounded. Others like von Gösseln carefully folded their jackets on deck before slipping into the sea. Detmers had kept enough gunners on board to handle four 5.9s just in case the enemy saw his burning ship and decided to investigate, but by 2330 all but the dead— only about twenty men died in the action itself—and those engaged in placing the scuttling charges were off the ship. At 2400, when reports reached him that the mine deck was filling with smoke, Detmers took his flag and climbed down into the last waiting boat. Thirty-five minutes later the mines blew up with a gigantic tongue of flame several hundred feet high and *Kormoran* went down as thousands of metal fragments rained out of the sky.

In the morning Detmers surveyed his new command, which, over-loaded with sixty-two men, was shipping water and had to be bailed continuously. Each man was to get two zwiebacks and a bit of water three times a day while they steered for Australia, many of them certain that *Sydney* had reported them and that they would be rescued soon. Those in the rubber boats had no other hope; they could not sail, only drift. But even sailing a boat was difficult, Detmers found, because the slightest heeling forced the overloaded boat's gunwales underwater. By then, there were 317 Germans and three of *Eurylochus*' Chinese who had signed on as laundrymen, adrift in five boats and two rafts and most of those were overcrowded, meaning standing room only for some and short rations for all.

The beautiful *Aquitania,* last of the giant four-stackers of an earlier era, was on her way from Singapore to Australia on November 24, trooping for the second time in her twenty-seven-year career. At 0830 that day west of Carnarvon, she stopped her quadruple screws to pick up twenty-six men from a rubber raft. The thankful survivors were German navy, who said they had been in a fight with a cruiser, but *Aquitania*'s captain, assuming that the latter would have reported the action herself, kept radio silence and continued on toward Sydney, where he informed the signal station at Wilson's Promontory of the odd incident at 1320 of the twenty-seventh. *Trocas,* which, as mentioned, picked up twenty-five of Detmers' men a few hours after *Aquitania*

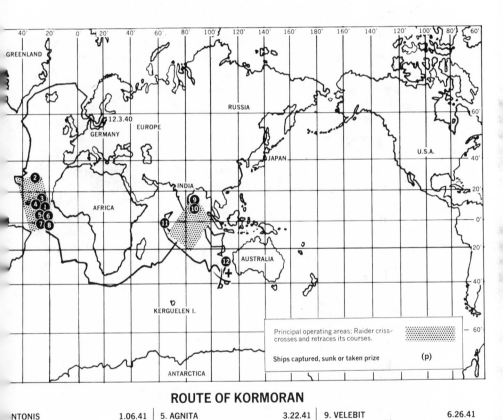

ROUTE OF KORMORAN

NTONIS	1.06.41	5. AGNITA	3.22.41	9. VELEBIT	6.26.41
RITISH UNION	1.18.41	6. CANADOLITE (p)	3.25.41	10. MAREEBA	6.26.41
FRIC STAR	1.29.41	7. CRAFTSMAN	4.09.41	11. STAMATIOS G. EMBIRICOS	9.24.41
URYLOCHUS	1.29.41	8. NICOLAOS D.L.	4.12.41	12. H.M.A.S. SYDNEY and KORMORAN SINK ✛	11.19.41

made her rescue, did announce her find and thus, by pinpointing the location of the survivors, undoubtedly saved seventy-three more Germans. Those men were fished out of a boat on the twenty-seventh by one of the four auxiliaries, the 990-ton *Yandra,* which had been sent out from Freemantle to search for *Sydney.* One boat with fifty-seven men, their feet swollen, backs burned, and some close to insanity, alternately standing or sitting for lack of room, fetched up about seventy-five miles north of Carnarvon on the twenty-fifth, and another with forty-six men landed nearby. Still another thirty-one survivors were taken from the sea by the 4,372-ton government motor ship *Koolinda.*

Detmers, with a lot of others as uncomfortable as he, chewing on buttons to keep themselves occupied and to relieve their thirst, was one of the last to make it in. They celebrated a mate's birthday on the twenty-fourth with two bottles of beer which the man himself had remembered to take along, and Detmers noted with pride that discipline was so good that much of the beer had been left for the birthday child after all sixty-two of them had taken a sip. On the twenty-fifth they saw a plane that was obviously investigating another boat over the horizon, and on the next day yet another plane, which also failed to spot them, was seen. Toward evening Detmers attracted the attention of the 3,222-ton Holt (Ocean Steam Ship Company) freighter *Centaur* with two star shells and soon found himself alongside with tea, bread, butter, and marmalade being lowered down to his boat. But their wary rescuer, Capt. W. F. Dark, whose "armoury was small," was not going to let more than nine of the sick or injured and a Chinaman on board. He would tow them at five knots. Pretty soon, Detmers remembers, they were going at seven knots, and early the next day the boat cut under, swamping everyone as it sank, until it came to rest on its flotation chambers. They cut the painter and waited until the steamer returned. They were then transferred to two of *Centaur*'s boats and by evening of the twenty-eighth were in port, down in the freighter's No. 1 hold, eating goulash and smoking, quite ready to turn in on some cots. The next morning an Australian commander called Detmers and his executive officer, Kurt Foerster, out. Did they know anything about *Sydney?* Why? Well, she was missing. Surprised, though rather elated at their success, Detmers told the man that he had been in action with a cruiser. Then he gave the R.A.N. his last position, hoping that a search. for the Australian ship might find some of his own men.

Though they had suspected as much, this confirmation that *Sydney* was gone, came as a terrible shock to the Australians. On November 30 Prime Minister John Curtin announced the sad news publicly, and then the questions and recriminations started pouring in from all quarters. How could a fast, well-armed, and armored cruiser, manned by experienced men and a competent skipper, be sunk by a mere armed merchant raider? *Thor*'s actions with *Alcantara, Carnarvon Castle,* and *Voltaire* had proven that those German vessels were dangerous adversaries and that it was difficult to identify the well-disguised ships. It was evident that *Leander* might have taken a hiding in February of the year if *Ramb I* had been better armed and a German rather than Italian, the Aussies noted, and that *Cornwall* had been hit by *Pinguin* in May. It was also true that *Neptune* could have been damaged by the Q boat she had stopped off Sierra Leone in January 1940, but that incident had never been widely disseminated through the fleet because of the secrecy surrounding those operations. And it was just possible that Burnett had taken a slight rebuke aimed at Captain H. B. Farncomb, of *Canberra,* by Adm. Ralph Leatham, commander in chief East Indies, to heart. The admiral had noted that Farncomb's expenditure of 215 rounds of 8-inch at a range of nineteen thousand yards in his encounter with *Ketty Brövig* and *Coburg* seemed "overcautious." Whatever the reasons for Burnett's carelessness, it had been, as the British history states, "courting disaster." It had been, and the only remnant ever found of *Sydney* was a shell-splintered Carley float that now rests in the lower gallery of the handsome Hawkesbury River sandstone Australian War Memorial Building at Canberra.

Unperturbed by the whys and wherefores, many of them posed by men without any knowledge of naval warfare, Detmers, who had had to fight the man, had a far more generous explanation for Burnett's disaster: "Just imagine yourself a cruiser captain. You have treated every one of the hundreds of ships encountered with the same precautions, and each one of them had turned out to be a harmless steamer. One moment of relaxation or carelessness, and then it's happened. That's war." To official investigators who, in trying to place the blame for the cruiser's loss, asked whether he would have acted as recklessly as Burnett, Detmers gallantly shrugged. "No," he thought silently, "but I was not about to denigrate a colleague, especially not one who had died in a horrible action."[3]

ONLY ONE WAY OUT

On the afternoon of the day the Australians announced *Sydney*'s loss, Captain Gumprich, still exasperated by the slow work done in the Kiel yards where *Thor*'s damaged bow had been repaired, conferred with the just-returned Eyssen. There was not a single raider operating on the high seas at that moment and the German surface fleet was simply a small, efficient, but bottled-up machine for which no one seemed to have much use. Not the British, to whom it was a thorn in the side, not Hitler, who feared the very thought of losing one of the gray monsters, nor SKL, which, hamstrung by the Führer's orders and Britain's might, seemed to have become timid. Dönitz's "wolf-pack" tactics and the U-boats' slashing attacks were terrorizing the Atlantic, but it seemed imperative that something more be done before the United States with its incalculable capacity to fight and to provide the means to fight entered the war. But conditions at sea had changed a lot since *Atlantis* had first put out, and the change was not in Germany's favor. SKL could juggle with one ship; and that little 3,862-tonner *Thor,* for example, would have to try to get out via the English Channel. There was no other way anymore. Britain's ships had been equipped with radar, their intelligence had improved, and the Royal Navy's surveillance of the northern waters had become nearly impenetrable. The Channel route, judging by *Komet*'s late experiences, was obviously not a very safe one, and the seas beyond it were not safe at all.

NOTES

1. The humorous, snappy Weyher, who now lives with his engaging, blond wife, Margaret (their son is a captain in the navy), in an apartment handsomely appointed with some of his own carvings and ceramics on Wilhelmshaven's Viktoria Strasse, was appointed Chief of Operations Naval Group South (Eastern Mediterranean, Adriatic, Aegean, Black Sea) after a stint with SKL. Between January and June 1944 he was head of escorts in the Black Sea and Chief of Staff, Romanian Navy. He then moved to Crete and in November to East Fresia as commandant, later becoming C-in-C and Rear Admiral in that area. After the surrender ("I had the distinction of surrendering in one war as the Kaiser's youngest Cadet, and in another as Hitler's youngest Admiral."), he worked with the Admiralty on a study of the naval war in the Black Sea. His money blocked (because he had attained Flag rank) and limited to menial chores for a while, he took up work as a ship chandler to support his family which had fortunately escaped from East Prussia. In 1961 he ventured on a private career as a political writer and lecturer, and now devotes much time to a society for the study of military science. Of his experience in *Orion* he says, "as long as there was a war going on anyway, it was the most independent and thus the finest command of all for a naval officer."

   Orion lasted until shortly before the war ended. Partially disarmed and renamed *Hektor,* she served as a gunnery training ship and was finally sunk by Russian aircraft off Swinemünde May 4, 1945 while engaged in evacuating military and civilian personnel from the slaughter in the Eastern Baltic.

2. *Komet*'s Eyssen, not overly popular in Berlin, served as liaison officer to Airfleet IV in Russia, later as Commander Transports in Norway, last as Commandant Military District III, Vienna, until retired early 1945. He died two days before his 68th birthday, and at his funeral, attended by officials from Bonn, his former Gunnery Officer Balser delivered a grateful eulogy: "You spared lives . . . you will live . . . as a beaming good friend." Adjutant Karsten wrote a dedication to a book on *Komet*: Eyssen was a revered commander, "Remembered with gratitude."

3. At first, Detmers feared the possibility of an unjust trial by a shocked Australia for sinking *Sydney*. Nothing came of the matter, however, because the Aussies were satisfied he had fought cleanly and nicely. His treatment at Camp Dhurringile was correct but dull, he says. If his captors said, "I will see what we can do," nothing ever happened. If they replied to a request with "I'll take a note of that," something favorable was on the offering. He was advised that he had been promoted captain and had been awarded the Ritterkreuz, and he and his officers were left pretty much on their honor. Across the pier from the liner in which they were to be repatriated from Port Melbourne, January 21, 1947, lay the real *Straat Malakka,* whose name *Kormoran* had borrowed for her last disguise. Detmers, partially disabled by several strokes, resided with his charming wife Ursula in a large house in Hamburg's Rahlstedt district, the "challenging days" a memory but not the byword with which he fought and lived—"there are no impossible situations." He passed away on November 4, 1976.

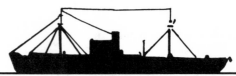

CHAPTER 10

1942, Part I:
Three Raiders Do Damage

"GOOD NIGHT!"   From what Eyssen had told him at the end
of November, *Thor's* Gumprich concluded that the situation at sea
"was not too healthy." He was fortunate in having a radar set and new
5.9-inch guns (their effective range of 15,800 meters was nearly twice
that of the raider's first, balky pre–World War I models), and he had
probably been lucky in ramming *Bothnia* because the weather at the
time scheduled for his original departure had not been propitious and
the British had, as he had feared, been aware of his moves. On the
second try, though discovered by aircraft and expected by Allied intelligence, he made it safely in stages, traveling mostly at night and heavily
escorted, to the Gironde, where he arrived on December 17. For a
number of reasons, atrocious weather and enemy activity being the most
compelling, several attempted sorties were aborted and it was not until
January 17 that he set out for his first assignment. It was to be another
effort against the whaling fleets near the Antarctic where *Pinguin* had
enjoyed such good success a year earlier. South, south, south he went
without the slightest pause or break, his gunports open, armament exposed at critical times, and his men, nearly 80 percent of whom had
never crossed the equator, standing special watches in dangerous areas.
South he went, past South Georgia, then east below Bouvet Island and
nearly to 30°E and close to the Antarctic Circle. He steamed 5,268
miles and spent nearly a whole month in icy waters, searching, finding
nothing, but nearly losing his plane along with Robert Meyer-Ahrens
and enlisted pilot Steenbock, who came back one day after one of their
eighteen Antarctic flights (more than eighty take-offs and landings in
all) with only one liter of gas in their tanks because of a compass failure.
At least the radar had worked. It could pick up bergs anywhere from

80 hectometers to 135 hectometers. By early March, he was ready to call it quits. On the fourteenth of the month he passed South Georgia northbound for a spell of raiding in the South Atlantic where he would operate until the arrival of his relief *Michel* (*Schiff 28*), which was that same day fighting desperately just for a clear passage to Le Havre. When she did, he was to move to the Indian Ocean, again to be followed by *Michel,* whose replacement in the Atlantic would be the long overdue and still abuilding *Schiff 23* (*Stier*).

The Tirpitzufer was by no means finished with its raider war. As they saw it in Berlin, every little bit helped, and Germany needed all the help it could get, even though Hitler and his new, independently banzaiing Japanese allies had made some stupendous gains in 1941 and the former had proclaimed that 1942 would again be a year of great victories. To help foster that promise SKL took stock of its surface forces. All they had in the water with which to do their mischief abroad—the glorious battle cruiser "channel dash," which had the London *Times* calling for heads to roll, notwithstanding—was a bottled-up pocket fleet-in-being, two raiders, another in the docks, and one ex-British merchantman.

The former lime juicer was *Atlantis'* prize *Speybank,* neatly renamed *Doggerbank* in honor of a battle cruiser action fought in the North Sea, January 1915. Though not a raider, her strange career merits some attention, it being closely interwoven with those ships' war against commerce. Commanded by *Tannenfels'* former thirty-eight-year-old first officer, Paul Schneidewind, whom Rogge had placed in charge of the prize (see p. 100), she had arrived in France on May 12, 1941. She sailed again disguised as one of her virtually identical sister ships, *Levernbank,* on January 21, 1942, with a mixed naval-merchant crew numbering 108 and again captained by Schneidewind. Her mission: mine Cape Town and Cape Agulhas; supply U-boats and raiders. On the afternoon of March 12, Schneidewind, then making his approach to Cape Town, was asked his name and destination by an aircraft. With deliberate clumsiness, he spelled it out: *Levernbank,* New York via Pernambuco to Cape Town. That night he laid sixty mines within sight of shore, then joined the normal traffic rounding the Cape. At 1945 the next evening he was approached by His Majesty's light cruiser *Durban* and questioned again. *"Levernbank,* New York to Durban; good night," the intrepid Germans signaled and were carelessly let go again. At 2012, when the cruiser was barely out of sight, they were already laying another field of mines. One of the fifteen dropped exploded. Less than fifteen hours later, at 1100 of the fourteenth, Schneidewind was challenged once more, this time by AMC *Cheshire,* which, on being told that the minelayer (whose arrival in the area had actually been predicted by British intelligence) was *Invernbank,* Montevideo to Melbourne, also let him go. "I wish you a happy voyage," the AMC flashed. Schneidewind responded in kind, unable to believe his luck, then disappeared into the Indian Ocean. The Royal Navy had become suspicious, however, and for several days aircraft were sent out in search of the strange Bank liner. Though they found nothing, the incident did stimulate the work being done on the prodigious "Check-mate" instant identification system. Schneidewind was back on the night of April 16/17 to lay another field off Agulhas where *Atlantis* had sown her eggs earlier in the war. Unlike Rogge's mines, which did no damage, *Doggerbank*'s accounted for 35,076 tons of shipping either damaged or sunk and their known presence created an immense amount of trouble for harassed minesweepers as well as the routing officers on shore. Rogge's idea for such a simple ship had worked.

"COPPING IT"

Thor's first victim in the South Atlantic was the Greek *Pagasitikos,* which was sunk on March 23 north of Tristan da Cunha after her crew of thirty-two men and one woman had been taken off. On March 24 the raider rendezvoused with the four-masted motor ship *Regensburg,* which had supported *Komet* and *Orion* (see Chapter IV), had run the blockade to France whence she had again departed on February 12, 1942. The raider's radar was tested at night with the supply ship acting as target, but the electrical marvel came out second best at 14,440 yards to the lookouts' Zeisses and the range finder. On the twenty-seventh the ships separated and *Thor* headed north to the central South Atlantic west of St. Helena, planning to operate there until *Michel* arrived around April 5.

On March 30 *Thor* found a second victim in *Wellpark,* whose master, Alexander Cant, was just a month from his thirty-seventh birthday. From Cant's 4,469-ton freighter, the engagement looked this way:

> At noon on March 30, 1942, we were in latitude 21°09'S, longitude 14°06'W, having just passed through one of the routed positions. It was a clear but cloudy day with good visibility and a cloud base of about 2,000 feet. At about 1300 hours Mr. Gray, the Second Officer, informed me that he could see another ship's masts just above the horizon on our port beam. . . . She appeared to be on a course parallel to our own and converging very slowly. . . . At about 1400 hours we could hear the throb of an airplane engine so I ordered

"Guns" crew to stand by the A.A. Gun. Shortly afterwards a sea-plane dived out of the clouds on our starboard beam and dropped something in the water which I first took to be a torpedo, but which later turned out to be a wire with hooks attached to tear the wireless away and stop any message from being transmitted. As the seaplane came in she machine-gunned right across the bridge, at the same time we opened fire with our twelve pounder. Meanwhile the auxiliary cruiser had closed us and opened fire; her first salvo was about 50 yards short and her second scored two hits, one shell penetrating No. 1 hold above the waterline, the other pierced the boiler casing under the funnel and burst over the boiler room. From then on it was a case of salvo after salvo finding their target and it was not until they saw our first life boat dropping astern of us before they ceased fire. . . .

From *Thor* it all naturally looked a bit different. The plane, whose tricky launching procedure usually tested veteran seaman and veteran of *Thor*'s first voyage Henry Militzer's skills and patience, reported a ship at 0744. *Thor* opened fire at 1403 and on the second salvo the British ship stopped. At 1413 Meyer-Ahrens reported her to be under way again and Gumprich ordered the plane into a renewed attack. When *Wellpark* responded with flack, gunnery officer Dr. Hermann Kandeler's 5.9's went into action. Thirteen minutes later, the ship lay stopped, two of her boats rowing across the water, their oars making them look much like beetles.

Gumprich's war diary shows that not much was learned from the British except that they had not expected a raider in the area. But the action itself had come off well and "silently" as far as the Germans were concerned. Gumprich was developing a style of fighting that was to stand him in good stead with many rewarding returns. It was really easy when it worked: sight ship, tear aerial, stop ship. And that is exactly what Gumprich did on April 1, his orders succinct for a tidy destruction of *Willesden,* which had first been spotted by the lads in the cockpit of the Arado at 0805. At 1721 it was "tear antenna." The plane did, but was fired on. In *Thor*, Kandeler got permission to open fire at 1738. *Willesden*'s gunners replied with six shots, while the rest of the crew took to the boats. One hundred twenty-eight of *Thor*'s shells later, the action was over, with one dead, three badly wounded, and three lightly wounded in the 4,563-ton ship.

Ernst Zimmermann, twenty-seven, was then on his first voyage serving as a cook in *Willesden,* which had left New York's seedy Bush Terminal bound for Alexandria. His observations of the attack are quite unlike the precise gunnery report Kandeler made out for his captain just two days after his inexperienced ammo handlers had nearly let him down by gawking at the action in progress. Salvo speed and fire discipline was good this time, the German lieutenant wrote. Zimmermann, who later sketched what he could observe of the raider's secrets hoping to pass the drawings on to British intelligence, recalls the contest:

> Plane trailing a hook—a dive out of the sun; our main aerial gone. Near misses with the first bombs, cannon shells set our deck cargo of oil drums on fire . . . smoke filling the alleyway. The Ceylonese cook packing in cartons of cigarettes, but with only life jacket and my banjo slung over my shoulder I made for the boat deck. Boat already in the water and jumping for the trailing ropes I slithered down into the boat burning skin on my hands in the process. . . . Ship burning fiercely. . . . Now the raider in full view in the falling daylight, bearded faces along her decks as her boats towed us to be taken aboard . . . investigated, identified, and check for personal belongings etc., knives taken away of course, and after a welcome hot shower given bedding and hammocks and installed in our prison quarters down one of the holds . . . one of the crewmen following [into the boat] was not so fortunate. He was hit by shrapnel and fell all the way to land with a sickening thud across the lifeboat side, was pulled in unconscious and later died aboard the *Thor*. Next day he was accorded a full sea burial by the Germans—our own Captain Griffiths officiated, the raider slowed and he was buried at sea. Our boatswain was also killed in the action—he went down with the ship.

Zimmermann spent two nights in his hammock below, happy that he did not have to sleep on the deck because sometimes the hand pumps for the latrine, which were below the waterline and were subjected to high pressure, did not hold and those sacked out on mats on deck would "cop it." Shortly before 1300 April 3, the prison hatches were battened down and the ventilators went off. Battle stations sounded and the merchantmen struggled into their clumsy life jackets to sit it out in the sticky heat hoping for the best. When the guns opened up, the light bulb blew out, but the ragged, worried men did not have to wait much more than two hours before new faces appeared in their quarters. They belonged to the multinational crew of the Norwegian coalburner *Aust*. That action, again, had been smooth. When scuttled at 21°00′S, 16°00′W, *Aust* became the fourth ship Gumprich had managed to take "silently."

It was "surprise" weather to Gumprich on the afternoon of April 10, the kind when you can come on a ship quite unexpectedly out of a bank of mist. He had almost given up that day as a routine one, and was just thinking that visibility must have been similar during *Thor*'s engagement with AMC *Alcantara* in July 1940 when Leading Seaman Westhues called out "Smoke in sight." Since high seas would have made it hazardous for the plane and poor visibility precluded its use, Gumprich had to forego his tried and proven tactics for a night attack.

Tracking by day, he turned to come down on the other ship in the inky darkness at 1828. "Alarm!" At 1925 a blip appeared on the radar —range 9,680 yards—and Gumprich moved in, using the set for the first attack of its kind. "Breathless silence," he logged, "will it succeed?"

Yard by yard radio electrician's mate Koudelka read off the distances as given by the magic eye. Finally, when the range was down to 4,500 yards, a black shadow just a shade darker than the night showed up in the binoculars. At 2007 when the range was only 2,420 yards, Gumprich ordered "Torpedo los!" and a minute later the guns went into action. The torpedo seems to have missed, as did Kandeler's opening rounds, but of the four shells fired in the second salvo three hit, lighting up the other vessel in flames. Gumprich illuminated. More hits until cease fire at 2011. Suddenly, the blazing vessel turned to ram. *Thor*'s combat officer of the deck maneuvered to evade and firing was resumed, the shells striking with "dreadful effect." At 2012, after the salvo gong had rung fourteen times, Gumprich ordered his guns silenced. The blazing steamer still had way on but the black water in its wake was dotted with dancing red lights clearly distinguishable through the glare of the burning ship. They signified survivors, and Gumprich stuck around for three hours with his deck and searchlights on to fetch what men he could from the sea. There were thirty of them (out of an original forty-six). One was *Kirkpool*'s Capt. Albert Kennington, another Shad Burley, the chief engineer, and O. Olsen, the first officer, still another.

Olsen had just stepped out of the wheelhouse when the first shells hit, setting the bridge on fire, leaving the helm unattended and thereby nearly causing a collision and a "dreadful" barrage. Commands to lower *Kirkpool*'s boats were drowned out by explosions that cut falls, blew some of the men attending them overboard, and killed the rest. Somehow Olsen made himself understood over the din and the racket of the anchor chain rattling out to effect the release of a few rafts, and after twenty minutes in the water he switched on his emergency light, then blew a whistle to attract the attention of *Thor*'s launch which was to take him into the tall Meckmann's big hands.

Burley had been in his cabin when the lights went out and he had hastened to the engine room thinking something amiss with the dynamo. There he found the second engineer, his right arm shattered, back torn open. By the time he got the dying man on deck, the action was over, the starboard boat splintered, the port hanging by its forward davit. He went below again to stop the engines, gather his haversack, a can of water, and some rubber mattresses, and he then collected a few men to make a raft out of hatch boards. Suddenly, he felt the ship give a "heavy shudder," and he noticed that things were "quiet," that his men had deserted him with the raft. He could not swim and the bare twelve feet to the water seemed like "twelve miles" as he jumped, strapped into a preserver. As he splashed to the raft, the body of a mess boy drifted by and Burley realized they had forsaken an Indian who was waving a red lantern from the doomed ship. After an hour and a half the raider backed down on the raft, its searchlight on. Helped aboard, Burley told someone about the Indian but he was either misunderstood or not heard because nothing was done by the Germans who otherwise seemed most kind to the sodden survivors of their fifth *"lautlos aufgebrachten Schiff."* Rendering assistance was no peculiarity of Gumprich's men; taking a ship without its radioing was. It seemed practically impossible to do any more those days.

FIRST "LOST BATTLE" FOR AN OLD HAND, NEW SHIP

Lounging in the saloon of the S.S. *Menelaus* one balmy mid-May evening, her first officer, B. L. Brind, and Richard Williams, the second officer, fortified themselves for what lay ahead. Their 10,306-tonner had just made port, and they were supposed to attend a dinner party in honor of heroic British seamen at the Roof Garden of the Commodore Maury Hotel in Norfolk, Virginia. They did not consider themselves particularly valiant, but practically anyone crossing the oceans those days had to be. Both of them had faced the enemy—the Luftwaffe and the Wolfpacks—and Williams had already been sunk once. Their encounter that evening would presumably prove to be somewhat trying as such affairs can be. To face it with equanimity, they poured themselves a glass of Guinness; but since the stout made them sleepy, they hit on the idea of adding a shot or two of gin to ward off tiredness. All would have gone well and they would have been able to join the rest of some seventy people who enjoyed the party if they had let it go at two shots. But they did not. By the time they had stumbled down the accommodation ladder past a series of inquisitive dockyard guards (Brind had a bottle of Gordon's stuffed up the sleeve of his bridge coat—just in case, you know) and to the yard gates, they had become a bit aggressive and were singing "Land of My Fathers" in guttural Welch. Once more they had to show their papers and at that, Williams, so Brind says, became downright abusive. The Norfolk police had to intervene, and Williams was dragged into a paddy wagon and carted off to jail. He, for his part, recalls that he had lost his pass and that he spoke Welch to the guards who, unable to comprehend either his words or the nature of his intentions, promptly took him for a German. That did infuriate him, but a lot of the problems could have been eliminated, he thought, if someone had had the foresight to provide them with transportation in the first place. Brind managed to let the party know that they might be detained a bit, and he then spent the rest of the night trying to spring his pal from the cell where he had fallen asleep on the floor—wrapped up in a coat borrowed from Brind. The cops were friendly, protective rather than punitive. All they really wanted to do was get all hands in their custody (there were many of them those days) back to their ships so that they could get on with the war.

Early next morning, Brind, gin on one arm, Williams on the other, struggled back to the pier. It was a long recriminative walk with one man peeved at the treatment the United States gave British heroes, the other sore at the treatment his coat had gotten. Neither of them felt very well, but they had most certainly had a good excuse for their private celebration. Just a fortnight earlier, on May 1, they and their shipmates in *Menelaus,* then en route from Durban to Baltimore, and still down in the South Atlantic some 720 miles southwest of St. Helena, had barely escaped the unmistakably hostile attentions of a disguised merchant raider. They did not realize it at the time, but their dull-gray assailant had been one of Germany's deadliest raiders, and theirs was the only ship ever to escape an attack once actually mounted by a Hilfskreuzer.

"The first we saw of him was his signal lamp winking at us from the starboard quarter," Brind, who had the watch at 0525 that morning, remembers. "The signal letters meant 'Stop instantly. I wish to board you.' I replied with the first two letters of our current challenge which require the remaining two letters of it in reply. They were not given. I knew then what he was, but asked him 'Who are you?' The reply was 'New British Naval Pattrol.' Two 't's! We signaled 'Repeat last word.' Again he gave 'pattrol' with two 't's." Brind ran into the wheelhouse to put the raider farther astern, rang down to the engine room for all the speed they could give him, called the captain, J. H. Blyth, alerted the radio officer, and ordered the gun crew to their stations (at one 4-inch, one 3-inch, and four 20-mm cannon). The ship's radio officer was meanwhile tapping out the mandatory "QQQQ" warning and his position (25°19′S, 13°21′W), and the message got through on several wavelengths despite frantic German jamming efforts. At 0543 the raider (it was *Michel, Schiff 28*), then still some five to six miles astern, fired several salvos but all missed, the shells falling harmlessly in the cargo liner's wake. Forty-seven minutes later, a fast motor launch flying the white ensign and its crew dressed in British duffle coats was spotted crashing through the waves in pursuit.

That ploy did not fool anyone on the Blue Funnel liner's bridge. Royal Navy personnel, they knew, would not be wearing duffle coats on a warm morning just south of the Tropic of Capricorn and they certainly would not be strapped in merchant navy-type life preservers. The boat sped past them at around thirty-five knots (it could do forty-two and a half) and dropped something into the water. Blyth, thinking it could be mines or torpedoes, bore off as his eighty-nine-man Chinese crew, responding to "plenty steam more fast othership," screwed down the safety valves and poured on the coal until a steam pressure of three hundred pounds (eighty pounds above normal for full ahead) was reached. That did it. *Menelaus* took off at fifteen and a half knots, one knot above her designed speed, and Brind had the satisfaction of seeing a job well done. It was he, after all, so his mates say, who had convinced the skipper to try to escape, and it was he who had vainly pleaded for permission to use the guns—at the very least, to blast the motorboat and its crew into their component aluminum and human parts. Down to Chief Engineer J. Blackstock and his sweating Chinese in the hot clanking engine room Brind shouted, "We've got the legs of her."

They had, and the Germans knew it. Shortly before 0800 they gave up the chase, and as they went about, the relieved engineers on *Menelaus* unscrewed the safety valves again to let off the now superfluous head of steam. It roared out of the pipes in the giant stack (a common feature of the company's ships) with an ear-splitting roar. It sounded derisive.

It was an abashed group of sailors that gathered aft around the raider's No. 4 hatch to hoist in the motorboat under the direction of its commander, the devil-may-care, witty aristocrat Malte von Schack who had held down a job as torpedo officer in *Schiff 21, Widder* as a lieutenant (J.G.), and now, advanced one rank, had the same position in *Michel.** They would have been even more embarrassed if they had known that Brind was later to report to Admiral Sir Percy Noble, Commander-in-Chief Western Approaches, that he thought the raider might have been Italian as it had bungled the job so badly.

The raider's skipper, reserve Captain Hellmuth von Ruckteschell, fifty-two, was not pleased, and no one could have blamed him if he had some doubts about the efficiency of his crew and the effectiveness of his

---

* It might be amusing to note that one Oskar Krink, though only a boatswains' mate at the time of the action, approached the Holt Company in 1950 to pass himself off as the boat's commander. Krink's tale, as recorded by the third officer of *Menelaus,* was rather erroneous, and then the man, according to Brind, asked for passage to Java for his fiancée and himself. The requested freeload was considered "a bit much," in fact "bloody cheeky," by Sir Lawrence Holt, a manager of the company and nephew of the founders.

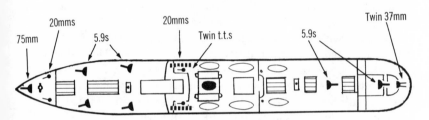

WIDDER, SHIP 21, ex-NEUMARK

Built:	1929, Howaldtswerke, Kiel
Tonnage:	7,800
Length:	477.0 feet, Lloyds Register
Beam:	63.1
Depth:	28.3
Speed:	14.8
Armament:	Six 5.9-inch; one 75mm; one twin 37mm; four 20mm; two twin 21-inch torpedo tubes*
Plane:	Two Heinkel 114
Complement:	317 (varied, due to prize crews and new drafts)
	*Shaded guns and tubes indicate a mounting below deck
Ships sunk or taken:	10 (including one prize = 58,464 tons BRITISH PETROL, KROSSFONN, DAVISIAN, KING JOHN, BEAULIEU, OOSTPLEIN, KILLORAN, ANGLO SAXON, CYMBELINE, ANTONIOS CHANDRIS
Length of cruise:	180 days, 5.5.40-10.31.40
Fate:	Returned to France

own leadership. The *Menelaus* fiasco hurt. It had, after all, as his world-wise executive officer, then Lt. Commander Wolfgang Erhardt (thirty-five), says, "a lost battle"—the first ever for any raider and the first and last the gaunt, graying captain, who was eventually credited with sinking twenty-three ships of 143,683 tons and capturing one 9,323-ton tanker, was ever to lose.

Ruckteschell was the same man who had fought so hard to make *Widder* a winner in 1940, but somehow, he and his men had botched the *Menelaus* job badly. Everything had gone wrong and, though *Michel's* officers still smile at their miserable performance or make excuses defending their or their captain's judgment and tactical skill, Ruckteschell could not at the time be expected to see any humor in the situation. They had sighted the British ship ahead of themselves and on a full-moon morning, and they had launched the thirty-seven-foot motor torpedo boat (LS-4) with orders to stop the ship with torpedoes. The boat's commander, von Schack, had tried, but missed. Its eighteen-inch torpedoes could only be reloaded on board the raider, and since that would have meant losing even more distance to their obviously fast quarry, von Schack was ordered to stop her by other means. He tried the white ensign and British coats; that did not work. He attempted to stop her by pretending to drop more torpedoes; *Menelaus* just rushed off. Finally, and in spite of the guns visible on the big ship, he wanted to rake her with his single 20 mm; it jammed. Worse still was that Ruckteschell had disclosed his intentions and identity when still out of effective range and had then continued an obviously hopeless chase while the quarry was bleating most accurately about the whole business—not just the attack but an excellent description of *Schiff 28* and its novel use of a small torpedo boat. The eighteen or twenty rounds fired by *Michel's* old 5.9-inchers never came within a mile of their target, according to those who were being shot at and who had an immense interest in the matter. It was obvious that Ruckteschell would have to leave the area. It had been a bad show; there was no question about its being a "lost battle," and it rankled.

NUTS AND BOLTS, A RUDE KNIGHT, AND A FRIED EGG

The dismal performance with the Blue Funnel liner, though an avoidable tactical error, underscored Ruckteschell's conviction that his ship, like *Widder,* was inadequate for the tasks imposed on it. It had a diesel that could drive the ship at only sixteen knots under the best of circumstances, and pre–World War I guns with an effective range of only five miles. There was not anything the hard-pressed navy could do to help, either. If Admiral Dönitz was commissioning less than half of the U-boats considered essential and possibly war winning, it was not surprising that priorities for *Michel* were disregarded—160 machinists, for example, needed for *Schiff 28*'s reconstruction, had not been available.

In December 1940, less than two months since his return with *Widder,* Ruckteschell had been ordered to the Schichau works in Danzig to take over command of the new raider. What he found when he reported at the lovely old Hanseatic town was a 4,740-ton, 443-foot freighter with a raked stem and powerful lines. She was unfinished and rusting. The vessel had been under construction for Poland's Gdynia-American Shipping Line as the fruit carrier *Bielsko* when the Germans seized her in 1939. At first they intended to refurbish her as the hospital ship, *Bonn,* but nothing much was done until it was decided to convert her into a raider. To arm the ship, Ruckteschell's old *Widder* had to be dismantled.

Schiff 28's main battery consisted of six 5.9-inchers. Two guns were built into the forecastle behind hinged sides which could be raised by means of counterweights. Gun No. 3 was sunk into a six-foot well in the second hatch (the ship's bulwarks folded inward on both sides to permit the weapon a clear field of fire). No. 4 was on the boat deck inside a deckhouse that could be rolled forward and fitted against and around the funnel to expose the gun. Nos. 5 and 6 were located aft in the poop behind hinged sides. A 4.1-inch gun, intended primarily for illuminating shells, stood on the winch house abaft the mainmast and was covered only by a tarpaulin. Twin 37-mm cannon, positioned on the forecastle and poop, were disguised as British 5-inchers by the simple expedient of lashing a stove pipe between the barrels. Four 20-mm were mounted one each on the forward winch house, the bridge wings, and on the rolling deckhouse behind the stack. Below in No. 2 hold there were four torpedo tubes, and in the bows, two underwater tubes, all of twenty-one inches. The raider also carried two Arado 196 float planes and a thirty-seven-foot, 11.5-ton motorboat that could do 42.5 knots, was manned by eleven men and armed with two 18-inch torpedo tubes and a 20 mm. (Though the torpedoes had to be launched from its stern, the boat was a vast improvement over the impractical minelayers carried by *Komet* and *Kormoran* and was the sort of craft Rogge had requested but found unavailable.)

To assemble and install all this equipment and the rest of the accouterments common to all raiders—from ammo hoists to X-ray tubes—took ten months, but much of that time was, without question, taken up in fulfilling Ruckteschell's exacting demands for perfection. He insisted on hundreds of alterations and though he managed to establish a good rapport with the yard's staff, he drove the efficiency experts crazy. It was September 7, 1941, a cool, cloudy day, before he could break out his pennant and ensign to the salutes of a stiff-legged crew and 150 high-ranking guests in Gotenhaven's Basin No. 4. Though long awaited at the front, this hard-fighting officer still had six months to go until he could get into action with the ship he had, much to the surprise of almost everyone concerned, named *Michel.**

That choice, much to the delight of the raider's twenty-two-year-old adjutant, Lt. Jürgen Herr, created quite a stir in official circles and served to endear the captain to his men. With his religious bent, Ruckteschell chose *Michel,* but to many Germans the name suggested the national sobriquet for the dull-witted, sleepy-headed burgher usually pictured in a stocking cap. It would not do, the teletype from Admiral Raeder's office clattered back; it just was not the name for a ship. Well, then let's call her *Götz von Berlichingen,* Ruckteschell countered disrespectfully.† Götz, of course, all Germans knew from Goethe's *Sturm und Drang* play, had responded to an enemy's challenge in a most unspeakably vulgar manner. No one would predict the outcome of the typically Ruckteschellian bit of heresy, and those who thought he would get his way with his stiff-collared boss were strictly in the minority. The laconic reply from Berlin was astounding; it was not what anyone would have expected from such a cold, formal type as the U. S. Navy's Adm. Ernest J. King or the Kriegsmarine's Erich Raeder: "Okay, then, good luck with your *Michel.*"

During twenty-four weeks of grueling working-up exercises, the men rushed to battle stations a hundred or more times; they studied damage control, practiced lifesaving, shooting at night, fueling at sea (from tanker *Wollin*), and taking a prize until they could do it blindfolded. Ruckteschell drove them hard, making "busts" when he needed and nearly meriting one himself when he refused to be disturbed by an admiral bent on a formal inspection. No such thing, Ruckteschell proclaimed, the visit would interrupt scheduled drills. But the admiral was welcome to either a fried egg for breakfast or a glass of wine. Sunny-side up or flowery Mosel—accounts vary as to what the admiral did or did not do suavely—such churlishness did little to improve Ruckteschell's relations with his superiors. There was no question about his feelings

---

* Diminutive for Michael—Archangel St. Michael, protector of the Jewish nation and the church militant of Christendom; patron saint of soldiers, fighter against Satan, victor over evil, often portrayed slaying a dragon.

† Berlichingen (1481–1562), an anachronistic Franconian—Imperial knight and/or well-born highwayman.

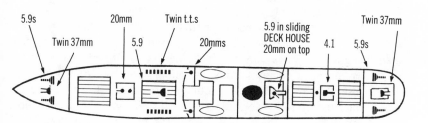

MICHEL, SHIP 28, ex-BIELSKO
(First Voyage)

Built	1939, Danziger Werft
Tonnage:	4,740
Length:	436 feet, overall
Beam:	55 feet
Draft:	24.6 feet
Speed:	16
Armament:	Six 5.9-inch; one 4.1-inch; two twin 37mm; four 20mm; two twin 21-inch torpedo tubes, two single submerged 21-inch tubes
Planes:	Two Arado 196
Complement:	400
Ships sunk:	14 = 94,363 tons
	PATELLA, CONNECTICUT, KATTEGAT, GEORGE CLYMER, LYLEPARK, GLOUCESTER CASTLE, WILLIAM F. HUMPHREY, ARAMIS, ARABISTAN, AMERICAN LEADER, EMPIRE DAWN, SAWOKLA, EUGENIE LIVANOS, EMPIRE MARCH
Length of cruise:	358 days, 3.9.42-3.1.43
Fate:	Arrived in Japan

(Second Voyage)

Ships sunk:	3 = 27,632 tons
Length of cruise:	HÖEGH SILVERDAWN, FERNCASTLE, INDIA
	170 days, 5.1.43-10.17.43
Fate:	Sunk by U.S.S. TARPON

toward the chicanery of militarism. He had hated his cadet times and now, middle-aged, he was often the bête noire of the high-collared traditionalists in the officer corps. Those gentlemen could not help noting that he sported handkerchiefs in his breast pocket and that he had appeared before Raeder in a light-blue civilian tie. Of more consequence were his supererogatory efforts to keep the naval mind on the ball. He annotated official correspondence and schedules—such as action reports and recommendations of other raider captains—as if he were correcting a student's imprecise thesis: with impatient scribbles that read "nonsense," "garbage," "ridiculous." Though German officers were encouraged to represent their opinions, the green pen was meant for those with high rank.*

His relentless insistence on perfection for his staff was time well spent, however. It also gave ample opportunity for weeding out those men thought to be physically or psychologically unfit with the result that there were never to be any serious disciplinary problems during *Michel*'s long cruise. The carefully culled four hundred men who remained and whose nucleus were *Widder* officers such as Navigator Ludwig Rödel, flier Konrad Hoppe, von Schack (who was planning to marry Herr's sister), prize officers Carl Cords and Adolf Wimmel, Dr. Friedrich Wilhelm Schröder, and some senior ratings hammered out the kinks they found in their procedures. They fired practice torpedoes at cruiser *Nürnberg,* worked with submarines, and developed a highly efficient lookout system ("our most important weapon"). Much of their labors were hampered by severe winter temperatures, and all did not always go well. The ship ran over a line which tangled around its screw, ran aground off Swinemünde, and was carried from its berth along Cuxhaven's Steubenhoft pier one morning by the pressure of tide-borne ice which tore a mooring bit from the deck plating, snapped the heavy bow, spring, breast, and stern lines with pistol-like reports. Sailing orders arrived on March 6, 1942: *Michel,* like *Thor,* and for the same reasons, was to break out via the English Channel, no matter how dangerous the route past Britain's front door might be, and no matter how alert her forces, stung by "Cerebus"—the Channel dash of battle cruisers *Gneisenau* and *Scharnhorst* and cruiser *Prinz Eugen*—would be; it was the only way out. Besides, it was short and would save fuel for a navy then already suffering from severe shortages of oil.

---

* Ruckteschell's flying officer Hoppe, who kept his skipper's war diary in *Widder,* thinks that the inane, sometimes asinine and non sequitur notations ("dirty, lousy folk," "I have had a grudge against the Greeks for a long time,") were intended to make someone read them and thus pay more attention to the more important entries.

BAPTISM OF FIRE

Though Ruckteschell did not believe it was still possible to deceive the enemy's espionage network, *Michel* stole out of Kiel without any fanfare disguised as *Schiff 26,* just another plain naval auxiliary. She lingered off Heligoland the night of March 9/10 and then set a course for the breakthrough. Three nights later, she grounded off Ostende, and though she was gotten free without assistance, Ruckteschell turned her back to Flushing to avoid being caught in narrow waters during daytime. Having picked up an escort of five 1,320-ton torpedo boats and nine mine-sweepers, he headed his blacked-out command for the narrowest part of the Channel on the night of the thirteenth, fully realizing that he would in all likelihood have to fight. His men, he knew, were standing to at their stations behind the guns, beside the hoses and wooden plugs of the damage control parties, by the pounding diesel and in the spotless 'tween decks operating room with the stainless tools everyone hoped would not be needed. Many had not been in combat and they worried about their own reaction to fear. Those who had could only hope and pray it would all be over soon. Topdecks, strapped into their life belts and helmets, they stared into the gloom and at the cold, dark seas rushing by, and down below, locked between scores of watertight doors, they fussed over whirring machinery or just sat, waiting for what would come. Up in the radio shack, the regular operators watched the highly trained, English-speaking petty officers of the "B-Dienst" who had come aboard just for the breakthrough. Specialists in British codes and communications tech-niques, the "B" boys were monitoring all of the enemy's chirping, beeping, and tweeting channels and they would be the first to know the Admiralty's and Coastal Command's intentions. Shortly after 0300 a message went to the bridge: The British were getting restive and their jabbering more frequent (six MTBs and three motor gun boats [MGBs] had roared out of Dover and orders were going to them). Those light forces, humming through the dark for a surprise attack, were easily beaten off amid drifting smoke, arching tracers, brilliant star shells, flashing automatic cannon fire, and the rumble of coastal artillery which tried to intervene. Intermittent skirmishing continued with little damage done on either side, and *Michel's* men, hearing that battle rations were to be distributed, thought the worst was probably over. In the dark wheelhouse, the officers knew better. The Royal Navy, they reasoned, would not give up that easily, certainly not if it had what was obviously an important convoy in its sights.

    The British did not quit. Five destroyers (three *Hunt* class and two older ships), which had been patrolling off Beachy Head, were ordered to close in. And a serious threat they were as they cut through the weaving German lines, their 4-inchers barking and their torpedomen standing by. So dangerous, in fact, that Ruckteschell had to unmask his battery, and risk disclosing the nature of his ship. His heavy weapons opened up in anger for the first time in the fierce, close-range fighting, shaking the decks and the dust off the beams while fast-firing gunners at the automatic guns shouted for magazines of 37 and 20 mm (an additional quadruple 20 mm had been mounted forward just for the breakthrough), and torpedoes dropped by *Walpole* and *Windsor* were avoided. Again, little harm was done; *Windsor* and *Fernie* took some hits, one German sublieutenant was killed, and *Michel* came out of the scrap pock-marked by small shells, paint-chipped by splinters. It had been, Ruckteschell noted, a most fortuitous baptism of fire. Nothing much had happened, he said, and the crew were "completely changed. When a soldier has seen action without getting hurt, he thinks it will always be that way."

As her men stood down, *Michel* coasted to St.-Malo, where she replenished ammunition, topped off her tanks for her final departure on March 20, and relinquished the prized quadruple 20 mm which the gun-short German Navy would soon lend to another ship. For security reasons no one got liberty and the men idling along the rails grumpily reminded each other of an old seaman's adage: "A sailor does not need to go ashore; he can see it from his ship."

Ruckteschell's orders read that he was to raid in the South Atlantic and the western Indian Ocean following in *Thor*'s wake, the times to be set by SKL, and it did not take him long to get to work. He rendezvoused on April 16 with the 1928-built *Charlotte Schliemann,* which had been lying in the Canaries since the beginning of the war and was scheduled to attend to the needs of *Michel,* later *Schiff 23.* Two days later, his men made a short, clean morning's work of knocking out *Patella*—and a messy job it could have been, for the Shell-owned tanker radioed and was loaded with 9,911 tons of Admiralty-oil. Her survivors, twenty-three British, one Canadian, and thirty-six Chinese (three men had been killed), were sent trooping down *Michel*'s ladders to tidy, scrubbed quarters two decks below the forward battery.

During the night of April 22/23 Ruckteschell employed a new stratagem to add Texas Company's 8,684-ton *Connecticut* to the long, dreary list of war casualties. The raider stopped after dark, and as she wallowed in the seas, her men horsed motor torpedo boat LS-4, which with Ruckteschellian touch had been named *Esau,* overboard for its first action. Von Schack's torpedo struck at 0210. *Connecticut* radioed shortly and her men immediately lowered three boats to abandon—not at all an unreasonable thing for anyone sitting on a cargo that consisted chiefly of hundred-octane gasoline to do. Another torpedo smashed into the tanker just as the last two boats were trying to round its stern, hoping to get to windward before the gas caught fire. But *Connecticut* exploded in a ball of fire hundreds of feet high and the flames spread over the water to engulf the boats and the men in them. *Michel* managed to pick nineteen shaken men from the remaining boat at dawn.* Ruckteschell had to and could accept the loss of life, but the radioing he could not; not if he wanted to stay afloat. Worse was still to come, however. Only a week later he bumbled after the big ship with the Spartan name *Menelaus,* whom he could not silence at all and those uninterrupted signals brought His Majesty's cruiser *Shropshire* and AMCs *Canton* and *Cheshire,* which had been dispatched from Simonstown, out after his neck.

NEW TACTICS, NO SQUEALERS

For the nervous Ruckteschell, determined to rack up 200,000 tons of Allied shipping (combining the results of *Widder* and *Michel*), the *Menelaus* affair had been a serious disappointment. He had to do better. It was essential, he reasoned, to silence the enemy, who had become "more skittish than young girls," instantly so that they could not "squeal"; he would have to attack at night with overwhelming firepower. Rough, perhaps, but since the enemy was not operating within the conventions set for merchant vessels, the only way. Gradually he and the affable Erhardt worked out some tactics that developed into as much of a pattern as was possible in as varied and dangerous a game as raiding. Once a ship had been spotted and tracked, she would be approached from the darkest sector of the horizon at night, preferably from ahead at an angle of about five degrees from either bow to make it harder for him to escape. As the raider closed to three thousand yards she would fire a star shell to illuminate the target. Once the technique improved, Ruckteschell would eventually go in as close as two thousand yards or less to snuff out any chance of opposition. The whole idea, he later explained, was "principally best described as a torpedo boat attack." Usually, *Esau* would be lowered at dusk with von Schack instructed to either shadow the enemy until the raider went into action or to act independently. Once an engagement was over, the boat would be handy in picking up survivors, "playing ragman," as its crew called it.

* Texas Company states that there were fifty-four men aboard; the Germans say fifty-two, but both agree that nineteen were saved. One died in the raider and two others succumbed to malnutrition in Japanese prison camps.

Following another meet with *Charlotte, Michel* crisscrossed the Cape Town–Montevideo track unsuccessfully until the afternoon of May 20 when *Kattegat* (home port Oslo), running in ballast for the La Plata, was sighted and followed into the dark, moonless night, the kind the Germans with their superior glasses and well-trained lookouts liked. The Norwegians were not zigzagging, and though they had three lookouts of their own (two on the bridge, one on the monkey's island above the wheelhouse), they did not see a thing until their radio shack, engine room, and bridge were shattered and blasted by sixteen screeching shells from gunnery officer Lt. Jacob Schwinn's starboard battery. Miraculously, none of the startled, terrified crew were injured (they never touched their radio or 4-inch gun), and they had the presence of mind to wave a white lantern. The minute they did so, the firing stopped, and they were all brought over to the raider. *Michel's* new tactics had paid off; no one had even been hurt!

Heading north, Ruckteschell had no luck until June 2 when he picked up a message that seemed outdated on an ocean haunted by drowned men and sunk ships. It was a genuine SOS, sent during the standard call period reserved for emergencies, and it was from an American, call letters WHPH, who was having engine trouble nine hundred miles to the north of the raider's position. The signals were loud and clear. The only thing the Germans could not figure out was her name (*George Clymer*). Ruckteschell was faced with a difficult decision. It would take him three days to get to the ship, and if he got there in good order and time, he might be running into a trap. He chose the bold course.

The fellows on the 7,160-ton *Clymer,* an American Liberty operated under the General Agency Agreement for the United States by American Mail Line, had a bad time on their way from Portland, Oregon, to Cape Town with a mixed cargo and twenty-four planes, and they were only a few hundred miles from the Ascensions and the presumed safety of air cover when their main shaft and thrust block bearings split. Their first SOS had been acknowledged by the Cape, May 30, but someone on the Ascensions had told them, "Sorry, old boy, no airplanes." They had then drifted two hundred miles. Suddenly at 2000 on June 6, a torpedo struck them to port on a line between the fire and engine rooms. A second torpedo hit the after end of hold No. 1 only seconds later. As the ship took a list and started settling by the head, some of the panicky crew rushed to the boats without formality or muster, deserting two of their mates trapped below and leaving the plucky naval gunners to sit it out on board. At 0800 the next day the ship was still afloat and the seamen, whom the captain thought a bad lot, reboarded. One day later, a British plane flew over them signaling that help was on the way, and at 1600 on June 7, AMC *Alcantara, Thor*'s old sparring partner, arrived on the scene to supervise the scuttling of the Liberty, whose salvage was thought to be impractical.

Not far away, the many men jammed between the humming sets in the hot, sticky radio room of *Michel* grinned. They knew the Americans had not been hit by a U-boat. Little *Esau* had done the job. Ruckteschell, who had not even gotten near to the crippled vessel with the raider and who was well pleased with von Schack's playing U-boat, hung around, hoping to finish the wreck off. But when he finally reached the scene of the attack, all that could be seen were two mast tops rapidly disappearing over the horizon. Undoubtedly they were *Alcantara*'s!

STIER, A GENTLY RUN BULL

> Dear Sir:
>
> This is to notify you that I (Saedi Hassan) am at present in the Val de Grace Hospital recovering from wounds, namely complicated fracture of the left leg and sundry flesh wounds.
>
> I would appreciate it if you would find it convenient to send me shoes, size 6½ and any comforts, also cigarettes, through the Red Cross or which is most convenient to you. I am being treated well here.
>
> I have no relatives to notice so I will close.
>
> I remain yours obediently,
>
> Saedi Hassan

When the people at Socony-Vacuum's (now Mobil) New York headquarters on lower Broadway received this letter from France on March 19, 1943, they did not quite know what to do with it. Then someone discovered that Hassan had been an able-bodied seaman in the company's Panamanian-flag *Stanvac Calcutta*. The tanker had been missing since she departed Montevideo in ballast for Caripito on May 29, 1942. She had been given up as lost, and War Risk Insurance benefits had been mailed to the next of kin.

Hassan got his cigarettes and shoes and a guarded, by-the-way sort of letter asking what had happened. His reply, censored by the Germans, did not say a thing.

After months, the company pieced the facts together. The first news came from a Norwegian who had been freed when the German blockade runner *Ramses,* out from Japan, was intercepted by the Australian light cruiser *Adelaide* and the Dutch *Heemskerk.* He said that he had met some of *Calcutta*'s crew on a German supply ship. Later, another Norwegian got a letter telling Hassan's tale through to New York via a released British prisoner of war. The War Shipping Administration hastily revoked presumptive death certificates for the entire crew, and the budget-minded government set about trying to retrieve some of the insurance that had already been paid out to grieving relatives. No one heard the whole story until after the end of the war, however, and it was quite a tale.

There was nothing unusual about *Calcutta*'s chief officer, Aage H. Knudsen, and Capt. Gustaf O. Karlsson having a cup of coffee in the dining room at 1012 on June 6, 1942. It was unusual, however, for them to hear shellfire near the equator, six hundred miles from Brazil and some twelve hundred miles from Liberia even though they were in the middle of the greatest war that had ever tortured mankind. They rushed to the bridge and saw another vessel emerging from a rain squall about four miles away to port. They could not make out her flag but they did notice an international code hoist telling them to stop. Thinking the other ship British, they had the answering pennant and the Panamanian flag set. Then, "Captain Karlsson and I took another look through the binoculars. It was then I made out the German ensign flying at the main gaff," Knudsen recalls. The captain rang for full speed and *Calcutta*'s propeller thrashed the water into a frothy, wide, white L as her helmsman, Nelson Okander, put the wheel over hard right. The merchantmen on the forward 3-inch opened fire as did the nine-man naval gun crew with a 4-inch aft. They got off about twenty to thirty shells, two of which hit their target, one going through its forward mast, the other entering the crew's quarters aft by No. 5 hatch where it exploded and wounded two men.

The damaged German (it was *Schiff 23, Stier, ex-Cairo,* of the Atlas-Levant Line) replied with 148 rounds of 5.9-inch and a torpedo that shattered the tanker. *Calcutta* quickly developed a list which Knudsen tried to correct by shifting ballast. Unsuccessful, he ran back for orders but found the captain and Okander dead, the charthouse a shambles. The radio officer had not had a chance to signal; he, too, was dead in the wreckage. Eleven more lives were snuffed out before *Calcutta* was abandoned (one man later died in *Stier* and another in a Japanese prison camp). Among the thirty-seven oil-soaked survivors picked up was Knudsen and a badly wounded man with small feet, Hassan.

Calcutta was the new raider's second victim, and her stiff resistance—she was honored as one of the eleven United States "Gallant Ships" by the Maritime Administration—gave her opponents much food for thought.* The first ship to fall into *Stier*'s hands had been sunk two

---

* The award is wrong in stating that one of the raider's guns was put out of action. The latter's diary states that many of *Calcutta*'s crew were angry at their skipper for having endangered their lives.

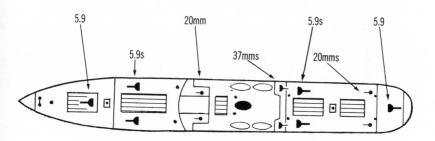

STIER, SHIP 23, ex-CAIRO

Built:	1936, Krupp Germania Werft, Kiel
Tonnage:	4,778
Length:	408.5 feet, Lloyds Register
Beam:	56.6
Draft:	21.4
Speed:	14.5
Armament	Six 5.9-inch, two 37mm; four 20mm; two 21-inch torpedo tubes (submerged)
Planes:	Two Arado Ar-231
Complement:	324
Ships sunk:	4 = 30,728 tons GEMSTONE, STANVAC CALCUTTA, DALHOUSIE, STEPHEN HOPKINS
Length of cruise:	142 days, 5.9.42-9.27.42
Fate:	Sunk by STEPHEN HOPKINS

days earlier. Her name had been *Gemstone* and her master was E. J. Griffiths. The captain had picked up his routing orders from Naval Control Officer Capetown but, unlike some skippers who were distrustful of both the Royal Navy's competence and the tightness of security in South Africa and who therefore simply steered as they saw fit, he followed orders faithfully, station by station. Those who did not, like the master of *Gemstone*'s company's *Sandstone,* felt justified in disobeying their orders, and pointed out that vessels that did were often captured or sunk. But with luck playing such a great part in war, it would be hard to make a case for either decision. At any rate, Griffiths was sitting down to breakfast on the morning of June 4 when he heard a shot that sent him rushing to the bridge. He brought his stern to the raider and had his wireless operator send out a "QQQQ" which the Germans at first thought to have been successfully jammed. It had not, for a few hours later they heard another ship repeating the message accurately and that ship's signals, in turn, were acknowledged on land. *Stier*'s diary shows that the Germans assumed that the second vessel had observed the action with *Gemstone* and had then waited prudently to send a signal when they were far out of sight. If, indeed, another ship had been able to approach so close undiscovered, SKL's annotation to *Stier*'s report was justified: "Lookouts?" it snapped.

And that is just the sort of thing that concerned the raider's Lt. Ludolf Petersen, who had been first officer of the Hamburg-Amerika Line's freighter *Kiel* and who had taken that ship through the blockade in 1939. He had then served as a prize officer on both *Lützow* and *Scheer* and had taken a flotilla of *Pinguin*'s whalers safely to Bordeaux before being assigned to *Schiff 23*. He thought *Stier*'s crew good kids but inexperienced and lacking in know-how of merchantmen. He found the lookouts wanting and felt the gunners had not had sufficient practice. The latter had not, in fact, hit *Gemstone* with any of their first salvos and had been fortunate that Griffiths, thinking a fight pointless against the odds, had called his men off the 4-inch and stopped to abandon. He had, after all, radioed, and in surrendering he enabled his entire crew to be taken unhurt to the raider where they were separated at his wish, the Germans say, according to race and rank.

To *Stier*'s crew the capture was a welcome change from the previous weeks and months and the troubles they had had when they first set out far behind schedule. Their captain was slim, good-natured, filled with a good sense of humor, and he was a better than average musician. Born on August 11, 1900, in Erfurt, he had always hoped for a naval career and when still in his teens he had seen that wish come true as he was posted to battle cruiser *Seydlitz* and became an ensign at

eighteen. Before World War II broke out, he served at naval headquarters in Berlin and then later as commander of an antisubmarine
vessel. In 1940 he was ordered to *Schiff 23* then being used as a picket
in the Baltic. In April 1941 he began to convert the ship into a raider,
first at the Wilton yards in Holland, later in Germany. Gerlack formally
commissioned her on November 11 and named her after his wife Hildegard's sign of the zodiac. He was proud to get a command considered
choice, albeit a "ticket to heaven."

Gerlach was satisfied with his young crew though they had not
had much time for working up and had been hampered by ice much of
the time. He found the ship generally to his liking in camouflage and
armament (six 5.9-inch, two 37 mm, four 20 mm, and two underwater
torpedo tubes) but at fourteen and a half knots too slow. And he was
skeptical of his chance of taking many ships. His role would be chiefly
strategic and in that he saw great promise. He was an optimist, his wife
says. But so were many of his officers like Lt. Rudolf Borchers, first
lieutenant and flak officer, who also would have liked more speed but
knew that they would have needed more oil to run the ship if they had it.
Borchers, still only twenty-two, was delighted to have been posted to a
raider and particularly *Stier,* which three of his Academy classmates
(Class 37A) had also drawn. He, like SKL, saw a purpose in the
proposed operations, and he along with the other young officers shared
their commander's enthusiasm. Their ship, they thought, without anything in their background to compare it with, was great. Not so Petersen, who had seen a lot of the world and a lot of fighting. He considered
his messmates pleasant but too young for their job, and he was not
happy with his billet. He told Gerlach that *Stier* was too slow, and he
felt that with the United States in the war, her mission virtually pointless. The disguises, he pointed out, were inadequate; none of the guns
were below deck.

Commander Gerlach (he was posted captain on June 1) had had
a few reservations, too, and what particularly distressed him was the
idea of steaming down to Rotterdam starting May 9, 1942, camouflaged
in an ordinary convoy whose average speed would be limited to seven
knots, and which would be subject to constant harassment by Britain's
MTBs and destroyers. Like Ruckteschell, he had an additional quadruple 20-mm mount and an excellent "B" group and he was to need
them both. On the twelfth he left the Dutch port and by evening his
escort consisted of four torpedo boats and sixteen R-boats (motor
gunboats). Two hours after midnight, the convoy came under fire of the
heavy 13.5-inch Dover batteries and by 0330 of the thirteenth it was
fully engaged by groups of MTBs roaring along on both sides. Star shells

cast an eerie glow over a dull, dark seascape rent by the flashes of thousands of tracers and the frothy whitish wakes of fast-maneuvering vessels of all sizes. In the fierce fighting, Britain lost MTB 220, and two German torpedo boats were snapped in half by torpedoes which killed 199 of their 287-man crews. Gerlach was calm, but Borchers will never forget the horror of seeing the men on the forward part of one of those ships screaming for help as it drifted past the onrushing raider. It was to him the most horrible moment of their cruise. Communications had broken down in the noise of battle and all those on the bridge could do was to "cry helplessly" as their "forward gunners, who had been instructed to shoot at every suspicious shadow, pumped shells into the wreckage and their own comrades." While those men died by error, *Stier*'s survived to sail from Royan on the nineteenth unaware that they were in the last raider to get out.

"MISERABLE TIME"

By the time Gerlach had taken *Calcutta* and Ruckteschell had seen the last of *Alcantara,* Gumprich had been in the Indian Ocean with *Thor* for over a month. Having sunk *Kirkpool,* he had moved south, passing the Cape on April 22 to carry out operations in an area west of 80°E and south of 10°S which had been arranged for him in long, protracted negotiations between SKL and the Japanese, who were overextended, had little understanding for the importance of commerce war, and had reserved a zone three hundred miles deep for their submarines off the East African coast, where they accomplished very little.

Late in the evening of May 4, when it was dark, *Wellpark*'s Cant, *Willesden*'s Zimmermann, *Kirkpool*'s Burley, and 159 other prisoners were transferred to supply ship *Regensburg,* and six days later *Thor*'s pilots sighted the old but stout Eastern and Australian Steamship Company's coal-burning liner *Nankin*. Three years, four months, and over a week later, on September 19, 1945, her captain, C. Stratford, "regretfully" submitted a report to his owners covering the loss of his ship. Written from records he had somehow preserved in Japanese captivity and an excellent memory, it jibes almost completely with *Thor*'s logs (German observations will appear in brackets). Stratford wrote in part:

> The *Nankin* sailed from Freemantle at 8 a.m. on the 5th May, bound for Bombay via Colombo with a full general cargo, 162 passengers, including 38 women and children, 18 Naval and 5 Military passengers, and a crew of 180. The passage was uneventful until

8.04 a.m. on Sunday, the 10th May, when a plane was observed. . . .

Passengers and crew had been exercised at "Take Cover" and "Actions Stations" on the previous day, and now they were exercised at "Boat Stations." . . .

At 2.35 p.m. my Second Officer sent Cadet Hulbert to report to me that an aeroplane could be heard. A few seconds later three machine-cannon bullets piercing the steel bulkhead on the port side of my cabin, exploded all around me. When I arrived on the bridge at 2.36 p.m. I saw a vessel on our starboard bow, bearing 045°, and a monoplane on our port bow; both were heading towards the *Nankin*. My Second Officer informed me that he had ordered the helm "hard-a-starboard" to avoid what he supposed was an aerial torpedo launched from the plane. I kept the helm in this position to turn the *Nankin* round until I had brought the approaching vessel astern. Orders were immediately given to the engineer on watch to increase to maximum speed and to prepare for scuttling ship. . . .

The plane made an attempt to fly over the ship, presumably to tear away the wireless aerial. [The plane's trailing grapnel failed.] This attack was frustrated by a sharp burst of machine-gun, rifle and revolver fire. The plane then flew once around the ship, close and low, keeping up a continuous fire with its machine-cannon. The first burst was aimed at the bridge, and the explosive bullets pierced the concrete protection on it. . . . Two Lascars, slow at taking cover, were killed. . . .

Wireless silence was broken at 2.36 p.m. (8.32 G.M.T.) when the plane attacked, and as the raider was jamming, distress messages were transmitted continuously on different wave lengths. . . . At 2.38 p.m. . . . when at approximately 13,000 yards range, the raider opened fire with a salvo of three, all of which fell short and wide. I then commenced zig-zagging and continued doing so throughout the action, keeping the raider astern; at the same time fire was opened with our gun at maximum elevation. ["Enemy evading my artillery splashes skillfully with constant zig-zagging . . . but his shots lie far too short."]

"At 3.00 p.m. the raider got our range; high explosive shells were now straddling the *Nankin* fore and aft and also bursting close on both sides, subjecting the ship to a heavy hail of shrapnel. A direct hit penetrated the shell plating on the port bow abreast No. 1 hatch, about one foot above the water-line. At 3.05 p.m., after firing twenty-eight rounds all of which fell short, I gave the order to cease firing, and decided to abandon ship in order to avoid unnecessary loss of life, particularly amongst the women and children. Thereupon the colors were lowered, and the gun crew instructed to take cover . . . and the following radio message transmitted: "*Nankin* abandoning ship Lat. 26°43'S., Long. 89°47'E." All secret codes and other Naval papers and the ship's confidential documents were cast overboard, locked in a perforated steel box.

During the launching of the boats the raider kept up a constant fire, but immediately the boats left the ship's side, it ceased firing. By 3.20 all the passengers and crew were safely away in the eight

lifeboats; they boarded the raider between 4.00 p.m. and 5.00 p.m.
["You will notice," Gumprich's gunnery officer explains, having been
read the report, "that she had struck, but continued radioing, which
had to be considered a hostile act; we could never be sure what they
might do next."]

Stratford and his first officer, Burnham Dun, the chief steward,
and chief engineer were taken back to *Nankin* by the Germans who
patched the shell hole and repaired the engines damaged by the ship's
company in their attempt at scuttling. The British party packed and
Stratford and Dun were then returned to the raider where they lived:

> . . . in crowded and uncomfortable conditions in a deck below the
> waterline, a little abaft amidships. Wooden bulkheads divided this
> deck into three compartments, one of which was used by the women
> and children, one by the male civilian passengers, and the other by
> the Naval and Military passengers and the officers of *Nankin*. All
> slept in hammocks. Lavatories and showers were fitted in two of the
> compartments, but the third, occupied by the male passengers, had
> lavatories only. The lavatories were rather difficult to flush on account
> of being below the water level. . . .
> . . . We were well treated, the food was wholesome, and adequate.
> The steward looking after us was a cheerful, friendly boy, who never
> grew tired or weary of attending to our wants. It appeared as if he
> could not do enough for us; in fact, everyone on board showed the
> same friendly spirit, and seemed to realize our unfortunate posi-
> tion. . . . [The captives were nice guys, we sympathized with them.]

Stratford found Drs. Otto Buchinger and Fritz Lehmann "most
attentive to wounded prisoners," and First Officer Dun still remembers
Prison Officer Meckmann as "a pleasant type of man." The big German
supervised the transfer of the five hundred captives (their number had
increased by the birth of a Chinese lad named Fritz in honor of the
doctor who delivered him) to *Regensburg* while his messmates directed
the unloading of *Nankin*. Nine hundred tons of the ship's cargo of wool,
walkie-talkies, and frozen foods and even some newly minted Chinese
money were taken. On the thirty-first, Stratford and 104 of his fellow
prisoners were again moved to relieve crowding, this time to *Dresden,
Atlantis'* old consort, which had left France on April 16 for Japan.

LONELINESS OF COMMAND

On June 10, in the week following Ruckteschell's narrow escape from
Alcantara, Gumprich's release of *Regensburg* and *Nankin,* and Gerlach's sinking of *Calcutta,* the latter Kapitän zur See met with tanker

Schliemann. Sixty-eight prisoners—all but *Gemstone*'s Captain Griffiths and the wounded from *Calcutta*—were shifted to the supply ship which was then dispatched to a waiting area for further availability. Gerlach, a lonely man, then, well-liked but often seeking company when it was not willingly proffered, spent the next few weeks meandering along the Africa–South America tracks, largely in bad weather and without luck due to his ship's slowness.

One of his worries could be traced to his two planes. They were tiny Arado 231s, designed for U-boats, but only six were ever built because it was found that they were underpowered, could not lift off in anything but the lightest winds and seas. For a raider, they were not worth a damn as Gerlach and his pilot, Karl Heinz Decker, found out. Try as he might, in several attempts during early July, Sergeant Decker simply could not get the machine airborne until its radio was removed and one fourth of its gasoline drained to save weight, and on landing a strut holding the starboard float broke, capsizing the frail contraption. A few days later, July 5, the port strut snapped and Decker's kite nosed over again. The second plane also failed to fly. The Arado 231, Gerlach logged, was "totally unsuited for the Atlantic even under the most favorable circumstances." He regretted that the hatch in which the planes were stored had not been enlarged to take the bigger Arado 196. That, margined SKL in the log later, was not so. *"Schiff 23* was to have gotten an Arado 196 A3 but the commander had preferred taking two AR 231s." Gerlach asked for the bigger model by wireless.

On July 27 *Stier* rendezvoused once more with *Schliemann* to which the remaining prisoners were transferred. *Gemstone*'s Griffiths was given a choice by Gerlach, whom he found jocular. Stay or go. The Briton had had no complaints; he had been given books, been well, courteously handled by Petersen whose attitude toward captives was that they were "colleagues." Jolly well go, it would be, he said, despite Gerlach's concern that he would regret it. Good-bye, the German replied, apologizing for sinking *Gemstone* and wishing the captain a speedy return to his family. Griffiths did regret not having heeded the Kapitän zur See's advice. *Schliemann*'s holds were filthy, filled with "rubbish, timber, wire, ropes, rats black and brown. More to be feared was the possibility that the ship might be ordered to Batavia, which, the German merchantmen knew, would be unfortunate for the prisoners.

During the next night while *Gemstone* and *Calcutta* personnel were trying to adjust to their new environment just east of Trinidade Island, their captors exchanged signals with *Michel,* and in the morning a testy Ruckteschell paid Gerlach a visit. What the former had to report about his experiences in the past few weeks was most interesting.

"BEST DAY YET"

He had shot J. & J. Denholm's *Lylepark* to pieces at close quarters during the night of June 11 and had then cruised south to within 550 miles of barren Tristan da Cunha for an exchange of foodstuffs, oil, torpedoes, and prisoners with the faithful *Schliemann* and Paul Schneidewind's proficient minelayer-blockade runner *Doggerbank* ten days later.* Discharging the two vessels after a week (*Schliemann* for further availability, *Doggerbank* to Japan), Ruckteschell turned north-east, boldly moving into the Gulf of Guinea, an area largely covered by air, and there he crept upon *Gloucester Castle,* Union Castle Line's smallest and oldest (1911) liner, which had already been retired when the war broke out and she was again pressed into service.

Gloucester Castle had steamed out of Birkenhead for South Africa with 154 souls and a cargo of machinery, military equipment, airplanes, and gasoline on June 21. She was armed with one 4.7-inch and several machine guns. On August 31 the Admiralty's Shipping and Casualty Department informed the company that their ship was "gravely overdue," and should be presumed lost. No one knew what had happened until after the war.

Tropical showers had not relieved much of the stickiness in *Gloucester Castle*'s many cabins and rooms on July 15 when night came on with the velvety black suddenness it does in the latitudes of Portuguese Angola. At 1900 it was dark, the ship blacked out, and the only sounds came from ineffective whirring fans inside and the foaming water rushing by outside. At that moment, the lulling quiet was interrupted by a loud report to starboard, followed by fire, terror, and death as heavy shells crunched into the vessel's inflammable superstructure and automatic cannon stitched nasty holes through the thin steel plating. The first shell struck just below the bridge, a second destroyed the neatly set dining room and set some gasoline stored in canisters on the foredeck on fire. The radio officer was killed instantly, and except for frantic commands and desperate screams, the ship was silent, listing first to starboard, then suddenly to port, glurking ominously in the sea. She sank so suddenly—four minutes, some of the shocked Germans say—that only one boat was gotten away. The raider, less than a mile away, sent her own boat to rescue fifty-seven crewmen and four passengers (two

---

* Twenty-two of LYLEPARK's men were saved, and a few of the remaining twenty-five reached safety at Freetown only to be torpedoed when reembarked in *Avila Star*. *Doggerbank* arrived in Japan and departed from there Europe-bound on December 17, still under the command of the daring Schneidewind. She was sunk by U-43 on March 3, 1943, leaving a bitter controversy over the responsibility for the sinking and mystery as to what had happened to all but one survivor who was picked up by a Spanish ship.

women and two children), many of whom were hauled to safety by German swimmers. The rest, eighty-two crew, six women, and two more children, perished—victims of a war that the New Zealand Commission had said did not permit the shipping of innocents and cargoes of destruction in the same bottoms. (Both British and German sources give the number of those saved at sixty-one, but the latter say there were only 151 persons on board.)

Fortunately for the Germans—the sad duty of destruction was getting on their nerves—*Michel's* artillerists were not given time to reflect on the deaths of innocents; they were back behind their sights less than twenty-four hours later. During the morning of July 16 *Michel's* lookouts reported several ships to Lieutenant Adolf Wimmel who had the 0800–1200 watch. One was thought to be Portuguese; the other two were tankers steaming along some twenty-five miles away on a parallel course. Ruckteschell, intending to snatch both of them, called von Schack to the bridge. "Today," he advised, "will be your best day yet." The two ships would be attacked at night simultaneously, the raider taking one, *Esau* the other. Shortly after 2100 they both struck. Schack, speeding through phosphorescent seas with *Esau* let fly with two torpedoes and saw two fountains of water rise from his tanker's slab sides as the missiles connected. At first the ship listed; then it righted itself and continued on at reduced speed as if nothing had happened.

While von Schack cursed his luck and damned the inadequate 18-inch aerial torpedoes which did not pack enough punch, *Michel* went into action against her own prey with all the weapons she could bring to bear. Only a few hundred yards across the water, Tidewater Oil Company's 7,983-ton *William F. Humphrey's* topsides, deckhouses, and starboard boats were smashed by around sixty shells that were being fired in salvos that seemed to be timed at intervals of thirty seconds, and hundreds of rounds of 37 mm and 20 mm. None of the tanker's three lookouts had seen anything of the raider except what they thought was a flashing white light before the explosions ripped their ship apart and changed their fates. Minutes after the initial assault, a torpedo hit their stern, another No. 5 tank, and a fire started at the bunker connections. *Humphrey,* with sixty-four men aboard, had not been a very happy ship; discipline, much to the grief of Second Officer Fritz Borner, was lax; the cocky gun crew could not get along with the merchantmen, and no one really seemed to respect the captain. She was an old ship (built 1921) and was steaming from Cape Town to Trinidad armed with a 5-inch gun which was manned, it should be mentioned, within seconds after the surprise attack occurred. Some say the gunners got off three rounds; Borner states only one shot was ever fired. At any rate, they were the only ones—but *Menelaus*—to have offered *Michel* any armed resistance until then. The brave effort did not do them any good, for their ship sank quickly when hit by a third torpedo after an action that lasted little over six minutes.

Michel's seamen, calling "come alongside, boys," picked twenty-nine survivors out of the water and from No. 2 and No. 4 boats, which the tanker's petrified crew had managed to lower (one died within a few days, and four others succumbed to disease and hunger in Japanese prison camps). Another eleven men, including the captain and Borner, drifted around on rafts and successfully avoided the raider. They heard her diesel, then saw the black hulk of a ship bearing down on them. It was the first they saw of the raider itself, and they did not want to get caught. Suddenly a flashlight one of them was carrying lit up, flickering brightly on the dark water. They let it sink, but it seemed hours before its evil, eerie glow vanished like a one-eyed monster in the depths below. Then, as *Michel*'s high hull towered over them, they could see men peering over the side looking for survivors. German-speaking Borner was relieved to hear a sepulchral *"Niemand hier"* (no one here) coming from the deck which seemed like a movie set. The next morning the raider was gone. *Humphrey*'s men, led by the badly injured Borner, found the deserted lifeboats, fixed up No. 2 with provisions from both, and set their red sails for Africa. They covered 450 miles in five and a half days before they were rescued by the Norwegian Wilhelmsen freighter *Triton,* which took them to Freetown.

Michel had meanwhile headed west along the presumed course of von Schack's damaged tanker, which, much to everyone's surprise, had made no attempt to let anyone know of her predicament. (Her radio equipment had been destroyed.) On the morning of the seventeenth it was in sight again, zigzagging. That night, the battered Norwegian *Aramis* was overwhelmed by the raider's guns and another torpedo, and ten Norwegians and thirteen Chinese (out of forty-three in the crew) were bundled over to *Michel* along with sacks of charts, routing instructions, merchant codes, and secret materials—the latter warning of German raiders that operated with torpedo launches. *Michel* churned off, and it was high time, too, Ruckteschell felt; three ships in as many days was pressing his luck. He pushed *Michel* back out into the Atlantic between St. Helena and the Ascensions where the United States was just completing an air base, and then motored leisurely to 21°S, 25°W near Brazil's Trinidade Island for another get-together with *Stier.*

"LEAVE YOUR SHIP"

At the rendezvous with Gerlach on July 29 the two raider captains decided to have a go at joint operations, their officers exchanged stories to clinking glasses, and some of the ratings developed wobbly legs in beery gab-fests. There were no results from the joint operations and the raiders then cruised separately, setting a new rendezvous for August 9. At 0815 that day, when the ships were still out of sight of each other, *Stier* gave chase to a vessel that was still out of range, vainly signaling her to stop. After Gerlach's opening salvo which, honoring custom, he had intended to miss, the new 7,072-ton *Dalhousie* ran and radioed, frantically replying to the German guns with a 5-inch which was unable to make any hits at a range of some sixteen thousand yards. At 1248, twenty-eight minutes after the first shot, the raider signaled "Leave your ship" and soon had the entire thirty-seven-man British crew on board.

Michel came up just in time for her men to watch the ship sinking, stern down, bottom up, but Ruckteschell did not dally long in the then badly compromised area and, always critical and demanding, he penned some doubts about Gerlach's tactics and character. He did not think the decent chap qualified to command a raider, and he felt that if anything should happen to him, there would be no one to take over because Gerlach did not discuss his plans enough with his subordinates. Ruckteschell planned to let SKL know this at the first opportunity and he later did.

ONE MAN

Back in June, while Gerlach and his pilot Decker were still fiddling with their miniature plane, and Ruckteschell was heading for a rendezvous with *Doggerbank,* the men in *Thor* had been quite busy in the Indian Ocean. Virtually in the center of that vast sea at 26°S, 77°E on June 14 they had had a traumatic experience. Early that night their radar had latched on to a target at 9,900 yards. Gumprich closed and at 1,760 yards opened fire. The first salvo struck and within seconds the other ship stood out on the water looking to Kandeler "like a floating wall of flame." The gunnery officer's most pleasant experience on board had been the day he was chairman of a court-martial of some Indians suspected of sabotage. Diligent investigation revealed the lads inno-cent—justice they had not expected of a white man—and Kandeler was happy to announce the verdict to them. His most horrible remembrance was the burning Dutch Shell Tankers N.V.'s *Olivia*. As in *Thor*'s year-before action with *Britannia,* only one man—one out of forty-six—was picked up. He was gunner J. D. Fischer. After the war Fischer testified that he had seen *Olivia*'s third officer, W. A. Vermoet, and gunner Cluclow lowering the starboard boat aft. Fischer went to his cabin to fetch life belts for Cluclow and himself and then helped slack away the boat. He lost track of it and therefore ran forward to escape the blistering heat that was charring the tanker and to climb on an over-turned boat. Washed off by a wave, he found himself swimming, shout-ing for help to the raider which had a searchlight on looking for survivors. He was the only one—one out of forty-six. The Germans were horrified. Henry Militzer, then on his second tour of killing or being killed, later wrote his previous captain, Kähler, "this sort of warfare was not to the liking of our former merchantmen"; no one else could have escaped.

Five days after that hellish nightmare, Third Officer Haagen Poppe, a twenty-four-year-old Norwegian, was sitting in his portside midship island cabin of the motor tanker *Herborg* reading. He does not remember what, but he can still hear the alarm bells. He had been through that before during his escape from Norway and in the sinking of *Thermopolae* in a Malta convoy. "Another ship seems to be following us," *Herborg*'s captain explained as Poppe reached the bridge. It boded ill to the latter:

> We hoisted our flag and were all standing on the bridge look-ing at him with our glasses when we saw a plane coming in from port, its machine guns chattering. It had a trailing line with which it tore out our aerial and then dropped two bombs. "Bak, bak, bak" went the other ship which we thought a jap. I ducked and heard the shells go "whuuum, whuuuum, whuuuuming" by overhead. They all missed but as there was little point in using our 3-inch gun, we abandoned with our crew of 38 Chinese. On board the raider we were searched by white-jerseyed Germans who, I must admit, were very nice and polite about it all. They were decent, probably thinking that they might be prisoners tomorrow. Taken below, we were placed in the hands of Heinz Müller, a rating from Leipzig who seemed terribly nice, always saying "Good morning, fellows, what can I do for you?" And he usually came through with our requests, say an accordion. We were never allowed matches, but everything was tried to keep a fire going to avoid having the wait for a German to give us a light.

A burning piece of rope made the latter mad, and an attempt with wires from a light bulb blew the fuse and that of the guard, too. Actually, Hoppe says, only the Indians ever got the best of their captors. They had their own customs, and while the Germans let them cook their own meals, no one looked kindly on their toilet habits, which ran counter to those recommended for warships. The fellows with the beards, too, for example, worried everyone. "Bugs, you know." Off with them, the Germans said. No, rather the whole head. Heads and hair stayed after an ample dousing with disinfectants.

THE CHEF DE POSTE DE FOULPOINTE

The same day *Herborg* was taken, but roughly 550 miles to the west, another group of nonwhites were giving some Europeans a lot of trouble. "Frequently we had to order the Chinese to keep the boat dry, as they appeared unable to arrange this amongst themselves. Whenever one of them was singled out, he was always very unwilling, a sailing report signed by W. A. Vermoet stated. Vermoet was the third officer of *Thor*'s "wall of flame" *Olivia,* and with him in the starboard aft lifeboat that Gumprich's prisoner Fischer said he had tried to lower, were three wounded Hollanders and eight Chinese.

Vermoet had run to his station when their captain had shouted "to the boats." Cluclow and Fischer had helped him lower away but an ear-splitting explosion had made the latter throw a turn off the forward bit and the boat had crashed into the water stem-first. Cluclow had then lowered himself to cut the lines of the after falls but had missed the boat and drifted into the flaming petrol. The same horrible fate seemed to have overtaken Fischer.

The third officer cut the lines himself and ordered some Chinese to "stand by the painter and oars" but not a single man moved an inch. "Even when I crawled forward armed with an axe, they still refused to hold the helm, nor would they row." And from then on, for a month, of torture, parched and starving, all but two of them continued to thwart Vermoet's efforts to reach land in a poorly maintained boat and with a larder of only fifteen pounds of corned beef, biscuits, and some chocolate that had spoiled. The Dutch stood watches, the Chinese were to bail. They did not and so the former had to do that, too. One European died, as did seven Chinese before they capsized in the rollers on a Madagascan beach on July 13. "At 0930 the 14th," Vermoet's boat log ends, the Chef de Poste de Foulpointe arrived . . ." and the four men were interned thirty days after that dreadful night when forty-one of their shipmates had been cremated more than two thousand miles to the east.

ON TO JAPAN

A week after the four indomitable but incredibly fortunate men reached safety—it had seemed impossible for anyone to have escaped—the cause of their horror, *Thor,* came across a ship that did not quit as easily as had the meek *Madrono* on July 4.* The latest victim ran, radioed, and

* Gumprich had had the undamaged *Herborg* renamed *Hohenfriedburg* and sent off to Japan where she arrived July 7. On the fourth of that month he

shot back until she was so badly on fire that a German boarding party could no longer search her. Her name was *Indus,* a reefer, and she belonged to Hain-Nourse, Ltd., of London. Her owners are not certain of all the details of her valiant end, but her Chief Engineer, Theodore L. Varian, one of the forty-nine survivors of a crew of seventy-one, has the answers. He was in his cabin around 1500 talking to Captain Bryan when they heard a heavy thud. Bryan ran for the bridge, asking Varian to maintain full speed, and the latter scrambled down to the engine room advising the engineers that they would be safer there than on the open deck. The near-mutinous natives ignored his advice; they were mowed down by shell splinters. *Indus'* gunners returned the Germans' fire with two ranging shots but before they could get off another, their gun was hit and the chief gunner mortally injured. (*Indus* did not, as mentioned in some literature, hit *Thor.*) Other shells set fire to the bridge and killed the radio officer. Once he had fallen from his keys and the ship had stopped, Gumprich's guns fell silent, allowing the British to take to the boats, a procedure that was hampered by the natives.

Indus' distress signals had been heard by shore stations and she was *Thor*'s last victim, bringing Gumprich's total to ten ships of 56,037 tons. Heading east, he met blockade runner *Tannenfels,* which had left France on February 12, for Japan, where she arrived on May 12 only to depart again Europ -bound on August 8. Varian, Fischer, Poppe, and the rest of the prisoners were transferred to the runner and Gumprich, by then without any prospects of replenishing his provisions and fuel, was ordered to Yokohama, where he arrived after a stop-over at Batavia on October 9. Far behind him, in the Atlantic, there was still a lot of action, and most of it was centered around *Michel.*

RED MOON GOES DOWN; BLOODY FINGERPRINTS; THE TENNO'S TROOPS

En route south one day after her hasty leave-taking from *Stier* on August 8, *Schiff 28*'s newssheet carried an important item: "Ritterkreuz bemedaled Captain Hellmuth von Ruckteschell, commander of the German auxiliary cruiser *Michel,* sank a unit of the *Rosita* class in a surprise attack yesterday." "Red Moon" was approximately ten inches across and was a record that moaned out one of the many selections of song bird Rosita Serrano, a favorite of many of the crew. Now it so

---

had taken the Norwegian *Madrono* without a fight—the eighth vessel he had captured "noiselessly." She, too, was renamed (*Rossbach*) and dispatched to Japan where she arrived August 5.

happened that Ruckteschell liked classical music and, being captain, he had reserved the ship's loudspeakers for it between 1900 and 2000. Aware of ordinary men's foibles, he had, however, let his men listen to pretty much what they wanted at other times. But the good Rosita offended his sensibilities and since he particularly disliked "Red Moon," he had requested that it not be played at all. Play it they did, and at noon when the entire ship was awake. It cannot be ascertained whether Ruckteschell was at that moment suffering from one of his awful migraine headaches or whether the past month of dawdling had gotten on his nerves. At any rate, he suddenly appeared in the wireless room, grabbed the record, stomped out on deck, and sailed it overboard. That was, his awed men decided, a command decision and, being far and a long time from home and more immediate news, they took it gleefully, savoring it as scuttlebut for once accurate. It was a delicious tale, better than the incident way back when they were working up with *Nürnberg*. At that time, so the story goes, Ruckteschell fell into the Baltic while on a visit to the cruiser. The exec, Erhardt, says it was he who splashed. What difference who it was; it delighted the seamen. By August 15 those healthy young lads were not particularly in need of a fillip; they had no reason to question the success of their cause even though some of their older messmates had already expressed uncertainty. The Axis' military machine's treads were still churning, its torpedoes still running true, but it was slowing, the men wearing down, the metal showing fatigue whether in good days or bad.

The fifteenth was a bad day in *Michel;* one and all were depressed, edgy and sick of war, and it did not help one whit that they had just added 5,874 tons to their record. That was just what had caused the gloom. Shortly before 2100 the previous evening, they had gone to their battle stations quite routinely and had launched LS 4 without more than the normal to-do. The raider had then veered in so close to their latest victim, *Arabistan,* that she had flashed a white light to prevent a collision. They had flattened her: "Arbitrarily considered sunk BZ F 3715 due to being overdue Trinidad since 8:29:42," her epitaph on an Allied naval tally sheet dated 11:10:42 reads. The Germans found not one man that night. But Ruckteschell had learned by then that it was wise for both morale and security to collect survivors, and his acquired concern paid off the next morning when *Arabistan*'s chief engineer was hauled out of a boat that was already awash. He was one man out of sixty! Less than a month later, after a final visit with *Schliemann,* *Michel*'s first division stood to again, cutting their fuses in earnest for an encounter with U.S. Line's *American Leader,* a new C-1-type freighter of 6,750 tons, manned by fifty-eight seamen and naval gunners.

American Leader, Capt. Haakon A. Pedersen, master, had left Cape Town at 1730 on September 7 with a valuable cargo of 2,000 tons of rubber, 850 of cocoanut oil in large tanks on deck, 440 of copra, 100 of spices, 200 of grease, hides, and assorted goods, and 20 of opium consigned to Newport News and New York. Heading west through increasingly heavy winds and seas that set the ship rolling and pitching so badly that the two boats lashed outboard for instant lowering had to be geared in, they passed several ships but none of them were spoken or seemed suspicious. At 1930 on September 10 Second Officer Walter Lee had just taken his evening star sights and had resumed his regular watch with the men in the wheelhouse and the lookouts in the bow and flying bridge. Captain Pedersen was up in the chart room and about to code the first position report as required by the Admiralty. Down below in the messhall, Bos'un Stanley E. Gorski was having a cup of coffee, and Third Officer George W. Duffy remembers that there was a great argument running. The chief steward had made a bet with the second cook that he alone could turn out a better meal than all three of the cooks put together. Naturally, everyone took a good deal of interest in the affair, but just as naturally, no one was about to pick favorites—the food had been poor all that voyage and the steward was not a cook. The big test was scheduled for the next day. It never came off.

Up on the bridge, Lee was staring into the dark, moonless night. Only a few stars twinkled through the thickening clouds, and visibility was low, perhaps a thousand yards. To the stocky Duffy, "it was the kind of night we liked—we could not see anything and no one *should* see us." Suddenly a dark shape materialized ahead and slightly to starboard. As the *Leader* slowly answered her helm starting to swing left, the other ship opened fire from what seemed about five hundred yards away, then came around her stern, its cannon hammering hot metal into her gun tubs (one 4-inch, several machine guns) and upperworks. The American vessel shook to the impact of the shells which instantly smashed lifeboat No. 1, killed the chief steward, splintered raft No. 5, destroyed the radio, and tore the armor plating off the emergency generator room. Kerosene drums caught fire, and diesel fuel, ignited by tracer, spilled blazing over the superstructure. Her whistle wailed horribly. On the shattered boat deck First Officer Bernard J. Hickey was trying to get the remaining boat away when it was shot off its davits, and down on the main deck Duffy, Gorski, and others ducked behind winches, resistor houses, and cargo as they struggled to free the rafts. Two torpedoes opened the ship's sides and she started to settle by the stern, listing to port. As she went down about twenty-five minutes after the first sighting, her whistle gurgled for a second or two in the black water and then there was silence, a deadly, uncanny silence in a black night broken only by flickering patches of burning oil and a splotchy phosphorescence where containers of oil, broken loose from the sunken wreck, shot through the surface and fell back with an enormous splash endangering the men clustered about the rafts. There was some panic at first, with everyone yelling at once and all hoping to get a favorable spot on anything that floated. One poor soul, who had had nightmares about being sunk and had taken to drink, simply swam off into the night to drown; another insisted that there was nothing further to be done but pray. "Bullshit," the tall, dark-haired bos'un roared, and gradually the men calmed down as Pedersen, Lee, Duffy, and Hickey, who was considered somewhat of a martinet by some of the crew, established discipline. Many of them did not know what had gotten them—some thought a sub; others knew that no sub could deliver such a volume of fire. Some believed it had been a pocket battleship, and those who feared it had been Japanese, did not want to be picked up. But the colder they got, the more advisable it seemed to get on a dry deck. They were roughly a thousand miles from shore and, as the bos'un said a bit inaccurately, "The nearest land is a mile away—straight down!" "Yeah," someone retorted, "what if we get machine-gunned?" "Well, let's get it over with," and with that they flashed lights and everyone started hollering.

After some time, the boys with Duffy saw a ship of some sort coming down. He flicked his light and the vessel stopped; its crew put a Jacob's ladder and a cluster light over the side and started tossing heaving lines. It was only then that those on the raft realized it was a German. Duffy, who had seriously considered concealing himself, thought better of it. He let go his revolver and camera, and when a boat appeared, he climbed into it. At last, after about six hours, forty-seven of them, wet, some wounded, and wondering what would happen, stood shivering on *Michel*'s deck. Nothing much did happen. Their wounds were dressed, hot bouillon was served, their valuables were collected to prevent fights and thefts, and they were deloused; they were told that their treatment would be according to their conduct. "It was strict and fair," Duffy says, and Gorski agrees though he lost his helmet to a souvenir hunter and someone pinched his ring. They did not have much time to test conditions before the raider's bells shrilled again the next evening as the Germans started their heavy-footed stampede up and down ladders to their battle stations. *Michel* was stalking *Empire Dawn*.

That was a motor ship only a year old, owned by the Ministry of Transport and managed by Walter Runciman and Company, of Glasgow. Capt. W. A. Scott and his thirty-three officers and unlicensed personnel had taken her from Birkenhead to the Mideast with military stores, ammunition, and planes. Their voyage had been rather typical for wartime. Four planes had been washed overboard in a storm, and another cargo vessel had torn a twelve-by-eleven-foot gash into their starboard side just opposite from where some twenty-five tons of gelignite was stored. Their four gunners had not had anything to do but tinker with their machine guns, an Oerlikon, a 4-inch, and some depth charges. Scott left Durban on September 4 bound for Trinidad to load bauxite for New York. When he was called to the bridge at 2000 on the twelfth, he had good reason to believe himself in safe waters. He was then well past the Cape's *Doggerbank* mines and the well-justified fear of long-range U-boats. Scott's account:

> The Chief Officer was looking through the binoculars at what he said appeared to be a merchant ship passing on an opposite heading. I went into the wheelhouse to check on the ship's course and as I turned around after looking at the compass I saw tracer shells coming over. My first impression was that they would go over the ship; they must be a warning. What should I do? Stop engines? Alter course? Send out my position by W/T? As these thoughts were passing through my mind there was a terrific crash and the compass seemed to break into small pieces in front of me. . . . I struggled up, blood pouring from my head. I passed my hand over my face to wipe away the blood and staggered against the side of the wheelhouse. My hand left a perfect imprint in blood on the paintwork. I stared at it and laughed hysterically, like a drunken man. . . . I watched fascinated for a second; they [the automatic weapons] left a series of 2-inch holes of red-hot metal which glowed in the darkness, and then they exploded inside the ship. By this time I realized that there was no hope of saving the ship, but I thought that if I could signal the raider he might give us time to get into the boats. I tried to signal from the boat deck with a torch, but the reply was a hail of 2-inch shells and both my legs were splattered with shrapnel and were extremely painful. The Third Officer who was standing beside me was killed and several others wounded. . . . It seemed as if the raider intended no survivors.

As Scott was being helped aft, he felt the blood from his legs "squelching" in his shoes. He noticed that the water looked cold and forbidding, and dazed as he was, he rather pointlessly asked his second officer how it was. To the reply "not too bad," he jumped and it seemed ages before he and twenty-one others were fished out of the debris-choked water. Scott and the other injured ended up in one of the raider's two white, tidy sick bays which were equipped with gimbaled beds.

Empire Dawn's men proved to be an unwelcome addition to the crowded ship whose prisoners then numbered nearly five hundred.

Water had to be rationed to a few cups per man per day and most washing had to be done with seawater—usually cold (to save fuel) and with saltwater soap, which, at best, is not too effective. As for the food—lunch for example—it differed a bit each day: One time it was soup with cabbage and hot dogs, the next hot dogs, cabbage, and soup; then stew, dehydrated potatoes, Brussels sprouts, and a slice of wurst. Sundays there was honey, a thicker soup, and perhaps some canned fish. Cigarettes were issued and those who did not smoke could trade them for candy bars. The only thing that could be said for it was that the Germans ate the same stuff. Duffy, who was responsible for getting their food in the chow line (he thought the job convenient for a little snooping) knows they did: "The Germans picked over our left-overs."

Contact with *Michel's* crew was strictly limited, but when they did get in touch the prisoners bartered for candy, cigarettes, and clothing—begged is as good a word—or they teased the Germans mercilessly. They told them that they would never win the war; they bragged about the Allies and the food served in their ships. They stole everything not attached to a living German, and allowed themselves the pleasure of shouting that they could see a "krooser." To those leaning over the bridge, the crowd below was fun to watch, but abstract. Adjutant Herr, who had spent 1937 at Connecticut's Kent prep school and even looked "white shoe," would have liked to have a chat: "They did not worry us in the least; we had our job to do and we were glad the tables weren't turned." For the prisoners who chose to work—for personal gain, "to get the air," to gather information, or for both reasons—there were compensations. A beer now and then, a mooched cigarette, and a glance at a strange collection of machinery and men. The Chinese rinsed in the laundry, the blacks in the galley; men like Gorski (with Pedersen's permission) painted ship. They were still dabbling in late September when SKL directed *Michel* to a meet with *Tannenfels,* tanker *Uckermark* (ex-*Altmark* of *Graf Spee* times), and *Stier*. Neither the raider nor the blockade runner lingered long, but *Uckermark* was kept in company by *Michel* for two weeks. On September 27 the two ships were lying stopped in the swells at 26°34′S, 27°37′W and Ruckteschell's radio operators were as usual monitoring the thousands of dots and dashes beeping in over many wavelengths. Suddenly one of them sat up straight to jot down a message flashed loud and clear on six hundred meters. It was exactly 1104 GMT. Interference by another ship's set garbled the signals a bit but it was quite evident that an Allied ship was in trouble and there was not the slightest hint of Germany's raider war nearing another big step toward its end.

CHAPTER 11

1942, Part II:
The Beginning of the End

WORRIED GERMANS; THEIR PRISONERS AND THOSE OF JAPAN The 1104 GMT signal was from an American ship—call letters KXWN—which said that she was being shelled and that she was at 24°53′S, 21°31′W, just below the Tropic of Capricorn and closer to South America than Africa. The message was repeated three times in as many minutes and was picked up by St. Helena and other stations despite some badly tuned jamming by another ship, purporting to be an Argentinian, with a communication reading *"Rio Corrientes ar Paranne descoia feliciatates familia ebrasca frederico oar caruch."*

At 1153 *Stier* could be heard with her usual nervous touch on both 600 meters and the special wavelength 8460 and signal KADW arranged between herself and *Michel.* Her coded message said that *Schiff 28* should come immediately to square GA 6130, a position approximately 110 miles away on the secret German grids. To Ruckteschell, it was obvious that someone had attacked the American and it was possible that it had been *Stier.* He certainly did not think it advisable to head for the very place where all the commotion was. Urgent British messages addressed to warships were already skipping across the ether, and it was a safe bet that they concerned KWXN's distress. He steered south at top speed with *Uckermark* and spent the next few days trying to raise both *Stier* and Germany. There was no reply, nothing for *Michel.* He was probably in one of the blind spots that unaccountably blot out communications, and he feared that *Stier* and *Tannenfels* had come to harm and the SKL was unaware of their fate.

Ruckteschell's worries, of course, did not faze his prisoners at all—in fact, they would have welcomed them if they had been informed.

234

Every day they were wakened by music, and it seemed that the P.A. system was never off: *Achtung, Achtung . . . Wecken* (reveille) . . . sweepers and cleaners, *Backen und Banken* (meals) . . . The special sea duty men will now . . . oompah music . . . Wagner, martial music, news from Germany, birthday greetings, quizzes, more music . . . all day until *"Pfeifen und Lunten aus."* The martial music had some effect in lifting droopy spirits, but the Americans wanted to hear something else. What, for example, was happening in the World Series, they asked supply-prison Officer Lt. (S.G.) Otto Saupe. He did not know and cared less, but when told of the significance of the American and National Leagues, he countered that that sort of preoccupation with trivia might easily cost the United States the war, conveniently forgetting the importance attached by his compatriots to Europe's soccer scores. Nevertheless, he got them what they wanted: St. Louis 4–1 over New York.

Since the prisoners did not have much to do, any change was welcome. News that the Germans incinerated most of their garbage and even chopped boxes and cartons into little pieces so that no one could trace their whereabouts was interesting. It made even better listening to hear that one of their numbers had gotten into an argument with a German and had created quite a stir, at least so the fellow said, while working in hatch No. 1 where a lot of gear from captured ships was stored. The dispute centered around something like Was Roosevelt or Hitler the greater bum? There were more immediately rewarding attempts to improve their lot. Gorski, being Gorski, almost regretted the effort if only for his own pride. He was down in one of the ship's storerooms shoring up supplies, when some jars of chocolate balls caught his fancy and he helped himself. The German chief supervising the work was, like his breed in any navy, eagle-eyed and suspicious. He caught the candy copper. "What would you expect me to do?" the discomfited prisoner snapped, counting on the chief to realize that "swabs" were the same the world over. The German grew indignant: "Why don't you ask, if you want some sweets?" Then Gorski got mad—it is never nice to be caught with your hands in the cookie jar: "Why didn't you tell me I could have some?" he said and with that insisted that he really did not want any of the damn things anyway. The chief then suggested he take some. Embarrassed, Gorski refused until he was convinced he should surprise his buddies with some of the goodies.

On October 7 SKL radioed Ruckteschell who was idling westward in bad weather and of similar mood and still anxious about *Stier.* "Whereabouts *Schiff 23* uncertain. Possible radio broken down." *Michel's* captain had his doubts and he was surprised that Berlin had not taken alarm (they had), but he agreed to wait until the tenth when he would be free to continue his own operations. On that day, much to the sorrow of his own crew, seventy of the healthier prisoners (including Scott who had been given the choice of remaining) were transferred to *Uckermark,* which took them to Tandjoengpriok, Java, Japanese captivity, and horror. They were punched, beaten, and starved from camp to camp, island to island, from Java to Singapore and Sumatra. Thousands died delirious, skeletonized by dysentery and swollen with beriberi, stinking cairns of bones to the inefficiency of the Japanese and a mockery of man. Tens of thousands were sardined into transports that crept from port to port hoping to escape Allied submarines. *Junyo Maru,* packed miserably with more than 2,000 POWs and some 5,000 natives, did not. She was torpedoed off Java by H.M.S. *Tradewind,* S.L.C. Maydon commanding. Roughly 750 to 800 people survived. Gorski was one of them.* By September 1945 when everyone who was anything was being saluted aboard U.S.S. *Missouri* for the surrender ceremonies in Tokyo Bay, only around 33,000 of an original 125,000 POWs remained in the East Indies and they, like Gorski's shipmate Duffy, were very, very lucky to have withstood being "kicked from pillar to post by Japs, Dutch or Limies, and, sad to say, our own people, too."

"AUSSTEIGEN, ABANDON SHIP"

Stier's officers never did share Ruckteschell's opinion that no one on their ship could take over if Gerlach should be incapacitated or that their captain did not consult with them on strategy or tactics. He did, taking advice graciously. Besides, the realistic Ludolf Petersen mused, "what tactics or strategy? They were forced on us by the enemy." They did, however, worry about his capabilities as a commander. "We were on a very exposed post out there all alone in the Atlantic and we often wished that we could have had a harder man for captain," says one. "Our faith in him as a strong leader was not sanguine." To another officer, he "was simply not up to the job, particularly that job." It was not in anger; they felt sorry; "he was such a fine man."

---

* There are conflicting figures in this as in most disasters, and it has been claimed that this sinking led to the greatest loss of life at sea ever. In early March 1945 the German *Wilhelm Gustloff* and *Goya,* carrying refugees from the eastern Baltic, were torpedoed by Russian submarines. Around 5,200 persons were lost with *Gustloff* and nearly 7,000 in *Goya,* according to German estimates. Lloyd's does not mention the Japanese ship. Gorski got a letter from Wraxall, England, in 1962. Signed by *Tradewind's* Maydon, it said: "I apologize after all these years for the indignity of having tipped you out of her for a swim."

Ruckteschell had, however, been right when he assumed that *Stier* was in trouble, bad trouble. When the raiders last separated, the cheers of their crews had been especially hearty, Petersen recalls, because "practically everyone felt that the chances of seeing each other again or getting home were very slim, indeed." Forced southwest by the disturbance created by *Dalhousie*'s wireless, Gerlach had gone to meet *Schliemann* north of Gough Island on August 27. It was a lucky day for *Gemstone*'s Griffiths, who had been told that the supply ship would be heading for Batavia where the Japanese were roughing about, but who was recalled to *Stier* by Gerlach to avoid Japanese captivity. Griffiths was "delighted" to shake hands with the German who met him at the raider's gangway, and "glad to get back to my clean old bunk." He was also pleased to see *Dalhousie*'s Captain Davies, whom he had known before, and a steward named Groves.

The contradictory title to a document signed by Gerlach reads:

Report of the Commander
'SCHIFF 23'
about the last successful fight by the ship
and its sinking

In this document it is stated that *Stier* was at position 24°44′S, 21°50′W in an area little frequented by shipping on September 27. At around 0800 that day, the executive officer advised the captain that the many men working outboard scraping and painting should be called in because of rain and rising seas. Visibility was poor (two to two and a half miles) and it would be a good idea to play it safe. Shortly before 0850 most of the lads had climbed back aboard, and just as Gerlach was leaving the bridge two minutes later, someone cried out, "Vessel in sight to starboard." Alarm! Germany's colors were hoisted and a visual signal telling the obviously enemy ship that had suddenly come out out of a squall line to stop was two-blocked. At 0850 the flack reported all clear and were given permission to open fire. At 0856 the 5.9s went into action, registering with their third salvo. By 0900 the enemy replied with four or five guns, or so it seemed: "It was immediately clear that this was not a normal merchantman . . . either an auxiliary, possibly even an AMC," whose armament was estimated as one 5.9 on the stern, two 4- or 5-inch on the bow, two of the same forward of the funnel, and two more behind it, plus some 40 mm and 20 mm. The enemy was radioing, too.

Stier was hit by fifteen heavy shells besides being peppered by smaller stuff. One shell set the coal bunker on fire, others the officer's section, both hospitals, and the bridge. The worst was No. 7, which tore into the crew's quarters near No. 2 hold and into the diesel-powered generator, setting fire to an adjoining compartment, wooden lockers, and mattresses. Ammunition hoists stopped when the electricity went off, fire mains were cut, leaving the snaking hoses flat across the deck as the men turned to squelch galloping flames with bucket brigades. Men trapped below by acrid fumes and heat had to be led out through narrow escape hatches. The main engine was dead, leaving the ship a drifting wreck with smoke choking everyone belowdecks. The splendid but unsoldierly Dr. Meyer-Hamme, Petersen's best friend, was killed. "It is easy to die," he said, "greet our friends." Men took splinters in their kidneys, lungs, and temples. Two more would die; five were badly wounded and twenty-eight suffered lighter injuries. At 1000, the enemy, at whom fifty to sixty salvos had been fired (not counting Borchers' flack which had hammered out some nine hundred rounds), was seen to be sinking by the stern. Raider *Michel* was called for help but could not be raised and nearby *Tannenfels* could not get her fire hose across the rough water. Prisoners Griffiths, Davies, and Groves were led on deck, where they found utter bedlam, smoke pouring from ventilators and ports, hoses limp without pressure. They knew *Stier* was doomed. Gerlach consulted for the last time with his officers; everyone agreed: abandon.

The captain calmly assembled his men. One "Sieg Heil" each for the Führer, the fatherland, *Schiff 23,* and their late enemy. Then they lowered the wounded (including *Calcutta*'s Hassan) into the boats. Lieutenant Petersen told the British to go overboard and at 1140 Gerlach left his command, heavy-hearted and miserable. At 1157 the first scuttling charge went off and two minutes later the second. As his raider went down over her stern, Gerlach managed another exhortation. *"Deutschland, Deutschland uber Alles,"* the shaken but disciplined seamen sang.

Up to that moment *Tannenfels'* trip from the Indian Ocean had not been too bad, taking everything into account. *Herborg*'s Haagen Poppe thought. Usually the prisoners had been allowed on deck all day, but that rainy Sunday they were kept below so that they could not see *Stier*. Suddenly a ship's gun opened up with a few rounds, and automatic weapons barked. After a while, there was a lot of commotion and then the singing of the German national anthem. Poppe thought it was all over—the Royal Navy must have arrived. But no; guards came rushing down all in a dither, shouting at the prisoners to leave everything, go aft to No. 5 hold which was filled with dunnage, a little cargo, and rats. There they had no blankets, no hammocks, no eating utensils.

Griffiths, Davies, and Groves, too, were pushed down aft, where they found *Indus, Herborg,* and *Madrono* men. "More than half of these were Indians and the stench was horrible," *Gemstone*'s captain lamented. "It was flour bags for bedding and bad food if any," until Gerlach paid them a visit and had Petersen straighten things out. With *Stier*'s crew forward in the former prison holds, and all the captives aft, *Tannenfels* simply had more men on hand than her Captain Haase had bargained for. He had not enough rations for all, and hardly enough oil to get home.

Haase and Gerlach searched first in the wreckage-strewn waters for enemy survivors—"no prisoners picked up due to poor visibility"—then made their way cautiously to France. And a bad trip it was, with overcrowding and everyone afraid they might not make it. One man did not. He was *Dalhousie*'s Steward Groves. Just before reaching the Gironde and when about twenty miles offshore, Groves took some life belts and jumped overboard in bitter-cold weather, determined to swim to Spain and get home. (Griffiths said he was never heard from again and this writer has been unable to trace him.) He was not missed until *Tannenfels* reached France on November 2. The rest of the Allied crews soon found themselves at Marlag and Milag Nord, where their treatment was just a bore. So much so, that Poppe, who was not required to work, volunteered to clean out some barracks. He found an old railway guide which he stuffed into his pants. Soon enough, a German party came along with a doctor who asked the tall, skinny Norwegian whether he had any "boogs." Poppe knew full well that the British called lice and such critters "bugs," but all he could think of just then was that somehow his theft of the guide book had been discovered. "Yes," he admitted. The doctor asked what kind (there had been a typhus scare) and Poppe spread his hands to show him how big it was. "Then I unlimbered my pants and wanted to pull the book out. I asked if he wanted to see it. '*Nein!!*' And off they went, thinking no doubt that I had been a prisoner too long."

Gerlach had meanwhile been ordered to form a precommissioning detail for a captured British merchantman which the optimists at SKL wanted to have in service the next year. Eighty percent of his men volunteered for another cruise, Borchers says, joining *Schiff 5, ex-Glengarry,* which was then in Rotterdam's Wilton yards being converted. Lieutenant Petersen, however, having had enough time behind the enemy's lines in *Lützow, Scheer,* the whalers, *Stier,* and *Tannenfels,* stood back. But navy personnel bureaus go by the book and the newly promoted lieutenant did actually have the necessary qualifications. He went to *Schiff 5,* a raider that would never fight.[1]

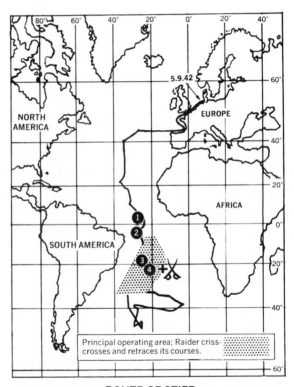

ROUTE OF STIER

1. GEMSTONE	6.04.42
2. STANVAC CALCUTTA	6.06.42
3. DAHLHOUSIE	8.09.42
4. STEPHEN HOPKINS & STIER SUNK ✛	9.27.42

"GALLANT SHIP"

On December 10 SKL attached an addendum to *Stier*'s log. It said the vessel Gerlach had fought was *Stephen Hopkins,* an American Liberty ship. "She may have sunk us," the realist Petersen reflected, "but she saved most of our lives. We would not have lasted much longer out there those days and there would not always have been a *Tannenfels* around to pick us up." SKL's top-secret attachment added that according to press reports six survivors of the United States ship had reached shore after thirty-one days.

Stephen Hopkins was one of 2,708 Liberties built. Her keel was laid at Kaiser's Richmond (California) yard where she was one of 821 of her class the company welded together with incredible war-winning speed. Known as Hull 247 and launched April 14, 1942, she displaced 10,708 tons and was delivered to the Maritime Administration on May 11 to be managed by the Luckenbach Steamship Company. She was not an AMC, nor did she mount the arsenal Gerlach thought. Her total armament consisted of two 37-mm, four 50- and two 30-caliber machine guns and a 4-inch aft. If SKL had read *The New York Times* or the New York *Tribune* on the tenth, they would have known that there were fifteen survivors, and though there were natural, war-time inaccuracies in both stories, they could have learned the names of thirteen of them from the *Times'* account. Two names were withheld because the men had relatives in Axis-controlled countries.

The *Hopkins,* Captain Paul Buck commanding, was on her first voyage which had taken her to New Zealand, Australia, and Africa, and she was steaming in ballast from Cape Town to Dutch Guiana to load bauxite. For Sunday September 27 the menu posted on the bulletin board listed turkey with all the trimmings, and iced tea for lunch. Some of the forty-one merchantmen and fifteen naval gunners (there was one passenger) skipped breakfast in anticipation. Gunner Paul B. Porter, who had had the 0400–0800 watch did not, and once he had finished, he hit the sack. Others had a dice game going, Ordinary Seaman Rodger H. Piercy, who was later promoted to acting third officer in another ship, remembers.

Porter had not been asleep very long when something like a sledgehammer hit the deck. He looked out the porthole of his starboard midship cabin and saw two ships, one of which was blazing away at *Hopkins,* and he could hear his own guns opening up. He grabbed a pea coat, sweater, and helmet—the gun crew slept in their clothes—and rushed aft to his 50-caliber mount, passing a deckhand whose buttocks had been shot off. But since his gun, wet under its canvas cover, would not function, he joined the 4-inch crew who were being cut down man by man, the dead and dying being replaced by volunteers. Piercy had seen two ships flying signal flags when "suddenly we received a blast and knew they were no friends of ours." The gunner ran to his station at the 4-inch which was temporarily in charge of Cadet Edwin O'Hara until Ensign Kenneth Willett, his entrails hanging out from a mortal wound, arrived to take over. Up forward, the 37 mm just vanished, Porter remembers, along with a friend who had mentioned German raiders in Cape Town: "I just feel that something is going to happen. I'm not going to make it."

Few of them did, for no matter how courageously they fought or how many of them tumbled to the decks "oozing breakfast and blood," *Hopkins,* her still revolving screw mangling a swimmer, was doomed. So much steam had escaped through ruptured pipes that her abandon ship whistle was barely audible.*

Porter, Piercy (the water was so cold he felt like a "Popsicle"), August Reese, a native German and one of the two whose names were later deleted from dispatches, nineteen others, and George Cronk, second engineer and senior survivor but not certainly a seaman, escaped in Lifeboat No. 1 despite *Tannenfels'* search. And though Cronk would later get much of the credit, it was Reese, then nearly sixty and an experienced Cape Horn sailing ship hand, who brought them through an eighteen-hundred-mile ordeal with unflagging perseverance, skill, some pemmican and malted milk tablets. By October 10, when two men had already died stinking of gangrene, and Gerlach was still pacing uncomfortably in *Tannenfels,* still another raider, *Komet,* outbound for the Atlantic, was fighting its way down the Channel.

"DEFINITELY NO SURVIVORS"

Komet's second attempt at raiding started on the night of October 7/8, lasted but two days and ended in disaster. She had returned to Germany less than a year earlier and since that time had been refurbished with late-model guns and a radar set. Her new commander, Capt. Ulrich Brocksien, forty-two, was first staff officer to Adm. Wilhelm Marschall in battle cruiser *Gneisenau* and *Scharnhorst*'s initial, November 1939 sortie in which AMC *Rawalpindi* was sunk, and had been slated to lead

---

* The posthumous awards: Willett, the Navy Cross; a destroyer of the *John C. Butler* class and a King's Point Merchant Marine Academy building named in his honor. Captain Buck and Cadet O'Hara, the Merchant Marine Distinguished Service Medal. Chief Officer Richard Moczkowski, a Liberty ship named in his honor.

fifty ships from Le Havre to England in the never-never-land invasion of the United Kingdom that wasted so much of Germany's efforts in 1940 and early 1941. She had only two of her original officers, the exec, Huschenbeth, who did not think much of her chances, and Signal Officer Wilhelm Dobberstein, on board.

She ran into trouble the first day after leaving Germany when she lost four of her escorting minesweepers (two others were damaged) to mines even though the passage had been cleared just four hours earlier. Brocksien therefore put into Dunkirk. Poor weather delayed the operation still further, and a Sperrbrecher was lost on another mine. Leapfrogging cautiously, he finally made it to Le Havre at 0500 on the thirteenth. But across the Channel, OIC were aware that the Germans were making unusual preparations to get an important ship out. A force of five *Hunt*-class destroyers, *Albrighton, Cottesmore, Eskdale, Glaysdale,* and *Quorn,* led by Comdr. J. C. A. Ingram in *Cottesmore,* and eight MTBs cleared Dartmouth to patrol off Cap de la Hague, and four more of the handy *Hunts* steamed out of Plymouth to close the trap.

By 1900 October 13, *Komet* sallied forth again, heading for Cap de la Hague and escorted by four torpedo boats in a circular formation with the raider in their midst, T-14, the flotilla leader, in the van. At 2100 they were close to Barfleur but had been detected by radar and a Swordfish plane which dropped flares. Their discovery made an order to put into Cherbourg for shelter imperative, the commander of T-14 felt. But the decision lay with Brocksien who did not alter course and who had precious little time to make up his mind. At 0205 of the fourteenth he radioed being in action.

It was a fast and deadly fight with the Germans almost immediately smothered by destroyer gunfire and desperately trying to avoid swishing schools of torpedoes fired by MTBs. All of the escort suffered more or less severe damage and fifteen men were reported missing or killed. Among the latter was the flotilla leader, Lt. Comdr. Hans Wilke. His death, T-14's skipper said, was, however, clearly due to panic or a communications failure in *Komet,* whose forward 20-mm gunners hammered shells into T-14 as well as T-4 and T-19 like wild men during the disarray of battle despite good visibility and ranges of only a bit over one thousand yards. Still, Brocksien would not alter course for safety, and his failure to do so when it was still possible, caused by either indecision or preoccupation, led to tragic consequences. Less than ten minutes after the scattered opening rounds, Sublieutenant R. Q. Drayson, R.N.V.R., bored in with MTB 236, its throttles wide open, to torpedo the raider. By 0215 *Komet* was seen to be on fire and the flames

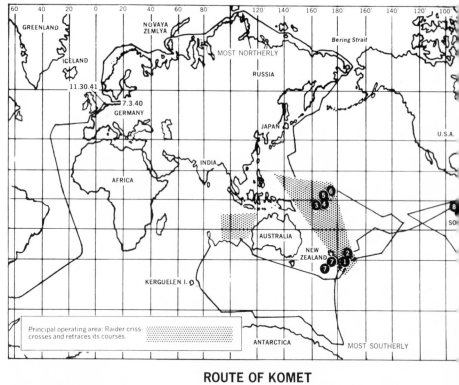

ROUTE OF KOMET

1. HOLMWOOD	11.25.40	6. NAURU
2. RANGITANE (with ORION)	11.27.40	7. Mines laid by ADJUTANT, ex POL IX
3. TRIONA (with ORION)	12.06.40	8. AUSTRALIND
4. VINNI	12.07.40	9. KOTA NOPAN
5. KOMATA	12.08.40	10. DEVON

spread with lightning speed. Fifteen to twenty seconds later, a ball of fire shot hundreds of yards into the sky and *Komet,* her back broken, her masts canted toward each other, and pieces of her wreckages whirling through the air, vanished, leaving only patches of burning oil to mark the grave of Brocksien and 350 men. "Definitely no survivors," T-14's commander reported when he put into St.-Malo.*

A BUTTERFLY

Way down in the South Atlantic not long after *Komet*'s annihilation, a tern fluttered into *Stephen Hopkins'* lifeboat No. 1 on one of those horrible days after the fifth of its suffering occupants had died. They had been talking about food all day and someone had mentioned that he could eat a skunk. "One of the fellows caught it," Piercy recalls, "and said, 'Well, here is the meal we wanted.' But not a man among us had nerve enough to hurt the bird. The poor thing had been fighting for its life and needed just as much help as we did." They allowed it to recuperate and when it flew away everyone "felt better for it." On October 25 the boat's log read: "Saw butterfly and two moths," and on the twenty-seventh, "Hurrah, sighted land at 4 a.m.;" a long, dreadful month, magnificently defied by a disciplined group of different ages and many ethnic backgrounds—Polish, Greek, Hawaiian, German—and many of them wounded. When they waded ashore near Barro de Stapapoana, Brazil, Porter was down fifty pounds, quite unaware that his *Hopkins,* which like *Stanvac Calcutta* was to be named one of the United States Maritime Administration's eleven "Gallant Ships," had sunk *Stier,* the last German raider to get out from Europe.

IT IS NONSENSE TO DIE

The only raider then at sea (SKL, either presumptuous or irrational, still had *Schiff 5* and yet another, *Schiff 14,* abuilding), *Michel,* had in the meantime been reassigned to the Indian Ocean for a few weeks after which she was to range the Antarctic for another *Pinguin* coup against

---

* The destruction of *Schiff 45,* her escort's officers decided, was probably due to gunfire which set off the aviation gas in hold No. 2 and resulted in an explosion of the forward magazines. None of the characteristic fountains of water usually thrown up by torpedo hits were seen, and none of the sounds indicative of such a hit were observed by any of the men serving below the torpedo boats' waterlines where they would have been most audible. The British, who suffered but two wounded and slight damage to a destroyer, however, assigned their success to Drayson's little boat and its 21-inch torpedoes.

the whaling fleets. Berlin's primary purpose in redeploying the raider
was to prevent her operations from interfering with a planned, and what
was to be a most successful, assault on South African waters by long-
range U-boats of the IX-c type. Ruckteschell was irked but he appreciated the strategic priorities. In fact, he frankly considered U-boats a
better weapon than raiders; "Tactically, an HK can hardly accomplish
anything anymore." It was a waste of time, men and materiél to throw a
ship like his aimlessly about with a good chance that she might end up
like *Stier,* sinking a few ships, perhaps, but virtually unable to affect the
dispositions of a by then overwhelmingly superior enemy. Since U-boats
were a better instrument for that, his four hundred men might best be
reemployed manning eight of Dönitz's gray wolves. What was more, he
was not about to go to the Antarctic at all. The timing was poor and the
distances too great, he said. In three words, much to the consternation
of his radiomen and the delight of the few in the know, he informed
Admiral Fricke, SKL's chief of staff, *"Antarktik ohne mich"* (Antarctic
without me). Bernau and Pillau radio stations acknowledged immediately, and Ruckteschell found it amusing that some careless decoder had
added a nonexistent sentence: "have not sunk anything." Right the next
day *Michel* received Berlin's reply in FT 80-1228/5; it said:

> *Einverstanden, Ruckteschell,*
> *Dann auch ohne SKL.*
> *Weiterhin nun gute Fahrt,*
> *Nach alter 28 Art.*
> (Loosely translated:)
> *Agree, Ruckteschell,*
> *Then without SKL.*
> *And furthermore, the best of luck*
> *With 28's proven pluck.*

Ruckteschell was delighted: "This message is refreshing and eases
the tension of the last few days." In mid-November, FTs 1 through 3 of
the thirteenth extended *Michel's* stay in the Indian Ocean until the end
of December, would have her back in France the end of February 1943.
On the fourteenth the raider dipped its ensign in reply to a salute from
the 9,925-ton tanker *Brake* (out from France on September 26), commanded by the cantankerous and very independent Capt. Otto Kölschbach. The tough, square-jawed merchant skipper turned naval officer
puttered over to the raider for lunch, stiffly saluted Ruckteschell and, in
a manner similar to the one affected by the latter, told his superior that
Brake's lookouts had spotted him one and a half seconds before *Mi-*

chel's had reported his own ship. Kölschbach had six tons of potatoes, three tons of fresh meat, beer, and oil for the raider, but no mail. It had been burned when his previous command *Passat, Pinguin*'s ex-prize and minelayer *Storstad,* had been bombed at St.-Nazaire. Kölschbach departed on the seventeenth and on the following day *Michel* rendezvoused with *Rhakotis,* a 6,753-tonner which had been in South America when the war started, escaped to Japan, and was then engaged in running the blockade to Europe. The management of that ship made an excellent impression on Rucktschell but he subjected the German authorities in Japan to the indisputably correct but vituperative scribbles of his pen. He found it "monstrous" that a ship like *Rhakotis,* loaded with valuable raw materials such as rubber, tin, or opium, was not sufficiently well armed (she carried two 20 mm), and that she was transporting Norwegians from *Kattegat* who had been in contact with seamen from *Patella, Connecticut,* and *Lylepark* and had met some of *Stier*'s prisoners as well. What was more, he noted, those men had seen both *Schiff 28* and *23* and *Doggerbank.* If any of them ever got through to the Allies, they would have a lot of secrets to divulge. It was utterly inexcusable, he argued, and he was right, as SKL belatedly agreed.* The ships parted company at 29°58′S, 65°05′E on the nineteenth and Ruckteschell turned west toward the suspected steamer tracks southeast of Madagascar. He had not accomplished anything for nearly two and a half months and he complained that SKL seemed to be treating each operational area as if it were a separate entity, an enclosed sea like the Baltic to which the prewar German Navy's experiences had been mostly limited. He was not getting enough intelligence from Germany, none from Japan.

November 29 found him slowly approaching a merchant route within easy reach of aircraft starting from Madagascar or Mauritius. It was a dangerous area and his raider's speed had been reduced to thirteen knots by wear and marine growths. At 1630 with visibility poor, a ship was sighted, its masts, stack, and bridge coming into view almost immediately. Ruckteschell sent his best observer, a former merchant officer, Lt. Edgar Behrend, to the foremast to conn the raider. *Esau* was ordered set on deck. That took an hour, and in that time *Michel* had forged comfortably ahead of the other vessel which was steering southwesterly at ten knots. At 1830 the motor torpedo boat was lowered with orders to keep tabs on the quarry and to torpedo it at will if the raider could not get into a favorable shooting position. Those instructions were

---

* When *Rhakotis* was sunk by His Majesty's light cruiser *Scylla,* on January 1, 1943, the prisoners got to Spain, where they naturally told British agents all they knew.

a mistake, Ruckteschell admitted, and could have led to trouble. Communications with the boat were lost, and unable to contact von Schack, Ruckteschell drove *Michel* in very close to the other ship. ("We had never run so impudently.")

> 2126 *Michel* starts in, her gunners waiting patiently, stiffly, sure of themselves. Their orders: Passing fight to starboard; aiming point waterline, bridge; 6-second salvos. 5.9-inch guns No. 3 and 4 use high explosive, delayed fuses; No. 1 high explosive contact fuses and tracer; No. 5 high explosives, contact fuses; the 4.1-inch high explosive and incendiary; 37 mm are to take bow and stern, keep enemy from manning guns; 20 mm work over bridge and flack positions. Do not spare ammunition.
>
> Still 2126: Enemy shows green light, starts sharp turn to port. Captain first thinks they are giving recognition signals, then decides that he has been spotted and that they have switched on their running light to avoid a collision. *Michel* shows green, too.
>
> 2138: "Feuererlaubnis!" distance 2,500 meters.
>
> 5.9s go over to 15-second salvos. Enemy topdecks and interior on fire. One torpedo let go by Second Torpedo Officer Schmolling's No. 1 above water tube hits as aimed ("a beautiful shot") just aft of the stack. [A second missed.] Ship lists. 2145 "Halt Batterie, halt!" 2147 resume fire; people running aft presumably to work gun.*

The battered target—*Michel*'s first salvo had destroyed her bridge and the 4.5 aft, the second had hit the engine room, boat deck, and cement-encased radio shack—was American Export Line's twenty-two-year-old 5,882-ton *Sawokla* (Capt. Carl Wink) with forty-one crew, thirteen naval gunners, and five passengers en route from Colombo to Cape Town with a cargo of jute and rough linen. How did it look from her?

\ Tough, stocky Dennis A. Roland, then *Sawokla*'s second officer, describes it without much pathos: It was a Sunday, the sea rough, wind force four to five (moderate to fresh breeze). They were ten days out of Colombo and they had been routed far out to sea, and that they did not like at all. Inshore, the trip would have taken longer but they would have had air cover, and if any of the subs often lurking off the ports had attacked, they would have had a good chance of pulling for land. Out where they were, their chances were not too hot if they got hit by something. At 2020 it was dark. Roland was visiting the chief officer, Elmar Saar, down in his cabin with conjunctivitis. At 2035 one bell was struck. (That signified either a vessel sighted to starboard or that it was 0430, 0830, etc.) Roland looked at his pocket watch. "It puzzled me

---

* Actually some plucky lad on the blazing freighter had emptied one drum of 20 mm at the dark, fire-spitting raider and one feeble "SSS" had been tapped out by the radioroom. It was heard only in *Michel*.

for a moment trying to account for the five minutes discrepancy between 2030 and that one bell. It never occurred to me that the lookout on the foc'sle head was making one bell because of something sighted." Two minutes later (*Sawokla*'s clocks were one hour behind the Germans'), "the ship suddenly jarred and the air was filled with a haze. She shuddered as if she had run over an obstacle and then continued onward." Roland took one look at his bunk, decided he would not be using it anymore, grabbed his helmet and went out into the alleyway then filling up with a bunch of men "expressing more curiosity than fear . . . nothing like one would imagine it would be with a ship in its death throes, ablaze and with acrid fumes permeating everything." He and some others managed to lower No. 2 but it sank as its air tanks broke loose. That left the men clinging to some oars, afraid of being washed away, afraid of being picked up by the raider for fear that it might be Japanese. Roland was not hurt; he just thought he would die from exposure; he was "indifferent," but figured it was "nonsense" to die. When the dark ship reappeared in their limited field of vision, all decided to call for help, regardless of who she might be.

Thirty-five of them were fished out of the drifting wreckage within three hours (longer than prudent for the Germans) and four more of their gunners were saved the next day when Ruckteschell returned for a check.

Once aboard the raider, the lads from *Sawokla* were showered; the wounded (including Saar with his bad eyes) were taken to the sick bay while the rest padded down steel ladders to their respective quarters below (the officers' room was about twenty-eight by thirty-five feet, Roland recalls, the crew's around twenty by twenty) to receive some coffee and a short interrogation. Roland, the senior healthy survivor, was appointed prison commander and he was told that they would be well treated as long as they behaved themselves. They were, too, for Roland cannot remember any unpleasantness: "They did all they could to make us comfortable." Their routine was simple: Lights on at 0630, breakfast; lunch at 1200,-an hour's stroll on deck, then supper and a visit from Saupe, who always entered with a curt salute to ask their wishes—they called him "Visches"—whatever they might be, dental care, more heat; 2030, hammocks, old jokes, stale stories, and mulling over worries.

SCRAP

Not many hours after Ruckteschell's men hauled *Sawokla*'s lucky gunners out of the water but five time zones to the east on November 30, a gigantic fireball rose over Yokahama and an explosion rocked the surrounding countryside. *Nankin*'s First Officer Dun, who was working at the Nisshin flour mill in Tsurumi, says he heard an explosion from the harbor which was fully six miles away. Everything shook. The big blast was the end of a raider, Gumprich's *Thor*.

Gumprich, with ten ships to his credit, had had no more luck following the release of *Tannenfels* back on September 29, and since the Germans could not and the Japanese would not steer any oil his way, he had stopped shortly at Borneo and had then entered Yokohama harbor on October 10 where his ship was to be refurbished for another cruise. November 30 most of the work had been done, and the raider was tied up alongside the *Uckermark,* on which Chinese coolies were cleaning the tanks. It was just after lunch and Gumprich had left in his launch for the prize *Nankin*. Henry Militzer was up forward where a group of German and Japanese journalists were taking pictures of each other, when an enormous explosion occurred somewhere nearby. He remembers everyone rushing about rather heedlessly, not knowing what had happened. When an even heavier explosion rocked *Thor* and great sheets of flame shot into the air, Militzer ran to the forecastle to cast off the heavy hawsers that held his ship to the tanker, and hoped that someone else had the presence of mind to do the same thing aft so that the raider could drift free. Turning to check, he heard and felt still another explosion and that one tossed *Uckermark*'s bridge up on that of *Thor*'s. He never got past hatch No. 2 where the aircraft he had so roundly cursed so often was stored. It was a sea of flames. Being an excellent seaman, but a poor swimmer, Militzer tore off his jacket, and for some reason he cannot remember, folded it neatly. He then placed it on the capstan, tidily put his cap on it and his watch on the latter. Only then did he jump.

Once in the water, he saw Gumprich returning with his boat to pull men out of the oily scum and free from the burning fuel which was rapidly spreading over the whole basin and eventually burned out *Thor, Uckermark, Nankin,* the 3,023-ton Japanese *Unkai Maru 3,* and some harbor boats, all of which became a total loss. Militzer managed to climb up on a pier but he then had to run to escape the large chunks of metal that were still hurtling down from the ships.

The cause of the explosion, which killed thirteen of *Thor*'s men, fifty-three of *Uckermark*'s, and countless Chinese and Japanese—the latter have no official figures available—was never explained, but it was presumed that the coolies had either been careless in chipping rust or had been smoking and had thereby set off gases escaping from inadequately cleaned tanks. It was a sad blow to most of the men like Sepp

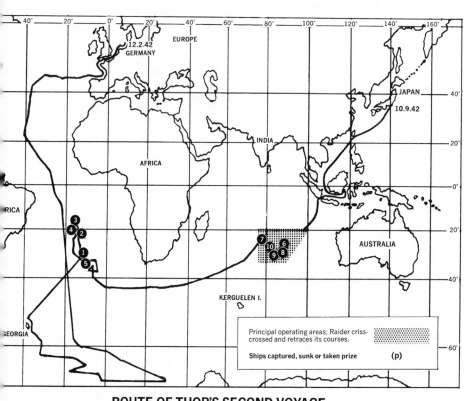

ROUTE OF THOR'S SECOND VOYAGE

KOS	3.23.42	6. NANKING (p)	5.10.42
K	3.30.42	7. OLIVIA	6.14.42
N	4.01.42	8. HERBORG (p)	6.19.42
	4.03.42	9. MADRONO (p)	7.04.42
L	4.10.42	10. INDUS	7.20.42

Gruber who made a long cruise in the raider and who openly wept at her loss. It was an even unhappier event for the executive officer, Fischer, who, having apparently been one of the first to leave the ship, was later sent home in the minelayer-blockade runner *Doggerbank,* a trip he did not survive. Militzer somehow retrieved his cap—someone quicker had taken a fancy to his watch—and a few months later he as well as a good portion of his shipmates found a berth in *Michel,* by then the only raider with which Germany could challenge the Allied might.

"HORROR AND SLAUGHTER"

That oceangoing predator was lying stopped, less than a fortnight after *Thor* had burned into scrap, southeast of Madagascar at 1400 on December 7 to let a bad weather front pass by when suddenly a vessel brushed through the curtain of a squall, coming so close that the German watchkeepers could clearly make out her details from the bridge. Its appearance was ironic, Ruckteschell sighed. "Flying master" Hoppe had covered 6,136 miles of the Indian Ocean in many flights, and he had discovered only one ship, and that could not be attacked. Ruckteschell veered off. He had *Esau* launched and his men fed at 1617. It was going to be a port-to-port passing fight, the loudspeakers gargled. Don't spare ammunition. Reason: Vessel is to be brought to "silently," there was to be no opposition; sink it quickly.

Down in Roland's circumscribed world, a burp-gun-toting guard appeared with "Visches." The officer was quite "solicitous. He explained that the prisoners had nothing to fear, and that if anything went wrong, he would come to their assistance." They nestled into their hammocks "and remained like scared children with long faces; no one talking; feeling the surge of the ship and the gentle rise and fall as she first went full ahead and then lay to. We could hear them trundle shells to the elevators . . . then the clatter of the bulwarks as they dropped; we supposed the vital moment had come which meant death to a lot of men, unsuspecting men." Second Torpedo Officer Willi Schmolling's weapon made one hit ("good shot, but too bad it struck where it did. Torpedoes that hit forward of the bridge seldom lead to fast sinkings"). But the second missed, "badly observed, that was a clumsy mistake." Ruckteschell had made one, too, and he admitted it. He had let the watch officer allow the still circling other ship, to lurch so close to *Michel* that the men on the raider's twin 37 mm aft had to give thoughts to "one hand for the ship, two legs for yourself." By 0515 the next morning, the excitement was all over, and a boat with thirteen men who had hoped to escape was captured. It was a mixed crowd, eleven Greeks, one Canadian, one Swede, one Egyptian, one Yugoslav, one Argentinian, and three British (the "most colorful" Ruckteschell had seen), that trooped down to the prisoner quarters that morning to join Roland and his men. *Eugenie Livanos*' men had been celebrating the feast of St. Nicholas, and when they had been attacked (the boatswain had the watch), some of them had helped themselves to a cargo of booze.

On December 20 SKL radioed: "Assume *Schiff 28* arranging return so that it will break through the Biscay during period of new moon (starting February 4, 1943). *Schiff 14* will leave during same period. . . ." Ruckteschell's comment: "I had personally hoped that *Schiff 14* would not be sent out anymore." He reasoned that it made no sense to risk another raider and a lot of men unless the ship went to Japan as a blockade runner, picked up *Thor*'s crew, and on its return trip engaged in a bit of commerce war. He feared that the British would institute a huge dragnet if *Schiff 14* were lucky enough to escape their attentions in the Channel and that *Michel* would be caught up in it while trying for home.

AND YET ANOTHER RAIDER

Schiff 14, which Ruckteschell thought had a lovely name, *Coronel,* had had an interesting career before it was ever decided to send her araiding. Built in 1938 at Bremen as the *Togo* for the famous Woermann Line, she was of 5,054 tons and could do seventeen knots. Two days before the war broke out, she was lying in Douala, French Cameroon, guarded by native troops and unable to get clearance papers. Her Belgian-born captain, Eugene Rousselet, was not, however, about to surrender the ship to France. He took her down the coast at night without a pilot to the dirty brown Congo. And there, his forty-odd German crew slapped mosquitoes, read by lanterns to conserve fuel, and idly waved at passing British merchantmen ("Seamen are not politicians," her third officer, Constantin Moser, puts it) while ninety "crooboys" (Congo tribe) stevedors wanted off—it had been rumored that France's *Sourcouf,* then the world's largest submarine, was waiting outside—and Rousselet went ashore to visit his Belgian friends.

One of his companions was a mail pilot and it was from him that the captain learned what the French Navy was doing. On October 25, the coast was clear and *Togo* was off for Germany. No one ever touched their transmitter (as published material would have it) to report their sinking and throw the French off the track but Moser does think that Rousselet planted the story of *Togo*'s being torpedoed with the press.

Serving as a trooper in the Norwegian campaign after her return to Germany, December 23, 1939, she hit a mine on April 21, but managed to get home. Once repaired, she was taken over by the Kriegsmarine, which employed her as a minelayer and patrol vessel until orders were cut to effect her conversion into a raider. Much of the work was done at Holland's Wilton yards, but the more sensitive installations were handled at Stettin, Germany. She was armed with six 5.9s, six 40 mms, eight 20 mms, two 21-inch torpedo mounts, three planes, and a *Bachstelze* (water wagtail) manned kite. But when she was ready for service, Grand Admiral Raeder reported on December 22 in one of his last Führer Conferences before his enforced retirement that the naval situation around the Channel had become nearly intolerable.

FRÖHLICHE WEIHNACHTEN

While Raeder was telling Hitler that things were not going so well along the coast—he might just as well have been saying that the only German craft that had much of a chance were the Red Cross-marked air-sea rescue boats—*Michel*'s crew were preparing for a sentimental Christmas. Their quarters were decorated, trees were turned out of wire, fringed canvas sprayed green, and each man spent hours making a present to be given to someone else by lot.

Roland was asked up to officers' country to discuss the captives' plans for the feast. They were not very elaborate, he said, because there was not much to work with. He had been up there a number of times and had even talked to Ruckteschell who he found a "perfect gentleman." This time he did not get to the captain, but he and "Visches" discussed Christmas—and President Wilson—over a couple of beers. Plans for the festivities at least turned out well.

Officers and men, Americans, British, Greek, and all the rest, spent the day in the larger crews' quarters. They had their own trees decorated with cigarette-pack tinfoil and some tiny candles given them by the Germans. They were treated to cakes, strawberries, and cherries. They were each given five bottles of beer and two bottles of cognac between them, two decks of cards, four harmonicas, and the loan of a record player. Each man's gift bag contained a two-pound raisin nut cake, one pound of dates, a pack of cigarettes, one pound of Dutch chocolates, a can of Italian peaches, a dozen large chocolate balls, and a quart of hair tonic—all of it items that both the British and the Germans would have had a difficult time finding at home. Some wanted to gulp it all at once, some saved the best, others "got drunk and many thought they were drunk." All in all, Roland had "personally one of the best Christmas Days I could recall, and it had to be in a German raider."

His captors were able to hold their celebrations undisturbed by anyone in the torpedo room. They were a thousand miles from Cape Town, southeast of Gough Island; it was appropriately cold outside (25° F.). They started with a selection of Handel's "Festmusik," followed by "Silent Night" and the reading of the Christmas story from the Bible. Among the presents the captain got was a portrait of himself. It embarrassed him and he did not quite know what to do with it without offending the donor. "I just cannot hang it in my own cabin," he lamented to Herr.

The next morning *Michel* was laid before the wind and the men mustered on deck for decorations (fifteen Iron Crosses First Class, fifty Second), advancements, and another short speech from their commander. Much to Ruckteschell's surprise, Erhardt then grabbed the word. He was happy, he said, to read them a radiogram (which had been decoded the day before but had been kept secret). The skipper, it read, had become the 158th German serviceman to be awarded the coveted Oak Leaves to the Ritterkreuz. Ruckteschell, cap in hand, bowed graciously to his cheering men, told them it was theirs; they had earned it for him. His own gift to them was a charming musical play which he had written himself. It was repeatedly performed by two seamen who had been sent to a school before leaving Germany just to learn how to operate the Punch and Judy theater.

On December 27, a Sunday, the prisoners held a ceremony in honor of their dead. It had been their own idea, but it had taken some doing to get it on the road despite the fact that the Germans encouraged it. The major difficulty: How does one salute? With or without caps? Each nationality presented its own views and argued them hotly. Roland got mad: "I just got everyone together and as I was in charge, I made the routine. We all saluted, hat or no hat." Roland asked them to show a bit more brotherly love while everyone was still around, not wait until a man was killed before saying he had been a nice guy and not a louse. "The ship then swung in a circle and the German honor guard in dress uniforms drew smartly to attention and we all saluted as *Michel*'s band played the equivalent of taps. A wreath was cast onto the sea as the ship's ensign rose back up to the gaff."

A day later, Erhardt informed the men that they would be home on February 2 but from midmorning of New Year's Day on it was obvious—in the inexplicable way of all ships or anthills—that something was in the wind. Even the prisoners felt it just a few minutes after a sighting had been reported to the bridge. Hoppe and his plane had skipped off the waves at 0821 to fly a basic parallelogram search pattern. At 1010 *Michel*'s foretop lookout spotted a two-masted vessel. The situation was serious but comical. *Michel,* not the plane, had seen the ship first and Hoppe was bound to fly right over it on his return. Ruckteschell feared that the plane would be spotted, yet he felt sorry for the "flying master" who had taken off on forty-one flights, had covered more than twelve thousand miles and had sighted only one steamer, and who would now most likely return with egg on his face. Hoppe did not. Three minutes before he was to let down in *Michel*'s wake, he saw the ship, banked away, radioed "have been seen by enemy" as a precautionary measure, then headed out of sight to the east where there were British bases from which a plane might have come. He then circled to get back to his own ship for a "well done" from Ruckteschell.

Ruckteschell launched LS 4 and called his men to quarters at 2005. *Feuererlaubnis* to starboard at 2147. The first salvo knocked out the other ship's bridge and radio. In the next five minutes Schwinn's boys smacked the vessel with 64 5.9-inch shells, 16 4.1s, 149 37 mm, and 191 20 mm, and about 80 percent of them were hits. "The impressions of this night attack are overwhelming" the experienced commander felt. (To Roland down below, it was a "symphony of death.") 2152 "Halt Batterie, Halt. The enemy is . . . an inferno from stem to stern, but still moving." To get him down quickly, Ruckteschell expended two of his torpedoes (one missed) and two of *Esau*'s. Short work. The ship had been *Empire March,* en route from Durban to Trinidad with a cargo of iron, tea, peanuts, and jute. Her twenty-five survivors (three had been killed), who said that they had seen Hoppe's plane but had thought it to be British because it had flown off to the east, were picked up. The next morning, *Michel* returned to search among the wreckages for anyone who might have been missed. One man was found in a battered lifeboat.

With only a month to go, Ruckteschell mulled over his chances of completing the final dash home, and found them poor. A wireless from SKL confirmed his gloomy appraisal, saying Berlin was contemplating orders that would send *Schiff 28* to Japan. Just before noon on January 8, he called the men together again to give them the bad news: We are going to Japan. They took it because they had to, but even the amicable, unflappable Erhardt still clearly remembers his thoughts at the time: "An order you could do nothing about. Whether you laughed or cried." And naturally, the bad news did not take long to sicker down to the prisoners. "Everyone's spirits dropped," Roland recalls, "the Germans' because they weren't going home and ours because we'd be prisoners in the east where we'd have to subsist on rice [he never did like it], receive no mail and no Red Cross. Everyone was gloomy and touchy."

FAR EAST

By the second day of February 1943, *Michel* had doubled the Cape again and was operating under the control of the German commander in chief Tokyo, Admiral Wenneker, who radioed recognition signals (Japanese challenge "HQ"; German Reply, "GR") and advised that the Japanese were a very sensitive people. Ruckteschell responded: "I do not know whether these suggestions are ordinary statements of fact or whether they are addressed personally to the captain of *Michel*. One thing is certain, however: your relations with your own wife are the least embellished, and you are surely the most polite with another woman. I . . . realize that the Japs have a different mentality: Prussia for the Germans, Samurai spirit for the Japs."

As *Michel* plowed through the warm seas, black nights, and spectacular tropical thunder showers, he had other things on his mind than the niceties of German-Japanese relations. At home bombs were falling on Hamburg, Wilhelmshaven, and the Ruhr. Montgomery's "set piece" battles were inching westward in Africa, and in Russia the last wretched sacrificial troops of the Sixth Army had surrendered at Stalingrad. (To honor their memory, all music was forbidden in *Michel* for three days.) He also had his own ship, then approaching Bali, to worry about. All watertight doors were shut, and anyone not essential to running the ship was ordered from the compartments below the waterline. Radical zigzag courses were laid on, the aircraft prepared for flight, and the *Esau* set out with depth charges to act as escort. An officer went into the mast top, additional lookouts manned the rails, and the prisoners were advised that they would be given ample opportunity to save themselves if need be.

Tense, silent, the men scanned the sea for Allied submarines as they entered the twenty-two-mile-wide Lombok Strait, with fabled Bali on their right. At 0525 on February 7 land was sighted, "the first land in 324 days." The men stared in disbelief as they weighed their chances of liberty with some of the nut-brown lovelies, a Rijstafel and strange drinks. At exactly 1240 (Tokyo time) on February 10, 1943, the anchor detail stood clear on *Michel*'s forecastle as the long-unused and rusty chain rattled out in the roadstead of Tandjoengpriok. Two hours later, much to the amazement of former prisoner Duffy, then laboring on

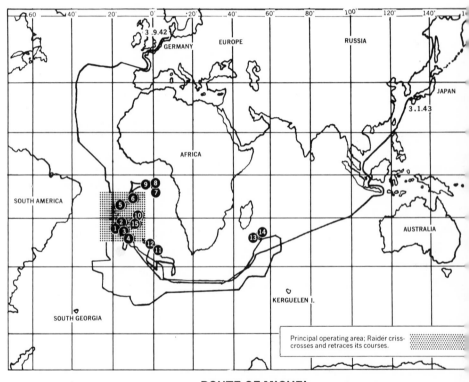

ROUTE OF MICHEL

1. PATELLA	4.19.42	6. LYLEPARK	6.11.42	11. AMERICAN LEADER	
2. CONNECTICUT	4.23.42	7. GLOUCESTER CASTLE	7.15.42	12. EMPIRE DAWN	
3. MENELAUS fiasco	5.01.42	8. WILLIAM F. HUMPHREY	7.16.42	13. SAWOKLA	1
4. KATTEGAT	5.20.42	9. ARAMIS	7.17.42	14. EUGENIE LIVANOS	1
5. GEORGE CLYMER	6.06.42	10. ARABISTAN	8.14.42	15. EMPIRE MARCH	

the decks for his new masters, the raider entered the harbor flying call letters DXEX. At 1526 she made fast at Pier 1.

Within minutes, Captain Maeda, Imperial Japanese Navy, came aboard in spotless whites to be introduced to *Michel*'s officers. Courteously, Ruckteschell thanked the Imperial Navy for its assistance and offered a toast to its future. Maeda returned the gesture, then advanced plans for the immediate future: movies in a shed on the dock; crew will be taken to resort hotel Sela Bintana. Regular liberty would not be allowed—supposedly because *Thor*'s crew had allowed themselves some boisterous excesses during their stay in a Japanese-controlled port, more likely because the Japanese wanted to avoid any contact between the Germans, natives, and European prisoners.

The movies that first night on the dock were better than nothing— if you like war pictures. The revue: A clean-cut young Nipponese joins the navy. The effect of his training becomes obvious in the reels of the Pearl Harbor attack. Early the next morning the first group of vacationers took off for a four-hour journey by bus to the hotel. Their tour was novel but about as relaxing and informative as a badly managed Caribbean tour package. When it was over—an hour and a half of tennis, etc.—it was back by the numbers for another four hours of squirming in rickety buses, one of which turned over, injuring three of *Michel*'s men.

By the fifteenth practically everyone was ready to go. They cast off at 1150, set antisubmarine and mine watches, and steered for Singapore. As they approached the city of the Raffles Hotel and countless less sophisticated pleasures on the seventeenth, the lower decks' hopes for liberty revived guardedly, but the captain, watch officer, quartermasters, and others were all tense, far more than average, on making a landfall. Navigator Rödel had, to be sure, been told by the Batavia Nipponese that he would have no trouble at all entering port, just like in peacetime, they had said. But that had not been reassuring at all. Important harbors, in those days, were usually mined, if not defensively, then by the enemy. The expected pilot did not appear off Pedra Branca Light, and Ruckteschell pushed slowly on, passing a Japanese minesweeper and trooper. Two miles off the roadstead a few wreck buoys were spotted and a steamer could be seen coming out of port, steering a course well to the south. Worried, Ruckteschell stopped, noting what appeared to be several sunken vessels ahead. After one of those interminable waits in which no one seems to know what to do and there is very little anyone could do but turn around, the other ship headed over toward *Michel,* pointing out a drifting mine.

Adjutant Herr was sent ashore to parley in English (in which all discussions were held), but he had a lot of trouble locating anyone. The local Imperial allies were celebrating the anniversary of the Crown Colony's surrender. Finally, when contact was made, the Germans were "so-sorried" for their inconvenience in making port. The pilot had gone out all right, but had climbed aboard old friend *Charlotte Schliemann*. *Michel* had been seen from the naval control tower and the excited spectators ashore avowed that they had been truly relieved when she had stopped just in time to avoid blowing up on a British minefield.

There was fresh food again, but no shore leave except for officers (too many spies, it was said), and Ruckteschell kept even them on board for the sake of the enlisted men's morale. While they chafed, he settled his prisoner problem. The Japanese Army was delighted to have them. Their fate was of a kind that makes wars indecent, more cruel than the killing itself, less natural than their recurrence.

As the scruffy men tromped down the gangplank with their few belongings, *Michel*'s crew felt sorry, and more than one German cried openly. Roland had all hands sign a letter of appreciation for their humane treatment. War is war, he thought, and he was willing to take his hat off to Ruckteschell and his men.

Japanese soldiers hustled the men off to Changi Jail with its unconcerned and, to the Americans, apparently selfish British POW Administration complete in polished boots and attending batmen. From there, they were driven into the horrors of life and death as slave laborers of the inefficient and callous "Greater East Asia Co-prosperity Sphere. The Japanese Army needed a railroad to link Burma's Rangoon-Ye line with the Singapore-Bangkok right of way and they chivvied some 330,000 men, 61,000 of them POWs, to build it—by hand. It cost the lives of an estimated 72,000 to 100,000 Burmese, Tamils, Malayans, and Chinese (whose half-buried bones stuck out of the mud), and around 16,000 emaciated POWs died. Diseased, weak, unattended, Roland (his appendix was taken out under hypnosis) was one of the few to count himself lucky to have survived cholera, malaria, diphtheria, avitaminosis, dysentery, stinking ulcers, and the whims of alien gang bosses. "Life went on," he wrote his brother from Singapore after the war, "with . . . mud to rest on, driven daily, seven days a week; floundering about in a perpetual sea of mud, irregular working hours, scanty food, loaded with dirt and grit. You wonder why so many POWs died?"—more than three hundred for each mile of track laid.

Michel left Singapore again on Saturday the twentieth for the final leg of its journey to Japan. Except for battering monsoons with wind forces up to nine, a few ship sightings, and one near collision with a carelessly run Japanese guard vessel (*Michel* had to back down "full" to avoid running it down), the ten-day passage up the China Sea, past Formosa and Tsushima was uneventful. At 1817 on March 1, pilot Higuchi reported on board for a rather disappointing night run through the spectacularly beautiful Inland Sea, and at 1310 the next day *Michel* was made fast to buoy No. 6 in hill-hemmed Kobe harbor.

NOTES

1. Gerlach, the only skipper not to be awarded the Ritterkreuz, relinquished his command of *Schiff* 5 to serve as Naval Commandant at Leningrad, then in the Peleponnese, and after October 1944, in Northern Holland where his wife, Hildegard, joined him as a Red Cross nurse. He was treated "indifferently" in captivity while his wife had to go on relief. His son, Klaus, was born Christmas Eve, 1945, "a true Christchild and just as poor." Misery, fed by adversity, increased: Gerlach drove trucks and shortly after he had finally succeeded to a bearable life and rose to take part in Nato maneuvers as a reserve officer, he suffered a stroke, dying in 1970. "I admired him no end; he never complained," his equally courageous wife says.

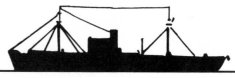

CHAPTER 12

1943: The End

"DO YOU SEE WHAT I SEE TO OUR LEFT SIDE? A RAIDER!" During February 1943 as the last beaten remnants of the Sixth Army were being driven like cattle eastward from the Volga into captivity, and as Ruckteschell was standing toward Japan, Capt. Ernst Thienemann, of the *Coronel*, ex-*Togo*, and his 350 men were experiencing a singularly unpleasant time. The balding forty-four-year-old had spent years in Berlin supervising construction of, among other things, raiders, and finally his own chance to test his work had come. Admiral Raeder had warned him just before retiring that this might be a last attempt, that the odds were a hundred to one against him, and that he would eventually have to go to Japan.

Thienemann's tribulation started with the coded cue "Morningstar 8998" at which *Schiff 14* set out from the Baltic at 0545 on January 31. She grounded twice near Dunkirk on February 9, was shelled by Dover's heavy batteries (thirty-three rounds), and was discovered by a British fighter bomber whose crew were overheard saying, "Do you see what I see to our left side? A raider!" Minutes later, another plane skimmed in over the sea, dropping a bomb which hit *Coronel* to port abreast the forward mast. Several compartments caught fire, water rushed in, the engine broke down, and No. 2 ammo locker had to be flooded. Considering the damage and reports that British surface forces were lying in wait off Dieppe, Thienemann put into Boulogne, arriving there with one dead and four wounded. A survey showed it would take four months to effect repairs, and it was obvious that those could not be carried out in a French port for security reasons.

That meant a return struggle through the Channel and it started with an air attack on February 13. *Coronel* was shelled again (twenty-three rounds), bombed by the RAF and the U. S. Eighth Air Force. On the twenty-sixth an attack by British Hudsons killed three men and injured three. One bomb destroyed a 20-mm magazine before tearing through the deck, rudder room, and out the bottom without exploding. By the afternoon of the twenty-eighth, Thienemann was back, anchored off Cuxhaven, convinced for all he had just been through that another try would be worth the risk. In retrospect, that appraisal seems rash, but SKL concurred—unmindfully, some say—thus permitting the raider effort to continue with nearly the resiliency of *Coronel,* which was still to be sailing (for foreign interests) thirty years later.[1]

"UNRESPONSIVE MAINMAST"

And it so happened that they had just the ship for the purpose, too, they thought. It was *Schiff 5, ex-Glengarry,* Captain Gerlach's precommissioning job to which the reluctant former merchant officer Petersen had also been assigned. The handsome 9,838-tonner with the tall stack so common to the company's vessels, had been under construction for Britain's Alfred Holt and Company at Copenhagen's Burmeister and Wain when the Germans invaded Denmark, and she was promptly requisitioned, serving as U-boat target ship *Meersburg* for the 27th Flotilla until ordered into the Wilton yards to be converted into the Kriegsmarine's most heavily armed raider (eight 5.9, numerous flack, and, profiting from her predecessors' experiences, a catapult and radar). But, frustrated by shortages of everything from labor to rolling stock and bombings that left the work unfinished two years behind schedule, SKL finally gave up. And a good thing it was, Petersen, who fought on as commander of torpedo boat 156 until bombed in March 1945, thought, "because the operation would have been senseless anyway." Renamed *Hansa, ex-Glengarry, -Meersburg, -Schiff 5,* served as a training ship and took part in the final desperate evacuation at Hela, returning on V-E Day.

On May 27, 1945, Capt. Frank C. Brown was given a briefing by Lawrence Holt, nephew of his firm's founder and manager of the huge concern which lost fifty-two ships during the war. Brown's instructions were the "sketchiest"; he was to proceed to Germany "to look after the company's interests and bring back the former *Glengarry* in one piece"—if he could find and claim her, that is. Once he had identified her (partly by the name chisel-cut into the stern plates and still visible under layers of gray paint), Brown went to work, skillfully employing a naval padre and compassion, insubordination and a little "help-yourself," guile and outright theft to thwart Britain's best, still stiff-lipped Admiralty bureaucrats who, considering her a lawful prize, were obstinately refusing to let him take her where Holt wanted—Buoy 10 at Gareloch, Scotland. As both sides became more determined to control the once-to-be raider, His Majesty's people had a writ served by the Cowes Customs Officer who, "finding the [steel] mainmast unresponsive," tacked the sheet on Brown's cabin door, thereby arresting the vessel in the name of the Admiralty marshal. Unbowed as he had been throughout the war, Brown hove up his anchor and stood out to sea: "No shots came across our bows as we passed the Needles. We had no pilot to dispose of; we did not stop. So we came to Buoy 10. From that day to this, I have heard no more of my infringement of maritime law. I assume that my juvenile delinquency was overlooked in the confusion of those days."

For some Germans, *Coronel*'s aborted sortie had been a close thing, and the drab, dragging affair with *Schiff 5* had been lucky for Petersen and Borchers, the rest of *Stier*'s volunteers, and owners Holt and Company, but it had been the handwriting on the wall for SKL. And being the caliber officers they were, its meaning was just as clear then as it is today to the historian with all the data and advantages of hindsight in hand.*

DESPITE THE ODDS, STILL ANOTHER TRY

It is relatively safe to state that Germany, in early 1943, did not have a chance of winning the war. In Russia, where, as the Wehrmacht said, you have to go if you want to know what snow and mud are, Stalingrad was lost; and in Africa some 130,000 of Germany's best peaked-capped troops had shuffled into captivity by May 13. At sea the war was as endless as the scend of the waves and the entire burden of the struggle was being carried by the hard-driven U-boats which had sent a whopping 627,377 tons of shipping down in March but were systematically being decimated by such refinements as 10-cm radar. In May they sank only fifty ships against a loss of thirty-eight of their own numbers—more

---

* Holt ships had had more than their share of brushes with German raiders and their *Glengarry* featured in much gossip, sometimes commanded by Graf Luckner, other times not. *Schiff 16* had been disguised as *Antenor; Troilus* had barely avoided *Atlantis* and the latter had claimed to be *Polyphemus* when brought to by H.M.S. *Devonshire. Hector* had steamed into Auckland while *Orion* was laying mines and she had joined the search for *Pinguin. Eurylochus* had been sunk by *Schiff 41,* whose captain was towed to Australia by *Centaur; Automedon* had been sunk by *Atlantis; Helenus* had rebroadcast her distress signals and had barely escaped Rogge's clutches herself.

than were being built as replacements. The Kriegsmarine's few remaining surface units barely existed as a nuisance-in-being after a December 1942 debacle against a Murmansk convoy, which cost Admiral Raeder his job. His successor, Dönitz, had only one ship abroad—*Michel*—in Japan, and that country was having its own share of problems. Her carrier pilots had been sent burning out of the skies and her ships bubbling to the bottom, and neither could be replaced. In April, Imperial Headquarters' land-oriented army and Mahan-indoctrinated navy were still quarreling about what to do.

On the last day of that month, when the last liberty boat fended off *Michel*'s side in Kobe and its unwilling cargo scrambled aboard with the usual boasts—the sake, hot baths with naked women, fried snakes that turned out to be dog meat—there were many indications that the ship was in all respects ready for sea. And when the first turns of the screw vibrated through the vessel and a rhythmic creaking and groaning and smooth rise and fall of the bow indicated that they had weighed, the next morning, it was obvious that there would be plenty to occupy the men's minds during the next few months. First there was the change of command.

Following their arrival that early March for a refit at the efficient Mitsubishi yards, the crew, though severely restricted and shadowed by suspicious police, had been to lovely Lake Biwa and the Takarazuka entertainment district for a good time while their commander, Ruckteschell, was being overwhelmed by official business—respects to the governor, a medal from the Emperor, Chamber of Commerce and Japanese visitors who found MTB *Esau* more interesting than the raider because they had seen *Thor*. It was grand to be ashore, he felt, rather than alone at sea "stealing geese like a fox" in a raiding venture that had been an "enormous psychological strain." And the strain had told. He still had migraine, his stomach bothered him, his heart was giving trouble, and he had been forced to ask for a relief. On the fourteenth he left for the popular resort Miyanoshita to discuss turning *Michel* over to *Thor*'s Captain Gumprich. His birthday fell on March 23 and on that day, cap in hand, he said good-bye, Godspeed, to the men he had led so long. An ideal raider captain to some, superb tactician, "a pastor, pirate, artist," who could not, however, have run a happy ship without the steadying influence of Erhardt and the other men who so patiently bore his idiosyncrasies.

The officers from *Thor* such as Navigator Ernst Siek, Dr. Buchinger, the ubiquitous Meckmann and Militzer, both of whom had already endured two cruises, simply had to acquaint themselves with *Michel*'s plank owners and a different, slower vessel which disappointed them as much as it did Gumprich. The raider's old crowd, Schwinn, von Schack, Schmolling, and Behrend, on the other hand, felt at home in their ship but soon learned that neither their new exec, Werner Trendtel, nor their skipper was at all like Erhardt or their old captain. The new second-in-command had been in Japan awhile, seemed impersonal, and was a new hand at raiding, innocent of the often brutal tactics it demanded. Gumprich, they knew, was experienced. He had sunk eight ships and sent two prizes to Japan. He had suffered no casualties during his ten-month cruise, and the loss of *Thor* had not been his fault. In fact, he had saved a lot of men from the holocaust. There was no question about his personality, either. Ten years younger than Ruckteschell, not of a philosophical bent, unbiased, uncomplicated, and cheerful, he was indisputably more fun to live with. He ran a "happy, tight ship," with drills to mold the mixed crews into a team and everything was done the way the Kriegsmarine and he, one of its regular line officers, thought it should be, even the formalities—no personal comments in the log, no light blue ties, for example. Happy-go-lucky he seemed to be, taking all matters in a much lighter vein and running his ship with less circumspection and deliberation than the canny Ruckteschell. Too light a vein, perhaps, as it turned out, the *Michel* men say, despite the man's record and hefty denials by *Thor*'s veterans.

NEW MAN, OLD TACTICS WORK WELL

On June 14* *Michel*'s plane, with *Thor*'s Ulrich Horn as observer, lifted off along the Africa-Australia track roughly thirteen hundred miles west of Australia and quickly reported a ship. Toward evening the vessel came into mast-top sight and Gumprich agreed with his officers that he would have to take her by surprise at night. It was not easy for him to come to that conclusion. All but two of his attacks with the fast, modern-gunned (model c-36 vs c-16) *Thor* had been launched in daytime and usually at the far greater ranges her newer guns permitted. Having been lucky, and not having suffered the humiliation Ruckteschell had with *Menelaus* before switching to night attacks, Gumprich found it difficult, Assistant Torpedo Officer Schmolling recalled, to accept the tactics pressed on him by *Michel*'s first-voyage officers.

   That night and forty-eight hours later, too, he did, after dark, suddenly and very fast. So fast and viciously that he was finished with Leif

---

   * *Michel*'s log for the entire following period was lost and, as a result, all times, positions, even some dates, are often based on conjecture, personal reminiscences, and a war diary reconstructed by the raider's only surviving officers, Behrend, Horn, Meckmann, Militzer, and Schmolling.

Höegh and Company's *Höegh Silverdawn* and its forty-seven-man crew and eleven passengers, most of whom thought they had been assaulted by a murderous Japanese intent on killing all, in forty-five minutes.* Twenty-seven men died in the action. Von Schack "rag-picked" six out of the sea with *Esau*. Another three—one of whom, John Bakkemyr, had survived forty-nine days adrift earlier in the war—first bounced into the raider's hull with a raft, heard the Germans talking, then spent over a week on their float before being saved by an American ship. Twenty-one others also escaped with Capt. E. Waaler in damaged lifeboat No. 4. Sailing and suffering thirty-one days and some 2,860 miles, he led nineteen of them ashore in India thirty-one days later.

The second Norwegian victim, Fearnley and Eger's 9,940-ton *Ferncastle*, went down on June 17, burning, trounced by shells and her bulkheads shattered by *Esau*'s torpedoes, with five of her thirty-seven men. Thirteen were captured and the rest sailed off with their captain, Thoralf Andersen, to arrive after thirty horrible days at Nosy-Varika, Madagascar, nearly three thousand miles from where they had been overwhelmed. Only thirteen dragged themselves ashore.

Gumprich, aware that the boats had escaped, decided to leave the Indian Ocean for the Pacific. At the end of July, he crossed the international date line and that was a big day—two Sundays in a row. An uneventful month went by as they do on raiders sometimes, but Sunday, August 29, was one of those days that make men—later on, at least shudder. It was United States light cruiser *Trenton* that *Michel*'s alert lookouts saw and identified as a heavy cruiser of the *Pensacola* class. *Trenton* (twelve 6-inch guns, six torpedo tubes, designed speed thirty-five knots), whose log, signed by Capt. S. C. Norton, showed her to be patrolling that day between 22°05'S, 72°46'W and 20°16'S, 74°56'W on a base course of 132°, secured from general quarters and "steaming as before." She had had an elusive radar contact the day before but it had disappeared from the screen within fifteen minutes.† It was *"Hackfleish* (minced meat), the fast, four-stacker could have made of our raider," Schmolling still remembered thirty years after the meeting. "It

---

* Their account, as published later, led Admiral Otto Kähler, then retired, to check with Militzer, his quartermaster during *Thor*'s first voyage. No, the latter replied November 4, 1962, Gumprich never tried to snuff lives out deliberately.

† There is some question about the date but *Trenton* was definitely the only Allied capital ship in the area during the period. She had four stacks, *Pensacola*, two, and the latter, part of Task Force 67, had been severely mauled by the tough, mustachioed Rear Admiral Raizo Tanaka's destroyers in the Battle of Tassafaronga, November 30, 1942. Her sister, veteran Pacific fighter *Salt Lake City*, was not in the area either.

seemed like a very long day" before the cruiser steamed away on a fortuitous zig.

A BALL OF FIRE, GHOSTLY SHIPS, AND NOTHING MORE

For Gumprich there was then obviously little point in hanging around that area not far from Chile. Besides, he knew that he would have to watch his supply of oil carefully; Germany had none to send, and the Japanese, already nearly surrounded, were not about to waste their small hoard or a valuable tanker to deliver any.

\ On September 10, when *Michel* was in the vicinity of Easter Island and its strange statues, she met with one last success of her trying cruise. It was a Texas Company-owned Norwegian-flag motor tanker en route from Talara, Peru, to Australia with a thirty-eight-man crew. She was spotted during the afternoon, shadowed and attacked in the manner Gumprich now found unavoidable. Within seconds of "Feuererlaubnis" and the puff of the first salvo, the tanker was a roaring wall of fire. The flames spread just as quickly as her oil poured out, and not a man could be saved. It was all von Schack with *Esau* could do to get near enough to the hissing, blistering hull to read the ship's name on its stern—*India*. Very little was said that night.

Black and silently, with just its ventilators and auxiliaries humming, its diesel hammering, the raider stole away on a heading that would take her across the heavily traveled United States–Hawaii–Pacific bases routes. On September 29 the bored crew were either hoping to get on with their job or, at the very least, get where they were going safely. They nearly ruined their chances of doing so that night.

Again, the claxons startled the men out of their bunks and sent them chasing to quarters. Once their eyes got accustomed to the dark, those stationed topside stared with incredulity. Dim black forms of ships were foaming by, ahead, astern, and on both sides. No one knew what had happened or why.

Throughout much of the war, the Germans, with their superior optics and rigidly trained lookouts, had been quicker on the draw than their foes. This time, the boys at the eye-straining glasses had somehow failed. *Michel* had bumbled into a convoy. Visibility had been poor and the watch were unaware of the trouble they were in until they glimpsed the vague outlines of what seemed to be destroyers.* They pressed the

* It is hard to determine exactly what happened because *Michel*'s log was lost. It is quite possible that the raider stumbled into U. S. Task Group 12.5

alarm button and tried to turn away as their standard orders read. But they could not get clear, and in no time at all, bulky shadows of transports took shape astern.

Gumprich relieved the O.O.D., and then ran along with the ill-met strangers for some awful moments wondering how to escape. While the chronometers seemed to stand still, he slowly and carefully shore out of line, hoping that his wake would not give him away, that no challenge would be made. Finally, his forward lookouts could see nothing but night as the ghostly ships and their unfriendly escort astern vanished into the gloom from which they had materialized. The unique event, probably the only one of its kind in the war, was an "exciting one," to Schmolling, "fantastic."

By the afternoon of October 16, the raider was only a little over one hundred miles from Honshu and while the men were preparing for liberty after their arrival the next afternoon, the officers met to discuss the next steps—getting there safely. That they might still run into trouble was perfectly clear. American submarines, they knew, had been raising hell with the Empire's shipping in the Pacific Basin areas. In fifteen months of campaigning, Japan's merchant marine had, despite a desperate building program, been reduced 71 percent below its 5.6-million-ton prewar total, and more than fifty ships had been sunk in waters adjacent to the home islands in the year ending August 1943. Gumprich could not have been aware of the exact figures, but both he and his exec, Trendtel, who had served a stint as German base commander Yokohama, were informed of the fact that the Japanese Navy's countermeasures were so inadequate that any ship making a landfall was fair game for the Americans. It was also evident that the same subs that were making the waters dangerous with their torpedoes were capable of contaminating the seas with mines. On the other hand, it was well known that over fifty

---

composed of destroyer *Braine,* destroyer escorts *McConnell* and *Miller* and destroyer-minelayer *Gamble* in the screen, and six transports in convoy. TG 12.5 was, according to Capt. F. Kent Loomis, U.S.N. (Ret.), Assistant Director of Naval History, Department of the Navy, the only convoy at sea at that time that matches the Germans' description—and the latter insist they saw destroyers and transports. It was steaming westerly en route from the United States to Hawaii and roughly on a line 33°–34°N on that day—if the date is correct. If, on the other hand, *Michel* was then still farther south, and it seems that she might have been, the highly accurate German historian Dr. Gerhard Hümmelchen may be right in assuming that the encounter was far more harmless than it had seemed to the men in the raider. Gerhard Hümmelchen, *Handelstörer,* 2nd ed. (Munich: J. F. L. Lehmans Verlag, 1967). Hümmelchen, also citing a letter from the courteous Loomis, who has been a steady source of this writer's information, states that *Michel* merely met up with four small ships, ATR-45, a rescue tug, APC-95, a coastal transport, and two submarine chasers, SC-1042 and SC-1046. His SC-1046 should, however, read SC-1045.

German supply ships and blockade runners had sailed unmolested, in and out, without any escort. Apparently there had been no recent submarine warnings, and Wenneker in Tokyo had requested neither a continuous air cover nor a surface screen for the seventeenth. The Japanese could not have provided one anyway; they simply did not have enough destroyers or antisubmarine vessels, say, like the 527-ton *Tidori* class, small boats, armed with 4.7-inch to cover all their overextended lines of communication—not even for friends close enough to be virtually in sight of Mount Fujiyama, fifty miles out. As it was, even the most important ships or convoys could usually obtain only a single, slow, and often inefficient escort, and had to rely on what aerial surveillance there was in the vicinity. That had supposedly been increased somewhat to assist the raider.

It had been planned that *Michel* would turn loose von Schack's boat to act as its own miniature screen when the raider was approaching the Izu-shichitō chain of islands that led right into Tokyo Bay, but for some reason, Gumprich did not order *Esau* launched. In the evening Militzer, a reserve lieutenant by then, raised the subject again with Trendtel, and other officers, too, were wondering why their underwater listening device had not been manned, why they were not zigzagging, why only the normal cruising watch had been turned out, why watertight integrity had not been established, or why the off-duty men were permitted to sleep in their bunks below. Ruckteschell, the officers of *Michel*'s original staff groused, would most certainly have taken more care. They could not figure Gumprich out. Though likable, far more so personally than the previous commander, they feared his carefree nature was leading to carelessness. Some of his own former *Thor* shipmates argue that zigging would only have slowed the vessel's progress down during the final stretch, and they say that lulled, perhaps by optimism and the lack of concern shown by the Tokyo-based authorities, Gumprich simply felt he was home free. But one officer, then on his third hitch in a raider, and the second under Gumprich, has the impression that the latter was not the man he had been during his first undertaking. He seemed to need the company of others more often and his drinking had become heavier. In fact, it appeared to that man that his skipper had been suffering from a premonition of death right from the outset of the cruise.

Flying Officer Horn, who had conned the ship many times during the journey, had the watch shortly after midnight when the lookout aft reported a streak of foam that could have been a torpedo. Nothing further was sighted, however. *Michel* was steaming at nearly her best speed close to the tiny islands and it was quite possible that the seaman had been misled by a line of waves broaching along a beach. By 0100 of the seventeenth (German time estimate), it was warm, and there was a bright moon shining through high clouds onto a smooth and apparently deserted sea.

Michel was not alone. Closing her predicted track, slowly and only six miles away, was, according to A. H. Clark, Jr., a former American torpedo officer, U.S.S. *Tarpon* (SS-175), a 1,315-ton submarine of the seven-year old "P" class (six 21-inch torpedo tubes, one 5-inch gun, and two 40 mms). She was commanded by Thomas L. Wogan (who was credited with sinking nine ships of 51,700 tons and damaging another 38,000 tons). The submarine, which was faster than *Michel* on the surface, was one of the boats of Pearl Harbor-based Submarine Division 44, was on her ninth war patrol with an assigned area of operation off Honshu, and on Sunday, the seventeenth, was stalking a prey. She had been on station at periscope depth within a few miles of Inamba Shima (one of the Izu chain), less than seventy-five miles from the mainland since 0400 the morning of the sixteenth, and had seen numerous small craft and daytime air patrols, but none at night. By her log, she surfaced at 1900, steering east, and, as Clark remembers, the bridge was manned, battery charge completed, and all four diesels available to go on line. At 0045, a ship was sighted, and radar, with which some difficulty had been experienced due to the screening effect of the nearby islands, picked her up at 13,450 yards, three minutes later. Wogan climbed up the tower to the bridge and stationed his radar and firing control approach parties whose ticking TDC (torpedo data computer) was clicking off the inputs of range and bearing of the target, speed, and course of the submarine to Clark, and transmitting the proper gyro settings to the torpedoes. *Tarpon* maneuvered for forty-five minutes, and then submerged (it took her only fifty-five seconds). There were no jokes, no humorous comments, just the hum of the electric motors and Wogan's commands coming through the line from his throat microphone as he watched the target through his periscope; "Making a run on target," the log says. At 0156, Wogan ordered "stand by to fire," then "Fire one, fire two . . ." *Tarpon* bucked as four torpedoes went swishing out of the tubes and were replaced by water to compensate for their weight of more than four tons. Tracked by sonar, the twenty-one-inch missiles churned toward the blacked-out, unsuspecting *Michel*. "Two hits. Target stopped."

Horn, on the raider's bridge, saw one of the torpedoes coming but there was not much he could do about it. As it struck just ahead of the bridge to port, bursting open two compartments with a sharp report, a high red column of fire shot up. The ship shuddered as if there had been a collision, then shore off course, losing speed and listing to port. More than one hundred German stokers and seamen sleeping in the smashed compartments died instantly in the explosion and under the inrushing water, and so did all of the nineteen prisoners from the two Norwegian ships. Only one man is thought to have gotten out. Within minutes, Gumprich and nearly three hundred of his disciplined men were at their stations, had closed all remaining watertight doors, moved the wounded, and cut the auxiliary generators into the circuits to provide light. Star shells were fired and the guns opened up, shooting fast and indiscriminately in the hope of keeping the sub down and away.

Wogan went deep—150 feet—as pieces of shrapnel bounced off the water near his scope and, as Clark remembers, clattered off the submerged submarine's hull, a most unusual occurrence, to say the least, and one reason why he can recall the incident. Obviously neither Clark nor Capt. Theodore M. Ustick, another *Tarpon* vet, nor Wogan thought their victim a German, and Ustick cannot remember the metal clanking on their hull. What he does still have in mind is that the slowly sinking, badly listing ship, though dead in the water, was well lit up, shooting wildly in all directions with guns of various caliber, and that there were hundreds of men in white clambering about her decks and sides. At 0218 Wogan fired three more torpedoes. One hit; "target badly damaged." Twelve minutes later he let loose one more; "hit same place as the first torpedo." Still no comments on the sub except the skipper's periscope-eye description of the dying but fast-shooting ship and a few "loud cheers and some uncouth remarks emanating from the torpedo room as each 'pickel' ran 'hot, straight and normal.' "

On *Michel,* listing fifteen degrees to port, they were just getting things squared away, the many alarming damage reports were in and they were about to get off a signal from the emergency radio room, when one of the second spread of "pickels" hit. Some of the Germans thought they saw several others glancing off the hull aft and they so reported to Berlin in a wireless sent from Tokyo on the twentieth. The one torpedo that did go off opened up the cavernous holds Nos. 3 and 4 where the plane and *Esau* were housed. With that, the auxiliary generators sputtered out—no distress signal could be sent—and the ship settled by the stern, her main deck awash. Gumprich ordered *"Alle Mann aus dem Schiff, Rettungsboote und Flösse zu Wasser."* (All men out of the ship, lifeboats and rafts into the water).

Obeying quickly, Lieutenant Behrend, whose abandon ship station was the starboard cutter (the port boat had been destroyed in the blast), worked hard to clear the craft from wreckage, then managed to lower it in the midst of a group of swimming men who all promptly tried to climb aboard. He jumped down to establish order and prevent his boat from swamping, and then tried to haul clear of the rapidly sinking ship. As he did, another torpedo exploded, the compiled survivors' report says. The message to Berlin, however, had that explosion, the third, taking place to port and forward of the bridge (in the vicinity of the first hit). Both accounts agree that a second torpedo slammed into them to port, but the former claims it to have been the fourth and last. The wireless mentions only three hits out of a total of six torpedoes observed. The submarine's patrol report shows that eight torpedoes were fired and four hits were claimed, with the first two and last apparently striking in the same place, and the third at the stern.

The last shot spelled *Michel*'s end. Her forepeak rose steeply and she sliced under by the stern with a horrible screeching, tearing, and crashing as machinery and equipment tore loose and the last bulkheads gave way. The hundred or so men struggling in the oily water to cling to casks, timber, air tanks, and anything else that would float, and the others who had managed to clamber into the boats and onto the rafts or were holding on alongside, gave a cheer for the ship and three hurrahs for the dead and those still alive who were going down with it—their comrades with whom they had shared monotony and terror for years. Captain Gumprich, who had directed rescue operations to the end, did nothing to save himself. He was last seen on his bridge with navigator Siek, just seconds before the raider rushed to the bottom. The gallant von Schack, a man always good for games and sport of all kind, led three hurrahs for Gumprich—strange in a war of machines, maybe, but chivalrous, spontaneous, and from the heart. Very few of the disciplined lads survived, however, and only 110 of them, 70 in Behrend's boat and another 40 on several rafts commanded by prize officer Meckmann, managed to reach the safety of nearby Izu Peninsula during the next three days.

Behrend, who had gotten free with his boat, maneuvered about to pick up as many of the helpless men that he could (a total of 70) and then proceeded to save them in the most practical manner he knew. He got out a chart, entered the last known position, checked his provisions, had the mast stepped, the compass broken out. Some of them could not understand why he headed out to sea and not for the close-by islands, but Behrend, an old sea dog and long-time merchant officer, knew very well what he was doing. Local currents were unpredictable, and he wanted to get ashore to report the disaster as quickly as possible so that rescue measures could be undertaken. During the first day, some rubber boats with Lieutenant Meckmann in charge were still in sight astern. A badly injured man died. Several low-flying planes were seen but neither red nor white flares attracted their attention, and a fishing boat, spotted toward evening, passed the Germans by. The night was cold, windy, and wet, and off to starboard they could see the dim glow cast by the lights of still unblacked-out Tokyo and Yokohama. On the next morning, fabled Mount Fujiyama and later the contours of the mainland could be seen. A coaster, which passed them at only a few hundred yards, paid no heed whatever to the stripped men waving their shirts, but the villages on Izu Peninsula were getting bigger and they could already distinguish individual homes and trees. Behrend picked out a tiny bay in which there seemed to be a boat harbor, and he steered for it. A launch came out from behind the small jetty and its occupants showered the Germans with questions they did not understand, and made it evident that they were not welcome. Behrend ignored them and set his boat on the soft sand where a large threatening crowd equipped with clubs and scythes had gathered to prevent the round-eyed men they thought Americans from landing. Once the identity barrier was broken, however, the Germans were taken to a schoolhouse, treated to food, drinks, and smokes, while a report was telephoned to nearby Tokyo to initiate a rescue action for the rest of *Michel*'s survivors.

Forty of them were with Meckmann on rubber boats, one of which had no bottom and its unhappy occupants no choice but to ride astride its bulging, slippery sides. Meckmann had the same intentions as Behrend and was trying to follow him, but he could not control his clumsy craft as well and it was obvious to him the second night that they were in trouble. The next day he saw what was probably the same fishing boat that had ignored Behrend. This time, it reacted, but it took some time before the swastikas that Meckmann's wet, miserable men tried to draw had any effect. Finally, the fishermen took them on board and to the same place where Behrend had landed.

After their arrival, there was no further news from the hundred-odd men thought to have been left splashing in the large field of oil wreckage where *Michel* had gone down. The Japanese Navy had been alerted within thirty-six hours of the disaster by Behrend, and the Chief of Naval Station Yokosuka had been ordered to fly search patterns. Nothing, absolutely nothing, was ever found. Germans at all the bases and in the embassy in Tokyo pleaded and argued, complaining bitterly— despite the personal assurances of the Emperor's Navy Minister—that not enough was being done. (The Japanese would, according to the Germans, not even permit the latter as observers in their planes.) It was incredible, they thought, that the pilots could not even locate the wreckage. Nothing was seen, nothing was reported, the Japanese Navy said; nothing was done, the Kriegsmarine countered.

The recriminations began hardly a few days after the sinking.

There were searching inquiries from Berlin, where they could not believe the laxity with which *Michel*'s return had been handled, and the communications passing between Naval Attaché Tokyo, Admiral Wenneker, and his capital were unpleasant. Besides casting doubt on the provisions made or not made, by the raider's captain and the command on shore, it seemed evident to Berlin that too little action had been taken by the Japanese to assure the ship's security. "Arrival of Japanese submarines in Biscay entails major action here with sorties by all available vessels," SKL radioed on the twenty-eighth, adding that "lack of Jap. safety measures cannot be understood here." When he learned of the sinking, Dönitz's chief of staff, Rear Admiral Eberhard Godt, said that the carelessness had been "unbelievable" and "extraordinary."

For all the charges, accusations, and agitation for more rescue attempts, it appeared for days that there were no further survivors. A few men, Behrend's people thought, might have been picked up by the sub to verify its kill, and they were sure they had seen the American's slim dark silhouette shortly after the sinking. They may have seen *Tarpon* at one time, but in their hopes for their buddies they were deceived. Wogan had surfaced after his thirty-four minute attack, but he had not seen or picked up anyone. He thought they were Japanese. In fact, some of those on the sub remember that they had been tempted to hammer away at the many men engaged in abandoning the stricken ship, which seemed obviously to be some sort of Japanese auxiliary, with their 40-mms, but had been stopped by their skipper who had no hankering for revealing himself. *Tarpon* did remain on the surface but not in the immediate vicinity for several hours, and she later made two more attacks (both unsuccessful) before leaving her patrol area on October 23 after twelve days on station. By the time Wogan had arrived at his base on November 1 to be congratulated on an "aggressive" and well-conducted patrol and for "sinking a valuable enemy ship," only seven more of *Michel*'s men had managed to save themselves.

When the "valuable" ship went down, von Schack, as senior officer present, immediately set about with boundless energy and courage to keep as many men as possible alive. About one hundred of them were then still clustered about a cutter, one rubber boat, and a couple of rafts. Schack hoped that he could keep them all together in one spot where they would be more easily found once rescue operations got under way. Untiring and selfless, he pleaded, rescued, and ordered those who were able to make more floats from whatever material was drifting about. He jarred some to consciousness, he helped some swim, and he encouraged them all. A few planes were seen the first day, but they took no notice and apparently did not see the slowly dwindling number of survivors or the flares they shot off. The next night it breezed up, and

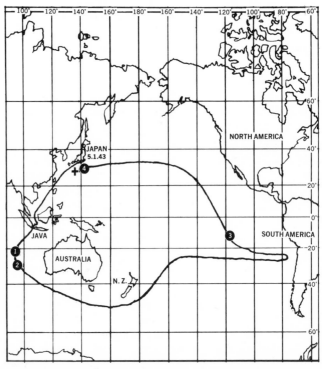

PRESUMED ROUTE OF MICHEL'S SECOND VOYAGE

1. HÖEGH SILVERDAWN		6.15.43
2. FERNCASTLE		6.17.43
3. INDIA		9.11.43
4. Sunk by U.S.S. TARPON ✛		10.17.43

the rising seas tore apart the hastily built floats and the struggling men off them. Schack realized that something would have to be done if anyone were to survive. He therefore ordered Militzer to take the only craft that could be paddled or steered—a rubber boat with eight men and a float with another four—and make an attempt to reach land and get help. Militzer was to be accompanied by only three men, and they were to take no provisions because Schack hoped they would make land within a reasonable time. He himself would stay in the oily water with the majority of desperate men. It was the last anyone ever saw of that heroic officer and the other survivors whom he had tried so hard to save.

Militzer could not bring himself to drive the superfluous men on his raft into the water, and so he set off with Schmolling, Dr. Buchinger, and five others on what he describes as an "adventurous and very difficult journey," often in sight, but never, due to the currents, in reach of the maddeningly close islands. The steel raft they were towing, with its four helpless men, was a constant threat to his fragile rubber raft, and though no one ever said it, they were lucky when the line holding it finally parted: "I'll never forget," Militzer recalls, "those poor miserable men, and their desperate reproach, 'You murderers!' " With only seaweed, small fish, and tiny crabs for both food and water, they were soon exhausted. One died; another, delirious, crawled overboard. In the morning of the seventh day at about 1000, a motorboat tuckered out toward them from Hachijō Jima, roughly 120 miles from the mainland and not too far from where *Michel* had sunk. There, at a small temple, most of them were carefully nursed and were then transported in a patrol boat along with urns containing the ashes of two of their friends to the hospital in Yokohama where *Michel* and *Widder*'s former Dr. Schröder attended to them. The ashes, reverently carried by the Japanese, were those of Warrant Officer Walter Emmel and Dr. Buchinger, who had helped spank the little Chinese lad into life on May 12, 1942, when *Thor* was in the Indian Ocean. He was the last of 15 officers and 248 ranks who had died with the last of the German raiders. Only a few Japanese and Germans in the Orient or in Berlin could immediately mourn them. The former were not concerned (the search for survivors was called off after a storm on November 6), and the latter, though anxious to pin down responsibility for the loss (no one was ever found guilty), were hoping to keep their loss from being known—no wire privileges for survivors until a later day—and their bureaucrats were soon hard at work. What, they wanted to know, with rising inflation, would be the compensation for each man's personal property? That was the end of World War II ocean raiding.

Conclusion

On the Allied side, there were very few even in the intelligence community who knew that *Michel* had again been at sea. There was no one who realized that she was gone until early 1944 after the last of the blockade runners, *Burgenland, Rio Grande,* and *Weserland* (which put up quite a fight, shooting up one United States plane and another down), had been tracked down by the U. S. Navy. Some of the German seamen in them had heard about *Michel* or had even served in her. A few talked and it then became evident that the last of the raiders had been sunk months earlier. At that stage of that great war, neither Washington nor London cared very much. Germany was losing the war and it was a safe bet—with D-Day only a few months off—that she could no longer field such a strange ship. SKL were the first to agree; they could not.

To those Germans involved with the raiders' struggle, it must, at times, have seemed a tale of woe not unlike the children's story of the ten little Indians. Only eleven of an envisioned twenty-six ever entered the yards to be rebuilt and that too late. Ten were completed and sailed to fight splendidly. But only nine served their hell on the high seas. Three were decommissioned while the war was still slaying, one blew up in an accident, and six were sunk in action. No, decisive the raiders were not, but then no single weapon except the A-bomb of 1945 ever has been. And it was not needed at the time, has now resulted in a trade-off, like machine guns and gas.

Few as they were and anachronistic, too, in a contest determined by science, production, and body counts, the raiders served their mission well. Their toil paid off handsomely for an underdog navy unprepared for a global conflict. The Hilfskreuzer sank a cruiser, an armed merchant cruiser; they forced two more of the latter to disengage and were responsible for more than 890,000 tons of shipping destroyed, damaged, or captured as prizes during the forty-three months of their peculiar war.

279

And that was better than 7.3 percent of the tonnage wasted by the terrible U-boats which nearly brought Britain to her knees a second time during that period.

But sheer destruction, as advantageous as that proved to be (one ship, for example, sank with 15.6 million weekly wartime rations of butter, 3.5 million of meat, and hundreds of tons of cocoa, milk, and cheese; another with 10,000 tons of gasoline; others with trucks and planes), was not their primary purpose.

That, as conceived by SKL and Admiral Raeder, was to create disarray in the distribution of Allied naval strength—to draw off warships engaged in breaking Germany's stranglehold on Britain's vital maritime transport. And it worked: If a heavy cruiser spent weeks searching the Indian Ocean as far south as the Kerguelen Islands, its one-thousand-man complement could be of use neither in clearing the Mediterranean nor in convoying in the cold Atlantic; nor could another 8-incher on escort duty between Mombasa and Colombo help trap the *Bismarck* near the Bay of Biscay.

The disruption the Germans in their singular and lonely ships created was punishing, in squandered effort, lost opportunities, in the number of fighting ships allocated to their annihilation. It was severe in the extravagant rerouting procedures, the spent time and manpower, the dissipated bottoms and overdue cargoes forced on the merchant ships. If a freighter, laden down to its marks with guns, ammunition, apples, or manganese, had to wait in port for a week or more while the navy assembled a convoy in which she then had to steam from port to port at the speed of its slowest member, she might be two months making a passage that normally took two weeks. That meant, in effect, that it would take four ships her size to get the same amount of cargo to its destination. And if she were then delayed again or routed evasively over longer distances, her voyage might last six months instead of one while her intended freight stapled at its port of origin, clogging warehouses, and the fighting men ashore to whom her bills of lading were addressed marked time.

A war against commerce furthered by diversions was the grand plan envisioned by Admiral Raeder, who, while lacking the numbers necessary to triumph, was burdened with internal politics and the necessity of making a name for his fleet. There were those in high places—and they cannot easily be refuted—who held that Raeder and his operations staff had been following the wrong concept right from the start, had been basing strategy on faulty tactics. If Germany lacked an adequate and integrated fleet, capital ships, destroyers, planes, the critics said, she should have frittered away what little she did possess in ships and manpower. Every ounce of strength, every bit of productive capacity, should have been concentrated in U-boats. Some of the officers in the raiders concurred but they still carried out their part of the war extremely well, with élan, proficiency, and, as one British prisoner put it, "a damn good bit of gallantry and chivalry."

But skill and courtliness alone could not set back the calender or make up for squandered opportunities and political mistakes. Nor could they, in the end, offset logistics in a war that had turned as it was bound to against a minuscule fleet that did not have the resources to back it up.

It was obvious late in the fourth year of the war that there could not be any more raiders, just as it is likely today that there will be no more of those terrifying but romantic craft to test the mettle of instant nuclear alert in the future. But then there were similar doubts raised in German naval circles after World War I. And did not the badly managed U.S.S. *Pueblo* and the exposed *Liberty* ply their trade successfully until nabbed? And did not the $300-million Hughes-built *Glomar Explorer* grapple up some of the coldest cold-war secrets, when rival industrial experts who had seen her once were bent on discovering her whereabouts and exploiting the oceans' oil and manganese, in an age of hostile navies and sophisticated satellites and electronic devices?

NOTES

1. *Coronel,* ex-*Togo* with a romantic pre-raiding career but a failure in getting through the Channel to raid, was again rebuilt after Thienemann returned her to Germany. Loaded with electronic gear and looking much like floating Cape Canaveral, she reverted to her old name *Togo* and was employed as a radar fighter-control ship for the rest of the war. In 1945 she was bombed several times while bringing back troops from Poland and East Prussia, but she survived to be allocated to the United States. Used for a while to repatriate Polish prisoners of war, she was sold in 1947 to the Norwegian government which rechristened her *Svalbard*. With little but reinforced decks to tell of her time as a raider, the ship was then employed by the Royal Norwegian Navy in transporting occupation troops to Germany. In 1954 she was sold to private interests, for whom she sailed as *Stella Marina* and *Tilthorn* for two years until her original owners repurchased her. As *Togo* again and handsomely refurbished, she was back on the Africa run for 12 years, after which she was sold to Taboga Enterprises, Inc., of Panama. Renamed *Lacasielle,* she was still in the early 1970s in tramp service.

2. Von Ruckteschell's fate was to be as different from the other raider commanders' as was his character, and he blamed the former in part on

his having been the only nonregular navy officer. (nonestablishment). Having turned over command of *Michel* to Gumprich, he spent the rest of the war in and out of hospitals in Tokyo, Shanghai and Peking, and was finally repatriated as a prisoner-of-war working in the mess line of U.S. C-4 transport *Marine Robin.* At the British interrogation center at Minden, August 20, 1946, he was listed as a "war criminal." A court would decide whether he would be taken to task for his warningless attacks on shipping, he advised his wife, "but I want you to know that my conscience as a human being is clear. So please pray for us." He was sick of heart and heartbroken; the examination he was to face was not one he could prepare for, and its results were legally, technically and ethically debatable. Held in Hamburg's University district Curio Haus, the trial lasted from May 5 to May 21, 1947, and the judgment passed down by the British Military Court opened up one of the many cancerous and acrimonious post-war disputes, the issues of which are clouded by personalities, prejudice and vindictiveness.

Prosecution, headed by a Royal Army Major, alleged that *Widder* continued to shell *Davisian* after her radio had been knocked out and the ship had acknowledged an order to maintain wireless silence. *Davisian's* Second Officer, John M. Jolly, said the raider continued to press his attack for several minutes and that three men had been killed as a result. Defense, using *Widder's* war diary, argued that no signal had been perceived and that firing had ceased after seven salvos. It had been resumed only after a few of the freighter's crew were thought to be running to man their gun. Much attention was, for some reason, paid to one of the irrelevant personal opinions about superiors, subordinates or enemies that Ruckteschell vented in his log with imperious irreverence and impartiality. In this case, he had opined that the 50 survivors he had picked up were "Englishmen—not Scots—insolent and noisy."

The Court charged that *Widder* fired on the lifeboats of *Anglo Saxon,* and failed to assure the survival of the men in them. The allegations were based on an affidavit of Seaman Robert G. Tapscott, one of the two men who lived through that incredible ordeal in the small lifeboat after their ship's sinking, but he could not be located for the trial. Defense countered, saying it had been difficult to stop the gunners, who had been firing over the heads of men in the boats, because of the noise of the battle. By the time the action was over, it was argued, darkness had set in and all the men in *Widder* ever saw of the survivors were two lights, apparently from boats speaking to each other in Morse code. No distress messages were observed; the men in the boats attempted to escape and thus made rescue impossible.

A second accusation regarding the safety of survivors involved the Norwegian *Beaulieu.* Prosecution, in this case, relied entirely on Ruckteschell's own log, and the owners of the tanker, Bjørn Biørnstad & Co., were not represented at the trial. Defense said it had been dark at the time, that only one boat with 18 or 20 men was seen drifting at the stern of the crippled ship, and that anyone remaining in the vicinity would have been picked up by the boarding party. *Widder,* stated Dr. Zippel, the defense attorney, had backed and filled for two-and-a-half hours while searching for men in the dark. Ruckteschell's contention that it would have been pointless to lower his own boats to aid in the rescue attempt was supported by a British Naval Captain and Admiral Rogge who, inter alia, pointed out that very little can be seen from a boat rising and falling in a high Atlantic swell.

The last charge, continuing to shell a vessel after it had already surrendered, concerned *Michel*'s attack on *Empire Dawn*. The ship's skipper, W. A. Scott, who had thought all Germans came in two categories—"either kind, well-mannered and loveable, or utter and absolute swine"—said that he had tried to signal the raider with a torch from the boat deck. He had hoped, he explained, that he would be given time to abandon ship, but the Germans had continued to fire on his burning vessel. Defense argued that there was no proof that the torch had worked and, even if it had, that it would have been impossible to see it against the background of a blazing ship by Germans already blinded by their own gun flashes. Ruckteschell said he saw no signal. *Michel*'s Executive Officer, Wolfgang Erhardt, one of the few German witnesses ever allowed to testify at the trial, which he as well as many others considered badly conducted by technically inexpert prosecutors and judges, accounts for one of the strong post-war contentions and, in doing so, points out one of those tragic misunderstandings—whims of fate—on which men's lives depend. Brusquely asked in court whether any ship had ever tried to speak to the raider by blinker, he said no, convinced five years after the event that he was telling the truth. Only much later did he remember the incident—and then it was too late to help his former commander. (Apparently, no one ever mentioned that Ruckteschell immediately ceased firing when the men in *Kattegat* waved a white lantern.)

Erhardt had been standing on *Michel*'s bridge, he says, when he saw a few weak dots and dashes—certainly not an entire message—coming from the enemy. "I yelled, 'Dampfer morst.' As you know, our commander was a reserve officer and was not entirely conversant with our language of command. We professionals understood 'morsen' to mean light signals. Ruckteschell, however, thought I had said 'Dampfer funkt.' (Steamer is using her wireless.) He consequently ordered his men to continue to shoot to choke off the radioing, and before the guns could be stopped, another four salvos had gone on their way." A simple language failure that was never cleared up in the context of the proceedings, and was tragically similar to the many incidents during the war when ships of all nations shot up their own forces and friendly planes due to faulty communications. Judge Advocate said that even if the Court concluded that no signal had been read in *Michel*, Ruckteschell could still be convicted if they concluded that he had deliberately or recklessly made it impossible for the ship to make a signal. That statement, if considered against the backdrop of a naval engagement and the fact that merchantmen could be considered belligerents if they resisted a warship, seemed witless, and Ruckteschell was found not guilty on that charge.

On May 21, the Court announced its verdict: Guilty on three counts; prolonged firing on *Davisian* and failure to provide for the safety of the crews of *Anglo Saxon* and *Beaulieu*. A ten-year sentence to jail was reduced to seven by the confirming officer who would not uphold the charge concerning *Beaulieu.* Ruckteschell, gray-haired and bespectacled, cheerfully waved to his family whom he had previously written that the thought of being executed had not nearly been as hard to bear as "being condemned on false evidence." As an officer, he refused to ask for mercy; it was justice he wanted, he said. He may have "erred and now it is they. We both did it on orders and in the belief that we were right, and now we are both wrong."

In Germany, only the communist "Hamburger Volkszeitung" rejoiced publically in his fate—he died on June 24 in the Hamburg-Fuhlsbüttel prison just after hearing that he was to be released in consideration of his heart problem. The British stoutly hold to their original contention that Ruckteschell's methods were brutal. The defendant's friends and countrymen, on the other hand, in part, at least, maintain that the Court was acting in vengeance for Ruckteschell's escape from prosecution for the part he played as one of the U-boat commanders the Allies hoped to bring to trial for war crimes after World War I. His officers, most of whom were not permitted to testify, were angered—as were some of his associates whether or not they personally thought well of him—by what they considered to be an unfair treatment of a hard-fighting sailor. Still other parties, namely former prisoners in *Michel,* but neither asked to nor involved in the proceedings, take a more impartial though perhaps cynical stand. It is quite possible that the captain was railroaded, they allow, but whatever the reasons for the trial and the findings of the victors' Court, war is war, and any injustices arising from it are just part of the beastly whole. One officer, who spent more than 80 days captive in the raider, says, "War is a systematic method of killing one another, lawful on both sides . . . to us, at least, Ruckteschell was a Christian and a gentleman."

BIBLIOGRAPHY

An acknowledgment of thanks with the hope that none of the principal contributors has been overlooked:

Baasch, Hans
Bailey, F. W.
Bailey, H. T.
Bakker, B. B.
Balser, Karl August
Barker, M. N., Jr.
Beeham, P.
Behrend, Edgar
Berens, George R.
Blanc, Adalbert von
Borchers, Rudolf
Borner, Fritz
Brind, B. L.
Brown, Frank C.
Cameron, D. V.
Cant, Alexander
Clark, A. H., Jr.
Davison, S. S.
Detmers, Theodor
Duffy, George W.
Dun, Burnham V.
Dupuch, Sir Etienne
Erhardt, Wolfgang
Frame, Charley
Gafos, George
Gerlach, Hildegard
Gorski, Stanley E.
Greter, Joachim
Gruber, Sepp
Gundersen, Gunnar V.

Haines, Thomas
Harrel, Mrs. Charlton
Heinicke, Günter
Hemmer, Hans Karl
Herr, Jürgen
Herzog, Bodo
Hoppe, Konrad
Jung, Carl
Kähler-von Friedeburg, Ursula
Kandeler, Dr. Hermann
Karsten, Wilfried
King, G. T.
Koppen-Boehnke, Werner
Krüder, Ingeborg
Lievense, A. L.
Lingen, K. C. van der
Loomis, F. Kent
Lutken, Thor
McClory, George
MacVicar, William
Meckmann, Bernhard
Meyer-Ahrens, Robert
Militzer, Henry
Mohr, Dr. Ulrich
Moser, Constantin
Müller, Theo
Myklebust, Board
Nash, Alfred R.
Nishimura, Susumu
Nolan, Edward

285

Petersen, Ludolf
Piercy, Rodger H.
Poppe, Haagen
Porter, Paul B.
Poulson, H. L.
Povey, George W.
Ramstad, Henry
Rehwinkel, M. J.
Rogge, Bernhard
Roland, Dennis A.
Schmidt, Otto
Schmolling, Willi
Schoon, Gerhard

Schröder, Dr. Friedrich-Wilhelm
Smith, George E.
Steele, H.
Thornberg, Egon
Tuinhout, Siebren
Ustick, Theodore
Varian, Theodore L.
Wesemann, Heinrich
Weyher, Kurt
White, J. Armstrong
Williams, Richard
Zimmerman, Ernst

OFFICIAL DOCUMENTS

Australia

"Notes on Interview with Capt. J. Callender Master *Triadic* and A. Jensen, Chief Officer *Vinni*," Melbourne, 28/12/40
"My impressions as a Prisoner aboard the *Manyo Maru* and the *Tokyo Maru* by G. W. Dillon Passenger to Nauru per *Triadic*"
"Notes on Experience Aboard German Raiders by G. R. Ferguson Passenger to Nauru per *Triadic*"
"Diary kept by Mr. Jensen, Chief Officer of the Norwegian Vessel *Vinni*"
"Translation of the log re the sinking of M.S. *Vinni*"

Germany

Kriegstagebuch (KTB) *Schiff 5*
KTB *Schiff 10* (Erste Fahrt)
"Bericht über das Gefecht und die Vernichtung des brit. Hilfskreuzer *Voltaire*"
"Bericht über das Gefecht mit dem brit. Hilfskreuzer *Alcantara*"
KTB *Schiff 10* (second voyage)
KTB *Schiff 14*
KTB Marinegruppenkommando Nord und Flottenkommando B. Nr. GKdos 431/43 Chefs (concerning the attempt of *Schiff 14* to break out)
Marinegruppenkommando Nord teletype communications with Kpt. z. S. Thienemann (concerning the attempt of *Schiff 14* to break out)
Operationsbefehl für den Hilfskreuzer *Schiff 14* B. Nr. 1 SKL 1K 2573/42 GKdos
KTB *Schiff 16*
Schiff 16—Bemerkungen des A. O. zu mehreren Gefechten
Schiff 16—Bericht über den Untergang
KTB *Durmitor* (prize of *Schiff 16*)

KTB *Schiff 21*

KTB *Schiff 23*

FT Bericht von *Schiff 28* über Verlust von *Schiff 23*

KTB *Schiff 28*

The German High Command file of special signals relating to *Schiff 28*, mainly information concerning its sinking off Japan

Kriegsmarine documents such as SKL IK 203/42 Op. GKdos Chefs, Operationsbefehl für den Hilfskreuzer *Schiff 28*, 1 SKL 21020 GKdos Verschl. Tel. aus Tokio, 255, 262, 267, 359, etc.

Compilation of accounts of survivors of *Schiff 28*'s sinking

KTB *Schiff 33*

KTB *Schiff 36*

KTB *Schiff 41*

Ergänzung zum KTB *Schiff 41* (concerning rescue and conditions in camp)

KTB *Schiff 45* (first voyage)

Short Battle Report of the 3rd T Flotilla concerning the attempt to escort *Schiff 45* (second voyage) out through the Channel

Report of the acting Flotilla leader (Commander of T-4), Commanding the 3rd T Flotilla concerning the battle off Cap de la Hague

Report of T-14's action off Cap de la Hague, submitted by the Flotilla Engineer in the absence of the commander who was wounded

Report of the action off Cap de la Hague by Commander of T-19

Report concerning shore-based artillery such as Battery *York*, 722, 706 to See Kommandant Normandie

Report concerning loss of *Schiff 45*, Adm. Marschall C-in-C Marinegruppenkommando West to SKL 15/12/42; Report of the See Kommandant Normandie; KTBs of Escort Division 2

Comment of SKL on attempt to get *Sperrbrecher 12* (*Schiff 45*) out

KTB SKL Teil A., Oct., Nov. 1943

Oberkommando der Kriegsmarine 1 SKL B. Nr. 841/43 GKdos Chefs, Mar. 1943

KTB U-A

KTB U-126

Operationen und Taktik; Heft 5; Die Fahrt des Hilfkreuzer *Schiff 16* (*Atlantis*), Berlin, Feb. 1943. M. Dv. Nr. 601 GKdos

Operationen und Taktik; Heft 6; Die Fahrt des Hilfkreuzer *Schiff 33* (*Pinguin*), Berlin, Apr. 1943

Operationen und Taktik; Heft 7; Die erste Fahrt des Hilfkreuzer *Schiff 10* (*Thor*); Berlin, July 1943

Operationen und Taktik; Heft 8; Die Fahrt des Hilfkreuzer *Schiff 21* (*Widder*); Berlin, May 1943

Operationen und Taktik; Heft 14; Die erste Fahrt des Hilfkreuzer *Schiff 45* (*Komet*); Berlin, July 1944

Operationen und Taktik; Heft 15; Die Fahrt des Hilfkreuzer *Schiff 36* (*Orion*); Berlin, Oct. 1944

Rogge, VAdm. a.D. Bernhard, files
Ruckteschell, Hellmuth von, letters to various people
Weyher, KAdm. a.D. Kurt, files

Great Britain

Britannia: Report on sinking of, by William MacVicar, Third Officer, and
    Sub-Lt. McIntosh; c. Mr. MacVicar
Lifeboat No. 7: Log; c. Mr. MacVicar
Clan Buchanan: Report on the sinking of, by S. S. Davidson, First Officer;
    c. Cayzer, Irvine & Co.
Empire Dawn: Account of the sinking of *Empire Dawn,* by W. A. Scott,
    Captain; c. Walter Runcinam & Co.
Gemstone: Notes on the loss of *Gemstone,* by E. J. Griffiths; c. Mrs.
    Griffiths
Kirkpool: Letter to Messrs. Sir R. Ropner & Co. (concerning loss of the
    ship) by Shad Burley, Chief Engineer; c. Sir R. Ropner & Co.
Kirkpool: Report of the sinking of *Kirkpool* from Shad Burley to Messrs.
    Sir R. Ropner & Co.
Kirkpool: Report of the sinking of S.S. *Kirkpool* to Sir R. Ropner & Co., by
    O. Olsen, Chief Officer
Report on Interview with Oscar Krink; c. Alfred Holt & Co.
Supplement to the London *Gazette,* July 9, 1948 (concerning the sinking
    of *Atlantis* and *Python*
Supplement to the London *Gazette,* July 12, 1948
Report: The adventures of *Maioma*'s Engineers; c. Shaw Savill Line
Menelaus: Report to Alfred Holt & Co. (concerning attack on *Menelaus*) by
    B. L. Brind, Chief Officer
Extracts from the abridged proceedings of the British Military Court Ham-
    burg, 5/5/47–5/21/47
Nankin: Report on the capture of S.S. *Nankin* by a German Raider by
    C. Stratford, Captain; c. Eastern & Australian Steamship Co.
Port Wellington: Report by Mr. F. W. Bailey, Chief Officer, later, owing
    to the death of Captain Thomas, Captain F. W. Bailey; c. Port Line.
Wellpark: Report on sinking and survivors of *Wellpark,* by Alexander Cant,
    Captain; c. Mr. Cant
Wendover: Report of sinking, by E. Winter, Captain

Netherlands

Olivia: Report of the sinking of *Olivia,* Tamatave, July 20, 1942, by Th. J.
    Brouwer, Fourth Engineer; c. Shell Tankers, N/V
Olivia: Report of J. D. Fisher, (A.b.); c. Shell Tankers, N/V
Olivia: Report of sinking of *Olivia,* by C. Ringelberg, Fifth Engineer, July
    20, 1942
Olivia: Report of shelling of M.V. *Olivia,* by W. A. Vermoet, Third Officer;
    c. Shell Tankers, N/V

Olivia: Sailing report of S.B.-Aft lifeboat of M.V. *Olivia,* signed by W. A. Vermoet, Third Officer; c. Shell Tankers, N/V
Tela: Report of sinking of *Tela,* by C. J. Huijsson, Chief Engineer; c. Maatschappij Vrachtvaart

New Zealand

Komata: Report of the sinking of *Komata,* by Angus Macdonald, Chief Engineer; c. Union Steamship Co. of New Zealand
Komata: Report of the sinking of *Komata,* by N. C. McGreggor, Third Officer; c. Union Steamship Co. of New Zealand
Komata: Report of the sinking of *Komata,* by W. W. Fish, Captain; c. Union Steamship Co. of New Zealand

Norway

Krossfonn: Report of Henry Ramstad, First Officer; c. Sigval Bergesen Co.
Krossfonn: Report of Simon Svendsen, Captain; c. Sigval Bergesen Co.
Krossfonn: Report (on the capture of) by Kare Tjensvold; c. Sigval Bergesen Co.
Ole Wegger, Pelagos: Reports concerning loss of and *Solglimt;* c. Thor Dahl, Inc.
Svalbard: Files of the Royal Norwegian Navy, concerning *Svalbard,* ex-*Togo;* c. Royal Norwegian Naval Attaché, Washington, D.C., Capt. Ch. O. Herlofson, R.N.N
Talleyrand, Tirranna: Reports concerning the loss of; c. Wh. Wilhelmsen

United States

Braine, U.S.S. DD-630, War Diary
Kirling, Campbell, Keating; extracts of files from lawsuit vs. United States Lines
Department of the Navy, OP-09B/CRP Ser 82 PO 9B92, Feb. 25, 1969
Department of the Navy, OP-09B/CRP Ser 138 PO 9B92, March 21, 1968
Department of the Navy, OP-09B/CRP Ser 374 PO 9B92, July 11, 1969
Department of the Navy, OP-09B/CRP Ser 68 PO 9B92, Feb. 23, 1967
Department of the Navy, ONI-222-J The Japanese Navy, June 1948
Report on *Raider 28,* U.S.N. OP-16" Command File World War II, Department of the Navy, Office of the Chief of Naval Operations, Final Report, Surface Craft G/Serial 4
Department of the Navy, Office of the Chief of Naval Operations; various files concerning losses of Allied ships
A list of Japanese Merchant Ships, Second Edition; Short Title
PSIS-100-1 Publication of the Pacific Strategic Intelligence Section—Commander in Chief United States Fleet and Chief of Naval Operations (OP-20-3 G 50), Feb. 1, 1945
Japanese Merchant Ship Recognition Manual, Department of the Navy, Office of the Chief of Naval Operations, ONI-208-J, Aug. 24, 1942

Stephen Hopkins, Log of Lifeboat No. 1, by Cronk
Submarine Forces, Pacific Fleet Endorsement FF 1210/2
Trenton, U.S.S. War Diary
Tarpon, U.S.S. 175 War Diary
Tarpon, U.S.S. (SS-175) A16-3 Report of War Patrol Number Nine—
    Comments FB5-44/AI6-3, Nov. 1943
Account of a surviving member of the crew of *Stephen Hopkins,* U. S. De-
    partment of Commerce, Maritime Administration

COMMUNICATIONS WITH GOVERNMENT AGENCIES

Australia

Australian War Memorial
Commonwealth of Australia, Department of the Navy
Mossman, Town Clerk

Germany

Bundesarchiv, Militärarchiv
Bundesministerium für Verkehr
Bundesministerium für Verteidigung
Militargeschichtliches Forschungsamt

Great Britain

Board of Trade
Chamber of Shipping of the United Kingdom
Imperial War Museum
Ministry of Defence (Navy), Material Division 1 (Naval)
Ministry of Defence, Naval Historical Branch
Ministry of Defence, Naval Home Division
Ministry of Defence, Head of the Home Division
Ministry of Transport
Public Records Office

Japan

National Defense Agency

Netherlands

Ministerie van Defensie (Marine)
Ministerie van Verkeer en Waterstaat, Directoraat-General van Scheepvaart

Norway

Det Kongelige Departement for Handel og Skipsfart

Royal Norwegian Navy, via Capt. Ch. O. Herlofson, R.N.N., Naval Attaché, Washington

United States

Department of the Navy, Bureau of Naval Personnel
Department of the Navy, Office of the Chief of Naval Operations, Naval History Division
General Services Administration, National Archives and Records Division
U. S. Department of Commerce, Maritime Administration
U. S. Department of Commerce, Maritime Administration (U. S. Merchant Marine Academy, Kings Point, N.Y.)

OFFICIAL HISTORIES

Australia

Gill, Herman G. *Royal Australian Navy 1939–1942*. Canberra: Australian War Memorial, 1957.

Canada

Schull, Joseph. *The Far Distant Ships*. Published by Authority of the Minister of National Defense, Edmond Cloutier, King's Printer, Ottowa, 1950.

Germany

Assmann, Kurt. *Der Krieg Zur See 1914–1918*. Edited by Eberhard von Mantey. Vol. III. Published by Kriegswissenschaftliche Abteilung der Marine. Berlin: E. S. Mittler & Sohn, 1937.
Mantey, Eberhard von. *Der Kreuzerkrieg in Ausländischen Gewässern*. Edited by Erich Raeder. Vol. II. Marine Archiv. Berlin: Verlag von E. Mittler & Sohn, 1923.

Great Britain

Roskill, S. W. *The War at Sea*. Vols. I, II, III. London: Her Majesty's Stationery Office, 1954ff.

New Zealand

Waters, S. D. *The Royal New Zealand Navy*. Wellington, N.Z.: War Historical Branch, Department of Internal Affairs, 1956.

Union of South Africa

Turner, L. C. F.; Gordon-Cumming, H. R.; and Betzler, J. E. *War in the Southern Oceans 1939–45*. Cape Town: Oxford University Press, 1961.

OTHER LITERATURE

Alexander, Roy. *The Cruise of the Raider Wolf*. Garden City, N.Y.: Garden City Publishing Co., 1941.

Assmann, Kurt. *Deutsche Schichsalsjahre*. Wiesbaden: Eberhard Brockhaus, 1951.

Auphan, Paul, and Mordal, Jacques. *The French Navy in World War II*. Annapolis: U. S. Naval Institute, 1959.

Barley, Goeffrey Alan. *Caught by a Nazi Raider*. Published by New Zealand Shipping Co., London, 1941.

Bekker, Cajus (pseud.). *Kampf und Untergang der Kriegsmarine*. Hannover: Adolf Sponholtz Verlag, 1953.

————. *Verdammte See*. Oldenburg: Gerhard Stalling Verlag, 1971.

The Ben Line. *The Story of a Merchant Fleet in War*. London: Thomas Nelson & Sons, Ltd., 1951.

Bennett, Goeffrey. *Coronel and the Falklands*. New York: Macmillan Co., 1962.

Berthold, Will. *Getreu bis in den Tod*. München: Süddeutscher Verlag, 1957.

Blake, George. *The Ben Line*. London: Thomas Nelson & Sons, Ltd., 1956.

Boykin, Edward. *Sea Devil of the Confederacy*. New York: Funk & Wagnalls Co., 1959.

Bragadin, Marc' Antonio. *The Italian Navy in World War II*. Annapolis: U. S. Naval Institute, 1957.

Bredemeier, Heinrich. *Schlachtschiff Scharnhorst*. Jugenheim: Koehlers Verlagsgesellschaft, 1962.

Brennecke, Jochen. *Eismeer Atlantik Ostsee*. Jugenheim: Koehlers Verlagsgesellschaft, 1963.

————. *Gespensterkreuzer HK 33*. Biberach an der Riss: Koehlers Verlagsgesellschaft, 1953.

————. *Das Grosse Abenteuer*. Biberach an der Riss: Koehlers Verlagsgesellschaft, 1958.

————. *Haie im Paradis*. Preetz (Holstein): Ernst Gerdes Verlag, 1961.

————. *Kreuzerkrieg in Zwei Ozeanen*. Leipzig: V. Hase & Koehler Verlag, 1942.

————. *Schlachtschiff Bismarck*. Jugenheim: Koehlers Verlagsgesellschaft, 1960.

————. *Hilfskreuzer Thor*. Hereford: Koehlers Verlagsgesellschaft, 1967.

————. *Schwarze Schiffe Weite See*. Oldenburg/Oldb, Hamburg: Gerhard Stalling Verlag, 1958.

Busch, Fritz Otto. *Schwerer Kreuzer Prinz Eugen*. Hannover: Adolf Sponholtz Verlag, 1958.

Busch, Harald. *So War der U-Boot Krieg*. Bielefeld: Deutscher Heimat-Verlag, 1954.

Bushell, T. A. *Eight Bells* (History of the Royal Mail Lines). London: Trade and Travel Publications, Ltd., 1950.

Caidin, Martin. *The Night Hamburg Died.* New York: Ballantine Books, 1960.

Cant, Gilbert. *The War at Sea.* New York: John Day Co., 1942.

Carrell, Paul. *Verbrannte Erde.* Frankfurt/M—Wien: Verlag Ullstein GmbH, 1966.

———. *Die Wüstenfüchse.* Frankfurt/M—Berlin: Ullstein Bücher, 1964.

Charles, Roland W. *Troopships of World War II.* Washington, D.C.: Army Transportation Association, 1947.

Chatterton, E. Keble. *The Sea Raiders.* London: Hurst & Blackett, Ltd., 1933.

Chronology of the Second World War. London and New York: Royal Institute of International Affairs, 1947.

Churchill, Winston S. *Their Finest Hour.* Boston: Houghton Mifflin Co., 1949.

———. *The Gathering Storm.* Boston: Houghton Mifflin Co., 1948.

———. *The Grand Alliance.* Boston: Houghton Mifflin Co., 1950.

Cocchia, Aldo. *Hunters and the Hunted.* Annapolis: U. S. Naval Institute, 1958.

Cooper, Bryan. *The Battle of the Torpedo Boats.* New York: Stein & Day, 1970.

Coward, Roger. *Sailors in Cages.* London: Macdonald & Co., 1967.

Cranwell, John Philips. *Spoilers of the Sea.* New York: W. W. Norton & Co., 1941.

Dechow, Fritz-Ludwig. *Geisterschiff 28.* Preetz (Holstein): Ernst Gerdes Verlag, 1962.

Detmers, Theodor. *Kormoran.* Biberach an der Riss: Koehlers Verlagsgesellschaft, 1959.

Dönitz, Karl. *Memoirs, Ten Years and Twenty Days.* Cleveland and New York: World Publishing Co., 1959.

Eyssen, Robert. *Komet.* Edited by Wilhelm Wolfslast. Jugenheim: Koehlers Verlagsgesellschaft, 1960.

Farago, Ladislas. *The Tenth Fleet.* New York: Ivan Oblenski, 1962.

Frank, Wolfgang. *Die Wölfe und der Admiral.* Oldenburg/Oldb, Gerhard Stalling Verlag, 1953.

Gardner, Brian. *On to Kilimanjaro.* New York: MacFadden-Bartell, 1964.

Gasaway, E. B. *Grey Wolf, Grey Sea.* New York: Ballantine Books, 1970.

Gibson, Charles. *The Ship with Five Names.* London, New York, and Toronto: Abelard-Schuman, 1965.

Gibson, John Frederic. *Brocklebanks 1770–1950.* Liverpool: Henry Young & Sons, 1953.

Giese, Fritz E. *Die Deutsche Marine 1920 bis 1945.* Frankfurt am Main: Verlag für Wehrwesen Bernard & Graefe, 1956.

Görlitz, Walter. *Der Zweite Weltkrieg 1939–1945.* Vols. I, II. Stuttgart: Steingruben Verlag, 1951ff.

Gröner, Erich. *Die Schiffe der Deutschen Kriegsmarine und Luftwaffe 1939–1945.* München: J. F. Lehmann Verlag, 1945.

Guderian, Heinz. *Erinnerungen eines Soldaten.* Heidelberg: Vohwinckel, 1951.

Hashimoto, Mochitsura. *Sunk.* New York: Avon Publications, 1954.

Herzog, Bodo. *Die Deutschen U-Boote 1906–1945.* München: J. F. Lehmann Verlag, 1959.

Herzog, Bodo and Schomaekers, Günter. *Ritter der Tiefe Graue Wolfe.* München and Wels: Verlag Welsermühl, 1965.

Hocking, Charles, F.L.A. *Dictionary of Disasters at Sea During the Age of Steam.* Vols. I, II. London: Lloyd's Register of Shipping, 1969.

Holmes, W. J. *Undersea Victory.* Garden City, N.Y.: Doubleday & Co., 1966.

Hoyt, Edwin P. *Raider 16.* Cleveland and New York: World Publishing Co., 1970.

Hubatsch, Walter. *Der Admiralstab.* Frankfurt: Verlag für Wehrwesen Bernard & Graefe, 1958.

Hümmelchen, Gerhard. *Handelstörer.* München: J. F. Lehmann Verlag, 1967.

Jane's Fighting Ships 1940. London: Sampson Low, Marston & Co., Ltd., 1941.

Jane's Fighting Ships 1941. New York: Macmillan Co., 1942.

Jones, Guy Pierce. *Two Survived.* New York: Random House, 1941.

Kahn, David. *The Codebreakers.* New York: Macmillan Co., 1967.

Kemp, P. K. *Key to Victory.* Boston: Little, Brown & Co., 1957.

King, Ernest J. *The U. S. Navy at War 1941–1945.* Washington, D.C.: U. S. Navy Department, 1946.

Kloss, Erhard. *Der Luftkrieg über Deutschland 1939–1945.* München: Bundesminister für Vertriebene Flüchtlinge und Kriegsgeschädigte, Deutscher Taschenbuch Verlag, 1964.

Kölschbach, Otto. *K 'A' P'N Kölschbach, Der Blokadebrecher mit der Glücklichen Hand.* Biberach an der Diss: Koehlers Verlagsgesellschaft, 1958.

Kranke, Theodor, and Brennecke, Jochen. *RRR Das Glückhafte Schiff.* Biberach an der Riss: Koehlers Verlagsgesellschaft, 1955.

Langer, William L. *An Encyclopedia of World History.* Boston: Houghton Mifflin Co., 1948.

Lenton, H. T. *Navies of the Second World War (German Surface Vessels 2).* London: Macdonald & Co., 1966.

Lenton, H. T., and Calledge, J. J. *Warships of World War II.* London: Ian Allan, Ltd., 1962.

Lipscombe, F. W. *The British Submarine.* London: Adam and Charles Black, 1954.

Lloyd's Register of Shipping. Several editions, 1937ff.

Lüdde-Neurath, Walther. *Regierung Dönitz.* Göttingen, Berlin, Frankfurt, and Zurich: Musterschmidt Verlag, 1964.

Lusar, Rudolf. *German Secret Weapons of the Second World War.* New York: Philosophical Library, 1959.

McLachlan, Donald. *Room 39*. New York: Atheneum, 1963.

Mannstein, Erich von. *Verlorene Siege*. Bonn: Athenäum, 1955.

Marine—Offizier—Vereinigung (1970). Printed by Bonner Universitäts-Buchdrückerei, 1971.

Martienssen, Anthony. *Hitler and His Admirals*. New York: E. P. Dutton & Co., 1949.

Masters, David. *Epics of Salvage*. Boston: Little, Brown & Co., 1954.

Meister, Jürg. *Der Seekrieg in den osteuropaischen Gewässern 1941–1945*. München: J. F. Lehmann Verlag, 1958.

Merchant Ships 1942. New York: Macmillan Co., 1942.

Mohr, Ulrich, and Sellwood, Arthur. *Atlantis*. Jugenheim: Koehlers Verlagsgesellschaft, n.d.

Montgomery, Bernard Law. *The Memoirs of Field Marshall the Viscount Montgomery of Alamein*. Cleveland and New York: World Publishing Co., 1958.

Morison, Samuel Eliot. *History of United States Naval Operations in World War II*. Vols. I, II, III, IV, V, IX, X. Boston: Little, Brown & Co., 1949ff.

Murray, Marischal. *Union-Castle Chronicle*. London: Union Castle Line, Longmans, Green & Co., 1953.

Niezychowski, Alfred von. *The Cruise of the Kronprinz Wilhelm*. Garden City, N.Y.: Doubleday, Doran & Co., 1929.

Nimitz, Chester W.; Adams, Henry H.; and Potter, E. B. *Triumph in the Atlantic*. Englewood Cliffs, N.J.: Prentice-Hall, 1960.

Parkin, Roy. *Into the Smother*. London: Hogarth Press, 1963.

Peillard, Léonce. *The Laconia Affair*. New York: G. P. Putnam's Sons, 1963.

Pope, Dudley. *Graf Spee*. New York: Berkley Publishing Corp., 1956.

———. *73 North*. Philadelphia and New York: J. B. Lippincott Co., 1958.

Porten, Edward P. von der. *The German Navy in World War II*. New York: Thomas Y. Crowell Co., 1969.

Potter, E. B. *The United States and World Sea Power*. Englewood Cliffs, N.J.: Prentice-Hall, 1955.

Raeder, Erich. *Mein Leben*. Vols. I, II. Tübingen-Neckar: Verlag Fritz Schlichtenmayer, 1956.

Ringelnatz, Joachim (Hester, Gustav). *Joachim Ringelnatz als Mariner im Krieg*, Berlin: Rowohlt, 1966.

Rogge, Bernhard, and Frank, Wolfgang. *Schiff 16*. Oldenburg/Oldb, Hamburg: Gerhard Stalling Verlag, 1960.

Rohwer, J., and Hümmelchen, G. *Chronology of the War at Sea*. Vols. I, II. New York: Arco Publishing Co., 1972.

Roscoe, Theodore. *United States Destroyer Operations in World War II*. Annapolis: U. S. Naval Institute, 1953.

———. *United States Submarine Operations in World War II*. Annapolis: U. S. Naval Institute, 1949.

Roskill, S. W. *A Merchant Fleet in War*. London: Collins, 1962.

Ruge, Friederich. *Der Seekrieg 1939–1945*. Stuttgart: K. F. Köhler Verlag, 1954.

Schoen, Walter von. *Auf Kaperkurs*. Berlin: Ullstein Verlag, 1934.

Sellwood, A. V. *The Damned Don't Drown*. New York: Pinnacle Books, 1975.

Semmes, Raphael. *The Confederate Raider Alabama*. Edited by Philip van Doren Stern. Bloomington: Indiana University Press, 1962.

Sill, van Rensselaer. *American Miracle*. New York: Odyssey Press, 1947.

Smith, Eugene W. *Passenger Ships of the World Past and Present*. Boston: George H. Dean Co., 1963.

Steinweg, Günther. *Die Deutsche Handelsflotte im Zweiten Weltkrieg*. Göttingen: Verlag Otto Schwartz & Co., 1954.

Thomer, Egbert. *Unter Nippons Sonne*. Minden/Westf.: Wilhelm Köhler Verlag, 1959.

Thursfield, H. G. *Brassey's Naval Annual 1948*. London: William Clowes & Sons, Ltd; New York: Macmillan Co.

Vois, Paul. *Tausend Inseln und Keine für Uns*. Tübingen: Katzmann Verlag, 1954.

Vulliez, Albert, and Mordal, Jacques. *Battleship Scharnhorst*. Fair Lawn, N.J.: Essential Books, 1958.

Waters, S. D. *Ordeal by Sea*. London: New Zealand Shipping Co., Ltd., 1949.

West, Frank. *Lifeboat Number Seven*. London: William Kimber & Co., Ltd., 1960.

Weyher, Kurt. *Vagabunden auf See*. Cooperating with Hans Jürgen Ehrlich. Tübingen: Katzmann Verlag, 1953.

Whiteman, Marjorie M. *Digest of International Law*. Washington, D.C.: Department of State Publication 8367, Vol. X, 1968.

Winterbotham, F. W. *The Ultra Secret*. New York: Dell Publishing Co., 1974.

Woodward, David. *The Secret Raiders*. New York: W. W. Norton & Co., 1955.

———. *The Tirpitz*. New York: W. W. Norton & Co., 1954.

CORRESPONDENCE WITH CORPORATIONS

Alfred Holt & Co., Liverpool
Alva Steamship Co., Ltd., London
American Export-Isbrandtsen Lines, New York
Ben Line Steamers, Ltd., London
Sigval Bergesen, Stavanger
Biørn Biørnstad & Co., Oslo
Blue Star Port Lines (Management), Ltd., London
Bowring Steamship Co., Ltd., London

BP Tanker Co., Ltd., London
British Phosphate Commissioners, Melbourne
Cayzer, Irvine & Co., Ltd., London
Chandris (London) Services, Ltd., London
Chilean Iodine Educational Bureau, London
Commodore Maury Hotel, Norfolk, Va.
Curaçaosche Scheepvaart Maatschappij, Emmastad, Curaçao
Dahl, Thor, A/S, New York
J. & J. Denholm (Management), Ltd., Glasgow
Deutsche Afrika Linien, Hamburg-Altona
Deutsche Dampfshiffahrts-Gesellschaft Hansa, Bremen
Eastern & Australian Steamship Co., Ltd., London
Ellerman Lines, Ltd., London
Fearnley & Eger, Oslo
Getty Oil Co., New York
Glen Line, Ltd., London
Glover Bros. (London), Ltd., London
Granges Rederiet, Stockholm
Hain-Nourse Ltd., London
Hamburg-Amerika Linie, Hamburg
Herlofson & Co., A/S, Oslo
Imperial Oil, Ltd., Toronto
Kaiser Aluminum & Chemical Sales, Inc., New York
Kirling, Campbell & Keating, New York
Klaveness & Co., A/S, Lysaker
Koninklijke Rotterdamsche Lloyd, N/V, Rotterdam
Lief Höegh & Co., Oslo
Longstaff & Co., Ltd., London
Maatschappij Vrachtvaart, Rotterdam
Mobil, New York
New Zealand Shipping Co., Ltd., Wellington and London
North German Lloyd, New York and Bremen
Norwegian Cruiseships, A/S, Oslo
Oldenburg-Portugiesische Dampfschiff Reederei, Hamburg
Port Line, Ltd., London
Sir R. Ropner & Co., Ltd., Darlington
Royal Mail Lines, London
Walter Runciman & Co., Ltd., London
Wm. Ruys & Zonen, Rotterdam
Shaw Savill Line, London
Shell International Petroleum Co., Ltd., London
Shell Tankers, N/V, Rotterdam
South American Saint Line, London
Texas Co., New York
Tidewater Associated Oil Co., New York

Union-Castle Line, London
Union Steamship Co. of New Zealand, Wellington
United States Lines, New York
Unterweser Reederei, Bremen
Wilh. Wilhelmsen, Oslo

PERIODICALS I

American Aviation Historical Society Journal, Spring 1967.
Der Anker, published by the Unterweser Reederei, Oct. 1954, Apr. 1955,
     Oct. 1955, Dec. 1955.
Collier's, July 29, 1944.
The Compass, published by Mobil, Sept.–Oct. 1960.
Drei Flaggen Post, published by Reedereien John T. Essberger and Deutsche
     Afrika Linien, Feb. 1966, Mar. 1966, Feb. 1968.
Fore 'n' Aft, published by the Kaiser Richmond (California) Shipyard,
     May 5, 1944.
Hamburger Volkszeitung (Communist), May 7, 1947; May 24, 1947.
Imperial Oil Fleet News, published by Imperial Oil, Fall 1952.
Imperial Oil Review, published by Imperial Oil, Fall 1943, Winter 1945.
The Journal of the Institute of Navigation, London, Oct. 1956.
Life magazine, June 23, 1941.
The Lookout, published by the Seamen's Church Institute, New York, Apr.
     1960.
Nassau Daily Tribune, Bahamas, Nov. 9, 1940.
Petroleum Today, Fall 1966.
Reader's Digest, Oct. 1941.
Stanvac Meridian, published by Mobil, Sept. 1951.
U. S. Naval Institute Proceedings, Mar. 1953, Nov. 1954, Feb. 1969.
Die Welt, May 5, 1947; May 8, 1947; May 20, 1947.

PERIODICALS II

     Among foreign and United States magazines, newspapers, and wire
services examined, the following proved very valuable for following general
trends, communiqués, propaganda, specific actions and events during and
after the war. It was surprising to discover the many mentions of, and
misapprehensions about, the raiders and their activities.

Associated Press
Christian Science Monitor
Manchester Guardian
Newsweek magazine
New York *Daily News*

New York *Herald Tribune*
New York *Post*
New York *Telegram*
The New York Times
Time magazine
Times (London)
U.S. News & World Report
Die Welt (Hamburg)

Index